SPIRITUAL ECOLOGY INCLUDE DAAMA, RITUALS AND CUSTOMS

Himalaya Past and Present Series

MOUNTAINS OF THE GOD

(In Two Volumes)

SPIRITUAL ECOLOGY INCLUDE DAAMA RITUALS AND CUSTOMS

(Volume-1)

Editor
K.S. Gulia

ISHA BOOKS
DELHI-110009

Spiritual Ecology Include Daama Rituals and Customs

ISBN : 81-8205-420-6 (Set)
ISBN : 81-8205-421-4 (Vol. 1)

Published in 2007 in India by:
ISHA Books
B-63, Ist Floor, New Gupta Colony,
Near DDA Market, Delhi-110009
Phone: 9212142040
Email: ishabooks@hotmail.com

Lasertype Setting by: Tact Computer Graphics, Delhi
Printed at: Salasar Imaging System, Delhi

Contents

Introduction 9

1. **Himalayan Region** 13

Hindu Belt • Buddhist Belt • Islamic Belt • Christian Belt • Animism Belt • Benevolent and Malevolent Spirits • Death and the World After Death • Shamanism • Donyi-Polo (The Sun - Moon Cult)

2. **Temples and Culture** 47

The Architecture of Temples • Chiselling Life out of Stone • The Canons of the Shastras

3. **Badrinath: The Dhaam in the Himalayas** 53

The Prayags • Location • Myths and Legends of Badrinath

4. **Badrinarayan Temple** 61

Architecture • Temple Schedule • Sulphur Springs • Fairs and Festivals • Other Sacred Places • Sapta Badri • Joshimath • Hanuman Chatti

5. **Kedarnath-Gangotri-Yamunotri** 69

Location • Architecture • Gangotri • Yamunotri • Glossary

6. **Garhwal Landscape and Pilgrim's Progress** 79

Badrinath • Legend • Prayag

7. **Going on a Tirtha** 89

The Tirthas of Saptapuri and Chaar Dhaam • The Meaning of a Pilgrimage • Pilgrims through the Ages • Sacred Places

8. **Vishnu and his Dhaams** 101

Rig Vedic Vishnu • Vishnu in the Epics • Vishnu in the Puranas • Vishnu's Avatars • Vishnu's Image and Appearance • A Conversation with God • Vishnu's Chaar Dhaam

9. Religion—The Wonder World of Khasas **113**

Culture • Magic, Swearing and Nefarious Designs on Others • The Evil Spirits • Ceremonies during Epidemics and Calamities • Traditional Code of Conduct • The Bedwart (Rope Dancing) • Importance of Mahasu Deota • The Legend of Mahasu Deota • Attendants of Botha Mahasu (BIRS) • Some Gods of the Lower Order • The Institution of Baki • The Spirit World • Omens • Oaths and Ordeals • Festivals • Magh • Bissu

10. Gods and Godesses of Kumaon **145**

11. Nepal and the Gorkhas **159**

Religious Ceremonies • Birth • Names • Weaning • Cheor • Marriage • Betrothal • Wedding • Divorce • Widows and Widowers • Death • Inheritance • Festivals • Magh Sankranti • Basant Panchami • Shivaratri • Holi • Chait Dasain • Ram Nawami • Nag Panchami • Sansari Mai Puja • Sawan Sankrati • Rikhi Tarpan • Janamashtami • Tij • Sora Sarad • Dashera • Tewar • Sat Narain Puja • Pani Patiya • Bhor Patiya

12. Residence and Ritual in the Garhwal Himalaya **179**

Chhal Puja • Notes

13. Culture and Traditions of Himachal **213**

Food and Drink • Religion • Temple Dance • Evil Spirits • Hard Life • Song and Dance • Translation • Translation • Social Change

14. Fairs, Festivals, Rituals and Temples in Western Himalayas **221**

Fairs and Festivals • Dussehra • Shivaratri • Minjar • Renuka Lavi • Folk Songs • Love Songs • Religious Songs • Heroic Songs • Festival Songs • Seasonal Songs • Marriage Songs • Birth Songs • Dance Songs • Folk and Ritual Dances • Folk and Ritual

Index **301**

Introduction

The Himalayas are heaven on earth, the *swarga* of the Hindus. Hindu mythology says that this is the house of its pantheon of gods and goddesses. If humans imagine a place called heaven it would be something like the Himalayas. A dauntingly majestic landscape of soaring peaks covered in everlasting snow, emerald valleys and forests, fields of wild flowers, silver waterfalls and turbulent rivers flowing through deep gorges. The Himalayas are nature's very own *devalaya*, a landscape created like a temple to the gods. The Himalayan belt practices various religions like: Hinduism, Buddhism, Islam, Christianity and ever animism followed in different areas.

Foremost of these is Hinduism which extends from the banks of the Jhelum to the banks of the Lohita in the Assam valley. The cultural areas involved include: the Pahari, Gujar, Gaddi, Jhecha (in the pastoral cultural area) and the Lepchas, Aka-Nishi, Adi, Mishmi, Nagas it extends to the isolated valleys of Manipur and Tripura in the bamboo cultural area.

The Himalayan belt stands testimony to various temples and temple towns built down the ages. These have not only preserved Hindu religion but through their patronage they have also kept alive India's cultural heritage. Temple towns like Madurai or Varanasi have been great centers of scholarship and social life. The *Gurukuls* were based here. In these the students came from all over the country to leave ancient Hindu texts like vedas Upanishads as well as subjects like mathematics, logic, grammar, astronomy and medicine. That these ancient texts have survived till date is due to the dedication of count less scholars at these gurukuls.

Hindu tradition states that a *tirtha* is a place where you can gain *nirvana*, true enlightenment and also achieve *moksha*, a liberation from the endless cycle of life and death. The tirtha does not have to be a specific place or a temple. It can be anywhere—by the banks of a holy river, at the foot of a mountain, under a sacred tree and even at the feet of a great saint or guru. From the time of the Vedas, there has been a tradition of the veneration of river, and many tirthas came up beside them. For Hindus, the landscape itself is holy may it be – hills, rivers, trees, rocks, pools or the sea. The veneration of nature has led to temple, being built in especially picturesque places. When an aspect of nature is combined with other spiritual elements a great tirtha is created. For instance, Varanasi (also called Kashi and Banaras) is considered supreme among all Hindu *tirthasthanas*. It offers the pilgrims the combination of a great river, a powerful god and a venerable temple. Teerthas are also created by myths like the peethasthanas, the seats of the Mother Godden (Devi). Many of these are connected to the myth of the death of Shiva's wife, Sati. There are fifty-one *peethasthanas* where parts of Sati's body fell and here the temples of the Mother Goddes consecrate her *Shakti*, her divine power. Other myths are those of Shiva and his twelve Jyotirlingams which have temples with Shiva lingams. The Vishnu myths have created his four abodes – the Chaar Dhaams.

This volume includes an indepth study of the spiritual ecology of the Himalayan belt — its religious, temple, *Tirtha Sthals* and various cultures followed from Kashmir to the Garwal, Kumaon and Nepal.

Chapter 1 'Himalyan Religions' describe the ways in which different religions influence different areas of the Himalayan belt. The Hinduism belt forms the most extensive belt. Having its presence in the Kashmir valley since time immemorial. The Mata Worship forms a part of the Shakti cult. The Hindus in the Pahari cultural areas firmly believe in supernatural power. There are different categories of Pahari Gods, there is also a morbid fear of ghosts. The Gaddi cultural area also forms a part of the study. The description of Jhecha area of Kulu gives us an insight into their beliefs and deities. Their roots belong to the Austric or Dravidian culture. There has also been mention of the practice of the Naga cult in the Gandhara and Lahaul Region. The prevalence of Hinduism in Manipur, Andhra Pradesh, Narth-East, Nepal, Kinnaur and Lahaul has been mentioned.

Apart from the prevalence of Hinduism also included in the description are: the Buddhist belt with its extension in West till Taxila, Gandhara and the Hindu Kush region also having its prevalence in Kashmir, the Islamic Belt in the the worth-west Himalayan region; and the Christian Belt. The Animism Belt also forms a part of the beleifs in the Himalayan region. The fear of the unknown and deep rooted suspicion with curious customs is also prevalent with a number of benevolent and malevolent spirits affectiny the lives of the tribals. The cult of the dead among the various tribes residing in the Himalayan belt has also heen conceptualized. The techniques of using supernatural power 'Shamanism' also forms part of the beleifs. The animistic religion of the Adi tribe of Arunachal Pradesh 'Donyi – Polo' or the Sun-Moon cult also form an interesting reading.

Chapter 2 'Temples and Culture' is a description of temples as centers of social life and their role in preserving Hindu religion and in keeping the Hindu culture alive. The various Tirthas have also been described in detail in Chapter 3 to 7 which have dealt with Badrinath, the Badrinarayan temple, Kedarnath—Gangotri—Yamunotri and the various Tirthas along with the concept of pilgrimage. These chapter enlighten us on the concept of pilgrimage.

Chapter 8 'Vishnu and His Dhaams' is an extension of the topic of Dhaams. It details the various Dhaams of Vishnu. The four tirthas of the Chaar Dhaam are set at the cardinal points of the Indian subcontinent. In the north, the *dhaam* of Badrinaath is in the Himalayans; in the West, Dwarka stands by the Arabian Sea; in the East is Puri by the Bay of Bengal and in the South, Rameshwaram is an island at the point where the Indian Ocean touches the Indian shore. All four dhaams have temples dedicated to either Vishnu or one of his avatars. Badrinath is a Vishnu temple, Dwarka worship Krishna, Puri is the tirtha of Krishna as Jagannatha and Rameshwaram has temples dedicated to Rama.

Chapter 9 'Religion—The Wonder World of Khasa' gives us a description of the culture and various farms of religion being followed by the Khasas of Jaunsar – Bawar. While worshiping Hindu gods and goddesses, they also worship ancestor spirits, queer and fantastic demons and gods and also objects like stones, weapons, dyed rags and symbols. Also included are facts about their customary rites in temples, the manner and mode of sacrifice, the daily religions performances in the temples, the dimlighting, the burning of incense, the mysterious incantation and sing song monologues, all indicating Hindu origin and tradition. The ceremonies during epidemics and calamities, their traditional code of conduct, the *Bedwart* (Pole Dancing), the Mahasu Deota and and his importance are also studied in detail. Along with these — the Magh, Bissu and Mond festivals have also been discussed in detail.

Chapter 10 'Gods and Goddesses of Kumaon' accounts the predominant religion of the people of Kumaon. The temple bells ring here not only for the traditional gods of the Hindu pantheon – Shiva, Vishnu and Shakti – but also for a host of other gods and demons who have a very strong hold on the local imagination. The mother goddess Shakti is the most important deity of the area credited to having created not only the world but the three gods of the Hindu pantheon – Shiva, Vishnu and Brahma. Its incarnation Nanda Devi is also venerated out there, supposed to be the Kumaoni incarnation of Parvati. Maximum temples in Kumaon have been dedicated to Shiva followed by Shakti, Vishnu, Rama and Krishna. The chapter also includes a description of the Folk gods of varied origin having descended from pre-Aryan animism and demonism. The Kumaoni God of justice Golu *devta* of Goril is also famous in the region. Other folk gods include Airy, Chaumu, Kail Bisht, Haru and Saim. The Pahari belief in supernatural power also forms a major part of their faith.

Chapter 11 'Nepal and the Gorkhas' is mainly concerned with the important topic of religious customs and festivals. Included in it is a section on witchcraft. It also touches upon the fascinating subject of folk lore. The religious ceremonies and customs have been described in detail though there are many variations and not all customs are practiced uniformly.

Chapter 12 'Residence and Rituals in the Garhwal Himalayas' is an essay on research undertaken in Uttaranchal, Uttarakhand, in the Himalayan districts of the North Indian state of UP, specifically in upper Garhwal, bordered by Tibet on the north, Kumaon to the east, plains of North India to the South and the state of Himachal Pradesh to the West. Evidence drawn from Garhwali naming patterns, proverbs, language, traditional law interviews with local persons, marriage customs and folklore indicates that according to the folk ontology of Garhwalis, persons and the places where the reside have a great deal of influence upon each other. It contains extracts from the *Stridhamapaddhati* written by Tryambaka in 18th century stressing the importance of forgetting one's own family and never returning to one's father's house. Other interpersonal relations have been examined by students of Indian society. The ceremony of women visiting their natal home in Garhwal (*mait*) after marriage and the importance the Garhwalis give to this has also been included. The Chhal puja performed on this occasion has also been described in detail.

Chapter 13 'Culture and Tradition of Himachal' gives us an account of the Kinners lifestyle. What they eat and drink; their religion – vast majority of them being Buddhists; their beliefs and festivals. An insight into their hand life has also been included in the study along with the songs and dances which are performed to lighten their moods.

Chapter 14 'Fairs, Festivals, Rituals and Temples in Western Himalayas' is an account of the traditional fairs and festivals of the hill people. These fairs are a big draw not only to the village gods and the rural folk but also to the traders and visitors from far and wide. A major portion of the chapter includes a description of Folk songs, seasonal songs, marriage songs, birth songs and dance songs. Folk and Ritual dances and art also form a good part of the chapter. The study of Pahari Art of Painting has also been included with its various characteristic features and its inspiration from Bhakti Movement. The subject of Krishna cult forms the most important theme in Pahart art, other subjects like Shiva and his horms and subjects from the Hindu epics are also included in the Pahari art. A description of Rumal paintings another form of art has been given.

The role of Sansar Chand the great patron of art has been described in detail. The introduction of Shikhare style of architecture in the hills also is detailed in temple architecture along with the various important temples found in the hills. This volume sums up all chapters to form a comprehensive study on the spiritual ecology of the Himalayas.

1
Himalayan Religions

Hinduism, Buddhism, Islam, Christianity and Animism are practised in different areas of the Himalayan belt, a brief account of which follows:

Hindu Belt

The Hindu belt is most extensive. It extends from the banks of the Jhelum to the banks of the Lohita in the Assam valley. In fact, the Hindu belt of the Himalayas is an extension of the Hindu belt which runs through the Punjab plains, Gangetic plains and Assam plains. The cultural area involved is the Pahari, Gujar, Gaddi, Jhecha (in the pastoral cultural area) and through the Lepchas, Aka-Nishi, Adi, Mishmi and Naga cultural area it extends to the isolated valleys of Manipur and Tripura in the bamboo cultural area. Manipur and Tripura, however, have recently switched to Hinduism. Hinduism has been in existence in the Kashmir valley since time immemorial. This is evident from ancient literature like the Nilamatapurana which refers to the sacred Hindu places in Kashmir. Similarly, Mahatmya refers particularly to Kashmir's Hindu *tirthas*, the Amarnath cave which is connected with Siva and Parvati. The Saivite influence in the valley appears to be there since ancient times.

Kashmir: Avanti Varman (855 - 56 A.D.) established Avantipura (presently known as Vanipara) where the ruins of a Siva temple still exist. The Naga cult was in existence in Kashmir in the remote past. Traces of this cult are found in Kulu. In Kashmir, several important springs are named after Nag. Similarly in the hilly regions from Kulu to Garhwal some important places are named after Nag. In Kulu valley, Nag culture is very prominent; its influence is seen in the social, cultural and religious life of the people. There are numerous temples after Nag. Hermann Goetz considers the Nag cult as representing the Koli layer: "In Kulu, Mandi, Suket, and Sumla Hills the snakes have often also been Hinduized as Rishis, probably this may represent the Koli layer of south Himalayan religion. The Nag cult is prevalent in Manipur as well as the Khasi Hills. Wular lake in Kashmir was known as Mahapadma Sara in ancient times. The name was derived from the Naga Mahapadma, the deity of the lake. Moreover, the word "Wular" is derived from the Sanskrit word "Ullala" which means turbulent. Prof. Buhlar assumes the Padma Naga to be identical with the Mahapadma Naga, which is considered the deity of Wular lake. Nag-worship is still prevalent in Kashmir and a few Pandit families have Nag as their surname. This surname is also found in Kangra, Kulu and Hamirpur in the neighbourhood of Kashmir.

The Kashmiri Pandits have retained Hinduism despite pressures to convert to Islam in the past. The Chharhi Yatra to Amarnath takes place every August. Hindu pilgrims from various parts of India take part in this yatra which is performed on foot through the interior valley of Pahalgaon passing from Chandanwari, Pishughati, Sheshnag and Panchtarani. The Shankaracharya temple and the sub-temple of Martand are again proof of Hindu influence in Kashmir. In Jammu, Kishtwar, Kangra, Hamirpur, Chamba, Mandi and Bilaspur, Mata worship prevails. The temples of Vaishno Mata (Jammu), Chintpurni Mata (Hamirpur), Bagulamukhi Mata (Kangra, Dechragopipur), Jawalamukhi Mata (Kangra, Jawalamukhi), Kangrewali Mata (Kangra Town), Chamunda Mata (near Dharamsala in Kangra), Tarna Mata (Mandi) and Naina Devi (Bilaspur) are famous places of pilgrimage for Hindus as well as others. In fact, Mata worship is a form of the Shakti cult which is prevalent in the entire Pahari cultural area from Kashmir to Nepal and further into the Brahmaputra valley.

Pahari and Assam Valley: There are numerous temples in the Pahari and Assam valleys' periphery attributed to the Mata: Kaliwari Mata (Simal Town), Tara Devi Mata (at Taradevi near Simla), Hatkoti Mata (Rehru in Simla), Lakshana Devi Mata (Bharmor, Chamba), Sakti Devi Mata (Chatrahri Chamba), Markula Devi Mata (Udaipur, Lahaul), Hidimba Mata (Dhungra, Manali, Kulu), Sandhya Devi Mata (Jagatsukh, Kulu), Mritunjaya Mata (Kumaon, Garhwal), Devi Mata (Patan, Nepal), Malinithan Mata (Arunachal Pradesh), Tamreshwari Mata (near Teju, Arunachal Pradesh). The existence of these temples and various others attributed to the goddess reveal the vast extension of the Mata cult or the Shakti cult in the Hindu belt. Animals are sacrificed in almost all the temples to the goddesse. In the Pahari cultural area, there are temples to Brahma, Vishnu, Siva, Rama, Krishna, Narayana, Hanumana or some rishi. The temple is the institution which unites the entire village socially. Community feasts, festivals and sacrifices take place there. In the Pahari cultural area, the Hindus have a firm belief in supernatural powers. The help of the supernatural is sought when they are in difficulty and the village deity is the medium through which this help is sought.

Sometimes, the Pahari shaman is engaged for aid. While having belief in a Supreme Being, the Hindus also appease both benevolent and malevolent spirits. They arrange sacrifices of animals or conduct puja by engaging a Brahmin or shaman. A shaman is a man who may be of any caste and who is devoted to a particular deity for whom he acts as medium in the diagnosis of difficulties . . . The Pahari shaman is primarily a diagnostician. To learn the art of a shaman one has to seek the guidance of a Guru. There are different categories of Pahari gods. Ishta Devta or household god is generally a family deity. The Kula Devta is the clan deity.

In Pahari area, the people also have morbid fear of ghosts, whose abodes are considered to be thick jungles, high peaks, river banks, drains and the dark interiors of abandoned houses. It is believed that a woman passing away in childbirth turns into female ghost (*Churhel*) and attacks males at night. The depredations of a ghost are checked by means of magic (*Jadu-Tona*). Mental disorder and physical pain is brought about for an enemy through magical incantations and rituals. In general, it appears that in the Hindu belt of the Himalayas, there is syncretization of Hindu, Dravidian and Austric religious practices. Hinduism here has been influenced by aboriginal religions much more than in the Indian plains. The Hinduism of the Gaddi cultural area is not different from that of the Pahari cultural area but the people here are more inclined towards Saivite practices. Mani Mahesh, the trans-Himalayan God, is supreme for them as he looks after their herds when they are crossing the high peaks and passes of the Himalayas. They offer goat and sheep sacrifices to Siva. The Gaddis before partaking of food or drink like rice beer offer it to Siva and sprinkle it in his name.

Jhecha Area (Kulu): In the Jhecha area in Kulu, there are three shrines of Jambalu Devta at Burua, Majharh and Kulang. The people make an offering of silver horses to the god. It appears that Jambalu is an animistic deity who has merged with a Hindu Rishi, Jamdagni, and now the god is named Jamdagni Rishi. Animal sacrifices are made to Jamblu and the slaughter has to be via the *halal* method. This is a curious Islamic element in the ritual. Another Jhecha god is the shepherd god Dani Deo to whom sacrifices are made every year in the months of April/May when they return from their winter abodes. Several lambs are slaughtered and a community feast arranged.

In the Jhecha area, there are nine villages and their central shrine is at Goshal village. The Austric or Dravidian culture must have prevailed in the distant past in the Jhecha area. When the Bhotias held sway over the area, the Fagali (Buddhist) festival was celebrated every year. Evidence of the Nag cult is still available in Goshal village. The cult is still traceable in Kulu. A snake is frequently punched on coins. The cult has been referred to in the Vedas. The Grihya Sutra prescribes many rites pertaining to snake worship. The Asva Layana Grihya Sutra states that the sacrificer should go out to the east, pour water in a clear spot and offer sacrifice with the following formula: "To the divine hosts of the serpents which are terrestrial, which are aerial, celestial, which dwell in the direction (of the horizon). To them, I have brought this *bait* (sacrificial offerings), to them I give over this *bali*." Banerjee says that snake worship was prevalent in India in the 4th century B.C. and Alexander came across this faith among Indians. He also says that Naga cult was practised in the Gandhara region. To support this, Buhler describes the Kharosthi inscription which records the construction of a tank in the month of Sravana, for the sake of worship of Nagas by Thera Nora, son of Dati, the Greek ruler. The Goshali Nag holds together the Jhecha community.

The devta system had a great socio-economic and socio-cultural impact on the community life of the Kulu people. In fact, they are ruled and controlled by these demigods. "Kullu still retains its age-old Devtas (demi-gods), though they have been reassembled into a more recent hierarchy under tutelage of the presiding deity Raghunath." Austric and Dravidian forms of religious practices are still prevalent and have been amalgamated with Hindu religious traditions. The main deity of the village shrine in the area is a god of the Hindu pantheon but the aboriginal gods are in the form of Jogini, Than, Patal and Athara Pede. Over the years the "malevolence" of the Hindu, and Dravidian gods was so exaggerated that a phobia was created among the natives about showing disrespect to any god. But this system was used for feudal exploitation. The Devta became the de facto controller of the society and through him the institution of a Regency was created. The Kardar became the manager of the god's estate and this right became hereditary. This system prevailed for a long time as Hindu reformers rarely visited the area. But now the Majariyat system (the tenancy of gods) has been abolished.

Lahaul: The Naga cult is also traceable in Lahaul, the language of the people here gives evidence that the land was once inhabited by an aboriginal tribe which spoke a dialect analogous to that of the Mundas of central India. In Lahaul, Naga Puja (serpent worship) is especially prevalent among the Sipis. But Ghepan, a god of the Naga cult, is worshipped by all the natives. Otherwise too the Sipis follow all Hindu rituals. The Bhotias in Lahaul perform both Hindu and Buddhist rituals. After Hinduism had its sway in Lahaul, Buddhism made its entry into the valley. The Siva temple of Triloki Nath has now been converted into a Buddhist shrine but only the idol of Avlokiteshvara has been installed. Otherwise the shrine is unaltered.

Kinnaur: In Kinnaur, the Hindu influence is very vital upto Kanam. The Kinnauras in lower Kinnaur follow both Hindu and Buddhist rituals. In each village there is a Hindu shrine and a Buddhist Gompa. In Kothi village near Kalpa, there is a shrine of Goddess Kali. At Sangla along with a Hindu shrine there is a Gompa. The names of Kinnauras living upto Kanam are Hindu, while those beyond have Buddhist names. When Buddhism spread to Tibet, then it had a major impact in upper Kinnaur but could not completely wean away the inhabitants of the lower Kinnaur from their Hindu moorings. Therefore, in Kinnaur, there is a syncretization of animism, Hinduism and Buddhism.

Nepal: Hinduism is the state religion in Nepal though Buddhist influence there is very strong. Geographically, Nepal is so situated that Islam could never reach the country. Buddhist influence has been strong in art and culture but it has not been able to completely change the Hindu matrix of religion. Hinduism has been in existence since ancient times but animism was also prevalent. Buddhism was introduced in the country in the time of Asoka through his Mahamitras. Then again, the Brahmic type of Hinduism was introduced in Nepal during Mallas (1200 to 1769). The royal support for Hinduism has been a major factor in its survival and growth. Nepalese temple inscriptions are the evidence of the spread of Hinduism in this Himalayan kingdom. The Cangu Narayana temple inscription of 329 A.D. of Mahadeva, the Lichhavi king, depicts Vishnu with his Srivatsa mark. Vishnu is also mentioned in the Lajapat inscription of 332 A.D. The Deo-Patan inscription of 370 A.D. describes the establishment of the Prabhu Kesvara Linga, the Tabahal inscription of 345 A.D. describes the installation of Surya image by Guhamittra, a trader. Deo-Patan inscription of 432 A.D. describes the installation of images of Surya, Siva and Vishnu. The Brahmanical sculptures in Nepal are testimony of the Hindu influence there. There has been Mauryan, Gupta, Tantric East Indian and Bengali impact on the Hindu art of Nepal. "Nepal's Brahmanical sculptures and paintings, from about the 8th century onwards at any rate, are of East India affiliation, and they are all basically Tantric in religious character." In the present day, Nepali Hindus are akin to the Pahari cultural area Hindus. The Nepalese too believe in malevolent and benevolent spirits, a Supreme Being, Jadu-Tona, ghosts, and shamanism. They observe the caste system as in the Pahari cultural area. The Narwaris of Nepal have their God named Adhji-jh Deo (father of the father). He is invoked during all ceremonies. Pashupati is worshipped as the lord of animals and regarded by all as the guardian deity of Nepal. He is represented by huge phallic emblem with five figures of Siva in different meditative mudras. Bhairava, the demon, half human and half animal, is also worshipped. In fact, Bhairava is a manifestation of Siva. The ancient Bhairavas were Pachali, Bhaktapura (Bhatgaon), Sange and Nagakot. Now there are five types of Bhairavas: Akash Bhairava, Kal Bhairava, Bag Bhairava, Pachali Bhairava and Mahakal Bhairava. Nepalese also worship Nags and believe that they are agents of rain and custodians of treasures. There are nine types of Nags in Nepal and each has a definite function. Karkotak Nag is considered the most important and is believed to live in Tandah, a big tank, where he has got a subterranean palace of gold, diamonds and jewels. The sacrifice of goats and sheep is common; in some cases, the buffalo is also sacrificed. The goddess Bisen Devi prefers buffalo sacrifice.

North - East: Beyond Kanchenjunga in the North-East, the Hindu belt extends mainly through the Assam plains (or Brahmaputra plains). It extends through the foothills in the periphery of the Brahmaputra valley in the north and the south bank of the great river. In the Bengal and Assam Doars Hinduism has been adopted by the Kochs and Bodo tribals. It is in an amalgamated form of Hinduism and animism.

Arunachal Pradesh: As far as religion in Arunachal Pradesh is concerned, Hinduism is found in the foothills (the Upgais), animism in the central stretch of hills (the Antagiris) and Buddhism in the higher Himalayan region (the Vahigiris). The Hindu influence is found in the peripheral lines of the Brahmaputra valley in Assam. The extent of the influence has enticed some of the tribals to come into the fold of Hinduism. But even today we find that the tribals in the Hindu belt follow elements of their indigenous faith though they identify themselves as Hindus. The Mishmis record their religion as Hinduism. The Adis, Nishis, Akas and Miris pay due respect to Hindu idols in temples in their area. In Tirap district, the Noctes have adopted Vaishnavism but also follow their traditional faith. Some Akas are also attracted towards the Vaishnavite faith through their Assam contacts. Several new temples have been constructed in the Hindu belt and elsewhere in the State without resistance from the tribals.

Manipur: Hinduism is even prevalent in Manipur, which is surprising considering its relative isolation. It seems to have been adopted after the period of animism. Some Buddhist icons are also to be seen. These are made of white marble, which is not available in Manipur. The artistic details (like mudra, head dress, robe and pedestal with convex top) resemble the Buddhist icons found in Burma during the seventeenth to nineteenth century A.D. But the art pieces probably were brought in by individual collectors and do not point to the existence of Buddhism here. Animism, again, was probably not completely replaced till the eighteenth century. As far as the Hindu influence is concerned there are different views. M. Kirti Singh believes that Angrichogba and black magic which were practised in the eleventh century A.D. in Manipur were Tantric cults. Nil Manta Singh also believes that Shaivism and Tantric cults were prevalent before Vaishnavism spread. According to the text "Chingurembi Khonglup" ("The Companions of Chingurembi") which claims Hindu influence as early as the second half of the seventh century, the Meitei king Naothingkhong, who ascended the throne in 663 A.D. married a princess from the west. Jalajit Singh also considers that cultural contact was established between Manipur and western India as early as the seventh century. The people of Manipur began to study the Ramayana and the Mahabharata from that period onwards.

The translation of the Phayena copper plates reveals that Shaivism existed in Manipur in the seventh century. These plates were made during the time of King Khongtekcha (763-784 A.D.) Paratt has described the medieval period in Manipur as the pre-Hindu period. She believes that during this period there are a number of references to the influence of Hinduism. But the influence seems to have been slight and ineffective in seducing the Meiteis from their indigenous faith. Royal sanction to Hinduism was given by Garib Niwaj only. Raja Jaising of Manipur visited the Assam court in 1757 A.D. A matrimonial alliance was effected when Kuranganayani, the daughter of the Manipur king, was presented to King Swargadev of Assam. The following recommendation was made: "The Manipur king has a daughter; her name is Kuranganayani. The Manipur kings are the scions of Babrubahan of the Kshatriya caste. Swargadev may be pleased to marry her." There were different stages in the introduction of Hinduism into Manipur. Jalajit Singh believes that the kings of the period 1467-1697 A.D. were devotees of Vishnu but they did not adopt Vaishnavism formally. Charai Rongba became king in 1697 A.D. He did not immediately adopt Hinduism. He patronised temples belonging to the old faith. A tableau was constructed by him before the temple of Laikasa and he also constructed the temple of Panthoibi which was dedicated in 1700 A.D. In 1704, however, he embraced Hinduism. Some subjects also adopted the religion along with their king.

A Hindu preacher is reported to have come from Puri with his family and started a mission. He was adopted as a Guru by the king. His descendants were called the Guru Aribom and a habitation of these descendants exists at Brahmpur where the king built a brick temple dedicated to Krishna. The image of Brindaban Chandra (Shri Krishna) is worshipped in this temple. A Kali temple called Manipur Kalika was constructed in the year 1707 in Imphal but is believed to have collapsed the following year. The second stage starts with the reign of Garib Niwaj (1709-1748 A.D.). In 1714 A.D. Krishnan Dase, a preacher, arrived in Manipur. Next year, about 36 Hindu monks, including a preceptor of the King of Assam arrived. The king got himself initiated into Vaishnavism in 1717 A.D. by appointing Gopal Dass as his Guru. In the second instance, the king underwent the sacred thread ceremony for the second time in 1729 A.D. on the occasion of the full moon in the month of Watching (December/January).

In 1728 A.D. Santi Dass, a Hindu preacher from Sylhet, arrived in Manipur and started propagating the Ramanandi cult of Vaishnavism. Some people took to this cult. But the king was not happy at this and punished them for following the new sect. However, later the King himself became a follower of Santi Dass. In 1737 A.D. in the month of Hiyangei (October/November) Dass initiated the king into his religion. This event marked the beginning of the Ramanandi cult in Manipur. Idols of Rama, Sita, Lakshman, Bharat and Shatrughan were installed in the temples. The king also worshipped Hanuman, for whom a temple was built at Mahabali on the banks of the Imphal river in 1729 A.D. The Vaishnavism preached by Santi Dass, however, ended with the king and the preacher. After the death of Garib Niwaj the throne was occupied by three kings in rapid succession till 1759 A.D. when Jai Singh or Bhagya Chandra became the king. He and his subjects accepted the Chaitanya school of Vaishnavism and royal sanction was accorded to the sect. Rup Pamanarda was appointed Guru to the king.

During this time several Brahmins arrived in Manipur from different parts of India like Mathura, Brindaban, Kannauj, Gujarat, Puri and Punjab. The royal deity was now declared as Govindjee. Raslila was introduced as a dance in temples. The Hindu belief in the trimanifestation of divinity: Brahma the creator, Vishnu the sustainer and Shiva the destroyer is subscribed to by the Manipur Hindus. Ram and Krishna being the principal incarnations of Vishnu, it is only natural for the people to follow the Krishna cult.

Buddhist Belt

The Buddhist belt exists from Ladakh to the foothills of Mishmi Hills in Arunachal Pradesh. It comprises of two parts: the Mahayana belt (from Ladakh to the Ishu Razi Pass in the frontiers of Arunachal Pradesh) and the Hinayana belt (Lohit and Tirap districts of Arunachal Pradesh and the Chittagong Hill tracts). The Mahayana belt mostly represents the Tibetan form of Buddhism. It covers Ladakh, Zanskar, Pangi, Lahaul, Kinnaur, Garhwal and Kumaon hills, Nepal, Sikkim, Bhutan and Arunachal Pradesh. The Hinayana belt covers tribes like the Khamptis and Singphos in Lohit and Tirap districts and the Chakmas of the Chittagong Hills tracts and Arakan Yoma. The Buddhist belt in the west extended to Taxila, Gandhara (present-day Afghanistan) and the Hindukush region in ancient times. After the Muslim invasions, Buddhism in these tracts was largely replaced by Islam, but still there is evidence of Buddhism being a popular religion in these areas.

Buddhism was prevalent in Kashmir as well, the *Rajtarangini* refers to vihars there. Asoka's links with the valley are attested to by the records of Chinese pilgrims. Kalhana attributes to Asoka the foundation of Srinagari. Kanishka held the third Great Buddhist council in Kashmir. The Buddhist teacher Nagarjuna lived in Kashmir at that time.

In general, throughout the Mahayana belt, the Buddhism is the Tibetan type both in practice and institutional function. But in philosophy it is basically Indian. Subsects like Gelugpa, Kar-gyupa, Sakya-pa, Nin-ma-pa and Zijed-pa are found here. The salient feature of the Gelugpa sect is that it considers the mythical Vijradhara as its Adi Buddha. The Lamas heading the monasteries of the Gelugpa were appointed by the Dalai Lama. The important Gelugpa monasteries are: in Ladakh: Basgo, Saspol, Shankar, Spituk, Tikse; in Zanskar: Rangdung, Mune, Phugtal, Karsha; in Sikkim: Tharpa-choling; in Kalimpong: Tirpa; in Bhutan: Tashi-Tselling, Tailing (Sanglem), Dung-ham, Golden Tselling (Mira); in Arunachal Pradesh: Twang, Arikadum, Sanglangphe, Lahagten, Padung, Taidung (Thanglen), Surcharg (Lumla).

The Kar-gyupa sect: was founded in the 17th century A.D. by Lama Marpa of Labrang who visited Bhutan and introduced the sect there. The teachings of Naro (950 A.D.) are followed by this sect. It believes in mystic order and mystic insight (To-wa).

The Sakya-pa sect: was established: in Tibet in 1071 A.D. by-Kon-dkon-Mchog-rgyal-Po. It had its influence in Ladakh especially. It accepts most of the teachings of Indian sages ranging from Nagarjuna to Vasuputra and claims inspiration from Manjusri. The school believes in the occult mystery of the Deep Sight and its mystic insight is called "The fruitful path". The sect preaches Arjurna Avatansaka and Vasubandhu's Paramartha and believes in the demon Vajraphurpa. The important Sakya-pa monastery is in Ladakh at Mathr.

The Nin-ma-pa sect reveals a syncretization of the Bon and Buddhist faiths, celibacy and abstinence are rarely practised. The Lamas wear red hats. The metaphysical Buddha or Samanta Bhadra is regarded as primordial deity and considered as the Adi Buddha. It derives its mystic insight from Mahutpanna (Dasg-Chen) or "The great ultimate perfection". The fearful vajra (Vajra-phurba) is the titulary deity and its guardian demon is "The lord Gur". The subsects are Dorje-tak-pa, Mindolin, Kar-tak-pa and Na-dak-pa. They are named after the founders of the concerned monasteries. The Nin-ma-pa monasteries are: in Sikkim: Penmayangtse; in Ladakh: Manggyu, Trag-Thog; in Himachal Pradesh: Urgeling, Sartgeling, Tserghling.

The Ziged-pa literally means "mild doers or passionless ascetics". In fact, these are wandering mendicants who have affinity with the Kar-gyu-pa. This sect was founded by Pa-dam-pa Sans-rygyas who visited Tibet via Kashmir around 1112 A.D. Before 1960 they were seen visiting the Kulu and Kangra valleys in winter and treating the sick. The sect now seems extinct.

The Lamas: play a vital role in the socio-cultural life of the Buddhist communities in the Himalayan belt. They are invited at the birth of a child, and give him his name. They give their blessings at marriages. Their services are sought in illness and death. A household feels very satisfied if one of the sons is initiated into Lamahood. The family believes that through this some contribution has been made to the Sangha. Due to the influence of the Lamas the region is very peaceful.

There are different types of Lamas: The clerical apprentices (Upasakas) are the beginners in the order. The Ge-tsul are not fully ordained but observe 36 rules. The Gelong are fully ordained and observe 253 rules. The Kan-po is the Abbot (Upadhyaya). A Lama is an expert in spiritual and hypnotic methods and treats the sick with his occult craft.

The most honoured is the incarnate Lama. In the Himalayas there are several monasteries with incarnate Lamas. The Chief Incarnate Lama is the Dalai Lama, who is considered the first celestial incarnate Lama (Avalokiteshvara). In fact, the Dalai Lama was identified with the most famous king of Tibet, Sron-Tsan-Gampo. The first Dalai Lama was dGe'-dun-grub-pa (1391-1475 A.D.). The belief in reincarnation has brought stability to the order in Tibet and elsewhere in the Himalayas. Waddel remarks: It seems to me that it arose no earlier than the fifteenth century, and that at first it was simply a scheme to secure stability for the succession to the leadership of the sect against electioneering intrigues of crafty Lamas."

The sixth Dalai Lama was born on Indian soil in a Monpa family of Tawang. His name was Tsangyang Gyatso (1663-1706). Taripe Dronme Lama's incarnations are reported in Arunachal as Lopsang Khenchun, Lopsang Tanpei Wezer, Lopsang Tanpei Gechan, Lodre Gyatso, Lopsang Thapkhe, Kechang Doyen Tanding, Kejang Jurme, Thudan Kechang and Tanzin Thrinbe Namgye. Almost all the big monasteries have a line of incarnate Lamas.

The air of the Buddhist land is sanctified by the mystic Mantra "Om Mani Padma Hum" ("Hail to the Jewel in the Lotus"). A peculiarity of Buddhist villages and houses is posts flying flags with mantras inscribed on them. The idea is that the air will be purified as it comes into contact with the mantras. The flags are of different types: Darsing (a tall one), Lungtog (a small one), Dumphan (a printed one), Chephan (without print) and Pohing (small one tied to bushes). Waddel believes these prayer flags to be the replacements of Asoka pillars with the aim being to keep the teachings of Buddhism alive.

"The change from pillar to post could be easily explained, as great monoliths were only possible to such a mighty emperor as Asoka. But everyone could copy in wood the pious practice of that great and model Buddhist who had sent his missionaries to convert them." Before the approach to a Buddhist village there is a pile of stones on the road, the function of which appears to be to ward off evil spirits. Passers-by offer flowers here.

A container called Chortan is part and parcel of Buddhist religious life. It is used for keeping the earthly remains of the deceased person. A Dungten is a Chortan containing the personal possessions of the deceased. Miniature Chortans decorated with silver, gold or precious stones are carried by individuals.

The Kakalinga (entrance gate) in front of Gompas and even some villages bar the entrance of evil spirits. In each house there is a small chapel where prayers are offered. On the altar are kept images, water and some sacred books. In the village shrine, the articles displayed are: miniature stupa, butter lamp, sacred books, sceptres (dorje), bells, a holy water vase, a ritual arrow (dadar) bound with fine coloured silk, copper blowpipe, drums, cymbals, jugs, metal plates (melong). At the time of rituals seven kinds of offerings are placed on the altar: drinking water, water for washing feet, flowers, incense lamp, perfume water and food (torma) made of dough, butter and sugar.

In Pangi, Lahaul and Kinnaur, the Buddhists follow a caste system because of Hindu influence. In Ladakh, Spiti, Sikkim, Bhutan and Arunachal there is no caste system. The Buddhist layer in Arunachal Pradesh is peculiar as both the Mahayana and Hinayana sects are found.

Islamic Belt

The Islamic belt is a broken one and does not cover the entire Himalayan region. It is found in the north-west Himalayan region in the cultural area of the Baluch and Pathans. Islam spread partially among Khasis and Meiteis of Manipur but did not cover the major portion of the population. In the south-east also the Islamic impact among the Kukis was rare. It appears that the Islamic forces got exhausted after the Indus river and spared the Himalayan tracts from forced conversions with the result that Hinduism in the Pahari cultural area and Buddhism in the Bhotia cultural area continued to exist unaltered.

Among the Assam Hill tribals some families have converted to Islam. "The presence of a small group of Muslim Khasi within the tribe is the result of sexual union between Khasi women and non-Khasi Muslims. Unlike the Christian missions, there has never been an organised body for the propagation of Islam among the Khasis." The Khasis first came into contact with Muslims around the 17th century A.D. when the Muslims started visiting the Khasi Hills for trade etc. They came from Kabul, Kashmir, Punjab, Jaipur, Allahabad, Madras, Calicut, Lucknow, Varanasi, Chapra, Gauhati, Nowgong, Kachar, Silchar, Sylhet and Dacca.

Some Muslims also settled in Manipur. They entered the valley as servants, traders and artisans. Their advent did not change the homogeneous Manipuri culture. It was during the reign of Raja Gambhir Singh and Chandra Kirti Singh that most of the Muslim influx into Manipur occurred. Many among these Muslims married local girls and settled down. The descendants are similar to the Meiteis in physical features. They have Mongoloid and Aryan features. The Muslims are settled at places like Idlong, Miyang-Imphal, Ukhrul and Thoubal and Imphal. A village may be occupied by both Meiteis and Muslims, but they live in separate localities.

Christian Belt

The Christian belt also does not cover a continuous well-defined area. In the Khasi, Jaintia, Naga, Manipur, Lushai and Chin Hills the religion has been adopted by some families—at some places to the extent of 80-90 per cent of the population of a village. But no village has an all-Christian population. In remote areas, the impact of animism is too strong to allow the presence of any other faith. The greatest contribution of Christianity to the tribals has been education and literacy.

Hinduism and Buddhism have been able to spread among the tribals only by virtue of syncretization. This element has been lacking in the case of Christianity and has affected its spread. Because Christianity has not been able to keep in tune with the local faith, it appears alien to the tribals. Its spread among a few tribal groups in the bamboo cultural area is the result just of a religious vacuum. Christianity spread in the hill tracts of the north-eastern region as a result of the British policy in the area. Religious faith for the most part in this area consisted of animism with the general population considering Hinduism as a religion of the high classes. But interest in an 'advanced' religion was always there and the British took advantage of this to further the cause of Christianity with a view to transforming the tribal way of life to the Christian way of life.

To adopt Christianity would mean reading the Bible and this would necessitate a knowledge of English. This, in turn, would bring the tribals closer to the British view of things. Sir James Johnstone remarked: "I pointed out that Nagas had no religion; that they were highly intelligent and capable of receiving civilisation; that with it they would want a religion, and that we might just as well give them our own, and make them in that way a source of strength, by thus mutually attaching them to us. Failing this, I predicted that, following the example of other hill tribes, they would sooner or later become debased Hindus or Musalmans, and in latter case, as we know by experience, be a constant source of trouble and annoyance... A fine interesting race like Angamis, might, as a Christian tribe, occupy a most useful position on our Eastern Frontier... the late General Dalton, CSI, when Commissioner of Chhota Nagpur, did his utmost to aid the Christian mission among the wild Kols, his argument being like mine, that they wanted a religion and that were they Christians, they would be a valuable counterpoise in time of trouble to the vast non-Christian population of Bihar. In the same way, it cannot be doubted that a large population of Christian hillmen between Assam and Burmah would be a valuable prop to the state. Properly taught and judiciously handled, the Angamis would have made a fine set of Christians, of a type superior to most Indian native converts and probably devoted to our rule."

As far as Manipur was concerned, the British religious policy was very clear. They know that the princes of Manipur were staunch Hindus and almost all in the valley had accepted Hinduism. They know that Hinduism was the faith of the biggest section of the society. Therefore they did not want to forcibly propagate any other religion there. Sir James Johnstone's viewpoint was only in relation to the hill Nagas and Kukis. Christianity, thus, penetrated the hills, from Ukhrul, but indirectly it was initiated from Imphal.

William Pattigrew, a young, dynamic and ambitious Scottish missionary came to Silchar in 1891. He came to Manipur and visited Imphal in 1894 and continued there not as a missionary but as a language scholar. He could pick up any language very quickly. During his stay in Imphal he learnt the Meitei language. He managed to convert one Poran Singh and made him an adopted son. The greatest contribution of Pattigrew is that he rehabilitated the Meitei language. He started a primary school in Imphal where Meitei was the medium of instruction. He also authored a grammar of Meitei. A Meitei-English dictionary followed. Pattigrew also translated the Bible into Meitei for the convenience of British officers and others. He also wrote a history of the Meiteis. Two more schools were opened in Imphal and Pattigrew was appointed the Honorary Inspector of Schools. By the time he left Imphal in 1920, a Christian village had come up. But he did not extend his missionary activities beyond Imphal. He shifted his headquarters to Ukhrul to fulfil his evangelical objective. Pattigrew, after marrying in Calcutta in 1897, returned with his wife to Ukhrul. But by now opposition had reared its head against him and one day his hut was attacked and the couple maltreated. The political agent intervened to calm tempers. Pattigrew was then made the administrator of Ukhrul. He learnt the Tankhul dialect and translated the Bible into it. After this he diverted his attention to the Thado and Kuki dialects and again translated the Bible. After World War I, with the permission of the Maharaja of Manipur, he shifted his headquarters to Kongpokpi and started a small dispensary there which has now grown into a big hospital for lepers. People now think of him as a Meitei born in Scotland.

The Khasis came in contact with Christianity by virtue of the missionary efforts of Krishna Chandra Paul, a Bengali Christian, in 1813 A.D. He was the disciple of Father William Carey, the founder of the Serampore Mission. Paul was the first Christian Missionary to enter the Khasi hills. The Bengali translation of the New Testament of William Carey was introduced among the Khasis in 1824. Paul was succeeded by Alexander B Lish who opened schools at Cherapunji and Mawshmai. The Welsh Mission started in the Khasi hills in 1841. Its leaders were Thomas Jones and his wife. They started a missionary house at Cherapunji. William Lewis and his wife joined them in 1843. All of them converted a good number of Khasis to Christianity. In 1874, Maw Khari Chapel, was built in Shillong.

In 1890, the Roman Catholics also entered the Khasi hills. They established schools like Loreto (1909), St. Mary's (1913), St. Edward, (1905) and Don Bosco (1923). Later, Shillong became the centre of higher education in the north-eastern region. The socio-cultural changes in the Khasis to a great extent have come through the influence of Christianity.

Animism Belt

Animism is decidedly older than any religion of the world. As a matter of fact, Hinduism, Buddhism, Islam, Christianity and other religions of the world have all evolved from animism. Every civilization has originally followed animism. In the Himalayan region, animism is very conspicuous in the bamboo cultural area. The religion of the Indus valley was an animistic faith. The Harappan deity in human form with bull horns surrounded by animals is comparable to the Pashupati or Shiva of the Hindu Trinity. This deity has its influence in the Himalayas. It is a fact that Harappan culture and religion extended its influence into the ligions like Hinduism, Buddhism, Islam and Christianity. In practice Christianity does not approve of syncretization or continuance of animistic or aboriginal rituals, customs and traditions but we find that it has failed to impose such restrictions. Christian tribals do not change their names for instance. In fact, the Himalayas preserve the mysteries of animism. The Vedas talk a lot about sacrifices and in Himalayan animism sacrifices take a prominent role. The Hindus in the Himalayas have a gang of animistic gods. Nature worship is still prevalent here. The Supreme being exists in different forms and with different names among the Himalayan tribes. The Baluch believed in a Supreme Being, Khuda, who determines *taqdir* (fate). The Pathans, too, believe in Khuda. Among the Kafirs, the Supreme Being is the Imra, who is considered as the creator. For the Gaddis, the supreme god is Siva. Among Jhechas, the supreme god is Bhagwan but this appears to be new thinking and it is possible that earlier they paid obeisance to Jamblu like the Malanis. They also believe that their supreme deity can turn malevolent if he is not shown reverence. In the Pahari cultural area, the majority have faith in the Hindu Trinity of Brahma, Vishnu and Siva. In most rituals with borrowed aboriginal practices, Siva is the supreme deity and all prayers are conducted in his name. Among Newars, the supreme deity is Adnje-ju-Deo. He is the creator and given the status of grandfather. In the Bhotia cultural area, the concept of a supreme deity is prevalent. It is, however, not expressed in Buddhist rituals. In Bon rituals the worship of a supreme god is essential.

The Lepchas have their Great Mother Creator, Itbu-Moo or It-moo, who is believed to have Kanchenjunga and other mountains. Geoffrey Gorer names her as Itpomu. She is never directly worshipped. As far as the Akas are concerned, they do not have any supreme deity but they identify deities with major forces of nature. Khabrou-Pho-jSogo is the lord of the earth; Huphuliti the lord of the mountains and Sik-Siliaao the lord of the waters. Their father's name is Matti-Dan, who lives in the sky in Ban-Nebine, the place from where the rain comes. They believe in Tcharo, the benign ruler of the human and animal kingdom.

The Daflas believe in Ane-Duisi, the Sun mother. She is considered all-powerful and everything grows, survives and flourishes because of her will. She is, however, not involved in their daily affairs like other spirits. She remains busy keeping the world in motion. The Hill Miris also believe in cosmic deities. They believe in Doniyi, the sun-mother in the Sky and Si the earth-father. The Tagins believe in Donyi-polo, the Sun-Moon cosmic deity, as also the Adis. The Mishmis, however, do not believe in any cosmic deity. Arya is their God, the creator of human beings and others. Similarly, the Singphos do not have a Supreme God. They have adopted Hinayana Buddhism but also follow some animistic practices. Mathun Mathwa is the deity which provides them good fortune. He is not the supreme deity, but is considered as the protector, holder of power and 'onlooker' of all things. The Tangsas believe in a cosmic supreme deity. According to Dr. Parul Dutta, their supreme being is invisible, but created and cares for the world. They personify him by the names Sikia; Pra or Rang Kan Hawa. He lives in the sky and bestows blessings on mankind.

The Noctes believe in a Supreme God called Jongkan or Tesong. For them Kal Jouban is the lord of the sky. There are also Ram Jauban, Wang Jauban and Ha Jauban. The benevolent Kal Jouban resides in the sky and the other Jaubans reside in other places. Among the Wanchos the supreme god is the sky god Rang. The Sema Nagas' supreme god is Athou (Timilhou). He is a benevolent, remote creator who interferes little in human affairs. The Lhota Nagas do not particularly believe in a supreme being but have a sky god called Potso. The Ao Nagas' god is Lung-Kijingna who is considered the chief of heaven. The Kabui Nagas believe in a supreme deity. They say that man was created by Dumpa-Poee on the direction of this supreme deity. The Quireng Nagas have Kampinu as their supreme god, who established forests for their habitation. Some Kukis call their supreme god Pathian (Pasian). Sacrifices of dogs, pigs and hens are made to him.

The Khasis' supreme being resembles the deities of the Hindu faith. Their gods are U. Blei Nongthau, the creator, and his consort Ka-Bhei Synshar. The Khasis also worship the serpent god U. Thlen and other spirits. The Garos' supreme god is Tatara-Ralenga who is the creator and ruler of the world. He controls the lesser spirits and directs them for the welfare of human beings. Shiva is worshipped by many tribes as their supreme deity. As a matter of fact, as already stated he is an animistic god generated in the religious faith of the pre-Harappan period. He is today worshipped almost in the entire Himalayan belt and his abode is the mountain passes and the high peaks of the Himalayas.

Benevolent and Malevolent Spirits

The Himalayan tribal world, haunted by the fear of the unknown, is subject to deeprooted superstitions and has curious customs and intricate rituals. A number of benevolent and malevolent spirits are supposed to be affecting the lives of the tribals. For each action, a particular spirit is held responsible.

The Baluchs believes in good omens and attribute these to good spirits. They believe in the spirits of saints and visit their graves. The Pathans also believe in the good spirits of saints and their burial places are called Ziarath, where they make vows and tie a piece of cloth to mark the making of the vow. They also believe that ghosts attack a person in dark places. They believe that bad spirits, as the angels of death, roam around the earth and affect a person when he is not favoured by good spirits. Sacrifices of animals, however, can ward off the bad effects of the malevolent spirits. A sheep or goat is usually sacrificed in the case of illness, after which the blood of the animal is sprinkled over the doorstep by the sick person to ward off death.

Among the Kafirs, Imra is the supreme god and then they have other gods like Moni (the prophet), Gish (the war god) and Baghisht, Krumai, Dizane, Nirmali (the tribal gods). Their gods are all benevolent and animal sacrifices are offered to them. The Kafirs also believe in malevolent spirits and call them Yush. A person affected by evil spirits can be treated through animal sacrifice. The Kafir gods are Imra, Moni, Gish, Baghisht, Arom, Sauru, Sataram or Sudaram, Inther, Duzhi, Nong, Parado and Shomde. Their goddesses are Suranji or Sauranji (goddess of village), Dizans (goddess of crops, daughter of Sataram), Nirmali (protector of women and children) and Kurmai or Shumai. The Gujjars have their benevolent god of the forests and mountains to whom they offer milk products. Bad spirits are warded off with the aid of Mullahs. Sometimes a *tawiz* (small silver or copper container with mantras worn on the arm) is used to ward off the evil effect of spirits.

The Gaddis believe in Siva and Parvati and offer sacrifices of sheep and goats. But they also have shrines of Kuldeo on mountain passes. The Gaddis believe that bad spirits can attack an enemy if recourse is taken to Jadu-Tona. The evil effects of Bhutas and Pretas are warded off with the help of the village shaman. The Jhechas and Malanis believe in the benevolence of Jamblu Devta. For the Jhechas, Kana Nag or Goshali Nag or Gautam Rikhi is the benevolent deity. Dani is the shepherd god who looks after the welfare of herds. Yearly sacrifices are offered to him in April-May. Jhechas also believe in Khawaja (god of water), Bansheer (god of the forest), Grih Kulj (god of the household). Than and Patal (titulary deities) as well as Joginis (titulary goddesses) are considered helpful and are also syncretised with the Hindu faith. Hidimba, an aboriginal goddess, with her shrine at Dhungari near Manali is also worshipped by the Jhechas. They offer sacrifices of goats and sheep to her. In the Pahari cultural area there are numerous benevolent deities of aboriginal or Hindu origin. Fanjbirs are mostly the Kuldevtas. Saints like Kartiyayan, Parashar, Kashyap, Gautam, Vyas, Vashisht, Manu, and so on are also considered as Kul Devtas. Among the Gaddis and Jhechas, of the Pahari cultural area, there are numerous malevolent deities. Each locality may have a variety of these.

Alamashans are the bad spirits of cremation grounds who roam in the nearby village in search of a victim. Churhels are the malevolent spirit of women dying in childbirth; Gethu Rakshas are the spirits of dead children. Narsingh is believed to be a wandering spirit which attacks women. Bhoot-Prets are the spirits of bad persons who continue to perpetuate their evil ways.

The Buddhists also have numerous benevolent and malevolent spirits. The bad effects of the malevolent spirits are warded off by Tantric practices. The Buddhist "demons are insatiably greedy, vicious, predatory creatures who roam the world causing trouble—illness, death and destruction. They were in the world before humans came into being, and exist independently of any human endeavour." The Sherpas term their demons as Di. According to Heimendorf, the malevolent spirits of the Sherpas are called Shrindi and are of two types: those who have never been human beings and those who were great souls in an earthly life but whose spirits have became malignant. Among the Lepchas, Kangchen junga is a benevolent deity who provides shelter, water, rain, etc. Narzongnyon is the goddess responsible for the geography of the land and the growth of flora and fauna. Akas believe in benevolent spirits which look after their interests. Their malevolent spirit is Sikchi, a spirit of underworld. They also believe that disembodied souls enter this world under the direction of this spirit. The Nishis have Yulo as their benevolent spirit and Dojing and Yahem as the dangerous jungle spirits. Among the Hill Miris, the Kiri and Doje are the benevolent spirits. They reside in forests and look after the fields. Nit and Potlakera are aquatic spirits which live in streams, lakes and rivers. They provide beauty and ability to human beings.

The Hill Miris' malevolent spirits are: Chir-Mur-Chut who provides strength to evil spirits, Liri-Miri who damages crops, Giri-Situ-Tam who causes disasters, Jigri-Larem who causes death, Muri-Nichi who destroys wild bananas, Chulu-Tam who lives in the jungle and destroys livestock, Liri-Pirte who destroys crops and Yapoun who lives in the jungle and brings misfortune if seen by any human being. The Sulungs have a large number of malevolent spirits. Thakhyeng-Kanyeng and Dodok cause colic pain, Siki and Miyo cause stomach swelling, Pikhei lives in house beams and causes pains in joints, hands and legs; Sangtam lives in the walls of the house and causes fever and shivering, Kamnu lives in the roof and causes high temperature and diarrhoea. Kabla also lives in the walls and causes chickenpox and skin disease, Aram causes headache and pain in the body and heart, Yobo causes irritation in the body, Bari-Massuwai and Liru live in the kitchen and cause body pain, Nyongpo lives in the forest and attacks pregnant women and kills babies in wombs, Senyek also lives in the forest and causes vomiting of blood and bleeding through the nose, Miodo lives in the air and accounts for headache and burning sensation in the body, Pomji lives in the sky and causes shocks, Sango lives in trees and causes pain in the joints and hands, Reken damages crops and attacks women to make them deaf, Parta lives in granaries and attacks foodgrains, Sukbayerta-Mussuwai lives in stream and causes back pain and fever, Abo dwells in graves and causes headache and body pain. The Sulungs also have benevolent spirits.

The Apa-Tanis god of prosperity is Tigoui and Guniyanui or Chiching-Ui the god related with misfortune. The benevolent god Yalu-Ui is their war god. Nir-Kor-leng resides in the sky and provides protection from hailstorms and rains. Angura Korleng dwells in lowlands and protects from diseases. Ui-Kasong and Nia-Kasong are also war gods. The Apa-Tanis believe in a land of the dead called Talimoko where a bad spirit, Igi, resides. It may fall in love with any beautiful woman on the earth, in which case a death also occurs. They also believe that during sleep a person's soul wanders on the earth and if at that time it is attacked by a bad spirit it may resist return to the body. The affected person remains unconscious till the soul is restored through the intervention of a priest. The Tagins have benevolent spirits like Bago, Yalo and Pakya. Their malevolent spirits are Done, who causes goitre and Yalos, dead men's spirits who are dangerous and may attack any human being. The Tagins believe that death is due to an attack by a bad spirit.

The Adis have a complex hierarchy of benevolent spirits. Dade Bote is the lord of domestic animals, Doying Bote is the father-sky, the spirit of rain. Shidking Kede is the mistress of the earth. Tori-Mone is the goddess of worldly wisdom. Kine-Nane is the goddess of wealth. Gumin-Soyin the god of the household, Kongki-Komang the god of human structure and life, Nui and Gamro the deity of archery, Bisi-Bote or Ninur-Bote the deity of smithy, Kar-pung the deity of the arts, Karduk the deity of music. The malevolent spirits are: Sili-Sidong, the spirit of water and rivers; Sikkom-Tanom, the spirit of the jungle; Dimi-Diyoor or Epom Ejeng, the spirit of mountains; Suseng Medeng, the spirit of fire; Mili-Minam, the spirit of disease of epidemics.

The Mishmis believe that their life is always at the mercy of the spirits (Khinu). They are everywhere—in the jungles, hills, rivers, lakes and mountains and are always in search of a human being. Goulo resides in the high hills and causes bleeding. Beka dwells in rivers and drags a person into the water. Asha dwells in tall trees and causes the death of its victims. Amraj and Khe-Npa live in deep gorges and claim their victims through slippery paths. Athru is a female spirit which strangles women during childbirth. Ashmo moves in the village during the late hours of the night and tries to kill with terrifying dreams in sleep. Mitu-Sipa is the guardian spirit of animals. Ambung causes dysentery and diarrhoea. Emo causes epilepsy and Ethri respiratory trouble or tuberculosis. Chidi causes Hansen's disease and Ereshu causes accidental fire.

The Singphos have a series of spirits called Nats. The benevolent among these live in the sky and look after the welfare of human beings. The household Nats look after the family. Ningse-Nat is the guardian of morality. Bom-Nat is the guardian of the fields. Mudai Nat provides victory in war. Mufung Dingna Nat is the giver of a child. Luka Nat makes crops prosper.

There are several malevolent spirits also. The Nats of cremation grounds are very dangerous and attack human beings and make them sick. Creem Nat kidnaps children to the jungle; Simfa Nat guides men to be mischievous; Ciyong Nat causes rheumatism and pains in the joints; Sithing Nat causes diseases like leukemia and enlargement of the spleen; Duman Murung Nat causes high fever and death;

Ningsam Nat causes forgetfulness; Susam Nat attacks women during delivery; Fun Nat causes grievous sickness or injury; Wakhap Nat also troubles women during delivery and causes miscarriages; Chowa Numtang Nat troubles women during pregnancy and steals the foetus. Cu-Nat is the soul of accidentally dead persons which visits the relatives and makes them ill; Singlap Nat makes men suffer from continuous fever; Sing Kham Nat gives pain in the chest and abdomen; Chingyo Nat causes rheumatism and muscular pain; Insam Nat causes a bad harvest; Chada Capat Nat causes serious accidents; Ningsum Nat attacks domestic animals; Cu Nat causes pneumonia and high fever; Inja Nat causes leucorrhoea in women; Ninum Nat gives indigestion and diarrhoea; Murang Nat makes men lethargic; Ching Kham Nat is the soul of men dying in accident. It causes stomach pains and dysentery.

The Tangsas believe in spirits called Sang. Matri Sang is a benevolent household spirit. The malevolent spirits are Sip Sang who causes fever, Sousang who gives headache; Sitsang who causes body pain; Rangren who causes fever and headache. Sakugam gives stomach trouble, Jechit causes dysentery with blood. Chowthang is the spirit of the dead.

The Noctes believe that the benevolent Jauban resides in the sky. The Wanchos also believe that their benevolent god Rangad resides in the sky. The Sema Nagas have Kungumi as the god of the sky and Teghomi as the spirit of the earth. A benevolent spirit is Ki chi Miya or Litsaba who provides good crops. Their malevolent spirits are: Muzamuza, the spirit of the jungles which is malicious and leads men astray; Tegha-aghuzuwu who makes men mad; Tega-Kesa who spoils the crops; Kukwobotitomi who causes miscarriage; Losilonitomi who causes quarrels in houses. Kitimi are the spirits of the dead who attack human beings and cause death of the victim.

The Lhota Nagas' benevolent spirits are: Sityingo, the lord of the wild animals, who brings luck in the hunt; Ngazo, the jungle spirit; Rangsi, who provides good crops; Techupfu, the spirit of water. The malevolent spirits are: Khyuham, the spirit of dirty acts who kills children; Isandh Ramo who makes men sick; Nangkamo the malicious jungle spirit.

The Ao Naga deities are: Lungkijinba, the chief of the heaven; Lizaba, the chief of the earth; Mojing the chief of the other world; Kimung-Tsungrem, the house site deity; Ki-tsung-tsungrem, the house deity; Arem-Tsungren, the jungle deity; Lizaba, the creator of earth.

The Mao Nagas believe that earthquakes are caused by Pekujike, a malevolent spirit.

The Khasi god U-Thlen is a snake. Every house has a sort of altar or a fixed place or a basket where the deity is worshipped. He is both benevolent and malevolent. The Khasis also believe in some guardian spirits; Iabei is the female spirit and Thawlang the male spirit. They look after health, happiness and prosperity.

Among the Garos the supreme god is Tatara-Rabuga. Next in line is Chorabudi, the protector of crops, who is a servant of Tatara-Rabuga. Saljong is the god of fertility and is represented by the sun; Goera is the god of strength; Kal Kama is his brother; he holds the life of all human beings in his hands. Asima-Dingsima is the mother of sunshine. The malevolent spirits are: Susima, who causes blindness and Nawang, who causes stomach pain, vomiting and diarrhoea.

The Kukis' supreme god is Pathian (Pasian), to whom sacrifices of dog, pig or hen are offered. They believe that plagues and misfortunes are caused by the goddess Khozing. The other goddesses are Lungjai, Khhanu, Vanchungmula, Pavana and Vanhrika.

Death and the World After Death

Death is a very painful experience for man. He has thus developed a cult of the dead from ancient times. E.C. James describes the genesis of this cult: "Since of all the mysterious, disintegrating and critical situations within which man has been confronted throughout the ages, death appears to have been the most disturbing and devastating; it is hardly surprising that the earliest traces of the religious belief and practices should centre in the cult of the dead." The cult of the dead is one of the rites of passage. The cult of the dead is expressed differently by all the tribes in the Himalayan belt, but the basic concept is similar. As far as the disposal of the dead body and rituals are concerned, each tribe has its own beliefs. The disposal is by burial, cremation or exposure. The Hindus of the Himalayas depart from the normal practice of cremation of the dead in the case of infants who may be buried. Cremation and exposure are followed particularly by the Noctes, Tangsas, Wanchos and Singphos.

Among the Akas, Khoas, Mijis, Daflas, Apa-Tanis, Hill Miris, Sulungs and Adis, the dead body is tied in such a way that the legs are folded over the chest. The idea is to make the dead body resemble the foetus in the mother's womb. Some tribes keep articles used by the deceased alongside the dead body. Tribes like the Nagas, Adis, Mishmis and Tangsas display the articles of the deceased at his grave. An enclosure may be made over the grave which differs from tribe to tribe.

The general idea among the Himalayan tribes is that there exists a separate world of the spirits to which the soul goes after death. Some tribal priests boast that their spirit can go to this world, have a dialogue with the spirits there and return to their body.

The Baluchs believe in heaven and hell but Islamic influence has weaned them away from the blind faith in a celestial world after death. The same is the case with Pathans.

The Jhechas believe in a Road of the Dead which passes through Hamta Dhar. According to them, heaven is somewhere on the Indra-Killa mountain where souls go after death. Bad souls are tortured by Rakshas (demons) on the road through Hamta but good souls are carried on palanquins.

Among the Dards there is concept of heaven and hell. According to their theology, the universe is divided into three worlds: Urdesh, the world above, is the abode of the gods; Mididesh, the earth, is the abode of the living beings; Yardesh, the nether world, is the abode of the mortals. Yardesh is divided further into paradise and hell. Good souls go to paradise or heaven (Bisht) and bad souls go to hell (Zozuk). At the entrances of Yardesh, a custodian, Marmalik, is stationed by Imra (the god). He directs the dead souls to heaven or hell. Most Himalayan Buddhists believe that heaven is somewhere in the mountains near their localities. A few believe it is in the sky near the high Himalayan peaks. Hell, according to them, is in the deep forest or under the water of rivers.

They also believe that the soul of a dead person enters into a form of life existing on the planet and to know the exact form they keep some grains or flour in a container outside the house for three days after a person's demise. The prints seen in the flour indicate the type of life assumed by the soul. But in advanced Buddhist belief the concept of heaven and hell is very complex. It is believed that death affects the body but the mind never dies. The mind is subjected to cyclic existence. Heaven and hell are accepted by the mind in its cyclic existence as per the actions in the previous life. your own virtuous and non-virtuous actions determind what your mind will undergo during death and afterwards. The effects of these actions follow the mind like a flower and its scent.

An act of anger can serve as a cause for rebirth as a hell-being, while one of desire can give rise to a hungry ghost, and another motivated by delusion can lead to rebirth as an animal. These three actions are the causes of birth in the three lower scales. The Hill Miris believe that the soul, called Yalo, leaves the body and goes to the other world of spirits called Neli. This world is under the earth. All souls go there and live in the form of shades. A soul may meet its departed near and dear ones. Each soul going to Neli has to face the hurdles created by the spirit around it. En route are the places called Nido Harboki and Chutu where the souls of the ancestors live, and it is a must for a soul going to Neli to report to them. According to Heimendorf, the Apa-Tanis have a Yamlok-like concept. They also believe that souls (Yalo) go to Neli, the other world. He also mentions that they believe in the birth and rebirth cycle and thus continuous existence of life asz postulated in Hinduism but the difference is that the Apa-Tanis think the underworld life a replica of earthly life.

The Sulungs do not believe in any celestial world or underworld. They believe that the soul (Ho) hovers around and takes shelter elsewhere in this world only. The Adis believe that the soul goes to another world after death. They believe that the souls of men and domestic animals after a fixed stay on this earth go to the land of the dead called Tagramiya. It lives there as a slave.

The Singphos believe that the soul hovers around the earth and later goes to the land of the dead after the Cu-Natca ceremony. The world of souls is called Minla by the Singphos. They believe that the human body is the abode of Ninety Souls, collectively called Khumpuila. The souls of the dead, while on earth, are dangerous to human beings. For the departure of the soul a Nagasat ceremony is performed and the priest recites the following mantra: "From today we have become separated. Henceforth, we have no concern with you. As you are dead, you also do not have any concern with us. Do not come to us and trouble us any more for your food and other requirements. Do not insist on taking any of us with you. Be content with this food now given to you."

The Noctes believe in another world after death. This is called Ulim or Balum and is a celestial place. The soul mounts to it in the form of a kite. The soul of a person perishing in an accident etc, may become an evil spirit and instead of going to Balum may stay in the jungles. According to Dr. Dutta, the Kologaon Noctes believe that good souls go to Lumlan and bad souls to Chalam. They also believe that on the way to Lumlan and Chalam an old lady shows the path to the souls.

The Wanchos also believe in another world. The soul (Lampu) goes to the world of dead (Napung-Lampu). Some believe that this land of the dead is underground while others believe that it is in the sky. In that land, the dead soul owns house, fields, rears pigs and fowls and cultivates crops. The Wanchos believe that the souls of the dead are afraid of light and can only come in darkness. The Sema Nagas believe that good souls go to the east where the sun rises and the bad go to the west where it sets. The Lhota Nagas believe that there are two sets of souls: the Omon just wanders about and can be induced to return. It may also go straight to the world of dead along the Road of the Dead; the Mongyi leaves the man at the moment of death and goes straight to the world of the dead, where it joins with Omon already there except of those individuals encountering sudden death. En route there is the spirit Et Chhi Livanthamo, which lies in wait for passers-by to catch and destroy. To appease it, every dead Lhota has a bead tied to his waist when buried, so that he can offer it to this spirit for passing by. The Ao also believe in a world of the dead. Life in the village of the dead is like life on earth, except that there is no sexual intercourse. According to Ao belief Min Ching or Mojing is the ruler of the abode of the dead. When a person dies, his spirit must pause at Min Ching's house, where it is judged and assigned its proper place. The Khasis believe in an abode of the gods where the soul of the dead goes. There it joins its predecessors. Before cremation, a sacrifice of animals is carried out. The charred bones are collected and kept in a small cairn. This is later on transferred to the family crypt where elaborate rituals are executed.

Shamanism

Shamanism is believed to have originated from the Tunguz tribe which inhabited the area between the Yen-isuei and Lena rivers in Siberia. The German explorer and naturalist, Peter Simon Pallas, visited the tribe in 1772 and observed the prevalence of Shamanism. It probably travelled to other countries via Buddhist monks. Shamanism eventually extended from Siberia to China and had its influence in Central Asia, India and Tibet. Benzaroff believes that shamanism originated from the Manchus in China. He draws an inference about this from seventh century writings when north Mongolia was dominated by the Yuan-Yuan who were of Tunguz-Manchu origin. Whatever may be its origin, shamanism provides a link between animism and polytheism. "Shamanism is a necessary stage in the progress of religious development. The traces of Shamanism may have survived in all of them (Buddhism, Brahmanism and Islam), as in the witchcraft occasionally met with in the modern Europe." The Brahmin priest, the Lama, the Mullah, the Christian priest are thus all shamans covered by the veil of advanced religions, shamanism is the cult of presentation of spirits. The spirit is a very complex substance and is beyond the sensory powers of human beings. Shamanism is the cult which replaces uncertainty and dilemma by the operation of certain techniques which represent the spirit and satisfy the human being. In other words, shamanism is the cult of the technique of using supernatural powers in curing the ailing human being and in resisting the effect of witchcraft or magic. In primitive society, belief in rites and superstitions is deep rooted. The life-cycle itself is based upon certain rites at certain stages of maturity. Van Gennep has named these rites as 'the rites of passage'. The supernatural ceremonies designed to help individuals pass from one stage of a life-cycle to another. Since every person passes through the phases of birth, puberty, marriage and death in this life, he needs the help of supernatural powers at every stage so that the next stage is successfully managed. Shamanism is not only for the society but for each individual as well. A shaman's utterances, incantations, physical expressions and movements have value and meaning. A shaman cannot be ignored even after death.

Among the Dauds, the priestly class is very prominent in society. Among the Kafirs, a priest has the same status as among the Mirs. All sacrifices and rituals are conducted by him. The Baluchs have a Mullah who conducts sacrifices, examines the sick, predicts the future and deciphers omens. The Pathans too have a Mullah who performs all rituals. Fakirs help sometimes to ward off the effects of bad spirits. A taveez prepared by a shaman or Mullah is sometimes worn. The Pathans believe that bad spirits do not glance at a person if he is wearing a taveez. A taveez is commonly used by the Gujjars and even by Hindus. The Gaddis also believe in shamans and call them Chelas. They draw a 'mandala' and on it are kept different articles of food, etc. Then the sick person is placed in the mandala and the sacrifice of an animal, especially goat or sheep, is offered. Such Chelas are sometimes expert in Muth (magic by which an enemy is afflicted by misfortune). The Chelas also function as a medium of a deity who might demand a ransom, sacrifice, etc. A lady involved in shaministic practices is called a Cheli.

The Jhechas call their shaman Tangiri as also the natives of Kulu and Mandi. In fact, 'Tangiri' means a person expert in tantric practices. Among the Jhechas and Malanis, the Gur or Chela of Jamblu Devta also functions as a Tangiri. A Gur or Chela of any Devta or Devi in Kulu, Mandi, Simla and Sirmour functions as a shaman but for this he has to be trained by a Guru. Shamans generally operate their rituals via '*Mandalas*' which are of different types: Navgraha Mandala, Devi Mandala, Jogini Mandala, etc. They tell fortunes with the help of mustard. The mustard is placed in the palm of a person afflicted by some disease or malevolent spirit amid incantations. Then the closed palm is opened and the placement of the mustard examined. The pattern indicates the solution: what treatment is called for, what sacrifices need to be made to a deity, and so on. Some shamans in the Pahari cultural area (including Nepal) use human skull, bones and hair for their rituals.

Among the Buddhists of Ladakh, Lahaul, Kinnaur, UP hills, Nepal, Sikkim, Bhutan and Arunachal, the Lamas carry out shamanistic rituals. In fact, the old type of Buddhism is purely tantric and it combines shaministic practices with Buddhist rituals. A shaman is called Thawa, Tib, Irapa, Mindung or Bonpa according to the area from which he hails.

The Lepcha shaman is called Mun. His main function is to ward off misfortune and disease caused by malevolent spirits. The Mun also gets "possessed" by the spirit of a deity and announces future events. Both men and women are entitled to become Muns.

The Nishis and Hill Miris call their priest Nyibu. Any person having a spiritual aptitude can become a Nyibu. He, however, has to undergo training with a master. Nyibus wear special costumes especially while carrying out certain rites. They are very honoured in society. They do not engage in any other profession. Their services are required at birth, death and other community or individual rites. They are given a share of a sacrificed animal.

The Sulung priest is called Pehe. A female priest or diviner is not common. The Apa-Tanis' priest is also known as Nyibu. His main functions are: the invocation of gods; the recounting of mythological events and performance of individual and community rituals. The Nyibu carries out his divination by examining the egg or the liver of a chicken. As a mediator between men and Ui (the gods) he directs on the kind of animal sacrifice to be made to the latter. Heimendorf comments on the Nyibu: "The ability to be in touch with gods and spirits is not acquired by accident, for unlike the deities of other people, those of the Apa-Tanis do not impose themselves on mortals, summoning them to their services. Priests, known as Nyibu, have to learn the art of communicating with the denizens of the invisible world by a lengthy process of training. They do not belong to a special class of people, but any patrician—though not a Guchi—can acquire the skill of invoking gods and spirits. This is usually done by apprenticing himself to an experienced Nyibu and by assisting him in the performance of rituals and sacrifices."

Among the Adis there are two kinds of priests: the Epak Miri is the curer and the Nyibu is the diviner. The latter executes his work during day time. He narrates the myths relating to the origin of a particular spirit. The Epak Miri operates at night. There is no restriction on any one entering the priestly class provided the person has sufficient spiritual knowledge. The Epak Miri wears special beads (Rogum) and special ornament (Laikjiu). He also wears a woman's skirt while performing a rite.

The Mishmi shaman is called Igu. He performs rituals and cures people with indigenous medicines. Singpho priest is called Dumsa and is a diviner. Another type is called Mithai and is a magician. Both Dumsa and Mithai have supernatural powers. The Mithai has to lead a more austere life than the Dumsa. The Dumsa has no magical powers, but can attract spirits. The Mithai can disassociate his soul (Minal) and send it to the concerned Nat to invite it to preside over the rite being performed.

The Noctes have two kinds of priests: those who divine things through omens and those who perform rituals. In one particular place (Laju), according to Dr. Parul Dutta, the Chief himself performs the rituals, particularly those connected with the dead or with head hunting. The priests are named as Roba, Ronu, Kamba and Romnu in Soha village and Lamba and Kamba in Lingwang village. They are required for marriage ceremonies only.

The Wanchos' priest (Zampa) is hereditary. He is engaged for prayers at individual and community rituals for attaining success over enemies and for performing last rites. The Zampa may hail from the ranks of the commoners but by virtue of their shamanistic expertise occupy a special position in society. Some are chosen by members of the village council. The Angami Naga shaman is called Zhen. Among many Nagas, the tribal chief functions as the priest or shaman. Among the Meiteis of Manipur, the priest is called Maiba (male) and Maibi (female). Maibaism is related to the animistic faith. It must have evolved as a function and system in the division of labour in society. Those who excelled in performing the rituals of animism were in demand. The Maiba and Maibis also treat the sick.

The Kukis' shaman is called Davi Thiam and is in fact a village sorcerer appointed by any family for domestic rituals and to conduct sacrifices to spirits and deities. Among the Khasis, the shaman is very important. He examines the yolk of the egg or liver of a chicken and pronounces on the spirit involved in a particular disease. He also suggests the type of sacrifice to be offered. The shamam also plays an important role in the last rites of a person. An egg kept on the dead person's stomach is broken and the yolk sprinkled over the funeral pyre. The Garos call their priest Kamal. Anyone can become a Kamal.

Donyi-Polo (The Sun - Moon Cult)

Donyi-Polo is the animistic religion of the Adi tribe in Arunachal Pradesh. It is a sun-moon cult the likes of which are found among many tribes around the world. The cult is as old as the Indus valley civilization.

The sun cult is prominent in Hinduism from ancient times. The Suryavanshis of the Mahabharata were the adherents of this cult. Vasudeva's Garuda and Chakra are the solar symbols. Garuda, the bird, is the vehicle of the sun god. It takes the Lord to three places; Suryodaya (sun rise), Dopahar (the sun at its zenith) and Suryasta (the sun at setting).

Among the Sema Nagas, the sun and the moon are called upon to witness oaths and assertions. The Angami Nagas personify the sun and regard it as a female, the wife of the moon, which they look upon as a male. Being a woman, the sun is afraid to go out in the dark and only shows herself by day. The moon, being a man, moves carelessly about in the gloom of the night. Elvin quotes J.P. Mills that the Lhota Nagas think the sun to be a flaming plate of hard metal which travels along its path in the sky by day and returns under the earth to light up the land of the dead at night. The moon is also regarded as a plate of flaming metal. Elvin further says that the Mikirs regard the sun and moon as divine though they do not specially propitiate them. The Ao Nagas worship the sun and moon by offering sacrifices of eggs, cows and pigs. They believe that the sun and the moon look after their crops and animals.

The Wanchos believe that once the moon was very hot, shining the whole night, as a result of which many creatures died of heat.

Jang Tai then threw mud on the moon and since then it has become cool and pleasant. About eclipses, their myths say that Luk, the enemy of the sun and the moon, swallows the sun, causing a solar eclipse.

According to Nocte mythology, Rango Kotakray created the sun and the moon when the first man and woman appeared on earth. The sun was the man and the moon a woman and lived as husband and wife. The heat of the sun used to destroy the children born of them. One day, in a temper, the moon threw mithun dung at the sun which led to the development of what are now observed as sunspots. However, it was decided between the two to change their sex for a few days every month. Another quarrel took place between the couple and this time the sun threw mithun dung at the moon, the marks of which, are still visible.

According to Singpho mythology, there were nine suns. All were hot and made life miserable on earth. Mathun Matta thus killed seven suns and also tried to kill the sun and moon. But they hid themselves behind the Himalayan mountain ranges at a place called Najoi-Singrabhum. The sun made a golden boat for itself and thus goes around in this. The moon, on the other hand, made a silver boat for itself. But its journey is not regular. It gets tired and sleeps and then starts on its rounds after some days. So we see it increasing and decreasing in size and shape. The Mishmis hold that the sun goes for a walk every day. In the morning he takes the upper path and in the evening the lower. Long back there were two suns, one appearing in the daytime and the other at night, causing great difficulty to the creatures on earth. One sun at last was killed by man, so there is only one sun now. The Mishmis also believe that the moon shows one of its sides to the earth and the other to the land of the dead. The spots on the moon are believed to be due to the shade of a tree.

The Adis believe that the sun and the moon are born of Pedong Nane, the great grand-daughter of Sedi-Melo. Sachin Roy writes: "Donyi the sun and Polo the moon are twins of hers. The luminous eyes of Irmyam Miteko a son of Sedi-Melo, were grafted on them one of each by Irsiye of the same family and so they became the luminaries they are now." Among the celestial deities, Donyi and Polo are not very high in the hierarchy but directly affect human beings, animals and plant life on earth. Verrier Elvin remarks: "Donyi-Polo emerged rather late in the scheme of things, and his origin was not altogether dignified: there were at first two suns, of an unbearable brightness, but the Prog shot at one of them with his arrow and reduced its radiance to the cool and gentle light of the moon. The sun-moon was created after the Wiyus and, according to some traditions, later even than mankind."

The Nishis say that the sun was very hot in the beginning. Dedu-Kombu damaged one of its eyes with an arrow. The sun in anger went under the earth. The marks on the moon, according to the Nishis, are due to the beating given to him by his wife, the sun. Elwin has mentioned that "the Buguns, like people all over India, shout, beat gongs and light fires at the time of an eclipse of the sun. But for a total eclipse of the sun, they go outside their houses and throw off all their ornaments and clothes, hide themselves and their children under bamboo baskets and do not allow any animal to come near them. For they think that at the movement of darkness their clothes, ornaments, daos or domestic animals will turn into demons and destroy them. After the eclipse they bathe and only then they resume their clothes."

The symbolic representation of the sun-moon cult is also prevalent in the Buddhist belt. The Monpas decorate their houses, doors, kitchen, etc, with a 'Karta' (literally "white mark") design. This depicts the crescent moon and the sun, combinedly termed Nyida or Nyima-Dawa. The sun element is called Nyima and the moon element Dawa. The Monpas believe that since both these celestial objects are the source of light, their symbolic representation on doors and walls will brighten their homes. The symbolic representation of sun-moon (Nyima-Dawa) is also prevalent among the Ladakhis, Lahulas, Kinnauras and Sherpas. Shepherds like the Gaddis and Jhechas of the Himalaya also worship sun and moon and offer goat and sheep sacrifices to these deities. Their seasonal migrations start as per the size of moon and its light.

The sun-moon cult is also prevalent in one way or another in the Hindu belt. On the occasion of Paus Sankranti, ceremonial bathing takes place at the Parshurah Kunda in Lohit district. Sankranti is represented by the lunar cycle. Archaeological evidence of a solar cult is found in the sculpture of Malinithan in West Siang district.

From all this it is evident that the sun-moon or Donyi Polo cult is prevalent in the Hindu, Buddhist and animism belts. It is, however, clear that the Adis' neo-theological approach centres more prominently around Donyi-Polo than that of the others. According to Sachin Roy, "the Donyi and Polo are endowed with light that illuminates the world and lifts the cover of darkness and are favoured with a position high above in the sky to overlook all. They are also extremely regular in their courses across the heavenly expanse. Naturally, they are looked upon as the custodian of law and truth. That is why they are invoked in the beginning of Kebang on disputes to reveal the truth and expose the false."

References

Banerjee, P., *Early Indian Religion,* Vikas Publishing House, New Delhi, 1973, pp. 100, 102.

Berreman, Gerald, D., *Hindus of the Himalayas,* Oxford Univer sity Press, Bombay, 1963, pp. 89-90.

Goetz, Hermann, *The Early Wooden Temples of Chamba,* 1955, p. 48.

Grierson, G.A., *Linguistic Survey of India,* Vol. III, Part I, p. 427.

Indian Antiquary, Vol. XXV, pp. 141-142.

Roy, Anita, *Art of Nepal,* Indian Council for Cultural Relations.

Sacred Books of the East, Vol. XXIV, p. 202.

Sanon, Arun, *Festive India,* Frank Bros. & Co., New Delhi, 1987, p. 88.

2
Temples and Culture

Temples have not only preserved the Hindu religion but through their patronage they have also kept alive India's cultural heritage. Temple towns like Madurai or Varanasi have always been great centres of scholarship. Here the gurus had *ashrams* and students came from all over the land to study at these colleges. At these *gurukuls* the students not only learnt the ancient Hindu texts from the Vedas to the Upanishads but also specialised in various fields like mathematics, logic, astronomy, grammar and medicine. For centuries the Vedas were not written down but taught through recitation by the gurus and memorised by students. As the Vedas were considered to be divine, great emphasis was laid on correct pronunciation, even when the meaning of the ancient Sanskrit text was obscure.

If these ancient texts have survived nearly intact it is because of the dedication of countless scholars at these gurukuls. The temples also became centres of the social life of a town. Spiritual leaders gave sermons in the halls of the temples, where dance and music recitals and big sacrificial ceremonies were also held. Temples fed people, ran schools and were refuges for the poor and the priests were influential members of the community. Traditionally the deity had to be entertained, so temples also welcomed musicians and dancers. All the classical dances from Bharatanatyam to Odissi have their origins in temples. Great poets received the patronage of temples. Among the greatest gifts of the temples of the south are the Tamil devotional poetry of the Nayanmars dedicated to Shiva and the Alvar hymns that praise Vishnu and these hymns are still sung at the temples. Important treatises on the systems of architecture and sculpture like the Shilpa Shastra and Vastu Shastra were written because of the many temples being built by kings.

Religious architecture became a symbol of power and kings built temples to gain punya, merit with the gods and also as monuments of their greatness. Dynasties vied with each other to build more magnificent structures to be patrons of great scholars and artists. They gathered the best craftsmen — sculptures, architects and painters to build these temples. Then invited great scholars, poets, musicians and dancers to become a part of these great religious institutions. The craftsmen working on a temple were called *silpin* and there were various kinds of *silpin*. The *sthapati* was the designing architect; the *sutragrahin* was the surveyor; the *takshaka* was the sculptor and the *vardhakin* was the builder-plasterer-painter. They all worked under the supervision of the *Sthapaka,* the architect-priest who was usually a brahmin with both a knowledge of the *Vastushastra* and also of the practical crafts of architecture and sculpture. Most of these great artists have remained nameless and have been forgotten by later generations but their magnificent creations have stood for centuries.

All the temples have grandiose inscriptions that praise the king who has had these temples built, but rarely do we find any mention of the talented *silpins* who actually built them with such devotion and covered the walls with carvings of such incomparable beauty. Ancient Hindu temples, especially those that survived in the South were created as a form of sculpture and the finest work of these nameless artists can be seen on the walls, pillars and the towering *gopurams.* It is a magical, mythical, world of gods, goddesses, celestial nymphs, prancing horses, royal parades, demons and legendary heroes. Then the interiors were embellished with fresco paintings and the ceilings and walls glittered with murals in jewel like colours. One of the greatest temple art traditions that has survived till the present is that of Chola bronzes; these are exquisite free-standing icons that were first presented to temples by the Chola kings. Religion has always been good for business and even today temple towns are also great commercial centres.

Take the silk weavers of Kashi and Kanchipuram, they were first employed by the temples to provide silk cloth for the deities and priests, as silk is considered the purest of textiles. Then sarees were woven for the *devadasis.* Today these two cities are leading producers of silk with a huge population of weavers. Big markets flourish at all temple towns to meet the requirements of pilgrims and provide a livelihood to the people. Important temples hold regular festivals like the *ratha yatras* when thousands arrive and it is also a time to shop and enjoy the pleasures of the city.

The Architecture of Temples

Most of the architectural elements are the same in all temples and each has a specific name. The sanctum sanctorum is called the *garbha griha* - the womb house. The *garbha griha* is a square cell that is usually plain and undecorated inside so that all the attention is focussed on the deity that is placed in the centre. The *garbha* griha has its only door facing the East so that it gets the first rays of the sun. Traditionally the other three walls have no openings. The garbha griha is surrounded by a rectangular corridor called the *pradakshina patha,* that is used for the circumambulation of the deity. On the outside walls of the garbha griha, in the three cardinal points of the North, South and West, there are niches for images. The tallest tower is always over the garbha griha, which is the *shikhara.* The earliest temples were usually just the garbha griha with a small porch before it. Then an open pillared hall called the *mandapa* was built facing the door of the sanctum. Here devotees could gather and large religious ceremonies like yagnas could be held. Over the centuries the garbha griha has remained an essentially simple chamber, the spiritual home of the great mystery.

It is the mandapa that has seen many elaborations and variations. A porch called the *ardha mandapa* was added first, then a second pillared hall called the *maha mandapa* appeared. The Orissan temples have a *natya mandapa* where dance performances were held and the *bhoga mandapa* where offerings were made to the deity and devotees fed with the *prasada.* Shrines to other gods and goddesses were added in the courtyard around the main sanctum. Then southern temples added a slightly smaller but equally ornate shrine for the consort of the min deity called the *amman temple.* So Shiva got an *amman* shrine to Parvati, Vishnu to Lakshmi. A mandapa was then attached to the *amman* shrine called the *kalyana mandapa,* where a celestial wedding ceremony is performed every year during the *Brahmotsavam* festival. During the reign of the Chola kings in the south the temples began to be enclosed and fortified by a high stone wall. The wall was pierced at the four cardinal directions by entrances and over them the amazing *gopuram* gateways appeared.

Soaring gateways teeming with figurative carvings - human and divine figures, animals, birds and demons, all painted in vivid, eyecatching colours. With each generation these pyramidal towers rose higher and became more elaborate till they towered over the main shikhara. The larger temples were then enclosed within a series of courtyards called *Prakaras*, each with *gopurams*, so that you walked under a row of gopurams gradually diminishing in height till you reached the final courtyard with the main temple.

Chiselling Life out of Stone

Our temples are as much a creation of sculptors as the work of architects. In Indian temples the basic structure of the building is concealed by a profusion of carvings and the finest works of Indian sculptors are to be found here. These forgotten artists remained anonymous and did not win any personal fame for their work. There is a vibrant exuberance in the shape and posture of figures and a frank enjoyment of every aspect of life in their work.

The Canons of the Shastras

Shastras are ancient treatises that laid down the rules of correct conduct and practise and they have codified many aspects of life from the rituals of worship to the layout of temples and the principles of sculpture. The Vastupurusha Mandala lays down the sacred rules of architecture, especially of temples. The *Vastu Shastra* was written down in the early years of the first millennium and copies of the treatise were widely circulated. Because of this, temples came to be built on the same pattern all across the Indian subcontinent. The temple is considered a sacred space, a mandala, where every structure has a fixed place, a specific direction and purpose. For instance, most temples face east so that the first rays of the sun can illumine the deity. Often temples are built next to rivers because running water is needed for ritual ablutions. The *Vastu Shastra* gives detailed and very specific instructions on where entrances are to be made, the direction of the niches where images of deities can be placed, the position of windows, gateways, roof beams and towers. It is finally a practical architectural code that is couched in esoteric religious terms.

A temple is conceived as a symbol of heaven. The heaven of the Hindus - *swarga,* is said to be located around a mythical mountain named Meru in the Himalayas. The pantheon of gods and goddesses, the *apsaras* who are celestial dancers, demi gods like the *yakshas* and *yakshis,* celestial musicians called *gandharvas,* all live in this *swarga.* The temples with their gradually rising towers depict this in Mt. Meru where the inhabitants of heaven, the gods and celestial beings, are placed around the temple in the form of sculpture.

Originally the *garba griha* held just one image but with the rituals and festivals becoming more elaborate, the number of icons grew. There is the main icon, the Mulamurti, which is immovable and worshipped in the sanctum. The Utsavamurti, the movable image is taken out in procession during festivals. Then, images of the consorts of the god, his famous devotees like the sage Shankaracharya or Bhakti poet Chaitanya were placed in the sanctum. Finally, even his weapons, like Vishnu's *sudarshana chakra,* found place and worship in the sanctum. In the temple sculptures an idealised image of heaven was created. Gods and humans wear richly pleated clothes, elaborate hair-dos and heavy jewellery.

The *apsaras* are perfectly shaped, with narrow waists, curvaceous breasts and hips and long sinuous arms. The demons are utterly ferocious with misshapen bodies, bared teeth and protruding eyes. This is a portrait of heaven, so the bodies are always youthful, their features perfectly proportioned and there is an expression of vivacity and cheerfulness on most of the faces. Even the wild haired ascetic is usually quite well fed and benignly smiling. A temple is what you want it to be. For the devotee it is the place where his god lives. For the connoisseur of sculpture and painting, it is like a living museum. For a dancer, the figures carved on the walls are the foundation of her art. For a musician or poet, the deity is both inspiration and the final audience. You don't have to enter a temple to pray, you can go there to savour the many aspects of India's rich and iridescent culture.

3

Badrinath: The Dhaam in the Himalayas

Badrinath is the Uttara Dhaam, the *dhaam* of the north, and this *tirtha* stands in a valley high in the Himalayas. On the map of India, the subcontinent wears a white, icy crown of these great mountain ranges. Hindu mythology says this is the home of its pantheon of gods and goddesses and if humans imagine a place called heaven it would be something like the Himalayas. A dauntingly majestic landscape of soaring peaks covered in everlasting snow, emerald valleys and forests, fields of wild flowers, silver waterfalls and turbulent rivers flowing through deep gorges. The Himalayas are nature's very own *devalaya,* a landscape created like a temple to the gods. The Himalayas are heaven on earth, the *swarga* of the Hindus. Somewhere among the peaks and glaciers, is the mythical Mount Meru around which the gods live and Lord Indra, the king of the gods, holds his celestial court.

Then there is the holy Mount Kailash where Lord Shiva has his home and with him lives his consort Parvati, who is the daughter of the Himalayas. Lord Vishnu also has his kingdom of Vaikuntha somewhere beyond the highest peaks and among the valleys of wild flowers. Here at the end of Indian rivers, the Ganga, springs from an icy cave at the end of a glacier at Gaumukh. The Himalayas are the source of the mightiest rivers of the north — the Indus, Brahmaputra, Yamuna, and the three streams of Alakananda, Mandakini and Bhagirathi that merge to form the most sacred river of all — the Ganga, goddess and mother to the people of the land. At an inaccessible valley high among the craggy peaks are the legendary Mansarovar Lake and Mount Kailash, that pilgrims reach after weeks of arduous trekking. So where else would you build a temple but in the Himalayas?

The *tirtha* of Badrinath stands at a glacial height of 3122 metres and here the Rishi Ganga river flows into the mighty waters of the

Alakananda, one of the main tributaries of the Ganga. Beyond Badrinath is nature's playground, the unforgettable Valley of Flowers where, every August, the grassy fields bloom with a bouquet of wild flowers and attended by hovering butterflies. The picturesque valley is transformed into a carpet of flowers circled by snowy peaks and topped by an azure blue sky. Nearby is the silver lake of Hemkund that is a tirtha of the Sikhs. The lake is at a height of 4328 metres and a thousand steps carved up the hillside lead to the ancient and sacred Sikh gurudwara of Hemkund Sahib, once visited by Guru Gobind Singh.

One of the names of the Badrinath region is Badrikashram, a hermitage for sages and seers, as the Himalayas have drawn pilgrims and mystics, artists, poets and wanderers for centuries. It is also called Tapobhumi, the land for meditation and among its rugged, remote hills the ancient Hindu ascetics and scholars, the rishis and munis, built their ashrams, and here many of the greatest ancient treatises were written. The mountains have a strange magnetic power that still calls the mystic and for centuries *sadhus* have meditated in inaccessible caves and worshipped the rising sun by bathing in the icy waters flowing out of the glaciers. (The saint Adi Shankaracharya answered the call of these mountains when he travelled from Kerala in the far south, climbed high into the Garhwal Hills to build a temple at Badrinath and establish a monastery and a theological college at Joshimath).

Most of the thinkers and preachers from the past, from Ramanujacharya and Nityanand to Guru Nanak have wandered here in search of the eternal truth. (The Himalayas have been the final destination of not just sages but even heroes and kings. Rama and Lakshman came here to perform the sacrifice of penance after the death of Ravana. The five Pandava brothers of the *Mahabharata* retreated into these hills when they decided to renounce the world after the great battle. The final chapter of the epic narrates the story of their last journey of penance into the hills beyond Badrinath and their ascent to heaven).

The Garhwal Himalayas, in the state of Uttaranchal, have the greatest concentration of *tirthas* in the country. Most of the important deities like Shiva, Vishnu, Rama, Krishna and the various aspects of the Devi have temples dedicated to them here. So this sacred region resonates with myths and legends and is called Devabhoomi, the land of the gods. As Lord Krishna says in the *Bhagavat Gita,* "Out of all immovable things, I am the greatest mountain in the world. I am the Himalayas." In the Garhwal Himalayas it seems like every mountain peak, glacier, valley or confluence of streams has its little shrine. And over the centuries, every temple has gathered its own myths and legends, many of them woven around the presence of the five Pandava brothers. In the mountains are four of the greatest *tirthas*—the Chaar Dhaam of the Himalayas—of Kedarnath, Badrinath, Gangotri and Yamunotri. Then along the confluence of the various streams that make up the Ganga are the *prayags* like Karna Prayag and Rudra Prayag. Finally, as the Ganga appears in the plains there are the tirthas of Rishikesh and Haridwar.

The Prayags

On the way to Badrinath pilgrims stop to worship at the temples of the five prayags. The Ganga that appears with such majestic power at Haridwar is the combination of a number of streams like the Bhagirathi, Mandakini, Alakananda, Nandakini, Dhauli Ganga and Pindar Ganga. As the meeting of two streams is considered very auspicious, these *prayags* are *tirthas* that are placed at the confluence of these hill rivers. The river that appears out of the glacier at Gaumukh above Gangotri is called the Bhagirathi, which is the main branch of the Ganga. Then there are *five prayags* along the river down to Rishikesh.

Moving up into the hills from Rishikesh, the first confluence is at *Deva Prayag* where the Alakananda meets the Bhagirathi and it is from here that the river is called the Ganga. Rama and Lakshman performed a penance here for killing Ravana who was a brahmin. Here the ancient Raghunath Temple stands above a steep flight of steps cut out of the hill. The temple is dedicated to Rama and has some intricate carving on the walls. There are two sacred pools, Vashishtha Kund that stands beside the Bhagirathi and Brahma Kund by the banks of the Alakananda. Myths say that Vishnu's navel lies in Devaprayag and that Brahma came to meditate here. The *prayag* is named after a sage named Devasharma who performed austerities, worshipping Vishnu here. Pilgrims also visit the temple of the four armed, Chaturbhuja Singavahini dedicated to goddess Durga, which is 22 km from Deva Prayag. At *Rudra Prayag,* the Mandakini river flows into the Alakananda and here the most sacred shrine, the Rudranath Temple is dedicated to Shiva. The sage Narada meditated here and Shiva was so pleased by his worship that the god presented him with the *ragas* and *raginis* of Indian classical music. There is also a Devi temple dedicated to Ma Chamunda here.

Above this *prayag* is *Karna Prayag,* where the Pindar Ganga meets the Alaknanda river and here Karna, one of the most interesting heroes of the *Mahabharata* is said to have performed austerities. The sun god Surya, who was Karna's father, appeared before him at this *prayag* and gave him the magical armour of *kavach* that made Karna invincible in battle. Among all the temples at Karna Prayag, the most popular are temples dedicated to Karna and Mother Goddess Uma, who is an aspect of Parvati.

Nanda Prayag is located at the confluence of the smaller Nandakini river with the Alakananda and then going up the Alakananda, at *Vishnu Prayag* the Dhauli Ganga meets the same river. At one time Vishnu Prayag was a busy pilgrim town as it stood on the pilgrim's trail to Mount Kailash and Lake Mansarovar. The *prayag* is named after Vishnu as Narada performed austerities to the god here and gained enlightenment.

Location

The *tirtha* of Badrinath stands by the banks of the Alakananda above these five *prayags*. As pilgrims head into the hills past Haridwar and Rishikesh, the road to Badrinath runs parallel to the Ganga till the confluence of the Bhagirathi and the Alakananda at Deva Prayag. From Deva Prayag the pilgrim's trail follows the path of the Alakananda, while the Mandakini leads them to another hill *dhaam* of Kedarnath. For centuries pilgrims dreaming of Badrinath have moved up this trail, listening to its roaring waters, as its raging torrents swirl over boulders and flow in a deep gorge that leads them to the great *dhaam* of Badrinath.

As the Himalayan hills get higher and more precipitous, a spectacular landscape unfolds before the traveller. Earlier pilgrims did this journey on foot. Long rows of determined men and women, bent over their rough walking sticks, trudging up the precarious hill slopes, wending their way through pine forests and fields blooming with wild flowers. Even today the road goes past villages with low stone houses with slate gray roofs, apple orchards and terraced rice fields. It is an unforgettable landscape framed by snowy peaks that change their colour with the movement of the sun. The Garhwal Himalayas have welcomed pilgrims and monks, ascetics and adventurers for centuries. Pilgrims who have wandered through this landscape of soaring snow-capped mountains, silver waterfalls cascading down craggy cliffs and the frozen expanse of icy glaciers, have been amazed by its majestic, ever changing beauty. In the Himalayas it is so very easy to believe that this is Devabhoomi, the true land of the gods. Before Badrinath is the Valley of Flowers and past it is the mythical land of Vaikuntha.

Like Kailash is the home of Shiva, Vaikuntha is the abode of Vishnu. So Badrinath is the gateway to Vaikuntha and here the Himalayas are imbued with his myths and the legends of his ten *avatars*. Picturesque Badrinath is also called Bhuvaikunth, Vishnu's Vaikunth on earth. Here every village priest will tell you of the Pandava brothers going past on their last journey or a visit by Krishna or the great sages. Many places have names that echo their-ancient past and links with the epics — Hanuman Chatti, Uttar Kashi, Karna Prayag and Vishnu Prayag. Here the mountains are worshipped as deities and named after gods — Neelkantha, Trishul, Nanda Devi.

Badrinath is mentioned many times in the epic, *Mahabharata*, which was written between 400 B.C. and 200 A.D. Once they had relinquished their throne, the Pandava brothers and Draupadi walked through this region on their last pilgrimage. Among the *tirthas* they visited were Kedarnath, Gupta Kashi and Badrinath. Bhima built a bridge for Draupadi over the Saraswati river called Bhima Pul. Their journey took them near the treacherous glacier ridden Satopant Lake, past a natural spring called Baandhara, created when Arjuna aimed an arrow at the earth to find water. The Alakananda river appears from a glacier beyond the Satopant Lake. Beyond Tapovan is the ancient pilgrim route to the Kailash mountain and Mansarovar Lake in Tibet but this route has been closed in recent times.

Myths and Legends of Badrinath

Badrinath is the heart of the land of the sages who meditated here in remote caves and by rivers and glaciers. Many of these reclusive seekers of truth, the true *sadhus*, can still be seen here. Rishis of ancient India like Gautama, Kapila, Kashyapa and Narada are part of the spiritual traditions of this land and that is why Badrinath is also called Badrikashram, the hermitage of Badri. Also as Narada attained *moksha* here, it is called Narada Kshetra. The Skanda Purana calls it Badrivishal, the great land of Badri and it is also called Keshava Prayag as Krishna loved this region. Over the centuries the scholars and sages have continued to come to Badrinath to meditate. In the 9th century it was visited by Adi Shankaracharya, then Ramanujacharya, one of the greatest *vaishnava-acharyas,* or teacher-saints, came in the 10th century. The philosopher Madhavacharya came in the 14th century and the vaishnava saint Lord Nityanand in the 15th century.

Badrinath also appears in many Buddhist writings, proving that at least for a while this was also a Buddhist place of pilgrimage. Legend has it that an ancient Vishnu temple that stood at Badrinath was destroyed 1200 years ago and probably replaced by a Buddhist vihara, which was also later destroyed. Then when Shankaracharya came here, he built the next temple. Badrinath is the ideal place for quiet contemplation and scholarship. The tirtha stands at the confluence of the two rivers of Rishiganga and the Alakananda in one of the most picturesque regions of the Garhwal Himalayas. The main temple dedicated to Vishnu stands in a valley cradled by a row of craggy peaks that are tipped with perennial snow. The peak of the sacred mountain Neelkantha, named after blue throated Shiva, is visible from here. Right below the temple flow the turbulent waters of the Alakananda and beyond the river are many beautiful waterfalls, pine forests and lakes. The peripatetic sage, Adi Shankaracharya arrived here in the 9th century with his disciple Padmapadacharya to meet a renowned scholar named Rishi Badrayan. This rishi had written a religious treatise called the Vedanta Sutra and Shankaracharya had written a *bhasya*, a commentary, on the text.

It is said that here Vishnu himself appeared to him in a dream in the form of Sri Narayan and asked him to retrieve the image of Vishnu that had once been worshipped in the old destroyed temple. In the dream, Vishnu also told him that this image was to be found in a pond, called Narada Kund, that stood by the Alakananda river. Shankaracharya asked Padmapadacharya to find the image in the tank and he called the retrieved icon, Lord Badrinarayan. He first established the image in a cave, the Garuda Gumpha, until a temple could be built for it.

He also began a *math*, a monastery and college of theological learning nearby and called it Jyotirmath. Today the town is called Joshimath. Shankaracharya got priests belonging to the brahmin community of Rawal Nambudris of Kerala to come and take charge of the *puja* in the temple and even today the priests at Badrinath all belong to this community. Over the years the original temple has been renovated and expanded many times by the kings of the region and today little remains that can be traced back to the time of the great sage except probably the sanctum, the *garbha griha*. The name of the *tirtha* comes from the local word *badri* which is a berry that is said to be a favourite of the goddess Lakshmi. Vishnu had come to Badrinath as the sage Narayana to meditate. When Vishnu was meditating here, she turned herself into a badri tree and shaded him from the sun.

Two famous philosopher-sages who meditated here are Rishi Nar and Rishi Narayan and the *Mahabharata* says that the sages in their next birth became Arjuna and Krishna. Badrinath was one of the favourite places of Krishna and the Srimad Bhagavat quotes him saying to his friend Uddhava, "Uddhava, take my order and go to my ashram called Badrika, purify yourself by touching and also bathing in the holy waters there, which have emanated from my lotus feet, rid yourself of all sinful thoughts with the sight of this sacred Alakananda River."

One of the myths of Badrinath explains the unusual image of Vishnu that is worshipped in the *garbha griha*. The weathered black stone idol sits in the yogic, cross-legged posture of *padmasana*. Vishnu is seldom shown in the *padmasana* pose, that is usually seen in the icons of a meditating Shiva or of the Buddha. It is said that once the god had allowed his consort Lakshmi to massage his feet and was chastised by a sage for giving in to such earthly pleasures. A penitent Vishnu fled to Badrinath and began severe penances by meditating in the yogic posture of the *padmasana*. He finally gave up his ascetic ways at Lakshmi's request but on condition that the Badrinath area remained a valley reserved for the meditating ascetics.

4
Badrinarayan Temple

Badrinath is considered one of eight self manifest *tirthas* that are called *'swayam vyakta keshtras'*. *Tirthayatris* doing the circuit of the *Mahaparikrama,* visiting all the four *dhaams*, bring the waters from the ocean at Rameshwaram to bathe the image of Vishnu here. Others carry the waters of the Alakananda river to Rameshwaram to pour as libation over the *lingam* of Shiva in the sanctum of the Ramanathaswamy temple.

The *tirtha* of Badrinath stands on the left bank of the Alakananda River and the valley is flanked by the two hills — Nar Parvat, the mountain of Man and Narayan Parvat, the mountain of God. The hills were named after two sages named Nar and Narayan who meditated here. There are a number of sacred hot water springs and waterfalls that are also visited by the pilgrims. The Badrinarayan temple is the main shrine in this *tirtha,* and it is one of the most popular *tirthas* of the country with pilgrims crowding its halls and sanctum all through the pilgrim season that is between May and October.

It is hard to imagine what the original 9th century shrine looked like as it has been rebuilt many times. Four centuries ago, Shankaracharya's original temple was expanded and embellished by the Garhwal kings and the *shikhara* was plated in gold by the Maratha queen Ahilyabai of Indore in the 18th century. The building was damaged in an earthquake in 1803 and was then repaired by the king of Jaipur.

Architecture

Built of stone, the facade has a row of arched windows, with a sweeping staircase in the centre leading up to the tall arched gateway to the first *mandapa*. The gateway is topped by a row of kiosks with curving roofs. The architecture of the temple resembles those of Buddhist *viharas* and like Buddhist buildings the exterior is painted in bright colours. Inside there is first the large hall of the *mandapa* that leads to the *garbha griha* and the walls and pillars of the *mandapa* are covered with intricate carvings. Though the temple has been renovated many times, the sanctum has remained unaltered. In the *garbha griha* of the Badrinath Temple is the bejewelled black stone image of Vishnu as Badrinarayan, the Lord of Badrinath, seated under a golden canopy. The icon of Lord Badrinarayan is self manifest from a black *shalagram shila* and shows Vishnu sitting in the meditative *padmasana* posture with his palms resting on his lap.

There is always a huge crowd surging forward to gain a *darshan* of the image and most pilgrims only manage a fleeting glimpse of the deity. There are fifteen icons around the temple that are also worshipped by pilgrims. At the door of the sanctum is the *gaddi* of Shankaracharya, the seat where he meditated. The images of Krishna's friend Uddhava and the sages Nara, Narayan and Narada are placed before the deity. Also in the garbha griha are images of Kuber, the god of wealth, Ganesha and the mythical bird that is Vishnu's vehicle, the Garuda. Vishnu's consort, Lakshmi has a shrine to herself to the left of the main temple. Also there are shrines to Narasimha, Vishnu's fourth *avatar*, the goddess Navadurga and an Ashtabhuja Ganesha, the elephant god is shown in an unusual form with eight arms.

Temple Schedule

The *puja* ceremonies in the temple go on from dawn to dusk but the Nirmalya Darshan, the first *puja* of the day that is held at 6.30 a.m. is considered to be the most auspicious. The temple is open from mid April to end October and once the snows come, the BadrinathTemple is closed and worship is continued at the Narasimha Temple at Joshimath. As the first snows fall at the beginning of winter and the priests prepare to leave, a lamp is left lighted before Lord Badrinarayan within the *garbha griha* and it is said that the flame still flickers when the temple doors are opened six months later in spring.

Sulphur Springs

There are a number of sulphur springs next to the river and pilgrims bathe in the hot water before going for the *puja* in the temple. In a miracle of nature these smoky springs stand right next to the icy water of the Alakananda and their waters have beneficial medicinal properties. These five springs are called Narada, Rishiganga, Kurmadhara, Prahlad Dhara and Tapta Kund. Among them a bath in the Tapta Kund is considered the most auspicious and pilgrims bathe here before entering the temple. Another hot spring, the Narada Kund, is where the image of Badrinarayan was found by Shankaracharya and Agni, the god of fire is said to reside in this *kund.*

There are five rocks standing by the Narada Kund that are also worshipped by devotees and they are called the Narada, Narasimha, Varaha, Garuda and Markandeya *shilas*. The Brahma Kapal Ghat is a platform with a flight of steps leading down to the river, where pilgrims perform the *pindadaan* ceremony when they worship their ancestors. Brahma Kapal means Brahma's forehead and one of the myths of Shiva is about an argument he had with Brahma in which he cut off Brahma's fifth head in a fit of anger and that severed head is supposed to have fallen here. A short climb takes pilgrims to the spot called Deva Darshini where it is said that the demigods, the *yakshas* and *yakshis,* come down from heaven to gain a view, a darshan, of the temple.

Fairs and Festivals

A fair called *Mata Murti ka Mela* is held at the Badrinarayan Temple every September. There is also a small temple beside the river called Mata Murti Mandir.'Mata Murti' means the image of the mother and some say that it is held to worship the mother of Lord Badrinarayan, though it is not very clear which goddess is considered the mother of the deity. In fact this fair is dedicated to the Mother Goddess as she appeared as the river Ganga. When the river goddess descended from heaven to earth she flowed through Shiva's hair and came out as seven streams and one of the streams that came to be called Alakananda appeared here at Badrinath. The government has also begun a cultural festival here called the Badri-Kedar Festival that is held in the month of June every year.

Other Sacred Places

There are a number of other sacred sites around Badrinath that pilgrims visit that are redolent with the mythology of the gods and the epics. The Temple of Charanapaduka has the footprints of Vishnu on a stone and Sheshnetra has the marks of his serpent Sheshanaag. The stream of the Vishnu Ganga begins at the majestic Vasudhara waterfalls. Its silver waters touched by shimmering rainbows, cascade from a height of 122 metres down a sheer cliff. They say that the eight sons of a *yakshi* named Vaasu, prayed here for Ganga to appear and save their souls and the river became the Vasudhara. The myth goes on to say that when people bathe in this cascade, the water does not fall on sinners. When the Pandavas went through this region on their last journey, the Swargarohan Mountain is said to be the place where they ascended to heaven. Chakra *tirtha* is where Arjuna prayed to Shiva before the great battle and he received the weapon, the powerful Pashupati Astra, that he used to defeat the Kauravas.

The Mana village is the last Indian village before the border with Tibet. The sage Veda Vyasa stayed here while he was collating and organising the four Vedas. He lived in a cave here, the Vyasa Gumpha, and pilgrims worship the image of the sage that is placed inside the cave. Veda Vysa is also believed to be the author of the *Mahabharata* and he is said to have dictated the epic to Lord Ganesha here. People will point to the hillside that is made of thin layers of stone and fancifully tell you that these are the petrified pages of Veda Vyasa's collection of these holy books.

The story of Ganesha taking dictation from Veda Vyasa also explains why the benign elephant god is always shown with one broken tusk. When Vyasa was composing the Mahabharata, he needed a scribe to take down his dictation and asked the scholarly Ganesha. The god was willing but he had one condition — Vyasa was not allowed to stop even for a moment or Ganesha would stop writing and leave. Then the little competition between the sage and the stenographer-god began. Vyasa dictating as fast as he could as Ganesha sat bent over the manuscript, his pen flying over the leaf pages. At times when Vyasa ran out of breath, he would say a couple of lines of very difficult and obscure words and as Ganesha pondered over the meaning or spelling, he would take a quick rest. Then Ganesha's reed pen broke but Vyasa refused to stop. At which Ganesha broke off one of his tusks and used it as a pen.

Sapta Badri

There are a total of seven sacred Badri temples in the area including the main temple. These are Adi Badri, Vriddha Badri, Dhyan Badri, Ardha Badri, Bhavishya Badri, Yogadhyan Badri and the main shrine of Badrivishal. The other six Badri temples are located in villages scattered across the region and some are quite remote and without proper roads. Pilgrims wishing to visit all the Badri shrines will have to trek for long distances and also be prepared to camp out in the open. When he established his monastery at Joshimath, the Adi Shankaracharya meditated at all these Badri temples.

The village of Adi Badri, as the name suggests, has some of the oldest shrines. The village is located in the hills beyond Karna Prayag and has a complex of sixteen temples out of which seven were built during the Gupta period between the 5th and 10th centuries. The main temple has the image of Adi Badrinarayan in black stone. In ancient times, when roads were primitive and were often blocked by landslides, pilgrims who could not reach the main Badrinarayan temple used to perform their *puja* here.

The Vriddha Badri Temple is located in Animath village on the Joshimath road. The myth around this simple shrine is that the sage Narada meditated here and Vishnu appeared before him in the form of an old man, a *vriddha*. So the image of Vishnu that was established here by Narada resembles an old man. The Dhyana Badri Temple is at a village where one of the descendents of the Pandavas called Urvarishi, who was the son of King Puranjaya, is said to have come to meditate. The region is called Urgam after him and he established the Vishnu temple here. Later Shankaracharya also established a Shiva temple here, like he did at Kedarnath.

The Ardha Badri temple is in a village on the road between Joshimath and Tapovan. The road is steep and pilgrims will have to walk along hill paths to reach this remote and quiet village. Here the black stone image of Vishnu is a tiny one and probably that is why the icon is effectionately called *ardha* or 'half Badri. Up the same hill is the Bhavishya Badri Temple. Pilgrims have to travel through dense forests to the shrine that stands in the village of Subhain beyond Tapovan, on the old pilgrim trail to Mount Kailash and Mansarovar.

The Yogadhyan Badri Temple is in the town of Pandukeshwar. This town is rich with myths connected with the Pandavas. King Pandu of the *Mahabharata*, father of the five Pandava brothers performed penances here to Vishnu and then he installed the image in the temple. The Pandava brothers were also born here and came back to build temples. Another myth about the Yogadhyan Badri Temple says that an image of Vishnu given by Brahma to Indra was then given to Yudhishthira and he established it in the temple at Pandukeshwar.

Joshimath

Joshimath is 44 km south of Badrinath on the road to Rishikesh. At one time Joshimath was an important trading post between India and Tibet and the *bhotiya* traders used to travel this route carrying

Indian goods laden on yaks and returned with salt from Tibet. During the winter months, between October and April the main Badrinarayan Temple is closed because of the snow and the seat of the shrine is shifted to the Narasimha Temple where the priests carry on the daily worship. The Utsava Murti, the image that is taken out of the Badrinarayan Temple, is installed in a temple in Pandukeshwar. Joshimath also has a Vasudeva temple dedicated to Lord Krishna.

Joshimath is where Shankaracharya meditated and then established a monastery and theological college that he named Jyotirmath. He meditated here in a cave and under a tree that stood before the cave and pilgrims worship at both places. Inside the cave there is a crystal Shivalingam that was brought from Kailash. The tree is said to be 2400 year old and is considered to be a wish fulfilling Kalpavriksha tree. Nanda Devi, one of the highest peaks in the Himalayas can be seen from Joshimath. The perpetually snow covered peak often has strong winds blowing the snow away and from a distance it looks like smoke. So the locals affectionately call it the Devi's kitchen.

The image in the Narasimha Temple has an interesting myth woven around it. The image, established here by Adi Shankaracharya is made in black stone and shows Vishnu's man-lion *avatar* of Narasimha seated in the lotus posture of *padmasana*. The left wrist of the image is very thin and is said to be getting thinner every day. Tradition says that when the age of the Kali Yuga comes to an end the wrist will fall off. Then the Jaya and Vijaya mountains that stand near Vishnu Prayag will crumble, blocking the road to Badrinath and the Nar and Narayan Parvats will collapse and bury the *tirtha* of Badrinath. Then Lord Badrinarayan will be worshipped in a new temple at Bhavishya Badri.

Another sacred shrine in Joshimath is the ancient Vasudev Temple that Vaishnavas of the south consider one among the 108 *Divya Desams,* the most sacred Vishnu shrines. The tall black stone deity of Vishnu is surrounded by images of his two consorts Shri Devi and Bhu Devi and by his son Kamadeva, the god of love. Near the entrance of the temple there is an interesting shrine to a dancing Ganesha, one of only two such deities worshipped in any temple in the country.

Hanuman Chatti

There are two villages called Hanuman Chatti in the Garhwal Himalayas. One is on the road to Yamunotri and the other on the road connecting Joshimath to Badrinath. One of the most interesting tales from the Mahabharata is about how the village got its name. One day Bhima, the strongest of the Pandava brothers, was travelling on this road and came upon an old monkey lying across his path. Bhima asked the monkey to move his long tail from the road and the monkey replied that he was old and tired and would Bhima kindly move the tail for him? An angry Bhima grabbed the monkey's tail and tried to lift it but in spite of his legendary strength he couldn't move the tail even an inch. Finally a humbled Bhima bent to worship the old monkey and the monkey revealed himself to be Hanuman, the devoted disciple of Lord Rama. Hanuman and Bhima were also brothers as they were the sons of Vayu, the god of the winds.

5

Kedarnath-Gangotri-Yamunotri

Among all the *tirthas* in the Garhwal Himalayas the four most sacred are also called *dhaams* and are very popular with pilgrims. These are the *tirthas* of the hill *dhaams* of Kedarnath, Badrinath, Gangotri and Yamunotri. Of these Badrinath is the most sacred as it is also part of the Chaar Dhaams that are the four sacred abodes of Vishnu, including Dwarka, Puri and Rameshwaram. Pilgrims with the time and energy can visit all the four hill *dhaams* that are connected by road. Lord Shiva as the mystic yogi, meditating in serene solitude in the hills is called Kedar and so his shrine is perched by the slope of the Kedarnath mountain in a remote part of the Garhwal Himalayas. In ancient times the *tirtha* was so inaccessible that they said that at Kedarnath "one finds oneself almost at the threshold of eternity". Kedarnath is one of the twelve *jyotirlingams* of Shiva, the self-manifest *lingams* that are considered the most sacred of his *tirthas*. The word 'kedar' means a field and it is said that this is the celestial field "where the crop of liberation grows". Shiva as the lord of this field is Kedarnath, the supreme *yogi* who offers salvation for the soul.

Location

As pilgrims follow the path of the Alakananada river to reach Badrinath, they travel beside the Mandakini to reach the tirtha of Kedarnath. Surrounded by craggy peaks topped by perennial snow, the gray granite temple stands at a height of 3500 metres, 400 metres higher than Badrinath. Kedarnath stands at a spot where four smaller streams flow into the Mandakini river and provide a panoramic view of the picturesque Mandakini valley. The streams are the Dudhganga, Madhuganga, Swargaduari and Saraswati flowing down the slopes from behind the temple. There are four sacred pools here named, Retah, Udak, Rudra and Rishi.

The sages Nar and Narayan worshipped Shiva here for the first time when they created an earthen *shivalingam* and placed it in a temple. Kedarnath was visited in the 9th century by Adi Shankaracharya, who meditated beside the river. Then he installed an idol of Lakshmi-Narayan in a new temple and he is also said to have attained *moksha* here. Though other traditions say that he died in Kanchipuram in Tamil Nadu.

Kedarnath is located between Badrinath and Gangotri and as the crow flies it is 42 km from Badrinath. There are buses available from Rishikesh, Uttarkashi and Joshimath up to Gaurikund and from there it is an arduous 14 km trek up a steep incline to Kedarnath. As Kedarnath is completely snowbound in winter, the temple is only open in the summer months from May to October. During winter the worship of Kedarnath continues at the Omkareshwara Temple in Ukhimath.

Kedarnath finds mention in the *Mahabharata* (400 A.D.-700 A.D.) and the Pandavas are said to have built the original temple here. After the devastating war of Kurukshetra, where their whole clan was decimated, the five Pandavas had no wish to rule. They renounced the world and began a journey of atonement that ended in the inaccessible reaches of the Himalayas. Atonement was not going to be easy for them as Shiva had been deeply angered by the death and duplicity at Kurukshetra and refused to listen to their prayers. The Pandavas first went to worship Shiva at Kashi but the god vanished from there to Guptakashi, where he hid by taking the form of a bull. This is why the place came to be called Guptakashi,'the hidden Kashi'.

As the Pandavas came to Guptakashi, Shiva as the bull began to sink into the ground to avoid them but Bhima caught hold of his tail and would not let him go. Finally Shiva relented and appeared before the Pandavas at Kedarnath and accepted their worship. The grateful Pandavas built a temple of Shiva here and meditated for salvation before continuing on their last journey. They performed a *yajna* sacrifice here before leaving by the path called the *Mahapanth,* the gateway to heaven. It is also called the *Swargarohini,* the path to heaven. The youngest Pandava, Sahadeva died at Kedarnath.

There are five *tirthas* called the Panch Kedar where the other parts of that divine bull appeared and many determined pilgrims visit all of them. The hump (*pindd*) fell at Kedarnath, the arm (*bahu*) at Tunganath, the face (*mukha*) at Rudranath, the hair (*jata*) at Kalpeshwar and the navel (*nabhi*) at Madhyamaheshwar. The Pandavas are said to have built temples at all the five *tirthas* of Panch Kedar. The upper part of the body of the bull appeared in Nepal where the great Pashupatinath Temple now stands.

Architecture

Like the austere aspect of the ascetic Shiva, the exterior of the Kedarnath temple is a starkly simple stone structure with the interior walls and ceiling covered with carvings and with carved wooden doors leading to the sanctum. It is built on a high stone platform below the Kedarnath mountain on a ridge that juts out above the Mandakini river. Built of dressed stone, lightly adorned by carvings, its real elegance comes from the classic design and the use of a dark gray granite. Unlike most temples that face east, this temple faces south. A flight of steps lead up to the arched doorway of the porch that opens into the main hall of the *mandapa*. Both the *mandapa* and the *garbha griha* have sloping stone roofs, with a *shikhara* rising above the sanctum topped by golden *amrit ghata*, the pot of holy nectar.

The *garbha griha* has the *jyotirlingam* of Kedareshwara, it is an irregular three faced stone shivalingam that represents the hump of the celestial bull. Pilgrims are allowed to touch the shivalingam, pour libations of water and ghee and decorate it with flowers in the ritual of the *abhishekha*. There is a figure of Shiva's vehicle the Nandi bull sitting guard at the doorway of the *garbha griha*. Before the main altar door there are smaller shrines to Shiva's consort Parvati and their son the elephant god Ganesha. Outside the second door leading into the *mandapa* there are carved figures of Lord Krishna, the Pandava brothers, their wife Draupadi and mother Kunti. In the temple there are the images of Lakshmi Narayan that were installed here by Adi Shankaracharya. There is a marble staff placed behind the temple marking the spot where the saint attained *moksha*.

Gaurikund, the last stop before the trek to Kedarnath has a sulphur spring where the tired pilgrims take a bath on their return. Gauri is another name of Parvati who performed severe austerities here to win the hand of Shiva and the Gauri Devi Temple is dedicated to her. This is also the place where Shiva cut off the head of his son Ganesh in a fit of anger and then had to replace it with the head of an elephant. So an intriguingly named temple called Sirkata Ganesh, 'Ganesh with a severed head', stands near Gaurikund.

Pilgrims take at least a fortnight and trek up narrow, treacherous hill paths for a distance of about 150 km to visit the five *tirthas* of Panch Kedars. Buses take pilgrims to access points but after that it is a climb up narrow hill tracks to reach the villages with the Kedar temples.

The Madhyamaheshwara Temple is the place where Shiva's middle part, the *madhya* or the *nabhi*, the navel fell. The temple is in the Mansuna village at a height of 3,497 metres and is 30 km from Guptakashi. Madhyamaheshwar stands in a picturesque green valley ringed by silver peaks and the *shivalingam* in the *garbha griha* of the temple is made of black stone, like at Kedarnath. There are two small shrines, one dedicated to Parvati and the other to the image of a half Shiva, half Parvati figure of Ardhanarishwara. Tunganath where the arm, the *bahu* of Shiva, appeared is at a height of 3680 metres. The temple is surrounded by a panorama of magnificent peaks — the Neelkanth, Kedarnath and the Nanda Devi.

The temple is reached after a climb from Chopta that takes at least seven hours. The Shiva temple is perched high on a stone platform with the stream of Akash Ganga flowing behind the temple. Inside there is a golden face of Shiva and five silver faces that represent Kedarnath, Rudranath, Madmaheshwar, Kalpeshwar and Parvati. Also there are temples dedicated to the Pandava brothers and images of Vyasa Dev and Kalbhairava, a demi god who is a follower of Shiva. There is also a small Parvati temple nearby.

To reach Kalpeshwar, where Shiva's hair, the *jata*, appeared, pilgrims take a bus to Helang village south of Joshimath. From Helang a 9 km walk takes them to Urgam and from there Kalpeshwar is a 1.5 km trek up a hill. This is a cave temple carved out of the hillside and the deity is also called Jateshwara. To reach Rudranath, pilgrims travel by road to the district headquarters of Gopeshwar and from there to Sagar. Then it is a 24 km trek to the temple of Rudranath where Shiva's face, his *mukha*, is worshipped. The stream of the Rudraganga flows by this temple, there is a small Vaitarini Lake below and from the temple one gets a magnificent view of the peaks of Trisul, Nandadevi and Hathi Parbat. Pilgrims can also walk between Kalpeshwar and Rudranath.

Gangotri

The temple at Gangotri celebrates the appearance of the Ganga river. Gangotri is at a height of 3140 metres. The real source of the river is at Gaumukh, 19 km above Gangotri where the stream first makes its appearance from a giant glacier. From Uttarkashi the road to the *tirtha* follows the path of the river as it cascades down the hillside, crashing over boulders and cutting narrow gorges through sheer rock. At the little village of Gangotri, the river meanders north and that gives the places its name of the Ganga moving *uttara*.

Here the river is called Bhagirathi because it is said that King Bhagirath prayed to the river goddess here at Gangotri and persuaded this celestial river to come down to earth. In the beginning the Ganga was a goddess, a celestial river that flowed out of Vishnu's toe and then spread her waters in *Swarga*, the kingdom of the gods. It is her descent to earth that brought life and plenty to people. The myth of her coming to earth begins with King Sagara, an ancestor of Lord Rama, who had become so powerful that even the gods had become envious. Then like all ambitious monarchs, Sagara performed the *ashwamedha yajna*, the sacrifice in which a horse is sent off to wander and wherever it goes unchallenged becomes a part of the kingdom of the king.

Lord Indra, the king of the gods, could not accept this growing power of Sagara and stole the horse and hid it in the hermitage of the sage Kapil Muni. Finding the horse missing Sagara sent out his sixty thousand sons to search for it. In their search they dug so deep into the earth that the oceans were created and that is why they are called 'Sagar'. Then Sagara's sons discovered the horse in the hermitage and believing that Kapil Muni had taken it, they insulted him. Angered at being disturbed at his meditations and then being accused of stealing a horse, Kapil Muni opened his eyes and the heat of his rage burnt the sons of Sagara into ashes.

The ashes of Sagara's sons lay by the sea and the king knew that the only way his cursed sons could gain salvation was when their ashes were washed away by the sacred waters of the Ganga. He and later his descendents prayed to the river goddess but she was reluctant to come down to earth. Finally Sagara's great-grandson, King Bhagirath went up to the Himalayas and performed such severe austerities that a reluctant Ganga finally had to agree.

The river goddess turned the path of her waters towards the earth but in her anger she flowed with such power that Brahma feared that her tumultuous waters would wash away all creation itself. In desperation he turned to Shiva for help and the great *yogi* obligingly placed his matted haired head in the path of the cascading river to break her fall. As she meandered through the "labyrinth of his matted hair, the river lost its force and descended gently on earth, bestowing life along her course".

The river came out as seven streams that flowed and merged along the path to finally become the mighty Ganga. These seven streams are Bhagirathi, Alakananda, Mandakini, Yamuna, Nandakini, Pindar Ganga and Dhauli Ganga and a pilgrimage of bathing in all their waters is called *Sapta Samudri tirtha.* Appearing in the plains at Haridwar, the Ganga now headed towards the sea through the plains of North India, spreading her blessings. Her journey ended at Gangasagar, where the ashes of Sagara's sons were finally liberated before the river merged into the sea.

At Gangotri, Parvati is said to have bathed in the Ganga's waters where the tank called Gauri Kund now stands. The Kedar Ganga merges with the Bhagirathi here and there is a waterfall called the Sahasradhara. The main temple at Gangotri is dedicated to Goddess Ganga and has marble and silver images of the goddess in the *garbha griha.* Also there are shrines to Lakshmi, Saraswati, Annapurna and Siva.

The simple granite temple was built by the *gurkha* general of Nepal Amar Singh Thapa in the 18th century and was later renovated by the kings of Jaipur. Here the most beautiful ceremony is the evening *aarti* when the image of the goddess in the temple is worshipped with the many flamed lamp and then the lamp is carried to the bank of the river and the river itself is worshipped with the holy fire. A similar *puja* can also be seen along the length of the Ganga especially at Haridwar and Varanasi. The Pandavas, who seemed to have visited every *tirtha* in the region, are also said to have come here, and there is a cave up in the surrounding hills called Pandava Gufa where they stayed.

Water collected from the river at Gangotri is used for the daily *puja* at the Ramanathaswamy temple at Rameshwaram. Right next to the temple is the slab of stone called Bhagirath Shila where the king is said to have performed his austerities and pilgrims worship there. The Gangotri temple is open from May to October, after that the *tirtha* becomes snowbound and the goddess is worshipped at the village of Mukhwa.

Adventurous pilgrims also visit Gaumukh, literally 'cow's mouth', which is a cave where the river first appears from a glacier. Gaumukh is at a height of 4200 metres above Gangotri and is reached after a tough 19 km trek along narrow, very steep hill tracks and patches of slippery ice, rocky moraine and glaciers. The trek takes at least two days and pilgrims usually stay the night at Chirbasa or Bhojbasa. Legends say that once the Gangotri glacier used to come right up to the temple but has now receded to Gaumukh. This is the largest glacier in the region, it is 24 km long and up to 4 km in breadth. It comes down the slope of the Chaukhamba Mountain and ends at Gaumukh — a daunting sea of ice with a forbidding beauty. The Mandakini and Alakananda rivers also come out of the Gangotri glacier.

Yamunotri

Yamunotri is the source of another sacred river, the Yamuna. This river takes an independent course across the Himalayas, flows along the plains of north India and finally merges with the Ganga at Allahabad. Yamunotri stands at a height of 3185 metres and on the west flank of the Bandarpoonch mountain. The road to Yamunotri from Uttarkashi ends at Hanuman Chatti and then it is a trek of 13 km that takes six hours to reach the *tirtha.*

At Hanuman Chatti there is the confluence of the Yamuna and the Hanuman Ganga. On the way from there to Yamunotri is the confluence of the Nil Ganga and the Yamuna at Shani Prayag. Here, there is a temple to *Shani,* the planet Saturn that pilgrims visit to ward off misfortune. Some pilgrims who are still getting acclimatised to the height prefer to make a night halt at Janakibai Chatti.

The Yamunotri temple dedicated to the river goddess Yamuna was built by the king of Tehri, Sudarshan Shah. Others say it was built by a queen of Jaipur named Rani Guleria. The temple needed major repairs after the earthquake of 1991. In the *garbha griha* there is an image of the river goddess Yamuna in black marble and of goddess Ganga in white marble.

The goddess Yamuna is the daughter of the sun god Surya and his consort Sanjana, and Yama, the god of death, is her twin brother. It is said that bathing in her waters saves the pilgrim from a painful death. Legends say that a sage named Deval had his hermitage here and his daily ritual was to bathe in the Ganga and the Yamuna. Finally the sage became old and could no longer walk up to the Ganga, so the river released a stream from the rocks that flowed past the old sage's hermitage.

There are a number of hot water springs near the temple and their waters are collected in tanks. The hottest is named Surya Kund after Yamuna's father and the water is too hot for bathing. Here pilgrims dip uncooked rice and potatoes in a cloth bag and it is soon cooked. This food is then taken to the temple and offered to the deity and consecrated as *prasada.* Pilgrims usually bathe in the Yamuna

Bai Kund. Nearby is the stone called *Dibya shila* where pilgrims first do *puja* before going to worship in the temple. Many pilgrims stay at Yamunotri for at least three nights as they believe it cleanses them of their sins.

The *tirtha* of Yamunotri stands at the foothills of the Kalinda Parvat. The actual source of the Yamuna is a remote lake called Saptarishi Kund at a height of 4420 metres in the slopes of the Kalinda Parvat that is extremely difficult to reach. It is called the lake of the seven *rishis* because seven sages—Kashyapa, Atri, Bharadwaj, Viswamitra, Gautama, Jamadagni and Vashishtha meditated there. From Yamunotri the lake is an extremely difficult 16 hour climb along narrow hill paths and very steep inclines and few pilgrims try to visit the lake.

Glossary

Aarti — invocation with lights
Amman — Mother Goddess
Alvar — Vaishnava poet-saint
apsara — celestial nymph
ashram — religious retreat
asura — demon
avatar — incarnation of a deity
Bhagavat Gita — philosophical treatise
Bhairava — terrible aspect of Shiva
bhakti — Hindu devotionalism
Brahma — Lord of creation
Brahman — the Absolute, the formless being
brahmin — priestly class
chakra — Vishnu's discus
darshana — viewing the deity
devata — god
devi — goddess
dharma — religious law and custom
gandharva — celestial musician
garbha griha — sanctum of a temple
Garuda — eagle mount of Vishnu
gopuram — temple gateway
guru — teacher, saint
Holi — spring festival of colours
Jyotirlingam — the Shivalingams of light

karma — past actions and their consequences
lingam — phallic symbol of Shiva
Mahabharata — epic poem of ancient war
mandapa — open pillared hall
mantra — sacred chants
marta — the earth
matha — monastery
Meru — mythical mountain
moksha — release from birth and death
Nandi — Shiva's bull
Nayanmar — Shaiva poet-saint
nirvana — enlightenment
prasad — ritual offerings
puja — worship of deity
punya — merit
puranas — collection of myths and rituals
Ramayana — epic poem about Rama
ratha — temple chariot
rishis — seers who wrote ancient texts
sadhu — wandering ascetic
samsara — cycle of birth and death
sannyasin — wandering ascetic
shaiva — worshipper of Shiva
Shakti — divine power of the Devi
shastra — ancient treatise
shloka — invocation
shubha — auspicious
shikhara — spire, tower
shuchi — pure
swarga — heaven
tirtha, tirthasthana — place of pilgrimage
tirthayatra — pilgrimage
vaikuntha — Vishnu's heaven
Vaishnava — worshipper of Vishnu
Vedas — oldest Hindu religious text
vihara — Buddhist monastery
Vishnu — Lord of Preservation
yajna — ritual of offerings

6
Garhwal Landscape and Pilgrim's Progress

From time immemoral Garhwal has been a destination for the devout. The five *Kedars* (seats of Shiva), the five *Badris* (shrines of Vishnu) and the five *Prayags* (holy confluences) are the cherished goals of the Hindu pilgrim. Deliverance from unhappiness is also promised to those who complete the arduous journey to the sources of the rivers Ganga and Yamuna. There are more than a dozen celebrated *tirthasthans* (auspicious places) located in two adjacent areas in Garhwal which have traditionally been identified as the domain of Shiva, Kedarkhand, and the realm of Vishnu, Badrikshetra. Although at times the entire Uttarakhand, particularly Garhwal, is referred to as'Kedarkhand', the term is more appropriately applied to the tract of land lying between the valleys of the Bhagirathi and the Alaknanda. The word *kedar,* it is speculated, refers in Sanskrit to a natural rock formation or glacial moraine. Kedarnath is in fact built on a huge platform of loose and uncon solidated glacial till.

The temple may have originally been built on the edge of a glacier which has since retreated about a kilometre and a half. The *Shiva Purana* contains an imaginative account of the origins of the five Kedars. The Pandavas were advised by the sage Vyasa, after their powers had waned, to embark on a Himalayan pilgrimage to purge themselves of the sin of *gotra hatya* (slaying one's own kith and kin). When the wandering brothers reached Kedarnath, Shiva—who had no desire to accept the homage of the fratricides—assumed the form of a bull and prepared to hide himself underground. The powerful Bhima clung on to the hindquarters of the departing deity and interrupted his vanishing act. (The *lingam* at Kedar is a natural rock formation which resembles the hump of a bull.) Shiva, never very difficult to please in the face of persistent devotion, relented and allowed himself to be propitiated. The forelegs had, in the meanwhile, travelled some distance and 'reappeared' in Kathmandu where they are worshipped to this day as Pashupatinath or Lord of the Beasts. Other parts of Shiva's body reappeared as fragments at different nearby places, giving birth to other Kedars—the navel at Madhmaheshwar, the arms at Tungnath, the face at Rudranath, and the matted hair (jatas) at Kalpeshwar.

1. ***Kedarnath*** is considered to be the holiest of Shiva's shrines in the Himalayas. It is likened in the *Skanda Purana* to Jahnavi (Ganga) amongst rivers, the brahmin amongst men, and gold amongst metals. Devout Hindus believe that whoever dies here becomes one with Shiva, and the properties of the sacred land are believed to cleanse the most hardened sinner.

The temple stands at the head of the Mandakini river in the shadow of the Kedarnath peak. It is dedicated to the worship of *Sadasiva,* the invisible form of Shiva. The symbolic phallus, the *Jyotirlinga* or resplendent *lingam,* one of twelve scattered over India, is in the form of a natural rock and is also called the Shankaracharyashiva. Beyond the temple stretches the snowy expanse known as the *mahapanth*—the highway of heaven. A short distance away is a precipice known as Bhairav-jhanp— 'Shiva's leap'. Until the first quarter of the last century, certain devotees would commit ritual suicide by throwing themselves off the edge in the belief that Shiva would thereby grant them instant salvation. Not very far away is the Chorabari Tal, now renamed the Gandhi Sarovar, where the river Mandakini originates. There are a number of glacial lakes within a radius of 5 km from Kedarnath.

2. ***Madhmaheshwar*** is at the base of the Chaukhamba peak at an altitude of almost 3,500 m and lies 29 km north-east of Guptakashi. The temple here is built in the classic Nagar style and Shiva is worshipped as a navel-shaped *lingam.* The sanctity of Madhmaheshwar is illustrated by the tale of Shambhuk, the hunter, who entered this holy tract accompanied by his dog. The dog fell into a pond and on emerging shook some water off his coat onto his master. By virtue of this partial ablution in the sacred stream both the dog and the hunter were transported to heaven.

3. ***Tungnath,*** where the arm of Shiva reappeared, is claimed to be the highest Hindu shrine, 5 km uphill from Chopta. The path to the temple winds up through a rhododendron thicket and alpine meadows, and another hour's climb leads to Chandrashila (3,930 m), renowned for its panoramic view. The river Akash Kamini ('sky-seeking') finds its source in three springs on the summit of Tungnath. The

Tun-geshwar Kshetra (the region surrounding the Tungnath temple) is considered to be an area of unsurpassed sanctity. According to a story in the Kedarkhand section of the *Skanda Purana,* Karmsharm, the debauched son of Dharam Dutt, himself a pious man, was killed in the neighbouring forest by a tiger. A crow carried his bones to Tungakshetra where the inherent power of the earth is said to have ensured his deliverance.

4. ***Rudranath,*** a natural rock temple, is situated above a rolling meadow. The trek traverses ridges as high as 4,000 m through orchards and pastures. Rudranath is perhaps the only place where Shiva's visage (Shivamukh) is worshipped. Facing the temple are the great massifs of Nanda Devi, Trishul and Nandaghunti. The shrine is surrounded by a number of pools—Surya Kund, Chandra Kund, Manas Kund. Behind the temple flows the Baitarani river which the dead are believed to cross when entering into the other world. Offering one *pind* (ritual offering to ancestors) here, the local brahmins claim, equals one hundred million at Gaya.

5. ***Kalpeshwar*** is situated at 2,134 m in a thick forest in the Urugam valley, where the sage Arghya is said to have performed austerities. Indra, the king of the gods, became apprehensive that the sage would acquire enough merit to displace him and sent some *apsaras* (heavenly nymphs) to tempt and distract him. The sage without breaking his meditation is said to have scratched his thigh and brought forth a stunningly beautiful girl, the nymph Urvashi, celebrated in many legends and the heroine of a famous play by Kalidasa. Kalpeshwar enshrines the head of Shiva with matted hair (*jata*) in a rock temple, the entrance to which is through a cave passage. It is told that sage Durvasa, notorious for his irascibility, had also performed austerities here beneath the *Kalpavriksha*, the mythological wish-fulfilling tree.

While the Shaivas (devotees of Shiva) are bound for Kedarnath, the Vaishnavas (worshippers of Vishnu) head for Badrinath. Most pilgrims, however, include both shrines in their itinerary, halting at the prayags (holy confluences) to perform additional rituals.

Badrinath

Badrinath is considered an *Adisiddhapeeth* — a place renowned for its mysticomagical power and hence considered conducive to the practice of spiritual-meditational exercises, tantric ritual or penance. There are interesting tales attached to its name. *Badri* is the Sanskrit word for a common berry, *ber*, usually offered to Shiva. The faithful believe that a gigantic badri tree is situated here which is not visible to mortals in the age of Kali.

Another legend places a badri wood here where the *rishis* or sages Nar and Narayan (Arjun and Krishna in an earlier manifestation) had their *ashram* or hermitage. This was originally the seat of Shiva. Vishnu, who had come here to perform *tapas* (penance), fell in love with the site. He devised a playful strategy to unseat Shiva. He assumed the form of a wailing child to attract Parvati's attention. Despite her husband's warnings, Parvati adopted the child, who then refused to be dislodged. The exasperated Shiva is said to have moved to the nearby Kedarnath peak to continue his meditations undisturbed.

Legend

Popular mythology recounts that the original temple was built by King Pururava and the icon of Lord Vishnu was carved by Vishwakarma, the engineer-craftsman extraordinary who served the gods. When the age of Kali began, the Lord declared that he would no longer be available for worship and immersed himself in the nearby Naradkund. The idol is said to have been retrieved by Adi Shankaracharya, the famed Malayali Brahmin scholar and founder of the Vedanta School of Hindu Philosophy. A gifted polemicist, he introduced the concept of *Maya* (illusion) to get the better of his Buddhist opponents. The more rational explanation for the concealment of the image may have been the threat of attack by iconoclasts encouraged by the spread of Buddhism. It is interesting to note that the idol is indeed mutilated. The nose, an eye and parts of the chin are missing. At the time of ritual worship it is restored through *sringara* (ritual adornment). The present temple has been restored by the royal houses of Scindia and Holkar in the late nineteenth century.

Considered one of the *Char Dham* or four principal places of Hindu worship, Badrinath is perched comfortably at an altitude of 3,122 m on the slope of a U-shaped valley, protected from avalanches by a rocky projection above. Nilkanth stands by like a sentinel, and below the temple flows the crystal-clear torrent of the Vishnu Ganga. A short distance and a hard climb away from the main shrine are the Vyas and Ganesh *gufas* (caves). The *Mahabharata*, according to tradition, was composed and dictated there.

Northwards and across the Vishnu Ganga lies Mana village, the last human habitation before the border of China. Once a flourishing centre of Indo-Tibetan trade, it is today shrouded in an air of desolation. At one time the pilgrim route to Mansarovar-Kailash via the Niti

Pass passed through it. Nowadays only the stray tourist treads the paved streets to catch a glimpse of the Vasundhara Falls. Even the Marcha *bhotiyas*, the original inhabitants, seldom climb up to Keshav Prayag, where the Saraswati meets the Vishnu Ganga. An army encampment inhibits the tourist from venturing further. Four other subsidiary shrines are associated with this dham and jointly justify the designation of the entire tract as *Vaishnava Kshetra* (Realm of Vishnu).

Narsingh Badri is located at Joshimath and is the winter seat of Badrinath. One of the arms of the icon at Joshimath is thinner than the other and devotees believe it is atrophying further. An interesting story seeks to explain the waning of the idol's arms. Once, it is said, Narasingh visited the consort of the Katyuri king in the form of a brahmin. The queen paid all due courtesies to the priest and after refreshing him with food and drink invited him to rest on the royal couch. When the king returned from his hunt he was enraged to find an intruder asleep in the royal bed. He struck the unwelcome guest on the arm, which began to bleed profusely. The Brahmin revealed his true self and ordered the king to shift his capital to Baijnath. The withering of the idol's arm is thus 'satisfactorily' accounted for. When the arm withers away or falls off it is foretold, the Lord will have to be worshipped at Bhavishyabadri ('the future Badri') in Tapovan. The latter site undeniably bears some resemblance to Badrinath.

Bhavishyabadri is at an altitude of 2,744 m, and there are two thermal springs in its vicinity. The Rev. Oakley, a Christian missionary of the early nineteenth century, claims to have seen more than 200 mendicants practising austerities at Tapovan, but these spiritual practices seem to have been discontinued.

The other two Badris are the Yogabadri at Pandukeshwar and Dhyanbadri near Hilang. These two are only of local importance. Some writers like Atkinson and Walton identify Vriddha Badri, 5 km away from Joshimath, as the fifth Badri while others opine that it is Adibadri situated on the Garhwal-Kumaon route.

Joshimath, the winter seat of Badrinath, marks the divide between two important valleys in Garhwal—the Alaknanda and the Dhauli valleys. The roads to Tapovan Malari, Auli bugyal and the Kunwari Pass branch out here. The name 'Joshimath' is a corruption of 'Jyotirmath' cseat of light'). A mythological tale connects this site with the eyes of Shiva's consort Uma or Sati. Her father Daksha, one of the ten *Prajapatis* (progenitors of man), was ashamed of his ascetic son-in-law, who appeared smeared with ashes, sporting a garland of serpents and followed by a retinue of uncouth companions. Accordingly, he scorned to invite Shiva to his *yajna* (elaborate family sacrifice). Sati was deeply humiliated to see Daksha's other sons-in-law being treated as honoured guests, and immolated herself in the sacrificial fire. At this Shiva was roused to uncontrollable rage. Wrecking Daksha's *yajna*, he slung the corpse of Sati over his shoulders and roamed the hills inconsolably. The gods feared that the world would be ruined if Shiva continued to grieve so wildly, and requested Vishnu to tear Sati's body away from Shiva by using his divine discus. Wherever the dismembered parts of Sati fell to the earth a *tirthasthana* (holy place) was created.

Joshimath has been for long the threshold of the Badrinath temple where pilgrims on foot rest and revive their energy for the final strenuous climb. Even today a festive multitude congregates here every year eagerly awaiting the opening of the temple gates after the winter recess. Joshimath is also the seat of one of the four Shankaracharyas, the chief ecclesiastics of Hinduism. A giant maple tree marks the site where the first Shankaracharya attained enlightenment. The temple at Joshimath is called Narasingh Badri, referring to an interesting mythological tale. It is mentioned in the *Puranas* that King Hiranyakashyap performed *tapas* (penance) at Joshimath to achieve the boon of near-immortality. Shiva ordained that the King could not be killed inside or outside his palace, by day or by night, by man or by beast. Drunk with the power of invincibility, Hiranyakashyap became a demon. The oppressor was finally punished. The Protector assumed the ferocious form of Narsingh ('man-lion'—i.e., neither man nor beast) and tore the king to pieces at twilight (i.e., neither day nor night) on the threshold of his palace (i.e., neither inside nor outside).

Another legend prophesies that the doors to Badrinath will close when the two mountains at Vishnu Prayag meet. According to geologists, the township of Joshimath sits insecurely on the rubble of an ancient landslide and has indeed been sinking over the years. With the Vishnu Prayag barrage project due to come into operation, the prophecy does not seem a fanciful superstition, at least to the residents of the town.

Prayag

The word *prayag* refers to the confluence of two or more rivers which, according to Hindu tradition, is a sacred site considered particularly propitious for certain prescribed religious rites (*shraddha*), ablutions (*snana*) and worship (*pujan*). The most important of the *prayags* in India is the mighty confluence where the Ganga and Yamuna meet—the ***Triveni-Sangam***, also known as Allahabad. Prayagraj and the *panch* (five) *prayags* of Garhwal rank next only to it.

At ***Vishnu Prayag,*** the Alaknanda (which from Mana to this point is known as the Vishnu Ganga) joins the Dhauli. The sage Narada is said to have worshipped Vishnu here. An ancient Vishnu temple stands here by a pool called Vishnukund.

Nanda Prayag marks the confluence of the Alaknanda and Nandakini. The trek to Tapovan branches out from here across the Kunwari Pass. Another path branches off to Roopkund via Ghat. Nanda Prayag derives its name from a legend about Nanda, the Yadav king and famous foster-father of Sri Krishna, who was childless. He and his wife Yashoda so impressed Vishnu with their devotion that the god appeared to them and offered to grant them a boon. Nanda and his wife asked for a son like Vishnu himself. This put the deity in a quandary as he had already granted the very same boon to Devaki, sister of the tyrant Kansa and wife of Vasudeva of Mathura. An ingenious solution was devised: The son, Krishna, would be born to Devaki but Yashoda would rear him.

Kama Prayag is at the confluence of the Alaknanda and the Pindar. According to the *Mahabharata*, Kama had practised austerities here to acquire the *kawacha* (armour) and *kundal* (earrings) which made him invincible. Surya, his father, pleased by his son's disciplined penance, had gifted him these. The junction of the two rivers is appropriately called Kama Kund. The hillside around Kama Prayag is thickly wooded and is believed to have been the meeting ground of Shakuntala and Dushyanta, the principal characters in Kalidasa's classic *Abhijnana Shakuntalam.*

Rudra Prayag is the junction of the Alaknanda and Mandakini. The place is named after Rudra (Shiva) and, according to local tradition, it was here that he humbled the garrulous sage Narad. According to the anecdote, Narad had become insufferably vain about his prowess in music and the gods entreated Krishna to remedy the situation. Krishna told Narad that his reputation had reached Shiva and Parvati and they were very keen to enjoy a recital by him. A smugly self-confident Narad immediately embarked on the mountainous journey. Shiva, in league with Krishna, in the meantime, had arranged a startling spectacle for him. On the outskirts of Rudra Prayag, Narada encountered several strikingly beautiful girls, all marred by severe mutilations. He could not resist asking them who they were and what beast had caused their disfigurement. Their reply sobered him. The damsels, he was told, were delicate *raginis*—musical compositions—ravaged by the insensitive handling of one sage Narad'! Chastened, the sage prostrated himself at the feet of Lord Mahadev and later devoted himself to learning the art of playing the veena from Shiva. Another legend associates the place with the penance of Sati, who was reborn as Parvati after her self-immolation. Notwithstanding the disapproval of her father Himalaya, Parvati performed stringent *tapasya* to obtain the boon of being Shiva's wife in her new life. She won over Shiva and Himalaya had to relent.

Rudra Prayag also has a secular claim to fame. A man-eating leopard stalked this region for almost eight years between 1918 and 1926 and accounted for more than 300 casualties in an area of about 700 sq km. The menace was finally ended by the famous hunter Jim Corbett on May 1, 1926—an event that was considered momentous enough to be mentioned in the British Parliament. The House was prorogued for the day to celebrate the deliverance of innocent men and women from this danger. A plaque commemorating the event marks the spot in Rudra Prayag.

Deva Prayag is where the tranquil Alaknanda embraces the tempestuous Bhagirathi and it is here that the Ganga is truly born. Devout Hindus consider this *prayag* second only to the Triveni in Allahabad. The most ancient stone inscriptions found in Uttarakhand are located here. The famous Raghunatha Math, one of the many names for the Rama temple, is also situated here and it is at Deva Prayag that the priests of Badrinath sojourn in winter. According to an old legend this spot is named after Deva Sharma, a poor Brahmin who performed rigorous austerities at this spot and obtained the favour of Vishnu's incarnation Rama. The hero of the *Ramayana* had come here to expiate the sin of *brahma hatya* (Brahmin-slaughter) after killing the demon-king Ravana. King Dashratha, the father of Lord Rama, is also said to have undergone penance here.

Some other towns in Garhwal are considered sacred even though they are not associated with a confluence or a major shrine. Srinagar, the traditional capital of Garhwal, is one such example. Srinagar is situated in a sprawling valley about 8 km long, and it is here that the Alaknanda spreads out as if preparing for its course in the plains as the Ganga. The town's name derives from Shri Kshetra, ascribed to the location here of a *sriyantra*—a tantrik device associated with human sacrifice. Through centuries the town has been transformed from a *chatti* (pilgrims' night halt) to a *durbar* (court) to a busy commercial centre which is its present status. Once it was an important centre of trans-Himalayan trade.

Srinagar is mentioned in the travel accounts of almost all the Europeans who visited Garhwal in the nineteenth century. But by the time it passed under British control it had lost much of its glamour. Maularam, the famous painter of miniatures, a poet and witty courtier, has written a moving lament for Srinagar. The reduction of the town to a ruin is attributed to the repeated ravages wrought by the Alaknanda and to an earthquake in 1803. The Gurkha invasion only hastened the process of it's decay.

Modern Srinagar was founded in 1896 and its architectural complexion has changed drastically in the last two decades. Gone are the rows of identical houses with slate roofs where the ground floor was used for shops and the first floor for residence. Only the old temples such as Kamaleshwar and Kilkileshwar preserve their quaint facades. Despite its urbanization Srinagar retains a strong rural flavour.

Another town intimately associated with the pilgrim's progress in Garhwal is Haridwar, variously referred to in the scriptures as Mayapuri, Gangadwar and Swargdwar. Although not strictly located in Garhwal, it is inextricably linked with the life and legends of the land. As an old traveller has written,

> To behold the Ganga at the moment in which, having forced its passage through the mountains, it glides in one broad stream along the plains, seems to the exhausted devotee who has suffered every fatigue and privation...as more than a recompense for all his toils.

7
Going on a Tirtha

"The gods always play where lakes are, where the sun's rays are warded off by umbrellas of lotus leaf clusters, and where clear water paths are made by swans, whose breasts toss the white lotuses hither and thither; where swans, ducks, curlews and paddy birds are heard and animals rest nearby in the shade of Nicula trees on the river banks."

— Places where gods dwell as described in the Brihat Samhita

The Chaar Dhaam are among the most sacred places of pilgrimage for Hindus, and these four sites are among their first destinations when they wish to go on a *tirtha*. For Hindus a place of pilgrimage is a *tirtha* or *tirthasthana*, a pilgrimage is also a *tirtha* or *tirthayatra* and a pilgrim is a *tirthayatri*. For Hindus a *tirthasthana* is a sacred space that they believe is charged with divine power and purity. A *tirtha* is resonant with three elements that make it so sacred — it is *shuchi*, pure; it brings *punya*, merit and goodness and it is *shubha*, auspicious. The act of pilgrimage is praised in many ancient texts, like the *Aitareya Brahamana* says,

"Flower like are the heels of the wanderer
Thus his body grows and is fruitful
All his sins disappear
Slain by the toil of his journeying."

Hindu tradition states that a *tirtha* is a place where you can gain *nirvana*, true enlightenment, and also achieve *moksha*, a liberation from the endless cycle of life and death. However for a Hindu, who worships every aspect of what is good and sacred in life and nature, a *tirtha* does not have to be a specific place or a temple. It can be anywhere — by the banks of a holy river, at the foot of a mountain, under a sacred tree and even at the feet of a great saint or guru. In the tolerant and life enhancing beliefs of Hinduism, a *tirthasthana* and a *tirthyatra,* are finally a state of mind and you find it where you seek it. A *tirtha* is a spiritual goal, as the *Skanda Purana* states, "Truth, forgiveness, control of senses, kindness to all living beings and simplicity are also *tirthas.*"

From the time of the Vedas there has been a tradition of the veneration of rivers and many *tirthas* came up beside them. However, for Hindus the landscape itself — hills, rivers, trees, rocks, pools and the sea are all holy. Rivers like the Ganga and Godavari are sacred, so are hills like Kailash and Arunachala, the river island of Omkareshwar and the island of Rameshwaram and Kanniyakumari on the sea are all *tirthas.* A temple often marks this sacred space and it houses the image of a deity in the sanctum but the sanctity of the place often begins with it being a scenic place because a Hindu sees the generous spirit of God everywhere in nature. Every aspect of creation is luminous with holiness, you just need the eyes to see them.

This veneration of nature has led to temples being built in especially picturesque places. One can discover the ruins of long forgotten temples in the most remote places of the country. Most often they are built near water, by the banks of rivers, by the seashore and beside lakes, because of the need for ritual purification before worship. The presence of flowing water and the confluence of streams makes the spot even more auspicious. Temples also come up on hills, on islands in rivers, in forests, beside waterfalls, in inaccessible caves and islands along the seashore.

When an aspect of nature is combined with other spiritual elements a *great tirtha* is created. For instance, Varanasi, (also called Banaras and Kashi), is considered supreme among all Hindu *tirthasthanas.* It offers the pilgrim the combination of a great river, a powerful god and a venerable temple—of the Ganga, the most sacred of the rivers, the presence of a great god, Lord Shiva and an ancient shrine, the Kashi Vishwanath Temple. Similarly, Puri has the presence of Lord Vishnu, the famous Jagannatha Temple and a sacred festival of the *Rath Yatra.* Then the ancient history and traditions of these *tirthas* make them even more sacred as the places are replete with myths and legends and vibrant with ancient rituals and festivals. To visit a great *tirtha* is to touch the very soul of this many faceted land called India.

The word 'tirtha' means a ford, a place along a river where it can be crossed easily. Many *tirthas* are in fact placed along such fords. However, the word has a much deeper significance. A *tirtha* is not just a crossing on this earth, it is a spiritual crossing between this mortal world of *samsara* and the heaven of *swarga*. Where you seek redemption for your actions and then seek liberation. So at a *tirtha,* as you row through the river of *samsara*, you move from the world of *marta* below to *swarga* above in a journey often described as travelling from 'this shore' of existence to the 'far shore' of *moksha.*

The *tirthas* of the seven *saptapuris* and four *dhaams* are called "mokshadayika" because they promise the pilgrim the supreme liberation of *moksha*. The Hindu believes that the soul never dies and that we are born again and again into an illusory mortal world of *samsara*. Our actions during our lives, which is our *karma,* often includes a multitude of sins, and it is our *karma* that will make us take birth once more on earth to atone for those sins. Going to these *tirthas*, worshipping in their temples, bathing in their rivers and tanks, frees us from this burden of sins and also liberates us from the endless cycle of births and deaths. A *tirthayatra* makes it possible for our souls to merge with the supreme oneness of the Brahman.

Surprisingly, *tirthas* are not just places where mortals reach out to heaven. Hindu myths tell us that they are like celestial pathways along which the gods also descend to earth. For instance, when evil is on the rise, Vishnu as the benign Lord of Preservation, often comes to earth in various incarnations to restore the presence of good. So wherever these incarnations, called *avatars*, were born, the places of their birth also became *tirthas*. Thus, Ayodhya where Rama was born and Mathura where Krishna was born and ruled are among the seven most sacred of *tirthas,* the Saptapuris. Then Varanasi is a *tirtha* because Shiva chose it as his earthly home and came to live there with his consort Parvati.

As it is a place connected to heaven, a *tirtha* is also a place where the devout come to die. For instance, many Hindus have a passionate desire to die in Varanasi because this *tirtha* is also resonant with the power of purity and goodness that makes the crossing easier. The auspicious presence of God helps further in gaining true *moksha*. In Varanasi, it is Shiva Himself who is the boatman on this spiritual river and it is he who rows the soul across as he intones the sacred *Taraka mantra* that gives absolute liberation.

The Jains also believe in the power of *tirthas* to provide *moksha* and they call their saints, *tirthankaras,* 'ford makers', as these saints release souls from the illusory world of *samsara* and take them to the serenity and peace of *swarga*. *Tirthas* are also created by myths, like the *peethasthanas*, the 'seats' of the Mother Goddess, universally called Devi. Many of these *peethasthanas* are connected to the myth of the death of Shiva's wife, Sati. There are fifty one *peethasthanas* where parts of Sati's body fell and here the temples of the Mother Goddess consecrate her *shakti*, her divine power. Then the places connected to the myth of the *jyotirlingam*, when Shiva transformed himself into an incandescent *lingam* of light, are also great *tirthas*. The twelve *tirthas* of *jyotirlingams* have temples with *shivalingams* called *swayambhu*, or self manifest and they are sacred to the worshippers of Shiva. Vishnu's myths have created his four 'abodes' — the Chaar Dhaam and 108 of his most sacred temples are called *Divya Desams*.

The Tirthas of Saptapuri and Chaar Dhaam

The *tirthas* of ancient times are mentioned in many books and one of the oldest is the *Mahabharata* which is one the largest sources for information on *tirthas* in the early years of the first millennium. The *Puranas*, written between the 4th and 7th century A.D. and books like *Kritya Kalpataru* of Bhatta Lakshmidhara written in the 12th century also list a large number of places of pilgrimage. The traveller Alberuni who came to India in the 11th century gives descriptions of many *tirthas* and the Mughal historian Abul Fazl, writing in the 16th century, lists many *tirthas* in the *Ain-i-Akbari*. Among all the lists there are ten *tirthas* that remain the most sacred — the Saptapuri and Chaar Dhaam.

There is a Sanskrit *shloka* that Hindu pilgrims recite when they visit *tirthas*. The simple verse lists the seven greatest *tirthas* of the land, the Saptapuris.

"Kashi, Kanchi, Maya, Ayodhya, Avantika.
Mathura, Dwaravati chaiva saptaita mokshadayika."

The *shloka* says that, Kashi, Kanchi, Maya, Ayodhya, Avantika, Mathura and Dwaravati are the seven *puris*. And these Saptapuris offer the liberation of *moksha*. These seven sacred cities are also called 'mokshapuris' and they are the *tirthas* of Kashi (Varanasi, Benaras), Kanchi (Kanchipuram), Mayapuri (Haridwar), Ayodhya, Avantika (Ujjain), Mathura and Dwaravati (Dwarka).

Next to the Saptapuris are the four *tirthas* of Chaar Dhaam. These *tirthas* are called *dhaam* as they are believed to be the sacred abodes of Vishnu and his *avatars*. The Chaar Dhaams are Badrinath, Puri, Dwarka and Rameshwaram. As the *dhaam* of Dwarka is also a

Saptapuri, it makes it even more sacred. So the list of the holiest *tirthas* of Hindus comes to ten places of pilgrimage.

In ancient times, pilgrims who ventured out on arduous journeys to the *tirthas* must have been the oldest travellers in history. For the devout Hindu, the attainment of *moksha* is life's truest purpose and so for centuries they have come to the Saptapuris and Chaar Dhaams seeking this elusive liberation. Most of them have managed to visit one or two of the ten *tirthas* in one lifetime but the dream has always been to visit all of them.

Visiting all the seven Saptapuris is not an easy thing to achieve as the *tirthas* are spread across the Indian subcontinent. Kashi, Ayodhya and Mathura are in the north in the Indo - Gangetic plains of Uttar Pradesh. Haridwar stands at the foothills of the Himalayas in Uttaranchal. Ujjain is in central India in Madhya Pradesh. Dwarka is in the west in the state of Gujarat and Kanchipuram is in the far south in Tamil Nadu.

The Chaar Dhaams span even longer distances. These sacred abodes of Vishnu are located in the North, South, East and West, at the four cardinal points of the Indian subcontinent. So the pilgrim's trail to them virtually covers the whole country. In the North, is the *dhaam* of Badrinath, nestled in a valley high in the Himalayan mountain ranges of Uttaranchal. In the East is the *dhaam* of Puri by the Bay of Bengal in the state of Orissa. In the West the *dhaam* of Dwarka stands by the Arabian Sea in Gujarat. Finally in the South, Rameshwaram in Tamil Nadu is located on an island at the southern most point of the subcontinent, where the waters of the Indian Ocean touch the land. So visiting the Chaar Dhaam is by far the most arduous journey that a pilgrim can undertake and because of this, the *tirthayatra* is called the *Mahaparikrama* — the great circuit of the land.

There is a shorter circuit of four *dhaams* in the Himalayas that is also a *tirtha* popular with pilgrims. This is an easier pilgrimage that can be done in one trip into the hills above Haridwar and Rishikesh. These *dhaams* are of Kedarnath-Badrinath-Gangotri-Yamunotri, all of them located in the higher reaches of the hills in the state of Uttaranchal. However, unlike the Chaar Dhaam, these *dhaams* are not all dedicated to Vishnu and his *avatars*. Kedarnath has a Shiva temple by the banks of the Mandakini river. Badrinath has a Vishnu shrine and it stands by the Alakananda river. The other two really worship sacred rivers with temples dedicated to river goddesses. Gangotri is the place where the Ganga emerges from the Himalayan glacier and Yamunotri is at the spot where the Yamuna river makes its appearance.

The most sacred tirthas since ancient times are these ten places of pilgrimage but in the present day the map of tirthas is a much larger one with an intricate maze of holy places spread across the land. There are tirthas of different sects like the Shaivas, Vaishnavas and the *peethasthana* of the Devi that total in hundreds. Also there are places sacred to local people that gather pilgrims from the region. Finally there are the tirthas around special occasions like the *melas*, or religious fairs, the largest and most famous being the great religious congregation of the Kumbh Melas that welcome pilgrims by the millions. The Kumbh Melas are held every twelve years at Allahabad, Haridwar, Ujjain and Nasik and millions gather for the gigantic celebration.

Tirthas also have this quality of rising and declining in popularity as newer tirthas gain more devotees because people begin to believe that these sacred places and temples have great powers to answer their prayers. Today Ujjain and Dwarka may not see as many pilgrims as later tirthas like Tirupati, Madurai or Vaishno Devi that attract devotees by the millions. Still for the traditional pilgrim, the ten ancient tirthas of Saptapuri and Chaar Dhaam possess a unique spiritual resonance and their dream remains to visit these tirthas and gain the *darshan* of their beloved deity while worshipping at their temples.

The Meaning of a Pilgrimage

The Puranas classify four kinds of tirthas. First are ***Daiva tirthas***, the sacred places that have been touched by the presence of the trinity of Brahma, Vishnu, Shiva and the Devi. Then there are ***Asura*** tirthas, these are the sites where the gods defeated demons, like Gaya where Shiva defeated an *asura* of that name. The ***Arsa tirthas*** have been created through the great penances and austerities of sages. Finally there are the ***Manusa tirthas*** that have been sanctified by the presence of great solar and lunar dynasties.

The most important reason for a tirthayatra is the darshan of a deity. A darshan can be explained simply as the seeing or viewing of an image, but for a Hindu it is a much more complex experience. It is a deeply personal experience where the eyes are like the doorways to the soul. A darshan is being in the presence of a god or even a great being and absorbing some of the aura of sanctity and goodness through this encounter. When a Hindu stands with folded hands before an image or bends to touch the feet of a wise saint they are reaching out to gather some of this holiness. And for a darshan of a deity the pilgrim heads for the temples, be it the Kashi Vishwanath to worship Shiva or to the Varadaraja Temple to pray to Vishnu.

The religious rituals during a pilgrimage have remained unchanged for centuries. The temple is the *devalaya,* the palace of the god and the pilgrims arrive at the doorway often after a purifying bath in a river or a tank. They buy flowers, sweets, incense, vermilion and lamps in the temple market and then enter the temple barefoot. They walk silently through the outer halls towards the sanctum concentrating their mind on the deity that waits for them in the *garbha griha,* resplendent in jewels and silks, decorated with flowers and wreathed in incense smoke. As the priest carries the pilgrim's offerings to the deity, they stand saying their prayers in a direct communion with their god. Then the offerings are returned to them consecrated as *prasad* that they carry home.

Pilgrims also attend the rituals and festivals at the temples. The rituals of puja begin at dawn with the waking of the deity and go on till the evening aarti and the worship with lighted lamps. These rituals take on a special significance on sacred days like the full moons. The festivals celebrate the myths of the deity like *Shivaratri,* when Shiva and Parvati were married or the *Brahmotsavams,* when the chariots come out in procession from the temples. As pilgrims crowd a temple town during a festival there is the ambience of a carnival with processions weaving their way through busy markets, music and dance performances and fireworks sparkling across a night sky.

Often there are more personal reasons for a pilgrimage. Pilgrims come to pray and ask for the help of a deity during a crisis and then if their prayers are answered they come again as an act of thanksgiving. This is especially true of temples that have gained a reputation for being generous with their blessings. People go by the thousands to Tirupati or make the demanding trek up a hill to Sabarimala and Vaishno Devi to ask for help or to thank the deity for prayers answered.

A pilgrimage can also be an act of penance for sins committed. Often in the waning years of their lives, penance, atonement and prayers for *moksha* bring pilgrims to a *tirtha.* Pilgrims bathe in the Ganga at Kashi and Haridwar with the belief that the holy waters of the river will wash away their sins. However, just a ritual dip in the river does not free those who do not lead moral lives. In Hindu belief one is responsible for one's actions and one has to always answer for sins committed deliberately in this birth and the next, as that is our karma. Not just ordinary people but even kings have gone on pilgrimage to atone for their sins. Rama went to perform a *yajna* sacrifice at Haridwar as penance for killing Ravana who was a brahmin. The Pandava brothers wandered from tirtha to tirtha after the battle of Kurukshetra.

Every landmark in a person's life is commemorated at a *tirtha*. Parents bring their newborn children to seek the blessings of the deity and name their child in the *naamkaran* ceremony. Young boys sit on the *ghats* of Varanasi and Ujjain getting their heads shaven before the sacred thread ceremony of *upanayana*. Newly weds carry flowers to the temples and the rivers and at some shrines like the Meenakshi Temple in Madurai the marriage itself is performed in the temple *mandapas*. Finally when life ends, the *shraadh* or funeral rites are performed beside the river by sorrowful families. Here ancestors are also worshipped with the *pindadaan* ceremony.

Sometimes a pilgrimage is a spiritual journey, a *yatra*. It is often undertaken as a vow and pilgrims trek for miles over arduous terrain, perilous hill tracks or sandy deserts to reach remote shrines like Amarnath or Sabarimala. They circumambulate sacred hills like Kailash and Arunachala bathe in the icy lakes like Mansarovar and walk for five day visiting 108 shrines in the Panchkroshi Yatra of Kashi. For them the physical challenges of the *yatra* make their spiritual satisfaction deeper.

Some fairs are sacred and a pilgrimage can be a *mela*. The greatest of all *melas* is the gigantic congregation of the Kumbh Mela where pilgrims arrive in millions and face great hardships for that joy of bathing in the sacred river at an auspicious moment. Every twelve years, the four *tirthas* of Prayag (Allahabad), Haridwar, Ujjain and Nasik come alive for the Kumbh Melas. It is a spectacular panorama of saffron clad, as smeared sadhus, villagers in turbans or veils carrying the possessions in dusty bundles, city people in track suits and carrying cell phones, young and old answering the call of a ancient myth of a pot of ambrosia being carried by Vishnu. At the Kumbh Melas the poor often arrive with nothing by the clothes on their backs and are provided with food and shelter in a gigantic enterprise of charity that is unrivalled to the world.

Pilgrims through the Ages

Pilgrims are the world's first tourists. For centuries they hava undertaken long, and at times dangerous journeys, to pray at sacred shrines. All the great pilgrimages — the haj to Meca the pilgrimage to the Holy Land of Jerusalem and the Hindu journey to the *puris* and *dhaams* have been the route for million of nameless, forgotten pilgrims. However, some of them too the trouble to chronicle their experiences and these pilgrim journals are an invaluable record for historians.

In ancient times pilgrims had to be a tough, adventurous breed. The roads were rough and physically demanding, there was the danger of robbers, bad food and disease. Some of the journeys took months — for instance the *haj* meant a voyage by sea and then a long trek across the Saudi desert. Hindus going to Mount Kailash and the Mansarovar Lake had to climb remote Himalayan mountains, traverse treacherous glaciers, face rain, cold, lack of food, altitude sickness.

Unlike most of the saffron clad men on the roads of India who are vagrants in the guise of mendicants, the true sannyasi often chooses to meditate in remote places like the Himalaya or deep in forests. These sadhus are by far the hardiest and the most committed of all pilgrims. These dedicated ascetics often flee from busy temple towns and one sees them meditating places no one will venture into. For these reclusive men religion is a personal search for enlightenment. However it is an unfortunate fact that many of the *sadhus* and priests to be seen at tirthas treat organised religion merely as a source of livelihood. For them religion is business and the pilgrim is the customer who can be fleeced.

For the true seekers of truth and inner enlightenment, the isolation and physical demands of their existence are the challenges of their search. One can see these matted haired ash smeared ascetics living in remote caves perched precariously by the edge of cliffs, in the deepest forests and bathing in the icy waters flowing out of a glacier, at dawn. No one knows how they survive or what they are seeking. Their enigmas of the spiritual world choose to remain a mystery of their psychic pilgrimage within their minds.

Pilgrims have also been the earliest travel writers in history. When pilgrims chronicle their experiences, their voices speak to us across the centuries. Their simple observations opening the window to a long vanished world. The two Chinese pilgrims Hiven Hsien who came in the 5th century during the reign of Chandragupta II and Hiuen Tsang who travelled through India in the 7th century during the reign of Harsha, came to visit the sacred sites of Buddhism. Today their writings are an invaluable record of the history of the time and the lives of the people.

The most famous Hindu pilgrim was of course the a mazingly peripatetic Shankaracharya. He began his journey from Kerala in the remote south and his travels covered just about every important tirtha in the land. Born in 788 AD this philosopher-theologian played a vigorous role in the revival of Hinduism and he was responsible for once again making it the cominant faith of the land.

Little is known of his life except that he was born in Kerala and began his journey of discovery as a teenager. He was a devotee of Shiva and belonged to the Mimamsa school of Vedic rituals. He was the founder and principal exponent of the doctrine of Advaita Vedanta, that propounded pure non-dualism. He died at the young age of thirty two and would gain *moksha* at the other end of the land in Kedarnath. During very short life he managed to organise and renew Hinduism by establishing his four monastic orders called *mathas* at the Chaar Dhaams.

These Shankaracharya *mathas* at three of the Chaar Dhaams are the Jyotirmath at Badrinath, the Sharada Math at Dwarka, the Goverdhan Math at Puri and the fourth is the Kamakoti peetham at Kanchipuram, that is now located at Kumbakonam. Even today these Shankaracharya *peethas* continue to be centres of Sanskrit scholarship and Hindu philosophy.

Once, *tirthasthanas* were the university towns of ancient India, centres of teaching and scholarship where philosophers, theologians, grammarians, even astronomers and mathematicians lived and worked.

Sacred Places

There are hundreds of *tirthas* across the country but there are some that are considered the most sacred. Here we give a list of the most important places of pilgrimage for Hindus.

Saptapur Kashi (Varanasi, Uttar Pradesh), Kanchipuram (Tamil Nadu), Mayapuri (Haridwar, Uttaranchal)), Ayodhya (Uttar Pradesh), Avantika (Ujjain, Madhya Pradesh), Mathura (Uttar Pradesh), Dwaravati (Dwarka, Gujarat).

Chaar Dhaam of Vishnu—Badrinath (Uttaranchal), Puri (Orissa), Dwarka (Gujarat), Rameshwaram (Tamil Nadu).

Chaar Dhaam in the Himalayas—Kedarnath, Badrinath, Gangotri, Yamunotri (all in Uttaranchal).

Jyotirlingams—Kedarnath (Uttaranchal), Vishveshwara (Varanasi), Vaidyanatha (Bihar), Mahakaleshwar (Ujjain), Omkareshwar (Indore), Nageshwar (Dwarka), Somnath (Gujarat), Triyambakeshwar

(Maharashtra), Grishneshwar (Aurangabad), Bhimashankar (Maharashtra), Mallikarjuna (Tamil Nadu), Rameshwaram (Tamil Nadu).

Sacred Shivalingams of the five elements—Ekambaranatha Temple, Kanchipuram (earth). Jambukeshwar Temple, Srirangam (water), Tiruvannamalai Temple (fire), Kalahasti Temple, (air).Nataraja Temple, Chidambaram (ether).

Sacred rivers—Ganga, Yamuna, Godavari, Saraswati, Kaveri, Narmada, Sindhu.

Four streams of the Ganga—Alakananda, Bhagirathi, Mandakini, Yamuna.

Places of Pilgrimage on the Ganga—Devaprayag, Rudraprayag, Karnaprayag, Nandprayag, Vishnuprayag, Rishikesh, Haridwar, Varanasi, Allahabad, Gangasagar.

8
Vishnu and his Dhaams

The Chaar Dhaams are called the sacred abodes of Vishnu and the main deity being worshipped in these four *tirthas* is of Vishnu or one of his *avatars*. Vishnu himself is worshipped in Badrinath. In Dwarka he is worshipped in his *avatar* of Lord Krishna, king of ancient Dwarkavati, the hero of the Mahabharata and the philosopher who spoke the verses of the Bhagavat Gita. In Puri the main deity is of Vishnu as Jagannath the lord of the world, with his unusual icon worshipped with the images of Balabhadra and Subhadra. Finally in Rameshwaram, it is Vishnu's seventh *avatar*, Lord Rama, the king of Ayodhya and the hero of the epic Ramayana, who receives the prayers of the devotees.Vishnu is a solar god and as the second god of the trianity of Brahma, Vishnu and Shiva, he plays the role of the great preserver.

In today's Hinduism the worshippers of Vishnu and his ten avatars are by far the most popular sects, with temple in every village and town of the land. In the Hindu pantheon Vishnu is probably the most benign among all the deities and because of his compassionate character, deeply loved by people. He is a benevolent, caring god who listens to your prayers, understands your dilemmas, forgives your sins and offers salvation and mercy. His worship has a joyful, and loving character, with devotees swaying to songs and even dancing during puja and making offerings of flowers, incense and food. As the sage Bhrigu wrote, "Here is the greatest of all the gods. He surpasses others by the most powerful of his weapons — kindness and generosity". Vishnu is ever-ready to intervene on behalf of righteousness and come to the assistance of those who ask for help. Among the great trinity of gods - Brahma, Vishnu and Shiva, he has the most human face. Brahma as the lord of creation who withdraws from the world once his work is done staying detached from the daily lives of people. Shiva is the lord of destruction, who begins the dissolution of the world, and is both loved and feared.

Even though he is often generous and loving, he is also a volatile god with a vengeful and angry face Vishnu is not that easy to anger, while he is much more forgiver and only a pure adoration is required from his devotees. As the Tamil poet Tirumalisai wrote around the 6th century AD,

"When the grooves of the senses are barred and sealed,
When the highway of knowledge is lit with wisdom's lamp,
When intense pity melts the heart and eases the bones,
Then only can Vishnu, the wielder of the sacred disc be seen."

Vishnu's rise to eminence is one of the most intriguing stories of Hindu mythology. In the Rigveda, (1200-900 B.C.) the first sacred text of the Hindus, Vishnu is merely one of the lesser aspects of the sun god Surya and only five hymns are dedicated to him. He is one of the twelve *Adityas* and is merely the manifestation of solar energy that follows *Surya* as the sun god travels across the sky every day. The only myth about him in the Rigveda is rather a simple tale of Vishnu covering the seven regions of the universe in three giant steps. From this unobtrusive beginning, Vishnu would evolve into this many hued, complex god whose many manifestations needed at least teen incarnations or *avatars*. Among these *avatars* being the two most popular deities of Hinduism — the hero-warrior-kings, Rama and Krishna. As Krishna described himself in the Bhagavad Gita, beautifully capturing his intricately imagined character,

"I am the Brihat songs of all songs in the Vedas
I am the Gayatri of all measures in verse.
Of months, I am the first of the year,
And of the seasons, the season of flowers.

I am the cleverness in the gambler's dice.
I am the beauty of all things beautiful.

I am victory and the struggle for victory.
I am the goodness of those who are good."

Rig Vedic Vishnu

The Rigvedic Vishnu represents the sun's disc and every manifestation of light — in the sun, in the fire and in lightning. He is the rising sun, the sun at high noon and at the setting. At times he is described as one of the companions of Indra, the king of the gods. In some of the hymns he is described as moving in Indra's entourage with the Maruts, the gods of storms, as Indra rides out to war against Vrittra, the demon of drought. The only connection to the later Vishnu, the god that is to be found in the *Puranas* (400-700 A.D.) and the epics (200 B.C.-200 A.D.), is his being referred to rather vaguely as "the unconquerable preserver". By the time of the epics he is not only the great preserver of every aspect of the universe including the sun but the Puranas even call him the creator, thus usurping the role of Brahma.

Vishnu in the Epics

Vishnu's mythology is given in the greatest detail in the *Vishnu, Vayu* and the Bhagavat Puranas and the story of his two most important *avatars*, Rama and Krishna are given in the two great epics. The history of Ramachandra of Ayodhya is told in the *Ramayana*. The exploits of Krishna of Mathura and Dwarka are found in the *Mahabharata* and in the *Harivamsa,* which is a supplement of the epic. The *Mahabharata* also contains the *Bhagavat Gita*, which is by far the most important religious text in Hinduism and contains the teachings of Krishna about the correct path of life and the attainment of salvation.

Vishnu in the Puranas

In the Puranas, especially the Vishnu Purana, Vishnu's character is described in great detail. He is the divine monarch, ever at work for the salvation of mankind, the perfect being who embodies all the *satvagunas,* the qualities of goodness and mercy that are the characteristics of the preserver. As this divine preserver he is called Narayana and is depicted as floating on the celestial waters of the Ananta ocean, lying on the coils of the seven headed serpent called Sheshanag. Ever smiling Vishnu always has this quality of calm and repose, a compassionate detachment that contrasts widely with the warm hearted but quick tempered and unpredictable Shiva.

Vishnu's Avatars

The most interesting element of the myths of Vishnu is his many incarnations called *avatars*. An *avatar* means a descent and in Hindu mythology it symbolises an incarnation, as a portion of the divine essence of Vishnu takes another form with superhuman powers.

One of the *avatars* of Vishnu is Krishna who in the discourse of the *Bhagavat Gita* explains the need for the *avatars*. Krishna explains that when the world is filled with iniquities Vishnu appears in a living form to save the good and destroy evil. As Krishna says to Arjuna at the battle field of Kurukshetra,

> "Whenever righteousness declines, O Bharata
> And unrighteousness holds sway;
> Then do I manifest myself in bodily form
> To protect the good, to destroy the evil
> To firmly establish *dharma*, the rule of
> righteousness
> I come into being from age to age."

The story of all his ten *avatars* from the man-lion Narasimha to Krishna have this common thread of good triumphing over evil with the intervention of a celestial aspect of Vishnu. When he is being a warlike god, Vishnu kills demons like Hiranyakasipu, Hiranyaksha, Namichi and Kalnemi. Vishnu and his *avatars* are so popular among worshippers because he is the champion of the good and a patient and compassionate deity who listens to the prayers of his devotees.

The worshippers of Vishnu are called Vaishnavas and among the greatest Vaishnava saints have been Chaitanya, Ramanuja and the Alvar poets of the south like Nammalvar, Peyalvar and the mystic poetess Andal. The Vaishnava sect rose in popularity from the 4th century A.D. and the first mention of the Bhakti of Vasudeva-Krishna can be found in the treatise *Ashtadhyayi* written by the philosopher Panini in the 5th century. Then the sect flourished with the patronage of the Gupta kings and King Chandragupta Vikramaditya called himself a *parama bhagavat* — a worshipper of Vishnu. He adopted the emblem of the Garuda Dhwaja — his flag had the image of Vishnu's vehicle, the mythical bird named Garuda. The Gupta period is the time when temples to Vishnu began to be built and a definite iconography developed with many images of Vishnu being carved at Mathura.

Vishnu and his consort Lakshmi or Sri, make a very attractive divine couple. She is the beautiful and gentle goddess of wealth and he is the wise preserver of creation. Lakshmi's aura dazzles like lightning and from her body emanates the fragrance of lotuses. They live in his heaven called Vaikuntha and his vehicle is the mythical half-human, half-bird Garuda, whose image is also placed on the god's ensign called the 'Garuda Dhwaja'.

In his icons Vishnu is depicted as a king, clad in silks and jewels often flanked by Lakshmi and Bhumi, the earth goddess. He is a very handsome god with perfect features and a smiling benign expression. He has a deep blue skin and wears yellow gold garments, a garland of lotuses and much jewellery — bangles, earrings, necklaces and a crown. On his breast he has a peculiar curl of hair called *Srivatsa*, he wears the famous *Syamantaka* jewel on his wrist and the *Kaustabha* gem on his chest.

Vishnu's Image and Appearance

Vishnu's image is called Sri Vigraha and it has four hands and carries the *shankha-chakra-gada-padma* — a conch shell, a discus, a mace and a lotus flower. The conch shell is the famous *Panchajanaya* that he blows at the beginning of a battle. The discus is called *Sudarshana Chakra* and also *Vajranabha* that he uses to vanquish the enemy. The mace is called *Kaumodaki* and the lotus is of course the *padma*. He is depicted in three postures — *Sthanaka*, that is standing; *Asana*, seated on a lotus with Lakshmi beside him and Say Sayaana, reclining on the coils of the *Sheshanag*, floating on the *Ananta* Ocean, with the serpent's seven great hoods flaring out protectively over his head. In the *Sayana* icon sometimes a lotus grows out of his navel and Brahma is shown sitting on it.

Vishnu's iconography is one of the most detailed with every element getting named and some like the *Sudarshana Chakra* even worshipped on their own. In spite of his benign appearance Vishnu is also quite a warrior and with his mace, he also has a bow, the Saranga and a sword, the Nandaka. His *avatars* Parashuram, Ramachandra and Krishna are all great warriors. Like Shiva has the symbol of the *lingam*, the stone symbol of Vishnu is the Salagram. These round stones that have been smoothened by the River Gandaki are worshipped as a substitute for the image of Vishnu. His favourite flower is the lotus and he likes the Tulsi plant, the *vata* or banyan and the *pipal* trees, that are all worshipped by Vaishnavas. Some of the greatest temples to Vishnu are at Srirangam, Badrinath, Kanchipuram, Guruvayur and Tirupati.

Vishnu may have ten incarnations but finally every aspect or *avatar* of Vishnu is the same eternal god. As Krishna describes himself in the Bhagavat Gita,

"In essence I am never born,
As I never alter.
I am the lord of all beings.
And the full master of my own nature.
Yet of my own power I come to be."

Unlike Shiva who lives like an ascetic in the hills, Vishnu's heaven is luxurious and gorgeous, deserving of a divine monarch. The *Mahabharata* describes Vishnu's abode Vaikuntha as being made entirely of gold, with pillars made of precious gems. The crystal Ganga flows through it and there are five pools with blue, red and white lotuses blooming in them. He sits on a throne that glows golden as the meridian sun; at times a resplendent Vishnu is depicted with Lakshmi on his right, seated on white lotuses. From the time of the Puranas, Vishnu has remained one of the most important gods of the Hindu pantheon.

As scholars studying the rise of this god have noticed, his growth comes from the ability to absorb the qualities of other deities, local cults and even the legends of heroes and great thinkers. So his mythology is a fusion of not just gods but also the history of great kings and seers. First he took on the role of the creator from Brahma and then he eclipsed Indra as a divine monarch. Later the legends of great kings like Ramachandra of Ayodhya and Krishna of Dwarka were incorporated into his myths when they were included as *avatars*. Finally great sages like Narayana were deified and became aspects of Vishnu. For instance some scholars speculate that the teachings of the Bhagavat Gita were the works of the great sages of the time.

While reading the myths of various gods and goddesses in the *Puranas* what is fascinating is the underlying conflict between the worshippers of Vishnu and Shiva.

The epic-Puranic times, between the 3rd and 5th century A.D. must have been a period of fierce conflict for supremacy between the two largest sects of the land and the thirteenth book of the *Mahabharata* is positively fraught with sectarian strife between Vaishnavas and Shaivites. Every Purana tries to prove the supremacy of one of the deities and there are innumerable myths that talk of one vanquishing the other. If Shiva triumphs by a show of his great yogic powers, Vishnu's successes come from a more subtle cleverness and a diplomatic demeanour. If the Skanda Purana tells the myth of the Jyotirlingam in which Shiva is shown to be supreme, the Bhagavat

Purana tells of the myth of Bhrigu in which Vishnu is worshipped as the greatest of the gods. The Bhagavat Purana story begins with an argument among the sages about who is the supreme god — Brahma, Vishnu or Shiva. Rishi Bhrigu is then sent to heaven to test the trinity and discover who is the greatest. He first visits Brahma and entering Brahma's court he does not greet the god with the correct rituals of obescience, and a furious Brahma is about to curse him when Bhrigu saves himself by quickly apologising. Then he travels to Mount Kailash and when Shiva comes up to greet him with a welcoming embrace, he turns away rudely and the volatile god promptly loses his temper and picks up his trident to kill him. Bhrigu is saved only because Parvati falls at her husband's feet and calms him down. Finally Bhrigu arrives at Vaikuntha and finds Vishnu asleep and he kicks Vishnu on his chest to wake him. Vishnu woken up so rudely springs up with a smile and welcomes the sage with kind words. He invites Bhrigu to sit down and then politely asks if he had hurt his foot when he kicked Vishnu and begins to massage it. Deeply ashamed, a repentant Bhrigu is left speechless by such kindness and his eyes fill with tears of devotion. He hastens back to earth to tell the other *rishis* that it was Vishnu who was the greatest of the gods. Diplomatic and clever, Vishnu is often shown triumphing by the use of his quick wit and a sense of humour and this quality is most evident in his Krishna avatar.

Among all his *avatars* it is Krishna who is considered to be a complete embodiment of all the qualities of the god. Vishnu became one of the pre-eminent gods, even eclipsing Brahma mainly because of his avatars. Vishnu and his ten *avatars* within themselves encompass just about every quality that makes a god popular. Rama is honourable and an ideal human being, Krishna is wise and clever and Vishnu himself is seldom described as being a vengeful or angry deity. He is kind and compassionate, a god who has the patience to listen to your prayers but he is not afraid of any conflict, as he is always willing to fight for the good and vanquish evil. His avatars span every stage of human existence, Krishna is a mischievous child, a divine lover and finally a majestic king. Rama is dutiful, just and the ideal king and there are ferocious Narasimha and the vengeful Parashuram to tackle the demons and the cruel kings.

Usually the avatars are believed to be ten in number but the Bhagavat Purana lists up to twenty-two *avatars* and then states that in fact the incarnations of Vishnu cannot be counted as they are as numerable as the rivulets flowing out of a lake. The ten most commonly accepted avatars are the following: (1) *Matsya*, the fish. (2) *Kurma*, the tortoise. (3) Varaha, the boar. (4) Narasimha, the man-lion. (5) Vamana, the dwarf. (6) Parashuram, Rama with the axe. (7) Ramachandra, the king of Ayodhya and the hero of the *Ramayana.* (8) Krishna, the king of Mathura and Dwarka and the hero of the *Mahabharata.* (9) Gautama Buddha, the founder of Buddhism and (10) Kalki, the god who is yet to come.

The first five incarnations are purely mythological and not human. Interestingly, the original myths of Matsya, Kurma, *Varaha* and *Vamana* were first credited to Brahma-Prajapati in the Satapatha Brahmana. But the next four, of Parashuram, Rama, Krishna and the Buddha show the deification of great kings, heroes and an influential teacher. The ninth avatar of the Buddha is the most confusing as some list Krishna's older brother Balarama as an avatar instead of the Buddha. There are three Ramas mentioned as avatars — Rama Bhargava who is Parashuram, Rama Dasarathi, the prince of Ayodhya and Rama Haladhara, that is Balarama who carries a plough as his weapon.

The inclusion of Gautama Buddha among the avatars of Vishnu has always intrigued scholars as his teachings rejected the rituals of Hinduism and opposed the supremacy of the brahmin priesthood. During the years of the rise of Buddhism when the ancient Brahmanical religion was on the decline, this was probably an attempt by the priesthood to combat Buddhism by introducing the Buddha into the Hindu pantheon. Buddha began as a teacher but was transformed into a god and by the time of the evolution of Mahayana Buddhism he was being considered a solar deity and that made it even easier to absorb him as an avatar. However, even though he is listed as an avatar, the Buddha was never worshipped by Hindus and no temples were built to him.

The concept of *avatar* was always a very amorphous one. Many of the writers and poets of ancient times created their own lists, praising gods, kings and sages they liked as avatars. Among the selections are Purusha, the primal man; *rishis* like Kapila, Narada, Dattatreya and Veda Vyasa and kings like Prithu and Rishabha. And even *Yajna,* the sacrifice itself, Nara-Narayan, the two aspects of Krishna and Arjuna, and Dhanvantri the physician of the gods manage to gain the status of avatars. In modern times the kings of Nepal are considered to be the avatars of Vishnu.

Both Shiva and Vishnu and his *avatars* were the inspiration for the greatest surge in devotional poetry in India. This stream of passionate devotion to a god began to be called Bhakti and it led to the composition of some of the most beautiful poetry from ancient to medieval times. From Nammalvar to Jaideva and Mira Bai, this poetry has been at the heart of the Hindu worship or *puja,* where there is a personal communion with God through rituals performed by the devotee and the singing of hymns. The songs of the Alvars who wrote in praise of Vishnu and the Nayanmars who worshipped Shiva through verse, are still sung in the temples of the South. The *Ramcharitmanas* of Tulsidas, the poems of Surdas and Mira Bai have become part of the spiritual heritage of the people. In North India the *Ramcharitmanas* has become the scripture of the common people, who read and recite its verses daily.

Among the greatest Vaishnava teachers and saints are Ramanujacharya who founded the Srisampradya sect in the 11th century. The most important centre of his sect is the Vishnu temple at Srirangam in Tamil Nadu. The sage Madhavacharya lived and taught in the 13th century. Chaitanya Mahaprabhu, who sang and danced in praise of Krishna, was born in Bengal in the 15th century and established the sect of the *Gaudiya Vaishnavas* and is considered one of the greatest Bhakti saints.

Vishnu has a thousand names and the recitation of his Sahasranama is considered a very meritorious act of devotion. Among his names is Achyuta, the imperishable; *Ananta,* the endless and *Chaturbhuja,* the four armed. He is Hrishikesha, the lord of the senses; Janardhana, the one men worship and *Purushottoma*, the ideal and supreme spirit. He is the handsome and long-haired Kesava and the king-like *Kiriti*, wearing a crown. He is Varadaraja, the giver of boons and Lakshmipati, consort of Lakshmi.

As he floats on the celestial waters, Vishnu is Narayana and because of the lotus that grows out of his navel, he is Padmanabha. His golden yellow garments give him the name of Pitambara. He is Madhav, made of honey or a descendent of *madhu*; Hari, the saviour and Mukunda, the deliverer. He is also Yajneshwara, the lord of the sacrifice and at a *yajna* he is the priest, the oblation, the hymn and the sacrifice itself. As cheerful bustle of life in the temples, full of chatter, song and the laughter of children capture its life enhancing character.

In ancient times kings built their palaces in perishable wood and brick but the temples were built in stone. And it is these temples that have survived as living records of great kings and famous dynasties. We know the history of kings like Narasimha Deva of

Orissa, Raja Raja Chola of Thanjavur and Krishna Deva Raya of Vijayanagar because of the inscriptions on the temples they built. We have discovered forgotten dynasties like the Pallavas and the Cholas because of their temples. These stone monuments to their greatness have stood the test of time, survived the onslaught of a cruel climate, the avarice of invaders and the bigotry of kings.

They are our history and our heritage, a vibrant kaleidoscope of sculpture, painting, music and dance. The *devalayas* are not just for the Hindus, they are for every Indian. When temples began to be built in the early years of the first millennium of the Christian era they quickly became the centre of urban civilization in India. A temple was always placed in the heart of a human settlement and a town would grow all around it. The main roads would lead off from the temple gateways and the largest markets would spring up along these roads. The temple would always be the tallest structure in the town, with its soaring spires reaching up to the sky and it would gather pilgrims and scholars, craftsmen and musicians within its walls.

Even today, in temple towns like Madurai or Varanasi, it is the spires of the temples that dominate the skyline of the city.

What is amazing at these temples is the unbroken religious tradition they have preserved for over a thousand years. As the bells ring, the priest raises the many flamed *aarti* lamp to illuminate the face of the idol and voices rise to the chant of *mantras*, what you experience is a continuing tradition that goes back to Vedic sages singing a hymn to the sun god Surya. Our temples are the living proof of the immense and venerable age of India's civilization and its remarkable power of survival. The temples of Luxor and Babylon stand empty and silent but in Varanasi and Madurai the walls still echo to the same prayers.

A Conversation with God

The Hindu way of worship is a personal communion with god, we do not have any tradition of congregational worship. Even when a crowd gathers around the inner sanctum to watch the priests perform the rituals of *puja*, each one prays on his own. This is a very personal faith, there is rarely any mass chanting of prayers or temple sermons, except the singing of *bhajans*, collectively. The Hindu holds conversations with god like they would with a spiritual guide, a family member or friend. There is Baba Vishwanath, the benign father in Kashi and Ma Durga, the understanding mother in Bengal and generous Ganesh, the benevolent godfather who's shrine finds a place in every Hindu home. The deities will listen to your prayers, share your happiness and also accept your anger with a stoic patience. For a pious Hindu going to the temple is not essential, you can pray at home at your personal shrine and worship by doing the *puja* without using the services of a priest.

> "Just as certain limbs of the body are purer than others, so are certain places on earth more sacred — some on account of their situation, others because of their sparkling waters, and others because of the association or habitation of saintly people."
>
> — *The Mahabharata*

At the heart of the *tirthas* of the Chaar Dhaam are four majestic temples that have drawn the pilgrims to their doorsteps for centuries. These temples are at the core of all the rituals of *puja* and *darshan* because in their sanctum stands the majestic, compassionate deity who listens to a devotee's prayers.

At Badrinath there is the great Badrinarayan Temple of Vishnu. In Dwarka stands the many tiered Dwarkadheesh Temple dedicated to Krishna, the eighth *avatar* of Vishnu, worshipped as the lord of Dwarka. At Puri is the legendary Jagannatha Temple of Krishna as the lord of the world. A temple that has amazed visitors with its elaborate rituals and colourful *Ratha Yatra* procession. Finally in Rameshwaram stands the Ramanathaswamy Temple dedicated to Rama, the seventh avatar of Vishnu, that is one of the jewels of Dravidian temple architecture.

For a Hindu, a temple is a *devalaya*, the palace of their god. Here, within its inner sanctum, they place the icon that is the earthly symbol of the deity. And to this image they carry their prayers in handfuls of flowers and lovingly perform the rituals of worship with incense and lamps. To their god they bring their hopes and fears, they visit him to share their happiness and sorrow, and they believe that if you come with pure intentions, God hears what is in your heart. Hindus have a surprisingly personal equation with their god, who is feared and propitiated but also cared for and loved. The deity is washed and given food, music and dance is performed for its entertainment and it is taken out for chariot rides. The gods have consorts, they have their favourite vehicles, trees, fruits and flowers. For a Hindu the temple is much more than a place of worship, where you ring the bells and chant the *mantras*. It is also a place where great minds gather to share their wisdom and it is a joyous centre of festivities.

Hinduism is a constantly evolving set of beliefs and it is more than a religion with moral precepts. It is a way of living. Its ability to evolve and accept new thoughts and its innate spirit of tolerance is what has helped it to survive the onslaught of more rigid faiths like Islam and Christianity. True Hinduism has place for all faiths and the builders and sculptors of our temples reflected this attitude as they worked on Hindu, Buddhist and Jain shrines with the same dedication. The *Nara Narayana* he is paired with a deified human being like Rama and Lakshman, Krishna and Balarama and Krisha and Arjuna.

Vishnu's Chaar Dhaam

It is said that the four *dhaams* are the favourite abodes of Vishnu on earth. The divine monarch bathes in the Alakananda River at Badrinath. He gets dressed at Dwarka. He eats a meal at Puri and then goes to Rameshwaram for a well earned rest after his arduous work of preserving all creation.

The four *tirthas* of the Chaar Dhaam are set at the cardinal points of the Indian subcontinent. In the North, the dhaam of Badrinath is in the Himalayas; in the West, Dwarka stands by the Arabian Sea; in the East is Puri by the Bay of Bengal and in the South, Rameshwaram is an island at the point where the Indian Ocean touches the Indian shore. All four have temples dedicated to either Vishnu or to one of his *avatars*. Badrinath is a Vishnu temple, Dwarka worships Krishna, Puri is the *tirtha* of Krishna as Jagannatha and Rameshwaram has temples dedicated to Rama.

The sage Adi Shankaracharya established monasteries, the *mathas*, at some of these *dhaams*. These are the Jyotirmath near Badrinath, the Sharada math at Dwarka and the Goverdhan math at Puri. His fourth *matha*, the Kamakoti Peetham was established at Kanchipuram.

Sometimes a very sacred place of pilgrimage is also called a *dhaam* to signify its great sanctity. For instance pilgrims visit four *tirthas* in the Himalayas which are also called Chaar Dhaam. These are Badrinath, Kedarnath, Gangotri and Yamunotri. These *tirthas* are not exclusive to Vishnu as Kedarnath has a temple dedicated to Shiva and Gangotri and Yamunotri are located where the rivers Ganga and Yamuna emerge from the Himalayan glaciers. Traditionally many other *tirthas* have also been called *dhaams*, like the Brahma Temple and lakes at Pushkar in Rajasthan. However, for the devout Hindu, the most sacred and ancient of the *dhaams* remain the Chaar Dhaam of Badrinath, Dwarka, Puri and Rameshwaram.

9
Religion—The Wonder World of Khasas

Culture

The culture of the Khasas of Jaunsar-Bawar has been deeply impressed by their contacts with the Doms, the aboriginal element in the population. The Doms belong mostly to the 'Austric' race and their cultural life greatly resembles that of the various tribes of pre-Dravidian or Australoid origin. While the Khasas claim to be Hindus and have been recently fast adopting Hindu surnames and trying to establish connection with the Rajputs and Brahmins of the plains (their contacts with outsiders have taught them the importance of their claims), their social life as well as their beliefs and practices connected with their religion do not identify them with the Hindus of the plains. They remarry widows, practise levirate, sororate and polyandry, recognize divorce as legal, and as against the Hindus of the plains intermarriage between the various Khasa groups is not tabooed and children born of such marriages do not suffer any social stigma.

While they worship Hindu gods and goddesses, they have a partiality for ancestor spirits, queer and fantastic demons and gods and for the worship of stones, weapons, dyed rags and symbols. On the other hand, their customary rites in the temples, the manner and mode of offering sacrifices, the daily religious performances in the temples, 'the dim lighting, the burning of incense, the mysterious incantations and sing song monologues', all indicate Hindu origin, and tradition in ritual and temple worship. The sun, the moon and the constellations are their gods. The sun is male and the moon female. The moon's pride on account of her greater beauty and her insulting behaviour towards the sun on that score, provoked the latter's wrath; his curse had the effect of disfiguring the moon's face resulting in spots which are said to be marks of leprosy to which the people are often victims. The Mundas of Bihar believe that eclipses of the sun or moon occur when their creditors surround the sun or moon for the debts of the Mundas; this represents the typical belief about eclipse among all the Austric-speaking tribes in India.

Among the Khasas, the sun and moon are said to have borrowed money from a Dom, but the interest swelled to such an amount that it could not be paid and the debt was repudiated. The Dom on that account worries them often by throwing a skin on their face. Though the average Khasa is always in debts, the stigma attaching to persons of higher castes who borrow from the Dom is great in Jaunsar-Bawar, and the elders belonging to the higher castes do not tolerate such practices in the village. The customary raising of *menhirs* and other stone memorials among the Khasas appears to be a relic of a megalithic cult which is an important feature of Austric culture. The Khasas appear to have, in all probability, borrowed this custom from the aboriginal element in these parts. It is customary to construct a terraced platform near a public thoroughfare on which they place a single upright stone to commemorate the dead. The belief in the transmigration of souls and in the doctrine of metempsychosis is an important feature of their religious life. They believe that the soul has to pass through as many as eighty-four lakhs of forms, including animals and insects. The activities of man on earth are carefully recorded by Yama whose messengers have to present the souls before him. As Dharamraj, Yama determines the form which a particular soul should pass into, in accordance with its activities on earth.

Their religion is a curious blend of Hindu and tribal beliefs and practices, and a functional analysis of these is sure to provide interesting material. Nowhere perhaps are magic and religion so closely interlaced and interwoven as in Jaunsar-Bawar. Magic plays an important role in the life of the hill people, by giving them confidence in danger and crisis, and by providing the incentive to organized undertakings. Not only in the main occupations of the people like agriculture and lumbering, in ordinary day-to-day life also magic is potent and effective. The importance of the evil eye and of the evil tongue is recognized by the hill people and oaths and ordeals have a significance hardly paralleled in savage society.

Magic, Swearing and Nefarious Designs on Others

It is possible to effect injury to person or to cattle or both by magical practices, to cause death in a family by mere swearing, and to cause houses to be burnt by magic. The courts of justice recognize the importance of oaths and ordeals, and when the necessary evidence in a civil case is not forthcoming the parties are allowed to decide the issue by means of oaths and ordeals. In some the image of the goddess Kali, or in any temple dedicated to Mahasu, their great god, and the plaintiff is asked to take the money. Should the defendant want to prove that the money he owes has been paid by him, he drinks the water in which the feet of the *deota* are dipped, and this is taken as conclusive evidence that the money has been paid by the defendant. In other cases, the plaintiff will light a lamp in a temple and the defendant has to put it out proving thereby that he has Paid the amount due from him. If a villager bears a grudgc against his neighbour and he wants to harm him or his effects, he takes a clod from his field, lays it on the altar of Mahasu, and prays for an immediate judgment. Should this neighbour meet with any accident or domestic trouble, he must leave his field, as otherwise the god invoked by his enemy may cause greater calamity to befall on him. The consequences of dishonesty and false statement on oath are terrible as the person is sure to be affected with insanity or leprosy, or some great calamity may befall his family, or he may die an unnatural death within a short period from the commission of the offence. People who are notorious for their wickedness are supposed to possess some power either inherent in them or derivatively acquired. For example, they are known to abuse people and swear against them on the slightest or no pretext and the belief is that such persons can do harm as their *ghat* (swearing) is usually very effective.

The Evil Spirits

There are certain gods whom wicked and anti-social people usually invoke for help in their nefarious designs on others. One such evil spirit is Narsin who is extremely mischievous and is readily invoked to harm or destroy cattle and crops and to afflict people with diseases. The *baki* (diviner) has to get in touch with this spirit and propitiate it whenever it is suspected of evil. Though it is a criminal offence in Jaunsar-Bawar to call any person a 'witch', it is commonly believed in these parts that witches exist, and whenever any person meets with a misfortune or contracts any serious illness, the members of his family may suspect any woman, young or old, to be responsible for it and she is dubbed a witch. Thenceforward, she becomes an object of close attention in the village and her family is branded as anti-social and consequently segregated from other families in the village.

The incidence of infant mortality is pretty high in Jaunsar-Bawar. It is traced to the influence of certain evil spirits. These are always after children and pregnant women and their attention is followed by disease and death of their victims. There are people specially versed in spirit lore who utter magic words and blow ashes over the child or woman believed to be affected by spirits and this is considered potent enough to cure the affliction. When a pregnant woman falls ill, it is believed to be due to the mischief caused by certain evil spirits and the woman has to undergo a course of treatment prescribed by the *baki* or *ghadiala* (witch-doctor). With her hair dishevelled and forehead painted lavishly with vermilion she is made to sit near the witch-doctor. The latter takes a bell-metal plate in his hand and starts beating it to tune, uttering simultaneously a number of incantations in a peculiar singsong tone. After half an hour or so, the woman feels heavy, starts shivering, indicating thereby that the spirit has entered her person. The woman shows signs of greater animation and moves her limbs to and fro, attempting to rise on her toes and eventually starts dancing to the tune of bell-metal music. Soon she forgets herself, her husbands and relations, and is metamorphosed as it were into the spirit which has taken possession of her. The *ghadiala* addresses the spirit in the woman and the latter answers on behalf of the spirit. The source of the attack, the name of the spirit, the necessary offerings and sacrifices that would appease it and any particular direction as to the manner and mode of disposal of the offerings are mentioned by the possessed woman and it is believed that as soon as these are offered as directed, the woman gets rid of the spirit possessing her. The spirit, however, leaves the victim in a spectacular manner. The woman shrieks, or strikes herself with some stick, or makes a violent attempt at escape and is often forcibly brought to rest by the people present. This and similar practices show the extent of the influence of tribal beliefs and practices on the cultural life of the Khasas.

Ceremonies during Epidemics and Calamities

When epidemics invade a village, the resources of the village are freely requisitioned by the headman concerned and custom prescribes an *astabali* (sacrifice of eight lives) to appease the godling of disease. Five different approaches of the village are selected for the purpose and at each approach an improvised bamboo gate is erected. At the centre of each gate is fixed the wooden effigy of a monkey and a vertical slab of stone (*menhir*) is firmly fixed in the earth. The menhir is crowned with a large round stone and two pieces of wood with flattened ends are tied on either side of the upright slab, the whole thing resembling a human figure from a distance. Five different sacrifices are offered at the five approaches to the village. At one, a goat is killed and buried near the *menhir*, at the second place a sheep is similarly sacrificed and buried. A hen and a pig are sacrificed at the third and fourth approaches respectively, while at the fifth, they cut a pumpkin into halves and bury the parts. After the sacrifices at the selected places, all the villagers assemble in the yard of the temple where a sheep and a vegetable (*gindoro*) are offered as sacrifice. The gindoro is cut into in the name of the village and the meat is distributed among the villagers. The elaborate rites of *astabali* are performed only when a major calamity is feared and the efficacy of this prescription is seldom questioned by the villagers. The village priest is in charge of this ritual and he recites hymns and prayers as well as magical incantations to invoke the aid of the gods.

Traditional Code of Conduct

They do not appear to be much concerned with rewards and punishments in the world to come, but they observe a code of conduct which, if followed, is believed to pave the way to a prosperous life in this world and uninterrupted bliss in the next. These refer to their food, sheep and sacrifice. They must not drink pure milk and they should abstain if possible from butter; butter is better burnt in the temple of the gods. It is on ceremonial occasions and festivals that they may eat butter after it is offered to the gods, and they should not sleep on beds with four legs; the usual practice in Jaunsar-Bawar is to sleep on the wooden floor. The principal occupations are safeguarded against interference by the forces of evil by a system of protective and productive magic. It is true that the efficacy of these magical rites is being trusted less by the people, but this has not caused any serious challenge to the traditional code of conduct so far as it relates to the observance of rites of protective magic.

Magic embraces practically all spheres of activity. When they build a new house, they have to protect it from destruction by fire, or from calamities that may fall on the inmates; the usual practice is to sacrifice a goat or sheep to the evil spirits and the blood is sprinkled round the house. When the bridegroom returns home with the bride, before the couple is allowed to enter the house, some relative, usually the maternal uncle, throws down from the roof of the house a live sheep in front of the couple below. The relatives and friends of the couple tear pieces of flesh and bone from the animal and there is a scramble among them for the heart and liver of the sheep, which when eaten raw ensures good luck to the eater. The bride and the bridegroom are then allowed to get inside the house. When the harvests are brought home or the first sowing takes place, the evil spirits are propitiated by individual families. Also a common sacrifice is made by the village to undo the evils of magic. Human sacrifice is non-existent, but the efficacy of it in theory is not denied by the Khasas.

The *Bedwart* (Rope Dancing)

The custom of rope-dancing, which formed an important annual festival in these parts, has become obsolete as it has been forbidden by the administration on account of the risk to life involved in the process. But in times of agricultural calamities occasioned by the vagaries of rainfall or by insect pests and diseases to crops and cattle, they remember the olden days when the annual *bedwart* (rope-dancing) provided the necessary safeguards against such supernatural visitations. Even a few years ago, in Rawain, *bedwart* was allowed to be practised under police surveillance, as the people had made repeated representations to the authorities not to interfere with the age-old magico-religious practice. The failure of rains and harvest was attributed to the non-observance of these practices and the government had to yield to their persistent demands. The *bedwart,* as it was practised in earlier days, was a cruel custom. It subjected the *beda* (dancer) to physical violence. Originally, a lengthy piece of rope, stoutly made, was tied to two peaks of unequal height and the rope was greased for days and weeks to allow the beda to slide smoothly from the higher to the lower end of the rope. The beda, after a ceremonial bath, was seated at the highest end of the rope and then given a push; the greasy rope did the rest. The beda glided down the rope at a terrible speed, somehow clinging to it, and the vast crowd gathered to watch the ceremony would break into loud cheers as the beda approached the end of the lower peak. If he accidentally missed his hold of the rope, it was fatal for him, for he would certainly dash against the ravines hundreds of feet below and be shattered into fragments. If he succeeded, as he usually did, because it was undertaken after long preparation and practice, he released his hold of the rope immediately before he reached the other end, and dropped down into the arms of a receptive crowd. They carried him on their shoulders and moved him through the crowd. The piece of cloth or rag he had on would be torn to shreds and each man collected a thread or two from this as protection against natural calamities and as a sign of good luck and prosperity. In the scuffle that would ensue to secure the token, the *beda* might lose not only his cloth but even a few tufts of hair from his head and receive other serious injuries. Other magico-religious rites include naked dances before sowing, during the growth of the crops and after harvests. Playing with red hot iron rods, swallowing burning charcoal and such other ordeals are some of the other precautions designed to safeguard their material prosperity and domestic bliss.

Importance of Mahasu Deota

The centre of religious life of the people of Jaunsar-Bawar is at Hanol, where the Mahasu temple is situated. The Hanolians are not orthodox Hindus, neither do they practise orthodox Hinduism. Mahasu Deota is their chief deity and a large majority of their beliefs and rituals centre round Mahasu. Like the Hindus, in general, the villagers believe in a supreme god, Mahasu in their case, but they also worship Ram and Sri Krishna. The Sayana of Hanol says,'Mahasu is our real *deota,* and for all practical purposes, he is their real *deota.* Every morning grown up men stand with folded hands and pray to him. In the evening, women of the village request the priest to give them a little of the ghee from *artipatra* with which they smear the forehead of each member of the family when retiring time draws near. It is Mahasu Deota who possesses the 'seers' and *bakis* and tells the people how to overcome diseases and the natural calamities. Mahasu is a powerful god, for it is he who sanctions the order of social precedence in Jaunsar-Bawar and controls the behaviour of the castes. The Bajgi do not till the land as it may incur the dis-pleasure of Mahasu. At Dangutha, a village on the Upper Simla Road in the Bawar range, a Kolta woman said, 'We cannot wear gold ornaments, only because our *deota* does not permit it.'

An incident in the same village brings out in bold relief the important place assigned to Mahasu Deota, as the traditional witness to oaths, and *chhinga* or *barjan*, the customary methods of expressing tension and social disapproval. A majority of the population of this newly settled village consists of Koltas and other immigrants. Traditionally, the rights of granting trees and timber to the inhabitants of Dangutha and Aithan were vested in the Sayana of Aithan. But sometime back, the Koltas of Dangutha approached the Sub-Divisional Magistrate of Bawar to allot them separate trees in the jungle which should be exclusively for the inhabitants of Dangutha. Their request was granted and an intimation of this was sent to the Sayana of Aithan. It happened that some inhabitants of Aithan were dissatisfied with their Sayana. The Koltas of Dangutha were also antagonized by this Sayana as he did not inform them, which he was asked to, that their request had been granted. Thus, an alliance was effected between the dissatisfied sections of the two villages on the basis of *lota-pani*. Each of them took a *lota* of water, put a little of salt in it and took a vow.

By making Mahasu Deota a witness, we promise, if we betray each other in our understanding, we should perish as salt gradually dissolves in water. We promise that we will not accept timber through the present Sayana of Aithan.' They proposed another man's name as the Sayana of Dangutha. On the other hand, some inhabitants of Dangutha went on the side of the Sayana of Aithan and thus complicated the problem. The forest ranger was ready to accept another Sayana to distribute the timber among the inhabitants of Dangutha, but the unwillingness of a section of the population of Aithan, bound by oath not to accept anything from the old Sayana, came as a hurdle. The ranger had no other alternative but to hand over the job of distribution for both the villages to the old Sayana. Ultimately, both the parties realized that it would be better if both the villages had separate Sayanas who could effect the distribution of the annual grant for their respective villages. But the *lota-pani* oath stood in the way, and its breach was feared to bring about the wrath of Mahasu Deota. The only remedy, therefore, was to go to Hanol, sacrifice a goat there, and request the *deota* to excuse them for going back on their promise.

The Legend of Mahasu Deota

Originally Mahasu Deota belonged to the valley of Kulu. An interesting legend is told regarding the establishment of the temple and the arrival of Mahasu Deota in Hanol from his original habitat. It is said that Bhimsen, with his mother Kunti and the other four Pandava brothers, came from the east and established the present temple and installed the god Vishnu in it. Afterwards they moved to Mahendrath where a demon by the name of Baghadanava had been troubling a local Brahmin woman. Having devoured six of her sons, he lay in wait for the seventh. The woman was weeping over the doom which awaited her seventh son when Bhimsen's mother Kunti asked the cause of her misery. The woman offered a gift of gold worth the weight of her deceased sons if somehow her seventh son could be saved. Bhimsen accepted the challenge at his mother's bidding. He ate up all the rice which the harassed mother had kept at six places in memory of each of her dead sons, and drank all the water. The demon appeared in due course of time and got infuriated at seeing that there was no food left for him. He declared that he would devour the whole of the village. All this time Bhimsen doubled up his body. He killed the demon in a duel that followed. Bhimsen then left for Bairat where he began to live in disguise.

This legend abruptly ends here and another begins. There lived at Mahendrath a Brahmin by the name of Oonrhan Bhat who married a Brahmini from Chatra, situated one mile above Hanol. Again there appeared a demon who devoured all the children born to the Brahmini. Once she had a dream that Mahasu Deota of Kulu and Kashmir could kill the demon and relieve her of the trouble. She persuaded her husband to seek the help of Mahasu Deota, whereupon the Brahmin set out on the errand and reached Ranrhin Thik. The Brahmin got hold of Chalda Mahasu and when asked to reveal the cause of detention he said,'At Mahendrath we are troubled by a demon. Please come there, kill him and establish your kingdom.'

Chalda Mahasu instructed Oonrhan Bhat to get a field ploughed by seven boys and calves who had been on fast for seven days. The boys on fast, however, could not go beyond the fifth day, and they ploughed the land with the help of the calves. Out of this ploughing the first to spring up was goddess Deolarhi who is said to be the mother of all gods. The Botha, Pabasi and Chalda Mahasus sprang up one after the other. The demon was caught at Kataeejan, a place in Jubbal state, and slain on a stone which is still there and is said to contain signs of weapons with which the demon was done to death. From there the gods started on a victory march, vanquishing the Ranas of Arakot in Garhwal, Hunredi Rani and Rana Arjun of Majhog in Bamar and a Rajput chieftain at Rayagi. They came back to Mahendrath. A temple for Kailu was built at Majhog and for Shirhkwihya at Rayagi. The gods then decided to march to Hanol for dividing the conquered kingdom. There they sat on the pavement which still stands in the southeast corner of the temple quadrangle. After a protracted wordy duel between the followers of Vishnu and Mahasu and a contest for display of wealth, Vishnu was defeated. He had to vacate the local temple, but Botha Mahasu took pity on him and gave him a little space outside the temple.

The temple referred to in the legend above has a long tunnel-like structure just at the entrance of the main gate. It has four apartments. Musical instruments and various other belongings of the temple are kept in the first and the second apartments respectively. Pilgrims are usually received in the second apartment. The third and the fourth being the darkest, they are visited but on rare occasions. Botha Mahasu is installed in the fourth and only the Pujagi (priest) can enter it. The flash of torch light is not allowed. At the time of aarti, when the silver plates shine, something seems to be written on them. Besides, there is a large collection of coins donated by different kings and officials. If these coins are studied, and the writings on silver plates are deciphered and the style of sculpture is examined in the Bhairon, Chharna, Mandanna, Lorha and Rangi and Tangi Birs are the attendants. An idol of Kali and other small elongated stones representing phallic symbols, like the Shivaling, are to be found. The temple at Hanol in which Botha Mahasu is installed is a centre of pilgrimage for visitors from Jaunsar, Bawar, Jubbal, Utroch, Bishar, Sirmur, Garhwal and other places in Himachal Pradesh. The expenses of the temple were shared by all the states which owed allegiance to Mahasu Deota of Hanol. One or two fields in every village are kept reserved for Mahasu, and their produce is collected by the temple managers. Final authority regarding temple affairs rests in an official known as Wazir. The Pujagi (the priest), Thani and orderly are three more servants of the temple. The orderly is a Rajput by caste and he acts as a menial and an attendant. The Thani too is a Rajput and is a helper of the priest. Every pilgrim who comes to Hanol is entitled to one meal from the temple storehouse and it is the duty of the Thani to provide them. Representatives of the Wazir, Thani and the Village Kolta often go out once a month to collect *kert*, the grain given in the name of god. The measure which is used for weighing grain is a silver cup known as *sorha*. This is the equivalent of one *patha* and contains more or less one seer of grain.

Pujagis are supplied from the Brahmin families of Chatra, Pultarh and Nenus. Each family is entitled to share the priesthood. Each family is allotted certain days in a year during which it has to send one person of the family who comes and resides in the temple and lives on only one meal a day. This meal is provided from the temple storehouse. The Pujagi is usually the eldest brother of the family for whom learning of the three R's is forbidden. The Pujagi learns the methods of worship from his predecessors. Whenever a priest family splits up, the days allotted to it are also divided amongst the separating members, like the Pujagi, the office of Thani rests in certain Rajput families, each of which sends its representative for a specific tenure of office. Out of every rupee donated by a pilgrim eight annas go to the Wazir, and two annas each to the Bajgi, Nath, Thani and Pujagi.

Chalda Mahasu keeps moving or touring with his train of hierarchical managers and servants. He lives for twelve years, alternately, in Garhwal and Jaunsar-Bawar. While in Jaunsar-Bawar he moves from village to village according to a traditional schedule. He is installed in tents in every village. He is in the charge of local Bajgis who take him from village to village and every village that falls in the itinerary has to provide for the maintenance of the whole party. The Wazir of Chalda Mahasu resides in Garhwal. Grains for this Mahasu also are collected from villages and all the donations are distributed in the usual way. Basik is also a roving deity. But he keeps moving within the four villages of Rarhu, Kunrhan, Bagi and Hanol. He stays in each village for a year and comes to Hanol only during the leap year. Pabasi is the Mahasu god of Tehri Garhwal. He comes to Hanol every year for a day and is worshipped like the other Mahasu gods.

The goddesses are mostly worshipped as local goddesses wherever they are installed. Older people of the village tend to surround local gods with an aura of mystery and superstition. In their system of beliefs gods do not allow Bajgis to till the land. When land was cultivated for the first time, the tradition goes, people suffered from fever. There was no harvest as land was left uncultivated for a long time. The instance of the death of Shibu's elder son has already been mentioned. Another story refers to the forcible entrance of an Englishman inside the temple and his great astonishment when the stony idol came to life and climbed the peepul tree under which the temple stands. It is also held that on the fifth of the last fortnight of the month of Bhadon or Bhadrapad, the stony idol comes to life and takes bath in silver and gold plates which are placed beside him filled with water. There is a good element of drama in the proceedings which were described to me by a Pujagi of Hanol. At the dead of night on the aforesaid day, the Pujagi enters the temple, closes the door behind him, implores the idol to take bath in water-filled plates of silver and gold, and, as a last resort, takes out the dagger praying, rather threatening, 'O God ! Take bath today or I will kill myself.' He now turns his back towards the god and hears the splashing of water indicating that his prayer has been granted. And the prayer is always granted, for, he must never turn his back to see the reality.

Attendants of Botha Mahasu (BIRS)

There are a number of spirits who are worshipped as gods of inferior order or spirits of superior order, such as Kailu and Shirhkwihya, who have already been mentioned. These are the attendants and closest associates of the god. Kailu is of black complexion, and resembles Kalu or Kalna Bir of the plains. These Birs usually occupy the outskirts of the villages and are worshipped by the local people. Lankura Bir is of fair complexion and beautiful in appearance. The features of other Birs, such as Chhaoni Ka Bir, Tangi Bir and Bhangi Bir, could not be recalled by the informants. The Birs are worshipped in the form of elongated, rounded, large or small stones which are found in the temple quadrangle. There are two large lead balls in the same quadrangle with which they are believed to play at times. They are worshipped with offerings of lat, a reference to which has been made in connection with the life cycle of the individual. Usual sacrifice to which they are entitled is either a cockerel or hen. Goddess Kali also has her seat in a small temple in one of the corners of the temple quadrangle. She, in no way, differs from the Kali of the plains and is worshipped on the occasion of Durga Puja.

Some Gods of the Lower Order

There are gods higher than Birs in that they do not attend and serve Mahasu. The role and duties of Kalu Bir show him to be a bit mischievous in nature and this seems to be a general characteristic of all Birs. These gods are not so important nor so high as Mahasu Deota. One such deity is Narsingh, whom the Hindus worship as an incarnation. He is regarded as the saviour of Prahlad and slayer of Hiranyakashyap. But whereas in the plains he is considered to have the head of a lion, in Jaunsar-Bawar he is imagined as a'Sadhu' who is ferocious because he wraps himself in a lion's skin and rides on a lion's back. Ordinarily, he does no harm, but he becomes furious if leather articles are taken to his small temple, situated by the side of the big temple, inside the quadrangle. He may possess the violater and cause his death. He is appeased by an offering of milk.

Bhairon, the next important among the gods of the lower order, rides on the back of a black dog like his counterpart in the plains. Both are supposed to render valuable help if invoked and propitiated. For both of them black dog stands as a symbol and, therefore, a black dog is never killed but regarded with due reverence. In Jaunsar-Bawar, worship of Bhairon is usually accompanied by the sacrifice of an ewe. Local Bajgis cherish a queer belief that centres round the god Bhairon. In the main temple, in a niche in one of the walls, an earthen lamp containing milk and ghee is lighted every night. The smoke causes a substance like black ochre to collect in the niche. According to them if a mixture of this ochre and ghee from the lamp is painted on the elongated stone representing Bhairon, a pilgrim is sure to arrive and offer a goat or sheep for sacrifice either on the same day or within a week. Whenever, as they say, they do not get meat for a sufficiently long time, they resort to this trick.

The Institution of Baki

A common sight inside the temple quadrangle in one corner is that of a person sitting with half closed eyes and shaking his body. The man is said to be possessed by the *deota* and is in complete trance. His words are not usually intelligible to an outsider. He is the *baki*, or the seer. He is consulted whenever there is a theft in someone's family or someone suffers from a prolonged disease, or on any other family trouble or quarrel. The local seer of Hanol belongs to a neighbouring village, Chatra, and is a Rajput by caste.

The *baki* folds his hands, closes his eyes and in a moment starts shaking his body, jerking it violently. His eyes become red and the voice hoarse. This is an indication that the *deota* has possessed him. And then he says to the questioner,'I know why you are here. Perhaps you want to put this question.' He starts answering the question, or if it be some malady, he begins suggesting prescriptions and remedies. It is remarkable how the *baki* is sometimes able to anticipate the questions or prescribe for maladies without even being told about them beforehand.

A *baki* is always from the Rajput or Brahmin caste, never from the Bajgis or Koltas. No one thinks of becoming a baki, unless through intuition, dream or visions, he becomes sure of the deota's favour. Once he becomes sure of it, he starts persuading the deota through feasts and sacrifices until one day he finds that his 'tongue is opened' (*jibh khul gaee*). Henceforth he is regarded as a seer or diviner.

The Spirit World

Of all the spirits of the unknown and intangible world the *bhut* and the *harh* are the commonest and most mischievous. *Bhut* is dark in complexion with long hair and two front teeth interlocked, one going up and the other coming down. People dying of sudden death are believed to pass on into *pret yoni* (sphere of spirits) in popular Hinduism and a similar belief exists among the inhabitants of Jaunsar-Bawar. Such individuals go neither to Hell nor to Heaven, but to the spirit world and become *bhut* if male and *harh* if female.

Harh may be regarded as the Khasa counterpart of churel of the plains.* This feminine spirit is also ugly but capable of changing herself into a beautiful damsel to lure able-bodied youngmen. No specific story of a particular youngman being thus entranced by a harh could be obtained, nor was there any young man or old man in the living generation who had come across such an exotic adventure.

Suggestibility of the environment is at the base of such beliefs. High hills covered with dense jungles standing around the village, dark and stormy nights and continuously roaring falls are constantly reinforcing such beliefs. *Bhut* and *harh* are malevolent spirits who may possess a child, a pregnant woman or any other person. A person thus possessed is diagnosed by the *baki* who also suggests remedies for appeasing them.

Pirs are spirits of a higher order, approaching gods and goddesses but not quite the same. Like all others of a higher order, they are not malevolent and do not harm anyone unless offended. The pir suggests a Mohammedan origin. In the plains, usually *Mo* medan'Sadhus' rising to divinity while alive are *believed* transform themselves into pirs. Such spirits are believed to dwell their graves or in old buildings lying desolate. Pir is not an important member of the Khasa pantheon of god spirits. It is a local phenomenon cherished by one Bajgi Dhan who has spent some years of his life in Sirmur state, now in Himachal Pradesh. Once a year in the month of Bhadon (September) invites his relatives as well as villagers to his residence. All village eat, drink and dance at his expense but Dhan Singh is possessed by

* Among the Harh of Singhbhum, Bihar, Churail, which is the disembodied soul of a pregnant woman who died at childbirth, is a malsficent and mischievous spirit.

'intoxication of' Sur' on the one hand and the pir on the other much hopping and jumping he settles down and is able to ask such questions as the villagers may wish to ask about their affairs, quarrels, diseases, etc. He says that the pir has been pitiated in his family since three generations, and it is in keeping his family tradition that he holds the yearly feast.

Worship of trees and animals is not so extensive and the Peepul is held to be sacred, for the first head-shaving ceremony formed under its shade. Whenever a cow gives birth, a member of the family is allowed to drink milk until a little of hulk is poured on the roots of the peepul or bkikhal tree. Like the in general these people also consider the cow as sacred and abstain killing it.

Omens

It is a bad omen to meet a person with an empty pot (ghilati) w is on his way home, or on some errand or work. It indicates obstruction in the successful accomplishment of the work. Seeing the face of a barren woman is highly inauspicious and *shavoided* on all important occasions. The carcass of a cow should not be looked at, and nobody in the village will take meals unlen it is removed. The same holds true for a human dead body. corpse has been taken away beyond the village boundary for cremation, no villager eats.

Oaths and Ordeals

It has been seen earlier how alliances are formed by way of is swearing by the deota. In the courts of the plains people swear by the holy river Ganga or by a religious book like the *Gita.* But as our informants told us, people of Jaunsar-Bawar in the Court at Chakrata have to swear by the god Mahasu. A small stone representing Mahasu Deota is put in the hands of those who present themselves as witnesses. Usually people swear by touching the *chaukhat* of the temple door.

Among ordeals designed to test a person's truthfulness the following two are usually mentioned:

(a) A man, if he is innocent, will be able to take out a rupee coin from a pan containing boiling water without being injured.

(b) An innocent person will remain unhurt if a red hot iron piece is placed in his hand.

In usual practice these methods of ordeal are not common. Shibu, who is about sixty years, told me of an old case to which he himself was not an eye-witness but had heard from someone. According to him Karn, a zamindar of Fanar, was accused of having illicit relations with a Kolta woman. To prove his innocence he took a red hot iron piece in his hands, walked five spaces forward and backward, and was unhurt and unburnt. These days the usual way is to swear by god.

Festivals

Festivals form an important part of the Khasa cultural life. They serve to mitigate, and more positively, to sweeten the otherwise severe round-the-year struggle with the elements, provide an occasion for the display of their gay, jovial nature, and for the periodic release of emotions, and help in renewing social contacts and in strengthening community relations. Most of the Khasa festivals are either inter-village or inter-Khat affairs. Apart from providing fun and frolic, these festivals help in maintaining social solidarity. Besides, as the following detailed structural studies of some of these festivals show, they are the crucibles of a mutually dependent economic life, serving to highlight the matrix of social relations and their intricate web.

Notwithstanding, even in defiance of, the hard lot that their inhospitable environment enjoins upon them, and the acute, competitive struggle for existence that it forces upon them, the Jaunsaris have, by means of social cooperation, evolved a network of festivals which aid them in sharing their hardships and fortunes. Social cooperation here helps in outdoing nature's niggardliness, and, if not overcoming it completely, it devises cultural means for circumventing it. Though by religion the Khasas are Hindus, their presiding deity, Mahasu, is not one of the Hindu pantheon. Worship of and around Mahasu, with its attendant local beliefs and faiths, rites and rituals, are all seen in these festivals. All these festivals indicate the need of social cooperation not for just economic sustenance but for cultural survival itself.

Magh

Of the four most important festivals of Jaunsar-Bawar, Magh, named after the winter month of January-February when the festival takes place, is of special significance. It is more than an ordinary festival: it is a season of festivities, extending well over a whole month, when after the Rabi crop has been fully and finally sown, villagers enjoy temporary relief from the hard agricultural activities, feast and celebrate, and avail of the time to meet their relatives from far and near. The fun and frolic not only helps in emotional release, but also in maintaining social solidarity. Like most of the other festivals, Magh is also connected with the local occupational pattern, being interlinked with the cycle of agricultural operations. After sowing the winter crop people have little to do in the fields for some time. Because of the snow and the extreme cold at this time of the year, it becomes almost impossible to carry out any kind of outdoor work. It is a time for rest, merry-making and enjoyment, symbolising victory over the most unfavourable natural environment.

Early Preparations: Some of the preparations for this festival start as early as a year in advance. For, it is on this day during the previous festival that a special goat or sheep may have been set aside and been specially fed for the coming season. At least one goat is killed in every house. A person who has a large family or expects many guests may kill more than one goat. As the current year's lot is killed another for the next year is separated and allotted for this purpose. Thus, a goat, a sheep, or a pig in the case of Koltas, is kept inside every house to be fed properly throughout the year, and to be killed on the occasion of Magh. Those who cannot afford it so soon, try to secure one some months before the actual day of killing the animal. For keeping the animal special arrangements are made in the building.

The animal is kept on the ground floor, and an opening is made through the floor of the upper storey so that it can be well looked after by the inmates, and after the family has taken meals, the left over is passed on to the animal. Thus, in addition to the ordinary fodder, these animals are also able to get some bread-pieces and other rich material to eat. The animal has also to be provided with fresh green leaves regularly. For this some person in the family is made in charge. Provision for keeping the animal inside the house for the Magh festival is thought out and made even while constructing a house. Often, green leaves and branches are hung from the opening through the floor of the upper storey in such manner that they look like live-plant and the animal has the feeling that it is eating from a plant in the forest. Similarly, arrangements for the preparation of liquor are made well in advance of the festival. On the occasion of 'Kimond', a large number of barley breads is baked, to be used for preparing liquor throughout the year. Also, loaves are made of coarse grain like *manduwa*, which along with 'Kima' loaves are used for distillation. Just before the Magh festival, liquor is made in large quantities.

Except for the Brahmins, who, as a rule, do not drink, all castes get the liquor distilled and stored for the festival. In every house, it is generally a lady who is in charge of the distilling process. She alone, unless absent or otherwise unable, will distribute liquor to the inmates and the guests. In her absence, the duty may devolve upon another lady. This charge is generally in the hands of the oldest woman or Sayani.'Moodi', made of rice and wheat grains, is also prepared and stored in advance for the occasion. Ghee, flour and other necessary food materials are purchased or procured and reserved for the festival. Salt is specially got from the market. Besides the food material, fuel, fodder and fresh leaves are brought and stored for the ensuing winter. Roofs of the houses are repaired and long green leaves placed in between the wooden sleepers to prevent leakage of water inside the building. The wooden roofs are tied together afresh by means of long plant roots, specially brought for the purpose from the jungle. Woollen clothes are so washed that they become thicker and stronger than before. All these preparations, some having started as early as the previous Magh, having been made, the stage is set for the season's celebrations.

'Lagada': The actual celebrations for the Magh festival begin a few days before the beginning of the month. The first day is known as 'Lagada', meaning the approach of the festival. This day, early in the morning, all the village Bajgis go together to the village deity's temple to play the musical instruments. They have to play the musical ins truments at the residence of the village Sayana(s) also, where they receive *dan*, often up to a rupee, and are offered drinks. This is to herald the day and announce the onset of the festival season.

'Masoj' or 'Maroj': On the day after 'Lagada', the Bajgis celebrate the Magh. The day is called 'Masoj' or 'Maroj'. All the Bajgis get their sheep or goat slaughtered by the Rajputs. These animals are not taken to the village *angan*. The Bajgis ask some Rajputs, usually from their *bera*, from whom they receive food every day, to slaughter these animals at their house. Sometimes, if they have so promised the deity, they may take the animal to the temple. A Bajgi has to provide a portion of the slaughtered animal to every Rajput of his *bera*. But this is only if a goat or a ram is killed. Everybody else who helps in skinning the animal must also be provided with a share of the meat. In case a sheep has to be killed, the job is done entirely by the Bajgis themselves, without any help from the Rajputs or the Badhais, as the latter neither eat sheep's meat nor even kill it. They do not even give any help in skinning a sheep.'Bedhi' or the sheep is considered sacred among the Khasas and the Rajputs and the Badhais will neither eat its flesh nor help in slaughtering it or even skinning it. Nor is a pig eaten by any one of the upper castes. The Koltas alone eat pork. Except for Brahmins, however, all other castes eat the wild boar's flesh, which whenever killed provides an occasion for rejoicing. Its flesh is distributed among the non-Brahmins.

'Bhatioj': During the next two days, called 'Bhatioj' and 'Adaka', the locale of the celebration changes for the Koltas, who take their animals outside the village. Accompanied by their women, they take the animals of all other castes to the jungle for grazing, returning on the third day of 'Sankrant'. All other castes, except the Koltas, celebrate the festival in the village.

According to the custom, the Rajputs, the Brahmins, the Badhais, and the Sunars, all get their animals slaughtered by those whose animals they will slaughter in turn. Among the Rajputs, there is a traditionally fixed system as to who should slaughter whose animal, all on a sort of reciprocal, interlinked and in-caste basis. Since the Brahmin does not take any other meat than that of a goat, he will not slaughter any other animal. As in the case of goats, there is no distinction between a sheep and a ram. The explanation put forward as to why these people get their animals slaughtered by others is that having fed the animal the year round, and having taken so much care to bring it up, it becomes too dear to them and they, therefore, cannot kill it with their own hands. They have therefore established a system of mutual help and assistance. Other castes too have a similar system of getting their animals killed, but, unlike Rajputs and Badhais, not by men of theirown caste. Thus, all the Bajgis and Koltas get their animals killed by someone outside their castes. The Brahmin gets his goat slaughtered by a Rajput, whose animal he, in turn, undertakes to kill. The Brahmins, as a rule, do not take ram's meat, but probably because of his close contacts and associations with Rajputs, Dei Singh of Baila has started eating it. His son Dharam Singh, however, does not do so. Even Dei Singh does not kill a ram in his own house. These Rajputs generally kill two goats per family. One more may be killed later at the time of 'Mendaura', when the relatives and friends visit a particular Rajput house.

For killing the animals, the Rajputs of Baila have a fixed chain of interrelationships among themselves. This chain has, sometimes, on account of a variety of reasons like poverty, serious illness, absence or lack of a grown-up male member in the family or his long stay away from the village, tended to break up. Thus, the Tegaik group due to its continuous absence from the village has almost completely disconnected itself from the village life. Again, Shibiya Doniyand suffers from 'Korh' and is therefore not able to participate in these celebrations. Danoo Debaik and Shiboo Chilaik are too poor to be able to continue their relationship of mutually killing the animals for the Magh festival. The Sidaik family has no male member to keep the continuity of these relationships, while in the Gurand family the two surviving members are too old to participate in these celebrations.

The Badhais too have a similar kind of mutual partnership chain for slaughtering their goats and rams, but the Bajgis and Koltas are required to get their animals killed by the Rajputs. Except for the pigs, which, if the Rajputs may not like to kill, may be killed by the Koltas themselves, all other animals must be killed by the Rajputs. They do not, however, kill a sheep, nor ever eat its flesh, this being a strict dietary taboo. This inter-caste pattern of killing the animals is accompanied in some villages by another inter-kin arrangement in the distribution of animal flesh.

In Lakhamandal, for example, the *jikuri* or the *kaleji* is reserved for the maternal uncle and other male members of his family. This is the best part of the animal and is given to the maternal uncle, emphasizing his special position in the Khasa kinship set-up. The *bukyan* attached to the *kaleji* is considered the next best part and is often reserved for the son-in-law. The *siri* is used on the eighth day after the 'Sankrant', which falls two days after the 'Maroj' or 'Masoj'. During the Magh season, a small portion of meat is prepared every day, particularly when the fellow villagers are invited for 'Bidaj'.

'Adaka': Every day begins with people, particularly the Rajputs and the Brahmins, paying social visits or returning these visits to each other's houses, where they are offered liquor to drink. While on the previous day they had to get their animals killed and skinned, on this day, known as 'Adaka', they start preparing bags out of these skins. Two kinds of bags are generally made, one for filling the corn and the other for filling water. For the first type, after filling some corn, they insert some sticks in it to enlarge it to its full capacity. For the water bags, animal skins are filled with a jungle root powder so that the skin is thickened and becomes stronger. While the ordinary corn bag is ready in a day or two, the water bag takes several days to prepare. All the persons who help both in skinning and in making the bag are entitled to a share of the animal's meat. Help from the Bajgi is particularly sought in cleaning the intestines.

'Pheeta': On the first three days of the Magh festival, people in some villages play a game, locally called 'Pheeta'. In Hindi, the term means a tape, but in village Lakhamandal the word is used for a crude football, shaped hard animal skin containing waste cloth pieces. Two parties of the *jethingya* (elders) and the *nanchhingya* (youngsters) are formed. It is an all-caste sport, wherein the old and the young male members of all the village groups are included. If there are, say, three brothers in a family, A (say, aged 70), B (say, aged 65) and C (say, 55 years old), then, according to the local rules of the game, A and C will join the jethingya party and B the other one. If, however, A is dead, B (65) will still be regarded as younger, and C (55) older for the purpose of the game. If A has no brothers, then he will invariably join the jethingya group. His or their sons will be similarly divided into two groups. All the village males thus get divided into two parties. In this way one may collide against one's own father while playing the game. The players may use both hands and feet but as the skin of the ball is hard, they generally use their hands only.

The *jethingya* are allotted one side and the *kanchhingya* the other, distance between the two parties being about 300 yards. The two parties defend their sides against the ball being thrown into their respective 'goal', which not infrequently is limitless. The field is uneven, and often consists of plots at different levels, covering even big stones and bushes. To start the game, the ball is dropped from a place of worship, and then the two parties run to catch and carry it. No specific rules are observed. One may snatch the ball from another by using any means or tactics, and, this often causes serious wounds and bruises. The game is said to end when one party scores a goal against the other, but this is not so strictly observed as the game is to be played for three days. The third day's game is more important because the hitherto intra-village sport becomes an inter-village contest, with the neighbouring villages also participating in it. 'Pheeta' is not played in the neighbouring Garhwal, and is an exclusive game of the Jaunsaris. Rati Ram of village Lakhamandal is emphatic that the game has not been imported but is of an indigenous origin. The day following 'Maroj' or 'Masoj', when 'Pheeta' starts, is called 'Sajha'.

'Sankrant': The fourth day after the festival has begun is called 'Sankrant'. The Koltas now return to the village, after giving charge of the cattle to their respective owners. Early in the morning, after having rejoiced and indulged in merry-making for two days, the Rajputs, the Badhais and the Bajgis go to look after their cattle and sheep. All the Koltas who had been with the cattle and sheep are given meals at their respective caste families. On their return these Koltas are expected to bring fuel for the Rajputs from the jungle. The Koltas, on return, get not only meals and liquor at the houses of Rajputs and other caste families, but they are also given some cooked meat and loaves to be taken for their evening meals. Having taken their meals and drunk the liquor, the Koltas bring their pigs and goats or sheep to their own *angan* and get them killed by the Rajputs. On all the four main festivals, namely Magh, Bissu, Mond and Dewali, the Bajgis are paid one loaf from every family other than the Koltas, who pay bora (uncooked food material) to the Bajgis. Those animals which are not killed by the Rajputs are later killed by Koltas themselves, but ram and goat must always be killed by the Rajputs.

If the Koltas have a goat or a ram killed, then they must provide the Rajputs of their bera a small quantity of meat. The Badhais and the Sunars too, like the Koltas and Bajgis, have to provide the Rajputs with a small quantity of meat whenever a goat or a ram is killed. This portion of meat given to the Rajputs is called *guthadi*. The Rajputs, thus, get *guthadi* from the members of all castes if they have a goat or a ram killed. The Rajputs in return give the other caste people liquor and cooked food. They are also invited at the time of 'Mendaura'.

'Khoda': 'Khoda' is the eighth day after 'Bhatioj'. The siri of the animal killed is taken out and cooked on this day. The Rajputs and the Brahmins provide the evening meals to all other caste people. Families more intimately related to the Rajputs get cooked meat, bread, rice and liquor, while the rest, who are not so intimately related, are given uncooked rice only. All the different caste people share the meat cooked out of the *siri*. Badhais and Sunars have to provide the same articles in a similar manner to all the lower caste people, namely, Bajgis and Koltas. Likewise, Bajgis are required to provide material to Koltas only, who, however, are not required to give anything to any one on this occasion. Thus, the Rajputs are the universal donors and Koltas the universal receivers on this occasion.

From this day onward the 'Mendauras' are arranged in different houses. People do not like to arrange these 'Mendauras' before the 'Khoda'.

'Mendaura': The term 'Mendaura' literally means 'a small fair', in which all those who are closely related to each other are invited for dinner at the residence of one of them. This is called arranging a 'Menda' or a *mela*. All through the Magh season, 'Mendauras' are arranged at different places in the village. There may be several 'Mendauras' at different places in one night. Not a day passes in this season when these celebrations are not arranged somewhere or the other. The feast given at a particular person's house is followed by a singing and dancing programme, lasting beyond midnight. This programme of singing and dancing continues as long as the people do not feel tired or sleepy. While only those who are close to a particular family are invited for the dinner, anybody may participate in the programme after dinner. Men and women from all castes, other than the Koltas, usually go to attend these programmes.

The Koltas have to confine their merry-making and enjoyments to themselves, because people from no other caste enter their houses. Their programmes are therefore limited to their caste only. There are three kinds of 'Mendauras', which may be arranged separately by anyone. Firstly, there is a 'Mendaura' for one's own caste or *aal* people, where one or more than one male member from each family of his caste or aal only may be invited. In case there are only a few people in a particular aal, as among the Lakhtate of village Baila, all the male members of that aal are invited. In all such matters as inviting, there is a relationship of reciprocity. A family invites as many people from other families of the same caste or aal as it would like or expect to be invited, when somebody else extends a similar invitation. Usually a person does like and try to invite more than one male member from other families, but if the number is reduced it is a sign of lack of means to do so. The Gurand family among the Horiyand Rajputs of Baila is not in a position to invite even one person from each family of the aal. Similarly, Dhyanoo Badhai of the same village neither invites anybody to attend the 'Mendaura' nor does he join the festivity at anyone's place.

The second type of 'Mendaura' is that for the 'Kamins', in which only those amongst the lower castes who are closely related to a particular higher caste family are invited for dinner. The information about a particular 'Mendaura' is given in advance to enable that invitees to reach in time. Whenever there are several 'Mendauras' in the village, the family members distribute themselves among the different ones. Very often all caste people, except the Rajputs, combine the two 'Mendauras' for convenience and economy.

Lastly, there is the 'Mendaura' for the *dhyantis*, in which they alone can participate. Usually all the *dhyantis* of a particular *aal* are invited to attend this special 'Mendaura' While sometimes *dhyantis* from another *aal*, related to the family, may also be invited to participate in this 'Mendaura', in no case is a *dhyanti* of another caste invited this occasion. It is thus, an intra or inter-*aal* social function, but always an intra-caste and never an inter-caste celebration. If a *dhyanti* from one *aal* is married in the same village and in the same family in which the *dhyanti* of another *aal* is married, then the two dhyantis of different *aals* are expected to invite one another. A significant point about the Mendaura is that while men of those families who have chhinga with one another are not invited to attend the party, dhyantis are invited everywhere. But the unmarried dhyantis are not invited those families of their *aal* or caste with whom their family has a *chhinga* 'Mendaura' for *dhyantis*, unlike that for men and that for Kamins seldom combined with other 'Mendaura'.

As in the cased 'Mendaura' for Kamins, that arranged for dhyantis is never follow by dancing and singing. In a number of 'Mendauras', dhyantis do not sing or dance; they simply watch these programmes from distance. When there happens to be a small number of Brahmin families in a village, they generally get associated with the Rajputs for 'Mendauras'. Their *dhyantis* are reciprocally invited at the other Mendaura'function. The Brahmins also invite the Rajput members for dinner on the day of 'Bhatioj'.

Among Rajputs of Baila, members of different aals are often in at this function. For example, members of the Sograik family of Lakhtate aal invite and are invited by the Dokrand family of the Rajput aal and members of the Bhyand family among Horiyand Rajput invite and are reciprocally invited by those of the Ravaik aal. It shows that inter-aal relations were formerly stronger, but now they are showing signs of breaking down. Members from the Sograik aal, for example are not invited now at the 'Mendaura' of Chaumbaik and Grand aals. The apparent cause of these breakdowns is the chhinga, but more the form rather than the cause of these intra-aal relations break down.

The Sunars are included among the Badhais, for they have to invited the latter for 'Mendaura'. The Badhais and the Sunars generally combine the first two types of 'Mendauras', as do the Bajgis, who have to invite one or two Koltas, besides members of their own caste. In case of death in a family, the 'Mendaura' must take place there first. No other family would arrange a 'Mendaura' before the one in the deceased's family is finished.

Dance Programmes: While the term 'Mendaura' is applied to the evening dinner party during the Magh festival, this party is not accompanied by dances or songs, which are arranged separately, and are a special feature of the festivities all through this season. Every evening after the 'Khoda' day, there are dance performances in the village *angan*. These evening dances are either followed or preceded by 'Mendauras'. Except for the Koltas, all other castes participate in these evening celebrations. Not only the male members from all the *aals* and different castes, but also the *dhyantis* join these dances. These dances in fact are the main attraction for the village young men and women, and all through the year, Magh festival is eagerly awaited by them. Older people also participate in these dances with as much gusto as do the young folks. As soon as they return from their work, people gather in the village *angan* and the programme starts. Ryantis are not expected to join these celebrations; if at all they come to the *angan*, they sit at a distance and just watch. These evening programmes begin with 'Lamads'.

The Badhais have specialized in these types of long songs. Children and *ryantis* do not participate in these songs. There is a sort of competition of wit here, and anybody may reply to a particular 'Lamad' sung by another. One by one, people come forward and sing these songs, which describe some old legends or narrate deeds of old disputes and fights. These 'Lamads' often relate to the work of old people and their relationships with outsiders. The first 'Lamad' with which the evening function starts is called 'Seva Ka Lamad' or 'Lamad of Service'. While these 'Lamads' are sung, the dances stop. The dances and the singing of these'Lamads' alternate. These songs serve as an interval between the dances for the serving of liquor. 'Lamads' are not easy to understand, and few people understand their meanings or their methods of recital. Singing 'Lamads' is in fact the right and the privilege of the elderly people.

For the dance, one person offers himself for the performance, while others sing or play on the musical instruments. Almost all the dances are of the same type, one person moving round and round, with his hands spread open, fingers making slow gestures. Gradually, the speed and tempo of the dance increases. The general pattern of movements remains the same, though the speed may vary from person to person.

Bissu

Bissu, the spring festival, falls in the month of April. This five-day festival is, unlike Mond and Jogra, a village affair, though at some places it takes the shape of a big inter-Khat meet. While the Magh festival is a season of rest and merry-making, Bissu, celebrated near about the Sankrant of 'Baisakh' comes to restore vigour, vitality and strength, and to set the villagers ready for the ensuing harvesting season. This is the bloom of spring, and lusty trees of red rhododendrons against the background of white snows provide a joyful scene for the celebrations. The festival is celebrated in the name of Mahasu, and 'Shilguru', the god of sheep, is worshipped. The preparations for this festival begin long before the start of the day. General cleaning of houses takes place, and fresh stocks of liquor are brewed which should last up to the next festival of Mond.

The festive occasion serves to replenish their stock of domestic goods and household materials. People either purchase cloth, or, sometimes, readymade clothing from the nearby market. For all these purchases, villagers start in groups to the market. It helps them to undertake the long journey without bothering much about shelter, for, in a group, they can lie anywhere on the way in a forest or on the roadside. At the time of these purchases, consideration is given to women's clothes and sweets for the children. The cigarette stock is filled up for the *ryantis* and the *dhyantis*. At this time various articles like household utensils, earthen pots for smoking, gold or silver ornaments, and iron implements for work may be included in the purchasing list. Women get busy washing clothes and cleaning utensils many days before the festival. This job of cleaning and washing is the exclusive concern of the women of the house. They have also to store sufficient water for the festival days. It is a hard time for women who have to fetch water from distant sources, clean everything and prepare liquor, etc. Men look after the outside marketing and other organizational work.

'Bow and Arrow': Men have also to make strong bows and arrows, required for the mock fights which are an essential part of this festival. Old socks, woollen pads for the legs, and other materials for this purpose are taken out, and repairs made. Men try to keep their old weapons intact, year to year, but these have to be made anew for the younger people. The Koltas do not always have all these sets of huge and strong lower garments, 'Jangel', and shoes, and so they have either to use whatever they have, turn by turn, or borrow some from those of other castes. The Bajgis do not play with bows and arrows as they have to be busy all the time with their musical instruments. These bow-and-arrow mock fights are played *aal*-wise. In village Baila, Bajgis do not play for the further reason that they are all from one aal. If some Bajgis from other villages not belonging to the same aal turn up on the occasion, the local Bajgis may play with them. The Koltas, if they be more than one aal in the village, play among themselves, or with their guests from outside, but they never play with the Rajputs or with those belonging to the higher castes. As a rule, playmates for these bow-and-arrow mock fights are pre-arranged and no attempt is made to change them. All the partners are selected by mutual consent and arrangement.

'Lagada': 'Lagada', meaning beginning, is announced by the Bajgis early in the morning. This is done by beating drums. They take a round from the deity's temple to 'Shiran'. No particular ceremony is observed on this day, except that the drinking of liquor starts, and good food is taken. This is a busy agricultural season, as potato growing is in full swing about this time. Also, fields are prepared for sowing 'Chauli', which is never sown until the festival is over.

'Bisauri': Early in the morning, after the 'Lagada', young boys and men go out to the nearby jungle to pluck 'Buras'. As the procession reaches the outskirts of the village, all the members start shouting and dancing. Women and old people who do not go with the procession watch it from their houses. 'Buras' flowers are plucked from the jungle, some of them are hidden there, and the rest brought back to the village. On return to the village, some flowers are offered to the deity in the temple, and some placed on the roof there. In the evening every Rajput has a goat slaughtered, before offering it ceremonially to Mahasu. The goat is brought to the village temple, and some water is sprinkled on it. If it shivers, it is believed that god Mahasu has accepted the offering, after which it is killed.

'Bagia Ka Bissu: The same evening of 'Burasani' when 'Buras flowers are plucked from the jungle, 'Bagia Ka Bissu is celebrated by young children. They go to 'Jubbad', a nearby hillock having some open space, to play with bow and arrow. The play is on a small scale but conforming to the prescribed rites and rituals. The deity Shilguru is taken to the place of the mock fights to watch the spectacle. It is done through the Brahmin priest who holds a silver staff in his hands and leads the procession. This silver staff with a red piece of cloth tied round its neck is considered very sacred. People consider themselves quite safe from any calamity when in the presence of the staff, which is taken to the scene of bow-and-arrow fights to the accompaniment of music played by the Bajgis. All through the way the music goes on, and on reaching the spot, the silver staff is placed on a high stone and the Brahmin sits by its side. The play begins and the young boys start their mock bow-and-arrow fight. The boys play in their everyday clothes, unlike their elders.

'Sankrant'

This day, the first of the month, has some special significance. Early in the morning the Bajgi announces the day by the beat of drums. Young boys go to the jungle to bring 'Buras' flowers they had plucked the previous day and hidden there. These boys return in the afternoon. They make garlands of the 'Buras' flowers, and place them at the doors of their houses. In the evening special non-vegetarian meals are cooked. Members of the higher castes offer food to those of the lower castes. The Bajgis do not have to give anything to anybody, but all the other castes have to give either cooked meals or *bora*, which is a raw food material, to members of the lower castes. The Rajputs give gifts to all other castes but do not receive anything in return. For beating the drum in the morning, the Bajgis get some special kind of bread. Some goats and sheep are killed on the occasion. One sheep is killed and offered to the deity. This is done by the Rajputs in accordance with their turn. Those who have taken a vow of making some offering to Mahasu at Asoi may do so while looking towards Asoi from their village itself. Offerings are also made to the Dlusta, who are regarded as evil spirits. These offerings are meant to drive away the influence of evil spirits from the village. A broken 'Tumba' containing some meat and kneaded flour is placed by the side of a footpath. It is believed that the evil spirits after taking the offerings will take shelter in the flour and go away from the village. Priests come from outside to collect their share of gifts from the village. They go from door to door and collect their due. All the functionaries of the village also collect their due.

In the village, after the garlands made of 'Buras' flowers have been placed at the doors of all the houses, the entire village gathers in the *angan* to dance. First, the men dance the 'Jooda' to the accompaniment of the beat of the drum. Every male member of the family has his 'Jooda' dress, which when he dies is cremated with him. Afterwards the villagers play the 'Toda', in which one person, who is standing, keeps lifting his feet alternately in quick succession, while the other tries to shoot at his feet. If the aim succeeds, he wins. This shooting is done turn by turn. The 'Toda' play continues for some time. This is called 'Chhota Bissu'. Throughout the day the villagers continue drinking wine at each other's place. A day after the 'Sankrant', young boys and girls of the village go in a procession for the 'Shilguru' yatra. The procession, accompanied by Bajgis playing on drums, goes dancing to the 'Shilguru Tibba', where dances continue for some hours. This is entirely a show of the young people, as the elders are busy in the fields. Their show, however, takes place next day.

'Bada Bissu': The main day of celebrations is called the 'Bada Bissu', when almost the entire village goes out in a procession to some previously settled open spot, where similar processions from other villages also gather. Women form a conspicuous part of these processions, their new, bright garments adding colour to the spectacle. The deity's silver staff and the Bajgis' band head the procession, followed by men, with the *dhyantis* forming the rear. On the way they all sing different songs. Reaching the festival spot, men get ready for their 'Toda' play, which is a mock performance of bow-and-arrow fight. Women sit around in groups, at a safe distance from the scene of the fight. Relatives from outside the village act as rivals. With their legs well shielded with thick woollen pads, the bow-and-arrow fights are a good training and test of marksmanship. Mock duels are fought alternately. Shooting above the legs is not permitted, violation of the rule often leading to serious fights. Women, *dhyantis* and *ryantis* both sit around and watch and enjoy the show. To break the monotony, *dhyantis* sometimes start dancing, but the *ryantis* are not expected to participate in the dance. When this 'Toda' play is over, the people return in a procession, shouting and rejoicing, eagerly looking forward to the next item in the evening, when the villagers gather in the *angan* to dance. Men and women join two teams for different dances.

The most important dance of the evening is the 'Jooda' dance, performed by men alone, with their naked, shining swords waving in the air, making fighting gestures. The scene is symbolic of a battlefield.

In solo performance, men follow their own movements and directions, but when together, forming a chain, performing 'Ras Lagana', they follow the leader who is towards one end of the chain. He gives all the directions with whistles and through movements. Save this, ladies join in all the other dances. Sometimes young boys of the village form a separate chain, without any swords, and dance. The day after 'Bada Bissu', there is again the children's 'Bissu'. On this day men, who have not gone back to the fields, spend their time drinking, and returning drinking calls.

Mond

In importance, 'Mond' is considered a major festival of Jaunsar-Bawar. While 'Bissu' is an important spring festival, 'Mond' is a bigger one still, organized on a large scale, crossing the Khat boundaries, unlike Bissu which is only an intra-Khat festival. At all places, 'Mond' attracts people even from outside Jaunsar-Bawar The 'Mond' at Dunghiara is said to attract the largest number of participants. Dunghiara is about five miles south-east of Chakrata, on Lakhamandal road, one mile ahead of Kharakhota. At Dunghiara there is no habitation except for two or three shops. In the month of 'Asadha', after a gap of many years, 'Mond' is held here. It is a social festival with an economic background. It is inseparably associated with fishing and, therefore, always takes place by the side of a stream. Fishing is so important an aspect of it that people call it 'a festival of fishing'. There is no fixed date for the festival. Different places celebrate it at different times. It has, however, a definite relation with the agricultural cycle. It is an occasion for, and manifestation of the temporary relief these hard-working people enjoy after harvesting the wheat-barley crop. It is the time for recreation and festivity.

The religious aspect is provided by god Mahasu who has to be propitiated on several occasions.

'Asadha' (May-June) is the time when the monsoon sets in. Rain water accumulates in 'Khadas', hollows in the earth, where the fish spawn. And 'Mond' is organized at important places in Jaunsar-Bawar such as (1) Dunghiara; (2) Manjghaon; (3) Masak; (4) Lakhamandal; (5) Kandoi; (6) Matiana; (7) Mohana; and (8) Menus. Out of these, the first is held once in eight years; the third, fifth, sixth and eighth after every two or three years, and the second, fourth and seventh, every year. 'Mond' is not a festival of a village, nor even of a Khat, but of several Khats, often extending to as many as five Khats officially participating. 'Mond' at Dunghiara, celebrated every eighth year, invites people from all over Jaunsar-Bawar. 'Mond' at Masak, held every two years, officially invites people from three adjoining Khats, namely Masau, Dhaneu and Tineu. But this 'official' invitation to these three Khats does not restrict people from other places from attending the festival. They may come and attend the festival, and, if there is otherwise nothing against them, may even fish there. But generally people from Khats which are 'officially invited' come at the instance of their relations in the Khat, which is organizing the festival and acting as the host.

These people come only one day before the actual festival. 'Mond' at Menus is organized annually by four villages in rotation: (1) Bhutnad, Tehsil Rinka, District Sirmur, Himachal Pradesh. It is about ten miles from Menus. The people of this village are known as Chandu. (2) Thukando, Tehsil Rinka, District Sirmur, Himachal Pradesh. It is about five miles from Menus. The people of this village are known as Thaktia. (3) Bhigrauli, Tehsil Jubbal, District Mahasu, Himachal Pradesh. It is about two and a half miles from Menus. The people of this village are known as Bigreu. (4) Baila, Tehsil Chakrata, District Dehradun, U.P. It is about five miles from Menus. The people of this village are known as Teneu. Among these four groups, there are two straight alignments: Thukando and Baila in one, and Bhutnad and Bhigrauli in the other.

Though Thukando and Bhutnad are neighbours and belong to one district, they are in opposite camps. Bhutnad and Bhigrauli are from two different districts, but form one group. Despite these differences, however, these different groups have worked out regulations for the celebration of 'Mond'. Each Khat gets a chance to lead every fourth year, thus all the four units get equal importance. The leading Khat enjoys certain rights and has certain obligations. For example, it becomes the sole organizer of the festival. It decides the date of the festival. It leads the procession on that day, and finally takes lead in throwing 'Timur' in the 'Khad'. No other Khat may reach the spot prior to the leading Khat. In case such a thing happens, it may lead to serious fights.

On the other hand, the leading Khat has certain obligations too. It has to provide 'Timur' powder for the festival. It has to collect 'Timur' bark from the participating villages, and to see that it is properly ground and powdered, and that it reaches the 'Khad' before the arrival of the procession. It has to get the date for the festival fixed by the 'Pandit', and then to have this information conveyed to the other Khats, whose Sayanas, in turn, have it further spread in their own villages. It has to arrange for the animals to be sacrificed during 'Mond'. It has also to meet all the expenses during the festival. The organizers of the 'Mond' are the Rajputs and the Sadar Sayana, or, in his absence, the Sayana of the village which has the privilege of organizing the festival in a particular year.

He is supposed to be responsible for the whole affair. No discrimination is, however, made among the Sayanas of the four groups during 'Mond'.

The first rite of this festival, which is inseparably connected with fishing and with 'Timur', is the cutting of the latter (Timur) in the month of 'Baisakh'. The host villagers' priest fixes a date for this and names the person who should strike the first axe at the tree. This rite is the first sign of the approaching festival. The villagers go out from the village and bring a twig of Timur tree, which is kept in the Mahasu's temple. The bark of the tree is crushed in *gutu* with *musso* and sent to the *ghrat* for grinding it into fine powder. This powder is used for fishing at the time of 'Mond'. It is suffocating and blinding for the fish, whose movement in water is stopped when this powder is thrown in the stream. Since this first cutting of 'Timur' bark, people in all the villages of the leading Khat of there year start cutting this bark, which has to be contributed to the common pool. This contribution is confined only to the Rajputs, for whom it is obligatory.

10
Gods and Goddesses of Kumaon

In Kumaon, as elsewhere in India, the predominant religion is Hinduism, but when the temple bells ring out here, it is not only for the traditional gods of the Hindu pantheon — Shiva, Vishnu and Shakti — but also for a host of other gods and demons, who have a very strong hold on the local imagination. In the very early period of Kumaoni history, the population, whether original inhabitants of the region or immigrants from other parts of India or outside, were forced to eke out a rough existence in a hostile environment. Inevitably, the elements that frightened them and needed to be propitiated became their gods. We do not really know what were the earliest objects of worship, but at some point there came a stage when they began to believe in superhuman spirits who were known as 'demons' and had to be propitiated. Local legend and mythology, and even historical characters, also provided them with gods. Interestingly enough, the *pahari* still worships these gods and demons and even in temples erected to Shiva, Vishnu or the mother goddess Shakti, the 'old' gods often have an honourable place. Incidentally, it must be pointed out that this is an all-India phenomenon, and though attempts are always being made to Sanskritize religion and bring it within the bounds of conservatism, rural India still continues to maintain a special place for its localized gods and spirits. They have either slipped into the traditional pantheon or maintained a separate identity, but they have managed to coexist peacefully. The anthropologist S.C. Dube, defines the religion of the Hindus thus:

> A textbook knowledge of the religious lore of India and an acquaintance with her ancient classics and their modern expositions will hardly give us a true picture of the actual religious beliefs, thoughts, feelings and practices of the people now living in the countryside. A classification of their religious beliefs and rituals is not an easy task. Folklore

> and myths, religious teachings of saint-poets, and contacts with persons having knowledge of scriptures and popular religious books have all influenced their ideology. Consequently their religion is a mixture of animism, animalism and polytheism with the occasional appearance of monotheism also. To these must be added a living faith in spirits, ghosts, demons, witches and magic.

To this worship of ghosts, spirits and demons, the term 'animism' is generally applied. The word really means the worship of spirits which could be either good or bad, but which are extremely powerful. They must be propitiated, and either persuaded to protect the worshipper, or dissuaded from harming him. Efforts of reformers or spiritual leaders from the plains, all directed at Sanskritizing the religious beliefs and customs of the *paharis* and generally bringing them in line with the orthodox religion prevailing in the plains, have made them sensitive about their original (and preferred) religious practices and, as a result, they will not discuss them with outsiders unless they are found to be sympathetic and uncensorious. The mother goddess or Shakti is the most important deity in this area, and ancient mythology credits her with having created not only the world but also the three gods of the traditional Hindu pantheon, Shiva, Vishnu and Brahma.

She is worshipped in several aspects all over Kumaon and Garhwal, and many local legends are centred round the goddess, the most popular incarnation being that of Nanda Devi. She is now linked with Naina Devi, but originally, Nanda Devi was identified with Parvati, the consort of Shiva, and Naina Devi was a borrowing from the Greek goddess Nana, who came into the Himalayas with the Indo-Greeks and Kushan kings. The temptation to trace these links between Kumaoni myth and mainstream Hindu legend (or, in fact, any other school of mythology) must be resisted as the stories clash in many areas. Scholars feel that this is the result of trying to incorporate the pre-Aryan deities who presided over these regions into the regular Hindu pantheon of gods and goddesses.

The Naina Devi legend as it exists in the Kumaon, runs thus. Her father, Dakshaprajapati, organised a great sacrifice, but he refused to invite her consort, Shiva, as he disapproved of his lifestyle and appearance. Daksha is supposed to have described him thus:

> He roams about in dreadful cemeteries, attended by hosts of goblins and spirits, like a madman, naked, with dishevelled

> hair, laughing, weeping and bathed in the ashes of funeral pyres, wearing a garland of skulls and ornaments of human bones, insane, beloved by the insane, the lord of beings whose nature is essentially darkness.

Undeterred, Naina went to her father's house for the ceremony, accompanied by her husband, but they were grossly insulted and turned away at the gate by Dakshaprajapati. Distraught, Naina committed suicide. A grief-stricken Shiva picked up her body, and danced with her all over the world. As he was carrying her away, her eyes fell out near the temple of Pashan Devi in Nainital. The temple that now stands near the Nainital lake is the temple of Naina Devi and she has given her name to the famous hill-station. Nanda Devi is supposed to be the Kumaoni incarnartion of Parvati, the wife of Lord Shiva. The local legend says that Nanda and Sunanda were both daughters of a local chieftain. One day they were attacked by a mad buffalo, and though they hid in a banana plantation, they were both killed. Nanda Devi, the highest mountain in the Indian Himalayas is now her abode. The feast of this goddess, which is very important in both Kumaon and Garhwal, is celebrated annually in the month of August. It was believed that the buffalo sacrifice that used to mark the occasion originated because Nanda requested people to give her a buffalo every year as one of the species had killed her.

The songs and *jagars* (a special type of religious chanting) that mark the festival actually relate to the story that Nanda Devi descends every year from the ice-cold mountain top where her husband Shiva has his home, and comes to her mother's house for a brief vacation. On the day of the festival she is sent back to his abode with all due fanfare, and with a plenitude of gifts. The annual Nanda Devi fair is celebrated with great pomp in Almora. The buffalo sacrifice has been replaced with the offering of coconuts, but the event is still impressive. While the priests chant the required *mantras* round a sacred fire, the young men dance desultorily to the beat of a copper drum. But the leisurely pace of events is maintained only till the *jagar* begins. The male oracle on whom the spirit of Nanda Devi descends, arrives on the shoulders of one of his companions and begins by settling problems of the villagers on behalf of the Devi. Soon, the climax of the ceremony is reached. Bill Aitken in his book *The Nanda Devi Affair* describes it thus:

> The Shilpkar drummer emerges from the shadows of the bonfire and suddenly assumes a presiding presence. His

small drum emits the most electrifying coda and one feels the hair bristle as "forces from the other side are challenged to appear in answer to these compulsive sorcerers" drum beats. Hissing, slavering and ranting, the possessed *shaman* is borne into the ring of fire. Popeyed with the vacancy of a soul dislodged, he shivers violently and has to be forcibly restrained from leaping off the shoulders of his bearers. Between his teeth is clenched the Devi's dagger to symbolise that the mouthpiece of the goddess will brook no obstacle.

As the drumming reaches its crescendo, the dancing intensifies. The dancers themselves seem possessed, and in the midst of grotesque shadows thrown up by the flames, mothers hold up their children to be blessed by the Goddess. Every twelve years (give or take a few years), a great *yatra* sets out to the foot of the Nanda Devi mountain. A four horned goat, which is provided by the villagers of Nauti in Garhwal — who incidentally organise not only the great pilgrimage but also the much smaller annual ones — is taken to a spot near the base of the mountain. When the pilgrims reach their destination, it is covered with garlands and sent off up the mountain trail. Legend has it that it runs straight up the mountain unhesitatingly. Bill Aitken's book describes one such *yatra*, the route it took and the rituals involved during the pilgrimage, which incidentally took place 19 years after the previous one.

The pilgrimages to Nanda Devi have been linked by anthropologists to a ritualized re-enactment of the *pahari* bride's (in this case, Nanda Devi's) return to her *sauryas* (her in-laws' home) from her *mait* (mother's house). All married women identify themselves with the event and, though they do not go on the pilgrimage, the songs sung at the villages and the Devi's procession traverses reflect the poignancy of the occasion.

Given below is a translation of one of the songs sung during the Nanda Devi *yatra*, quoted by William Sax.

> Victory to Nanda, Amba, and Jagdamba!
> Victory to Nanda and Jagdamba Bhavani!
> Victory to the Great Goddess, Bearer of the Parasol,
> Victory to the Mother of the World!
>
> May the sixty-four Nandas, the daughters of Daksa, the Lord of Creatures,

Sisters of the Royal Sages be generous!
In Nauti, Almora, Siroli and Pratyeka,
May the daughter of the gods be successful, Victory....

I will serve you by singing this song,
I will make offerings to your feet,
I will sacrifice buffaloes in your place,
Success will come to our village, Victory...

And so the song goes on, each verse reflecting the sadness of a young girl leaving her care-free girlhood behind and going back to the responsibilities of her married home. The most famous of the temples to Nanda Devi is the one in Almora. The British Commissioner of Kumaon, Traill, tried to shift the temple to a spot which he considered more convenient from the point of view of establishing a new township. A short while later, while on a trip to the Pindari glacier, he was struck by snow blindness and his advisors convinced him that this was an indication of the goddess' displeasure. He moved the temple back to its original site and his sight was miraculously restored. Another dominant deity of the Himalayas is Shiva whose abode has been Mount Kailash, but who seems to have evolved through the ages, accruing to himself the qualities of other local deities of Kumaon and Garhwal in becoming the figure he is today. Some early sculptures show figure swhich seem to be of Pasupati, who perhaps merged later with Agni and Rudra to become the Shiva of Kedarnath.

Many archaeologists feel that the Pasupati images were really early Buddhist or Jain icons. These artifacts are few in number and not easily identifiable, but it is believed that Buddhism was well established in Kumaon by the seventh century AD. The decline of Buddhism set in soon after, an event locally attributed to the arrival upon the scene of the Adi Shankaracharya, (788 - 820 A.D.) who is supposed to have visited Jageshwar and Gangolihat in Kumaon before moving on to Garhwal where he established the two large temples of Kedarnath and Badrinath.

Atkinson is of the view that the form of Buddhism prevailing in this region was also suffering from the ailments that assailed Brahmanism at this period — a decadence associated with Tantric practices — and Shankaracharya, in his great reformist zeal, eliminated the one and cleansed the other. In order to revive orthodox Hinduism in Kumaon and Nepal, Shankaracharya began by dispersing the Buddhist monks and nuns. He then established the worship of Siva at Kedarnath and of Vishnu at Badrinath. In place of the old Baudhmargi priests, who were disbanded, came priests from Kerala who manage these two temples even today. Pilgrimage to the two shrines was encouraged as the constant influx of pilgrims ensured that the area did not relapse into Buddhism again. In all fairness, it must be admitted that there seems to be no historical evidence that Adi Shankaracharya visited these regions, but popular belief attributes the establishment of the Kedarnath-Badrinath temples to him.

The maximum number of temples in the Kumaon are those dedicated to Shiva. Then come the temples of Devi or Shakti. Vishnu temples are comparatively few in number, and those dedicated to Rama and Krishna are modern in origin. Shiva is very obviously the god of the mountains, as his abode is on Kailash. Early texts described Rudra as the father of the *maruts* or the winds, or equated him with Agni, the god of fire, but later the two personae seem to have merged Professor Whitney, as quoted by E.T. Atkinson, says that the Kumaon Himalaya is responsible for the evolution of modern Saivism:

> The introduction of an entirely new divinity from the mountains of the north has been supposed, who was grafted in upon the ancient religion by being indentified with Rudra, or again a blending of some of Agnis attributes with those of Rudra to originate a new development. Perhaps neither of these may be necessary Shiva may be a local form of Rudra, arisen under the influences of peculiar climatic relations in the districts from which he made his way down into Hindustan proper.

The most important, as well as the most beautiful, Shiva temple in Kumaon is that of Jageshwar, 35 km. from Almora. This is a temple complex consisting of 108 temples built over a period of five centuries. Most of these temples are small but there are a few large ones as well. Magnificent deodar forests surround the complexes of Jageshwar and Dandeshwar (half a kilometre apart), thereby making them aesthetically as well as spiritually satisfying. The oldest temple at Jageshwar is the one built to Mrityunjaya, and it dates from the eighth century A.D., i.e. the early part of the Katyuri period The most important, however, is the one which houses the Jyotirlinga, one of the twelve all over India.

The old story associated with the establishment of the Jyotirlingas, runs thus. There are several versions of the legend, but the broad outlines are similar. This is the one current at Jageshwar, which is the Jyotirling associated with Darukavan in the ancient Sanskrit sloka.

सौराष्ट्रे सोमनाथं च श्रीशैले मल्लिकार्जुनम्। उज्जयिन्यां महाकालमोंकारे परमेश्वर।।
केदारं हिमवत्पृष्ठे डाकिन्यां भीमशंकरम्। वाराणस्यां च बिश्रवेशं त्र्यम्बकं गौतमीतद
वैधनाथं चिताभूमौ नागेशं दारुकावने। सेतुबन्धे च रामेशं घुशमेशं तु शिवालये।

This sloka details the various places where the *Jyotirlingas* have appeared and where they are now worshipped.

The temples are those of: 1. Somnath (Saurashtra in Gujarat), 2.Mallikarjun in Srisailam (Andhra Pradesh), 3. Mahakaleshwar on the banks of the Shipra in Ujjain (Madhya Pradesh), 4. Onkareshwar on the banks of the Narmada river in Malwa (Madhya Pradesh), 5. Kedarnath in Garhwal (Uttaranchal), 6. Bhimshankar near Ahmednagar (the old name of the hill where the temple is situated was Dakini in Maharashtra), 7. Vishwanath in Varanasi (Uttaranchal), 8. Trimbakeshwar near Nasik on the banks of the Godavari (Maharashtra), 9. Vaidyanath in the Samthal region (Orissa), 10. Jageshwar near Almora (Uttaranchal), 11. Rameshwaram (Tamil Nadu) and 12. Ghushmeshwar (or Ghrushmeshwar) near Veruk, the original name of the village where the Ellora caves are found (Maharashtra).

After Shiva and Parvati were insulted by King Daksha, Parvati immolated herself and became *sati.* In his deep distress, Shiva raged over the whole world, carrying her body in his arms. Later, appalled by the destruction he had caused, he settled down to perform penance at Vriddha Jageshwar, above Jageshwar. One day, the wives of the seven sages, (*saptarishis* saw him while they were cutting grass and, struck with wonder at the beauty and majesty of this unknown *rishi,* they fell unconscious. When they did not come home in the evening, their husbands came looking for them. Shiva was still meditating, and had no idea of what was happening around him, but the sages cursed him, holding him responsible for their wives dereliction of duty. Shiva suffered the punishment they inflicted upon him, and a great darkness fell upon the world, till Vishnu gathered up the darkness and dispersed it in the shape of the twelve Jyotirlingas, which are pilgrimage spots all over the country.

Another local legend says that when the original temple at Jageshwar was being constructed, a demon living in Vriddha Jageshwar made it a practice to come down every night and destroy whatever had been built during the day. The architect then had a brilliant idea. He got his men to provide the demon with mountains of meat every evening so that the demon was so busy eating it at night that he had no time to meddle with the temples. During the Rohilla invasion of Kumaon (1743), Jageshwar, already a very rich temple, was the only one in the area to escape being pillaged. Its salvation is attributed to swarms of bees that attacked the marauding armies and drove them away.

Folk gods of varied origin have also been added to the traditional Hindu pantheon. Some of these, as has been mentioned earlier, have descended from pre-Aryan animism and demonism, others from local legends associated with princely families or regional heroes. These are usually divided into various categories, i.e., those of *kul devtas* (family gods), *gram devtas* (village gods), *naga devtas* (snake gods) *bhumi devtas* (land gods) and *veers* (heroes). Harju, for example, is the name of a local village god who dominates in a group of villages near where the authors live in Ranikhet. Priests from Haridwar come once every few years (it is supposed to be every seven years, but the schedule does not work out with great regularity), to conduct a series of all-night *jagars*, and sacrifices. The animals for the sacrifice — goats or chickens — are provided by householders. The *puja* lasts for twenty-one days and, on the final day, a grand sacrifice of a goat, a pig and a chicken is performed. Significantly enough, the flesh is not eaten. It is buried on the outskirts of the village, which leads us to believe that this is one of the *gram devtas* whose job it is to protect the village. In addition to these gods, there are also ghosts and fairies who have to be propitiated on various occasions in order to prevent them from harassing human beings. Goril, or Golu *devta,* however, belongs exclusively to Kumaon and has no equivalent anywhere else. He is the Kumaoni god of justice.

The best known Golu temple is the one at Chitai near Almora, which is always thronged by supplicants and grateful devotees. Many of them sacrifice goats in gratitude for favours received, or in anticipation of boons to be granted. Thousands of bells donated by devotees hang from the ceiling and along the approach to the temple. There are also thousands of dust-laden documents dangling from the ceiling — copies of legal petitions to Golu *devta* asking for his intercession in personal disputes. In fact, on a recent visit, we found a copy of a supplicant's application form for recruitment into the Kumaon regiment with a small personal note to Golu asking him to ensure his success in the recruitment tests. There are three major temples in the Kumaon devoted to Golu, of which Chitai is the most famous. The other two are in Champawat and Ghorakhal, but a large number of small village temples have now reserved a niche for the idol of Golu.

The story of Golu stressing, as it does, the theme of justice has a legendary charm. It runs thus. Once upon a time, Jhalrai, a Katyuri king, went hunting. When he reached a village called Dubachaur, he saw two buffaloes fighting. He tried to separate them, but in vain, and then, as he was very hungry and tired, he sent his servants to look for some water. A servant found his way to a waterfall, but while trying to fill up the pot he was carrying, he splashed some on a beautiful maiden who was meditating nearby. Disturbed, she exclaimed angrily, "Obviously, the servants of a man who cannot even stop buffaloes fighting will be equally incompetent in everything else." Astonished at her omniscience, the servants begged her to accompany them. She did so, and easily separated the two buffaloes, which were still fighting. The king was very impressed with her. He enquired into her background, and found that her name was Kali, and she and her uncle, another local raja, had been engaged in austerities to propitiate one of the deities. She had been disturbed by his servants. The king went with her to meet her uncle, whom he found to be a leper. But Jhalrai was so struck by Kali that he was determined to marry her. After he had served her uncle for some time, the uncle commanded Kali to marry the king. Kali did so, and soon became his favourite queen. Soon she became pregnant, but when the baby was due, the king had to be away from his capital.

The other queens were very jealous of Kali, and so, when her son was born, they blindfolded her, took the child away, and substituted a pumpkin for him. Then they put the baby in a cage full of salt, and flung it into the river. The salt turned into sugar, and the baby was nourished on it till the cage was found by a childless fisherman, who decided that it was a gift from the gods, and took it home and raised it as his own. He was named Golu or Goril because the river from which he was rescued was the Gori Ganga. A few years later, when the boy had grown up a bit, he went to the river bank, taking with him his wooden horse. He made his way to the spot where the queens were washing clothes, and asked them to move out of the way as his horse wanted to drink water. They laughed at him saying can wooden horse drink water?" Golu replied, "If a queen can give birth to a pumpkin, a wooden horse can certainly drink water." This story was conveyed to the king, who immediately sent for the boy. Golu recounted in court the wrongs that had been inflicted on him and his mother.

The King immediately recognised him as his heir apparent, brought the mother back to court (she had been banished) and punished the wicked queens. In due course, Golu succeeded his father and ruled for many years, revered by all for his fairness and impartiality. He seems to have become an object of worship even in his lifetime Bholanath is another very popular folk god. He and his consort Barhini have now been identified with Mahadev and his consort, and have therefore intired the orthodox Hindu panthion, but Bholanath's origins are really in folk mythology and form one of the connecting links between the orthodox school of Hinduism and the world of ghosts and goblins that is common to all mountainous countries. He was reputed to be the elder son of King Udai Chand of Almora, who took to evil ways, and was exiled. The younger son succeeded his father on the throne as Gyan Chand and was very popular, but after some years, Bholanath re-entered Almora in disguise.

The news was communicated to the king, who ordered that he be killed. After his death he became a *bhut* or ghost, as did his wife Barhini and their unborn child. As they began to harass the villagers, they had to be propitiated. Many temples have been erected to them, where worship is regular and frequent. Soon after the British conquest of Almora, the ensuing confusion in the administration resulted in these temples falling into disuse, "but Bholanath showered such storms of stones on the British camp that the English gentlemen at once awoke to the importance of this deity and provided for his worship in a suitable manner". There are eight temples dedicated to Bholanath or Bhairav in Almora. Sometimes, a small iron trident is placed in a corner of a house as an emblem of Bholanath, and is worshipped when the family is in any kind of distress. Similarly, Gangnath, son of a Nepalese King fell out with his family and became a mendicant.

He fell in love with a Brahmin woman and, as a result, was murdered at the instigation of either her husband or her brother (legend is vague at this point). He began to 'harm' people and so rites were evolved to propitiate him and his lady love Bhana. Gangnath temples are found all over Kumaon. He harasses the young and the beautiful if they do not propitiate him. If anyone is troubled by wicked or powerful people, he prays to Gangnath, who invariably comes to his assistance. Sometimes Gangnath possesses a follower, and through him conveys to the world at large that anyone who gives him the following articles can achieve his heart's desire: to Gangnath himself, a kid, cakes, sweets, beads, a bag and a pair of earrings; for Bhana his mistress, a petticoat, a *dupatta* and a nose ring; to the child that was killed with them, a coat and anklets.

Airy is a sylvan god of repellent aspect. He has eyes on top of his head, and four arms filled with weapons. His chief attendants, Sau and Bhau, ride on dogs and always travel with a pack of hunting dogs with bells around their necks. They are also usually accompanied by hordes of fairies and goblins, all of whom have their feet turned back to front to distinguish them from ordinary mortals. Whoever hears the bells tinkling round the necks of the dogs is certain to meet with some calamity. Airy's temples are found in desolate areas and lonely hilltops.

Chaumu is worshipped in the Jhulaghat Pancheshwar area. The story goes that once a traveller proceeded to Champawat carrying in his turban a crystal Shivalinga. At one point, he wanted to drink water, so he put it down on the ground. Later he found that he could not pick it up again because it had "become so heavy. A temple was built on the spot, and it became a place of pilgrimage".

There is a touch of pastoral simplicity about the cult of Chaumu. He presides over cattle and, on all Hindu festivals, lamps are lighted and sweetmeats offered to him. People who have lost their cattle pray to him to help in their recovery. Haru and Saim are guardians of the village. Their temples are usually together, and prolonged *jagars* are conducted in order to request them to guard the boundaries of the village. Haru is a beneficent spirit who was, once upon a time, Raja Harishchand of Champawat. When he became old, he abdicated and went away to Haridwar, where he took *sanyas*, and gave himself up to austerity and good works. Saim was also one of his followers. When they died, they became good spirits. Kshetrapal too is the tutelary god of fields and boundaries. He is gentle and beneficent and harasses no one, but when a new crop is sown, a handful of seed is offered to him first to protect it from disease or blight.

There is a temple dedicated to him at Jageshwar because he is the guardian spirit of this area.

Kail Bisht, a gentle flute-playing folk god, has a temple dedicated to him at Binsar. Kumaoni drama troupes frequently dramatise the story of Kail Bisht, which has considerable local appeal. His story says that he was a cowherd. The official priest of the King of Almora, Srikrishna Pande, became very grateful to Kail for protecting him from the sorcery of one of his enemies, Naulakhia Pande. Kail achieved this by defeating the demon sent by Naulakhia Pande who was haunting

Srikrishna Pande and buried him under a huge rock. But Naulakhia, undeterred, continued his machinations to the extent that he created a wedge between Srikrishna Pande and Kail. Srikrishna asked the king of Almora to have Kail executed, but the king refused to oblige him for he saw the impression of a trident (*trisul*) on Kail's forehead and a *kadamba* flower at his feet. However, Srikrishna's efforts to kill him continued, and he did succeed finally in sending an emissary who killed him by deceit. Subsequently, he was deified, and the local tradition is that the milk of every cow or buffalo that calves must be offered to him before it is drunk.

There are scores of other gods and goddesses and demons of local origin who are worshipped in the area. Sometimes the distinction between the gods and demons is so slim as to be practically non-existent. Cairns, usually with a piece of iron sticking out of the top, have been erected all over Kumaon. These are intended to ward off ghosts and demons.

The average Kumaoni has little time for daily ritual. Owing to the exigencies of terrain and the general shortage of water, he washes his clothes and has a bath only once a week at the most, or on special *puja* days. However, he is emotionally attached to the *kul devta,* usually the main idol in the village temple, and not one of the major Hindu deities. Golu *devta* has a large following; so have Bholanath, Gangnath, Kalika *devi* and Nanda *devi*. The other gods get attention during their particular 'days' or festivals, and during the very special institution of a *jagar*.

The *pahari* belief in the supernatural is the belief of fear that spirits, ghosts and ancestral spirits can affect fate in a malign way. This must be avoided by rites and rituals or prayers which will restore the affected person to health and prosperity. Hence the *jagar* where a *shaman* identifies the spirit or god who has turned his evil eye on the worshipper as a result of which ill health, death or economic misfortune has befallen the family. The *jagars* take place on occasions other than those associated with the festivals of particular deities, and consist of the ceremonial recitation of a long folk poem, detailing the exploits of one particular god or goddess. The recitation can take either a few hours or a few weeks, and is a very specialised ritual as the jagar singer is traditionally identified, and each singer restricts himself to only a few themes or stories.

Devotees organise jagars in thanks-giving (on the birth of a son, for example), or to fulfill a vow or to propitiate a demon who has possessed someone or is deemed to be harassing the family. Incidentally, the harassing demon or deity has to be initially identified by a *dangariya*, an oracle or *shaman*, who is possessed by the deity called up by the *jagariya's* singing and drumming and who henceforth speaks on behalf of the deity. The *dangaruyas* are very often women, and he or she is not only the diagnostician but also recommends the treatment — either a *puja* for propitiation, or exorcism in cases where the diagnosis is possessed by a ghost. The *jagariya* is never a full-time practitioner as the income from this ritual is spasmodic and unspecified. The job requires years of preparation and there is no system of teaching the profession. Nor is it a hereditary occupation. Any boy who is interested learns by going to as many jagars as he can and committing the stories to memory. He also has to learn to play the drum though there is also a traditional drummer or *hurkiya* who can be called upon. Each jagariya becomes a specialist and in general, confines himself to one or two specific deities, whose,.chants he learns by serving an apprenticeship with a senior jagariya. The *shaman*, of course, just has to have a gift. This variety of Jagar singing is becoming rather rare these days, and the village people are not very forthcoming in satisfying the idle curiosity of outsiders about these very special rituals.

In recent years there is a growing tendency to hold elaborate rituals to appease the spirits of ancestors whose last rites have not been properly performed and who, therefore, have brought misfortune upon the family. These rituals can take several days, and in many cases, include animal sacrifice. Jagar singing associated with specific festivals (Nanda Ashtami, for instance) is of a different kind and consists of ritual songs sung to the goddess on the day of her festival. These *jagars* last all night, and incidents of possession by other gods take place throughout the ceremony. Bill Aitkin's description of one such *jagar* that he witnessed in Almora has been quoted earlier.

Certain diseases are supposed to be of supernatural origin. Specified practitioners diagnose the illness; others, called *jharnewale*, are supposed to have the power to cause the disease to reverse itself. Strokes, for example, are always treated by *jharnewale*. Men having been identified as having been born *ulta* — breech deliveries — can cure backache. The treatment varies with the disease but it usually consists of the chanting of *mantras*, and then alternately touching the patient and the ground with a feather, thereby grounding the disease.

We have already mentioned that Buddhism was probably dominant in Kumaon in the seventh century. To Shankaracharya is attributed the cleansing of Hinduism and the elimination of Buddhism from these regions. He dispersed the Buddhist monks and nuns, and disbanded the old Baudhmargi priests. Hieun Tsang, the great Buddhist traveller is supposed to have visited Kumaon in 633-643 A.D.

11
Nepal and the Gorkhas

Religious Ceremonies

Birth

As soon as a child is born a hen is sacrificed and the father makes a note of the time so that the Brahman may work out the horoscope. In villages where there is no watch or clock, the time is noted by the panigari or water clock. On the birth of the child, the *soreni* (midwife) severs the *nal* and is given some money. She then washes herself and receives a drink of liquor. From now until the eleventh day after the child's birth the mother is ceremonially unclean and must remain in a corner of the house. In Magar and Gurung villages, where the household work would suffer, the mother does at least some of it, but on no account may she husk rice or cut grass for cows. Thread wearers observe the eleven days most strictly. In the army the father of any child born in the lines is given eleven days line leave.

The day after the birth, the father informs the Brahman of the time it occurred and the latter then casts a horoscope to determine the name of the child. On the sixth day (chhainti), the Brahman binds a thread on the father's wrist and relations and friends are invited to celebrate. On the tenth day, *gaunt*, or urine of the cow, is prepared and is carefully kept in another house for the night.

On the eleventh day (gaunte), the Brahman arrives in the morning and at once says prayers and sprinkles the gaunt, diluted with milk from the heads of seven stalks of dubo grass, round the inside of the house and over the mother, in order to purify them. Until tnis is done, no food touched by the mother may be eaten. Should anyone inadvertently enter the house before this ceremony has taken place, he must drink gaunt himself. Close relatives are invited to the gaunte and are feasted. The priest, attended by the father, now starts his prayers outside in the courtyard, whilst the child is kept within the house. The Brahman is paid his fee, after which he makes a round cake of cowdung and pours milk into a depression in the centre of it. This is then blessed and the child, having been brought out of the house, has its big toes dipped in this milk. This is the *nauran*, or christening, ceremony and it is considered a good omen if at this point the child cries. The Brahman first gives the child its *rasi nam*, which is the name he has determined by his horoscope. This is the child's religious and official name and is entered as such on the *Janam Patra,* or birth certificate, and it is by this name that the child, when older, is married. The child may then, in turn, be given a name by its mother and father, by its relations attending the ceremony, and also by the *soreni*. The names given by the parents are entered in the *Janam Patra*, which is preserved with very great care.

The soreni remains in the house throughout the eleven days. She washes and anoints the child and massages the mother. On the eleventh day, after the naming ceremony, she is presented with her fee and takes her departure. All those present then drink a little gaunt and milk, including the mother, who is, at this point, brought out of the corner by the priest and is now considered to be ceremonially clean again. The night is spent in feasting and celebration.

Names

Parents who have previously lost children in infancy sometimes believe that this is due to an 'evil eye'. Accordingly, to protect the newborn child, they may try to convince the 'evil eye' that the child belongs, in fact, to a menial class and is not, therefore, worth harming. They do this by calling in a member of one of these classes and getting him to make, for the child, a metal or leather belt and by then giving to the child the name of the menial class concerned—Sarki, Chamar or Kami. An alternative safeguard is to feed the child on ceremonially unclean food and then to give it the name 'Juthe'.

Gurkha parents do not call their children by their names but, as is the usual practice in eastern countries, by the title of their seniority, e.g., *Jetho* (eldest), *Mainlo* (2nd eldest), *Sainlo* (3rd eldest) and so on. But amongst friends and acquaintances nicknames are common and these often come to be the only names used.

The sources of name are very varied. They may be drawn from any of the following religion: Maniram—Ram's Giant; names of gods: Bishnu, Durga, Rudra, Kishan; military: Rhandhoj—champion of war;

legend: Bhimbahadur, Pandhara—hero; manly virtues: Asbahadur—brave and reliant; astrology: Tula—scales, Kumbhasing—water-carrier; astronomy: Surja—Sun, Budh—Mercury; birthdays: Tike—born on Tika day; weekdays: Aitabir—born on Sunday, Sombahadur—born on Monday; or holy plants: Til—the sesame flower.

Most Gurkha names have two parts to them, e.g., Motibahadur rather than Moti, but this is not always the case. Certain endings, such as 'Man' and 'Bir', are common, and these endings can themselves be used to form names, e.g., Manbir, Birman. Names compounded from both Hindi and Persian can also be used, e.g., Jangbir, Bakhatbahadur. In Army documentation it is incorrect to split a compound name into two, though this practice is common in Kathmandu. For documentary and military purposes a Gurkha adds his tribe to his name. Thakurs, Chhetris and Magars, call themselves by their clan names, e.g., Jange Sahi (Thakur), Puransing Karki (Chhetri), Bhimbahadur Ale (Magar); other hill tribes do not. The custom of using titles, such as Subba, or kindred names such as Moktan, originated in Darjeeling schools.

Weaning

The next ceremony takes place, in the case of boys, after six months, and in the case of girls, after five months, and is the bhat khulai, or weaning, ceremony.

About a week before the ceremony is due, the father goes to the Brahman, who settles the exact day on which it is to be held. The day before the selected date, the father again visits the priest who tells him what articles he is to have ready and at what time the ceremony will begin. Those guests who were present on the eleventh day after birth, are again summoned. A meal is prepared for the child consisting of a little of all kinds of foodstuffs and including, if possible, some flesh, for preference the head of the *bhadrai chara*, a species of lark. The child is first fed by young, unmarried children, the priest stating the number, invariably odd, required for this purpose. then each guest puts a *tika* on the child's forehead, feeds it with a minute quantity of the prepared food, and makes a present of money. A child may not wear shoes until this ceremony has been performed.

Cheor

In the case of boys the next ceremony usually takes place when he has reached the age of five, though it may be delayed. This ceremony, known as *cheor*, is held when the boy has his haircut for the first time. The cutting is done by the boy's maternal uncle (*mama*) and if he has not got one, arrangements must be made for another person to assume a 'god'-uncleship. The *mama* first binds the lad's hair into five knots, one above each temple and one above and behind each ear, with the fifth in the centre where a man wears his *tupi* (topknot). The uncle then binds a piece of gold to the scissors, lights a small cowdung lamp, and cuts off the four corner knots. The centre knot is left and the rest of the head is then clipped, after which the child is washed by the parents. The uncle presents his nephew with a complete suit of white clothes and a pair of earrings, and the guests, again putting a tika on the child's forehead and present money. At the conclusion of the ceremony a Brahman may be called in to say prayers. The guests are then feasted, and, if the parents' means permit, a *nach* (dance) is held.

Marriage

A Gurkha may have as many wives as he likes, but he may only go through the long, formal marriage ceremony once. A wife so married is a *bihaite,* while all others are *lihaite*. A generation or so ago, it was customary for a boy to be formally betrothed by his parents. Eventually he completed the marriage with all pomp and ceremony, after which, if he chose, he was at liberty to take a second wife. Child marriages are uncommon, although betrothal may be made at an early age. Nowadays, although the girl should still be begged from her parents, the betrothal ceremony is becoming less formal and is not always regarded as essential. Elopements are becoming more common and, to preserve family respect, the marriage itself must often be hastened.

Betrothal

Known by Indian domiciled Gurkhas as *mangni*, the betrothal is known in the hills as *dahi theki lagaune*. Before it can take place both horoscopes must be compared and the *Janam Patra* (birth certificates) must also be produced. It is normal for betrothal to take place just before a girl reaches the age of puberty and when the boy is just a little older. Both boy and girl are represented by elders. Representatives of the boy, having given due warning, approach those of the girl in her parent's home. They swear on his behalf that he will be faithful, will refrain from ill-treating her, and will be a good and true husband to her. On agreement being reached, the boy gives the girl a complete suit of clothing and a gold ring, which she puts on while her father makes a statement that she is the promised bride and that he is responsible for producing her at the time of the wedding. Should she marry another, the father must refund any expenses incurred and is also liable to punishment for 'breach of promise'.

If one of the couple dies, the other is then free to marry someone else but if it is the boy who dies, it is customary, as a matter of courtesy, for the girl's father to ask the boy's parents if they have any objections. If a man has had several daughters who have died young, he may, to avert the evil eye, promise his daughter in marriage to a friend already married. Later the father may ask this man if he still wants the daughter and, if the reply is in the negative, she may be betrothed and married to another man.

Wedding

The most popular time for weddings is during the period from mid-January to mid-May. After consulting the horoscopes, the Brahman selects a day and the wedding procession, *janti*, sets out from the bridegroom's house, carrying him in a dooly. About 200 yards from the bride's house, the road is found to be barred by two guns placed muzzle to muzzle across it. The priest of the bride's party then arrives and sprinkles the procession with curds and rice, whilst the bride's guests bombard the procession with balls of ground rice, bananas and pieces of vegetable marrow. The priest of the procession now intervenes and asks for quarter, pointing out that they are attacking one who will soon be their own relation. The throwing thereupon ceases. Each party has in it a *kalas bokne*, that is a man carrying a metal vessel, the *kalas,* on his head, and these vessels the priests now exchange. The *dooly* containing the bridegroom is then brought forward and slightly lowered, whilst the bride's parents take up positions either side of it and pass an 'aarti' (a tray containing, amongst other articles, a small lamp) over and under it.

The bride's eldest brother now carries the groom into the house, where all sit down to a meal. The groom remains slightly apart, accompanied by his 'best man', known as the bridegroom's brother or *delaha ko bhai*, and is supplied with two helpings on separate dishes. Having eaten his own share, the groom sends the second plate to his bride. After the meal the couple are seated together on a dais, seconded by the best man, and the *gorha-dhoie*, or footwashing ceremony, takes place. The bride's guests wash the couples feet, place *tika* marks on their foreheads, and present the bride with money or jewellery. By now it is late at night and the two Brahmans again combine to decide the time for the *jagiya*. This is prepared in the courtyard and consists of a piece of cloth around which are set four small poles and on which are placed various articles. For this part of the ceremony the bride's guests must remain out of sight in the house, but the bride and bridegroom, accompanied by the best man and bridesmaids, and by the bride's sisters and girl friends, gather near the *jagiya*, and at this time the younger people frequently indulge in a little horse play.

While the priests are chanting prayers and singing hymns, the groom places red *sindur* along the hair parting of his bride, to show that she is a married woman, after which one of the priests covers her head with a white handkerchief over which the groom pours more *sindur*. The best man now steps forward and, drawing a sword, or *kukri*, cuts the four small poles of the jagiya, an act which symbolises the fate of anyone who dares to try to seduce the bride. During the night the bridegroom's house is the scene of a *ratoli nach*, in which only women take part, and which takes the form of suggestive songs and posturings. The following morning the groom is served with a double helping of rice and, having eaten his own share, he sends the dish to the bride. This she refuses to eat until her bridesmaids receive some forty or fifty rupees.

After the meal the procession is made ready to move off. The bride's parents give her the dowry and the presents received the previous day, after which her eldest brother carries her out and places her in the *dooly* in which the bridegroom arrived, whilst he mounts a horse and takes up his position on her right. Having been blessed by the priest, the procession then moves off to the husband's parental home. On arrival there the groom's sister, who has been barring the door, is given a present, and the bride is carried into the house by his mother. All present now enter the house and are entertained to a meal, followed by celebrations lasting late into the night.

On the third day the husband, accompanied only by his near relatives, takes his bride back to her parents, where she remains for that night. Considerable expenses are incurred on normal wedding ceremonies, and a family's reputation can be greatly enhanced, or considerably damaged, by the amount of food and drink supplied to the guests. Much gunpowder is also expended in firing salutes and one party, if not both, will have hired a Damai band. Runaway marriages are not uncommon, except amongst Brahmans, Chhetris and artisan castes. After such a marriage the husband must wait until his father-in-law sends for him and gives him his blessing, when, the boy having made obeisance, the wedding ceremony is often carried out with full ritual. In other cases, a couple who want to marry but have no money, may choose this easy way out of their difficulty. Gurungs are generally married by Gyabrings but Magars often employ Brahmans. Most Gurkhas can marry the widow of an elder brother as a 'lihaite' wife, but Gurkhas may not touch, even in passing, the clothes of the wife of a younger brother. This is a sin and involves purification ceremonies for both parties.

Divorce

Divorce is known as *sinka pangra* or *singo dago* and is permissible by either party. The grounds for the divorce are put up to a committee of elders, who also fix the compensation to be paid. Where proof is produced that the wife has been unfaithful, no fine is levied. On grounds of incompatibility a husband is fined Rs. 40 and a wife Rs. 80.

The actual ceremony consists of the husband and wife, each in turn, breaking a twig. A thread is then tied to the little finger of both parties and when this thread is cut by a third person the divorce is complete.

In the case of seduction, a divorce is automatically given. Until some years ago it was common for the husband to cut down the seducer of his wife with his *kukri*, and, though this practice is no longer permitted by law, reports of it occurring are still occasionally received. In such cases, however, pleas put forward in mitigation of punishment are often successful.

Widows and Widowers

There is nothing to stop a widower from remarrying, but a widow is not permitted to do so, though it is quite proper for her to become a member of another man's household. A man who has lost several wives through death is regarded as a *swasni-khane,* or wife-eater, and will have difficulty in obtaining further wives.

Death

Many tribes do not call in a Brahman to perform death ceremonies and the ceremonies in these cases include an animist element. Magars, however, do frequently call in a Brahman and the ceremony is then, as follows.

When it is obvious that a person is dying, *sun pani* is prepared and kept ready. This should consist of sea water, though ordinary water may be substituted, in which gold has been dipped and in which a leaf of the *tulsi* plant has been placed. If it is possible to avoid it, a man is not allowed to die on his bed. The ground close by is plastered over and on this the dying man is placed. In his last moments the *sun pani* is placed to his lips in the name of each of his relations in turn, and the son immediately discards his headgear and everyone takes off his shoes. All those attending the funeral sit up all night.

On the following morning the corpse is washed in *sun pani*, dressed in clean clothes, and covered with a white shroud. The procession, or *malami*, is then formed up, led by a man carrying in one hand a forked twig, tied with a white rag, and in the other a cloth containing barley, sesam seeds and copper coins. This man must never look back. Every ten or twelve paces he drops a few of the grains on the ground, whilst the rest of the procession follows exactly in his path. On arrival at the burning ghat, more barley and sesam are cast on the ground, and there the corpse is first laid, but the son himself moves it to the funeral pyre as soon as this has been half completed. An earthen vessel, containing milk and water, is placed nearby. The son then puts a small cake of camphor in the mouth of the corpse and lights it, but immediately extinguishes the flame with the milk and water. The pyre is then completed, being built up from the feet, and a piece of sandalwood is placed on top of it. After the priest has offered a prayer, everyone spinkles a little earth on the wood and takes up a torch. The son then lights the pyre at each corner after which all present also apply their torches, and ghee and camphor are added. The deceased's clothes, too, are burnt, and a ghee lamp is lit which, together with the earthen vessel, is left at the funeral site.

The procession now starts on its return journey which must be via cross—roads. Here one man goes ahead and with his *kukri* cuts a thorn of any type, which he places under a stone in the centre of the cross-roads. The remainder must now pass this spot, stepping on the stone with their left foot. They then proceed to a river where all wash and the son has the hair of his head and face shaved off. The procession now continues its return journey to the house, at a little distance from which they are met by the women, who have brought *gaunt* with them and have lit a fire. Ghee is poured over the fire and each man in the procession puts his hands into the smoke and flames and passes them over his face. Close by, the women have the *gaunt* ready and each man sips a little, sprinkles some over himself, and then leaves for his own home.

The ghost of the dead man is supposed to haunt the house and its surroundings for the following thirteen days. A friend of the son remains with him for this period, keeping close to him at all times. This friend also prevents any other living creature from coming into touch with him. The son, on rising each morning, first bathes and then cooks for himself the one meal a day he is permitted and which he must eat at mid-day. This food must contain no salt. Each day he divides the meal into two portions, one of which is wrapped in a leaf. Before partaking of his own meal, he places this leaf, together with some water, in the courtyard of the house or on the pathway outside.

On the eleventh day the priest is paid his fee and given a meal by the son. If the ashes of the corpse have not already been thrown into a river, a bone is removed on this day and is kept for disposal in this way at some later date.

The thirteenth, and final, day of mourning is known as *terui.* All those who attended the funeral are summoned to a meal and portions are set aside for absentees, one portion being placed at the burning ghat. His sisters prepare the son's meal, which is well salted and usually includes a fowl. He, on his part, presents them with money and clothes.

If there is a suitable river near at hand, the pyre may be built on its banks and the ashes cast into the water. If the relatives are rich enough, the corpse may be carried for some days to a particular river for this purpose. During the journey the corpse is watched over each night and the bearers eat only crushed rice.

If a son is absent from his parent's funeral, he may observe his thirteen days mourning either where he is or on his return home, and for this reason, in the Army special leave is normally given only where a death takes place in the lines.

If a childless son dies, the father performs the mourning rites. In the case of a wife, the husband does it, unless his father is still alive, in which case his father mourns. When there is no son, the rites may be performed by nephews or cousins. A child which dies before being weaned is only mourned for three days and is buried and not burnt. Only a son in mourning for his parent has his head shaved. Normal mourning lasts for six months and during this time women must wear white clothes and may not use any ornaments.

Gurungs employ Gyabrings and Lamas for funeral rites and often bury their dead. At the time of death a goat is sacrificed, and a small portion of the meat, as well as a small ball of rice, are eaten by each brother. They also cut a small piece of wood and place it at a bowshot's distance from the house.

An additional ceremony, known as *arghun*, is performed by Gurungs and Tamangs. This should be carried out between the third and thirteenth day after death but, if sufficient money is not available at the time, it may be postponed for several years. In this ceremony a ram is selected to represent a dead man and an ewe a dead woman. This sheep is dressed up and lengthy rites are carried out. The animal is said to show the habits of the deceased: if he was a hard drinker, for instance, the sheep would appear to be drunk. The animal is seated, and offered food and spirits, and when the mourners weep, it, too, is supposed to weep. The Gyabring places two branches in the ground, tied together at the top in the shape of a hoop. A crossbar is placed in position and from this a broody hen is suspended, head downwards. Samples of all the favourite foods of the deceased are then placed round it and the relatives sit in a circle. During this time the hen will have been hanging motionless, but when the Gyabring casts rice at it, it will fly out and crash on the ground at the spot where the deceased's spirit has arrived. The practice of using a ram or sheep to represent the deceased is now dying out and it is more usual to make an effigy of straw and plaster and dress it in the deceased's clothing.

Inheritance

The making of wills is unknown and, owing to the recognised law of inheritance, unnecessary. In the unusual event of a man wishing to leave part of his property to some person other than his direct heirs, he will inform his heirs and the village elders, officially, of such a desire, and the matter is then considered to have been legally settled. Should a Gurkha have no son and his chances of having one be remote, he will adopt one. It is usual for the choice to fall upon a son of the brother with the most sons. The adoption is first brought to the notice of the Mukhiya and village headmen, and then officially registered at the Adda. Such an adopted son, *dharmo chhoro*, is then entitled to inherit his adopted father's possessions and, more important, is the correct person to carry out the father's obsequies.

When a man dies, his house, fields, and other property, are divided equally between all his sons. His wife has the right to remain in the house unless she goes off with another man, and his unmarried daughters are the responsibility of the brothers. Should there be no sons, and as women have no right of inheritance, the estate goes to the nearest male heir, normally a brother or nephew. Doubtful cases are settled by the village panchayat, from whose judgment appeal can be made only to the Central Government.

Festivals

Magh Sankranti

This marks the end of winter, and occurs on the 1st of Magh (about mid-January). Near relations are summoned to a meal, which must include *khicheri*—spiced rice cooked in ghee. In the Army, one day's holiday is given.

Basant Panchami

This festival, held in honour of spring, falls in the months of January or February, and in the Army a day's holiday is given.

Shivaratri

Is held in February or March and, as its name implies, is a festival in honour of Shiva. It commemorates the occasion when he opened his eyes after long meditation and is celebrated by fasting during the day and by a feast at night. In many places, too, fairs are held on this day. One day's holiday is allowed for this festival.

Holi

Holi, a two-day holiday, has very much less significance in Nepal than in India, and in some parts of the country there are no celebrations. It takes place on the full moon of the month of Phagun (February to March), and is in honour of Krishna. Legends accounting for Holi are many, but the one most commonly accepted by Gurkhas is that there was an evil Raja, by name Hiranyakashyapu, who had a sister, Holika, and a young son, Prahlad. To the annoyance of the father, Prahald was continually calling upon the name of Vishnu and, in spite of threats and punishments, continued to do so. The father ordered an iron pole to be made red hot, and Prahlad to be bound to it. The boy, on approaching the pole, saw an ant walking on it, and taking this to be a sign from Vishnu, he clasped the pole to him without harm. As Parlad still invoked the name of the god, his father ordered a large fire to be built and commanded his sister to sit in the fire holding the boy. Although the girl was burnt to death, the boy again escaped unhurt, but to protect him against further ordeals Vishnu assumed the form of Marsing and killed the wicked Raja.

To mark the occasion, a fruit tree with a straight trunk and branches and which, when dressed, is round in shape, is selected. In the evening, after *puja* has been made, the tree is cut down and on the following morning is moved to a selected site where, after the branches have been dressed with innumerable small pieces of coloured cloth, it is planted in a hole. A much smaller tree, said to represent Prahlad, is then bound to it. On the fourth day coloured powder is sprinkled on the tree and on the following day it is sprinkled on all and sundry. In the Army, however, it is normally an offence to throw powder on anyone wearing uniform. On the seventh day the priest sets fire to the larger tree, snatching out the smaller one, which he dips in water. As the tree falls in flames, spectators rush to grab the pieces of cloth, which are then worn as talismans toward off evil. The ashes of the tree are collected and thrown into houses.

Chait Dasain

This one-day festival, for which no holiday is permitted in the Army, occurs in the month of Chait and is a day of great celebrations in the hills, particularly for the younger folk, who dance throughout the night.

Ram Nawami

Chait Dasain is followed immediately by Ram Nawami, which celebrates the birthday of Ram. In the Army one day's holiday is granted.

Nag Panchami

This is a festival for which a holiday is not given in the Army. It occurs in late July, before the outbreak of the real monsoon, and marks a period when, unless the need is very great, new projects should not be launched nor journeys undertaken. People hang up pictures of cobras, which have been blessed, and the day is dedicated to Vishnu. All debts must be paid up before Nag Panchami, a custom similar to that of Chinese New Year's Day, and normally considerable efforts are made to do so, because, if the debt is not paid before Nag Panchami, the creditor will not accept payment until after the following Mangsir, by which time interest will have considerably increased the size of the debt.

Sansari Mai Puja

A holiday is given for this festival, which takes place in April-May. Money, rice and firewood, are offered to the Goddess Kali for protection from smallpox. These offerings are not, however, collected from any house in which a pregnant woman is living.

Sawan Sankrati

This festival occurs at the end of July and is celebrated by a feast to which near relations are summoned and at which *khir* (sweetened rice boiled in milk) must be eaten. The feast is a *last* gathering before the monsoon really starts and travel becomes virtually impossible.

Rikhi Tarpan

Coming in August, this festival is also known as 'Janai Purne'. It is the day on which the holy cord, worn by thread-wearers, must be replaced and is therefore more particularly observed by Brahmans, Thakurs and Chhetris. The thread is first blessed by an Upaddhe Brahman, after which it may be presented by any Brahman. Non thread-wearers have the cord tied round their right wrists and make a monetary return to the priest. The cord is retained until Diwali. Thread-wearers take sufficient threads to last them throughout the year, so that they can be replaced when worn out or when they become ceremonially unclean, such as after attending a funeral.

Janamashtami

This day is in celebration of the birth of Krishna and occurs on the eighth day after the full moon of Bhadau (August to September). Images of Krishna are made and worshipped, and priests perform the birth ceremonies. The day is observed as a fast, although *phalar*, food that does not require the washing of hands for its preparation, may be eaten. The night is passed in dancing and celebration.

Tij

This festival is a continuation of Janam Ashtami and, coming eleven days after it, represents the ceremonial cleansing of Krishna's mother after his birth. It is therefore a women's festival, which they observe by fasting during the day and, in the evening, and after *puja*, by holding a dance to which men are not invited.

Sora Sarad

This period begins eleven days after *Tij* and lasts for sixteen days. Ancestor worship takes place and oblations are offered to deceased parents.

Dashera

Dashera, the most important festival of the Gurkhas' year, and called, by them, Dasain, is a soldiers' festival in honour of Durga, Goddess of War. It takes place at the new moon of *Asoj* (September to October) and lasts for ten days. In Western Nepal most Thums or parishes have a 'kot' where the major functions of Dashera are observed. In Eastern Nepal, however, where the houses of a village are far more scattered, these functions are usually carried out at some suitable place, often the *mukhiya's* house in the village, the *kot* as such does not exist.

On the first day, known as *Jamare Aunsi* or *Naurata Aunsi*, the priest sows barley or rice in the temple, in a dark place to encourage its growth, and close by prepares a shrine at which are collected *kukris, konras* and other weapons, which he ceremonially blesses.

The next day of importance is *Phulpati*, when the whole community marches in procession to fetch the, *phulpati*, which consists of leaves, vegetables, fruit and flowers. The cavalcade is led by a band, followed by a 'kalas-bokne' escorted by the men bearing the sacrificial kukris (*konras*) and swords. Attendants also carry yaks' tails, kindling material for the holy fire, curds and other necessary articles. Behind this comes a guard, equipped with an assortment of fire-arms which they fire frequently in salute. The Guard is followed by a choir, singing seasonal hymns, and by the *nach* (dance) party, behind whom come the entire population of the area. On arrival at the chosen spot, a mound of earth about 2-1/2 feet high, gently tapering from a base of some 2 feet in diameter, is erected. The officiating priest and his assistants, chatting the while, and with acolytes in attendance, prepare an altar, tracing symbols on the ground with curds, flour, rice and flowers.

A sacred fire is lit and prayers are offered. In the meantime, close at hand, the *nach* party dances and sings, the choir chants and the band plays. On the appearance of a party which had previously been despatched to collect the *phulpati*, a goat is sacrificed and the *phulpati* is blessed. The procession then reforms, each member carrying small green branches, and the *phulpati* is escorted to the kot. The eighth day is *Kalratri*, and in the early evening the whole population gather at the *kot* for celebrations lasting throughout the night. While the priest and his assistants perform the necessary *puja*, the *nach* party entertains the crowd. At about midnight a goat is sacrificed, and then, as the half moon disappears, a buffalo is decapitated and the rest of the night is spent in merrymaking.

The ninth day is known as *Balidan, Mar,* or *Naumi*, and is the day of sacrifice. After the necessary prayers have been said, buffaloes are sacrificed in numbers according to the custom and affluence of the village. Special goats, presented by individuals, are decapitated at the pile of arms in the *kot*, and others, bought out of common funds and numbering possibly forty or fifty, are let loose in an area and are cut down by any man or boy who wishes to show his dexterity with a *kukri* or sickle. Anyone who fails to strike the head cleanly off with one blow is greeted with jeers and catcalls and quickly has his face and body smeared with the blood of his unfortunate victim. The men who slay the buffaloes are specially selected for the task and are rewarded by the senior man present, normally the *mukhiya*, with gifts of money and a white *pagri*. Their success ensures a prosperous and propitious year for the assembly, and is acclaimed by cheering, clapping, salutes from every fire-arm available, and with much noise from the band. On their return home, many sacrifice goats with which to feast their friends and, with the blood, make an impression of a hand over their doorways.

The tenth, and last, day is *Tika* and is considered of great importance. The priest cuts the barley sown on the first day, and presents small tufts to individuals, on whom he also places the *maula ko tika* or special caste mark of the occasion. The rest of the day is spent in visiting relatives and in giving, and receiving, *tikas* and presents. In the evening the *phulpati*, together with various other articles, such as the baskets in which the barley has been grown, are ceremonially escorted from the *kot* to a nearby stream into which, after another goat has been sacrificed, they are cast.

In the Army only the following days of Dashera are celebrated as holidays: Jamare Aunsi; Phulpati; Kalratri; Mar; Tika.

Tewar

The last of the annual festivals to be described is Tewar, known in India as Dewali, which takes place in Kartik (October to November). It lasts for five days and each day has a special name and a special object for worship. These are the crow (Kag Tewar), the dog (Kukur Tewar), the cow (Gai Tewar), the ox (Goru Tewar), and the brother (Bhai Tewar). On the first day, and before the morning meal is eaten, rice is thrown to the crows and in the evening a lamp is burnt at the spot where the dirty dishes are washed and the crows gather. On the second day, dogs are given a special meal in the morning and are garlanded and marked with a *tika*. In the evening a lamp is placed at each side of the entrance to the house. On the third day, cows receive special favours, whilst the holy cords tied round the wrist on Rikhi Tarpan are cut off and tied to the cows' tails. In the evening special prayers are offered to Lachhmi, goddess of wealth, and parties of children visit houses chanting 'bhai lo, bhai lo', and receive alms. On the fourth day, special favours are paid to oxen and in the evening parties go from house to house chanting 'deosire, deosire', and receive gifts of food and drink.

Bhai Tewar is the most important day of the festival and on this day every man must visit his sister. If he has no blood sister he must find an adopted or god-sister, for it is she who performs the *Bhai Tika* ceremony. A carpet, on which are laid plates containing various fruits, sweets and nuts, and also vases of flowers and other articles, including a tray containing small bowls of coloured powders. This is placed in front of the seated brother. His sister, sitting in front of him, lights the incense, scatters flowers over his knees, shoulders and head, chants the necessary prayers, and passes the incense round him. Having anointed his head with oil, she breaks a walnut invoking a special magic against his enemies. The nut, sweets and currants, are placed in his hand and, after he has eaten them, he is presented with a coconut. His sister puts a little water into the bowls of coloured powder and mixes each into a separate paste. She places some of each colour, in turn, on her right thumb and, starting in the centre between his eyebrows, and finishing at the hairline, she affixes tikas to her brother's forehead. Her blessing ends the ceremony. That night every house is decorated, from courtyard to rooftop, with many small lights—a pleasing and beautiful spectacle. Gambling, which is strictly prohibited at all other times, takes place openly during Tewar, both in the villages and in the Army.

Sat Narain Puja

This is not an official holiday but is a thanksgiving service which can be performed at any time. Some religious minded people carry it out monthly; some after the granting of a prayer; some after a safe return from a journey; and so on. The ceremony lasts for one day during which the principal worshipper and the officiating priest must fast. An altar is constructed in the courtyard, at which prayers are offered and religious passages are read out.

Pani Patiya

This ceremony of absolution, or purification from defilement caused by going overseas, can only be sanctioned by the Raj Guru and is limited to those who have not exposed themselves to unnecessary defilement. It lasts for five days, the first of which is a day of complete fasting. Thereafter the quantity of rice which may be eaten is increased daily until it reaches a normal ration.

Bhor Patiya

This is somewhat similar to the above and is necessitated by unintentional contact with low caste individuals.

Witchcraft

The Gurkha has a strong belief in the witches, wizards and spirits, which are so numerous in his mythology. The ordinary wizard is known as *bokso* and a witch as bokso. It is no longer permitted to beat to death those suspected of witchcraft, but the exorcising of evil spirits is still practised. A man who has been bewitched will fall to the ground insensible and can be saved only with difficulty. He must be held by five others, four of them grasping his thumbs and big toes and the fifth the tupi on his head. Ground chillis are put in his mouth and nose, and a heated piece of metal is placed against his skin. This, it is said, will produce burns not on him but on the witch. Witches often cast their spells on young children and the parents must then carry out a special ceremony which varies according to the advice of the exorcist at the time. It may be necessary to go to a particular place at night and there, after scattering rice on the ground, to liberate a young hen. This hen will immediately be carried off by the evil spirit, which will appear in the form of a jackal.

A more common form is to sacrifice, after dark and after appropriate ceremonies, a black and white cock, the head and blood of which are left for the spirit. At night some spirits uproot clumps of bamboo and lay them across footpaths as a trap for the unwary, but these clumps are always replanted before dawn. Because of the danger from spirits it iscon-sidered advisable, at night, to travel in parties, carrying torches and singing. Nearly all sorcerers have a familiar which may take the form of a cat or a porcupine. These familiars, known as *chaura,* raid fields at night to find food for their master. Should a *chaura* be wounded, or captured and tied up, its protector will suffer a similar fate; if it is killed, its master will also die.

Wizards are of various kinds. Some, like the *gurau,* can turn themselves into animals at will; the *ulte* or *sankutte* has his feet turned backwards and is completely covered with hair; the *banjhankri* lives in dense jungle and carries his victims to his lair, occasionally releasing them later. Other wizards are fond of casting a spell on someone and then challenging a priest to exorcise it. A wizard will not, however, normally interfere with someone who knows them for what they are and a practised priest, with the aid of a bamboo divining rod, is generally able to detect them.

After a death, when a house is being ceremonially purified, the celebrant, and the occupants and their friends, using plates and dishes, scoop all the air from inside the house, out through the main door. Burning paper, or jets of kerosene, are also sometimes used to burn the air inside the house, and gongs or tin cans are beaten, conches blown, and much shouting goes on. This frightens the dead man's spirit and drives it outside. Often a bamboo framework structure is made, around which is wound a complicated maze of strings, forming symmetrical patterns. Into this is placed an effigy, made of dough, money, flowers, coloured paper and rags, which represents the evil spirit. A small offering of food is also put in the cage which is then taken some distance from the house and placed near the cross—roads. Confused by the maze of strings and by the roads, the spirit is unable to find its way back to the house and so is removed for ever. The cage may, however, also be disposed of by being burnt or thrown into a river.

To cure the sick, the exorcist, who is usually a man and who is paid for his services, goes into a trance, shivering and intoning incantations in a falsetto voice. Sometimes during the trance, he will whittle a piece of bamboo, a wooden stick, or a large feather, and ask questions of the spirit. The shavings fall to the ground and according to their disposition the questions are answered in the affirmative or negative. A male kid, chick, duckling or squab, is sacrificed. It is killed by a blow on the head with a stick, with no loss of blood, or a tap on the head with a finger, or its head is cut off with a *kukri*. Sometimes a vein is opened so that the offering bleeds to death. The animal is not killed until it has given its assent by nodding and if it is slow in doing so a few drops of water poured on its head normally accelerate matters. The sick person may be connected to the sacrificial animal by a cord so that, when magic incantations have driven the evil spirit out of the patient, it will enter the body of the animal. This is said to cause its death.

Those claiming to be able to exorcise evil spirits, keep their powers secret and only pass them on to those of their children who seem especially receptive. There are, however, some people in whom this special ability is believed to be innate.

The principal kinds of exorcists are:

Bijuwa—employed mainly by Rais and Limbus. The exorcist can be of either tribe, but is usually from the former. It is said that Bijuwa and Jhankri are the same.

Phedangma—chiefly employed by Limbus and is almost invariably a Limbu. But may occasionally be employed by Rais.

Jhankri—employed by Gurungs and Magars, but sometimes by Tamangs, Thamis, Sunwars, Limbus and Rais. Can be from any of the above tribes, but is seldom a Limbu. The Jhankri performs a dance step which, to look at, is not unlike a form of hopscotch.

Dhami—normally employed by the higher castes, such as Brahman and Chhetri, but may also be used by other tribes and may be a Tamang or a Rai. The Dhami normally beats out a rhythm on a tambourine-like drum (dengro) and mutters night-long prayers and incantations.

Gyabring—not a true exorcist, but is employed by Gurungs and is himself a Gurung.

Lama—also in a different category from those mentioned above; but is included here as many of his ceremonies are similar to theirs, in particular those of a postmortem nature and those connected with illness. In driving an evil spirit from a sick person he uses the metempsychotic method. He is a Buddhist, and is employed by Gurungs, Tamangs, and Sherpas.

Mun—employed by Lepchas, and may be a Lepcha of either sex. The methods used differ from those of all other types noted above.

The dress adopted by exorcists for ceremonies varies, but is sometimes a full length flared smock, a one-fold *pagri* with long feathers, and a mask. If a mask is not worn the face may be concealed by being blackened. Sometimes, too, a long iron trident, or *trisul,* is carried.

Folklore

Snakes

To see a snake eating its prey is a sign that a relative is about to die. If it is seen before mid-day the relationship is close. During the month of Kartik (October to November) a snake must not be referred to as 'Sarp' or 'Sanp' but only as 'Ghisarne'—the crawler, or as 'Lamkira'—the long one. Illness at home is presaged by a snake crossing the path when coming from the house.

Common beliefs are that a snake's bite does not have a poisonous effect until the tail has been erected; that after a snake has been killed the poison will keep the tail alive for some time; and that a decapitated snake can aim its head to inflict a bite.

12
Residence and Ritual in the Garhwal Himalaya

The research upon which this essay is based was undertaken in Uttarakhand/Uttaranchal, in the Himalayan districts of the North Indian state of Uttar Pradesh; specifically in upper Garhwal, bordered by Tibet on the north, Kumaon to the east, the plains of North India to the south, and the Indian state of Himachal Pradesh on the West. Until fairly recently, the rugged terrain and paucity of natural resources kept upper Garhwal relatively isolated from the rest of North India, both economically and socially. During as the 1950s, such basic necessities as sugar and salt were imported; carried for weeks on the backs of people and animals over long and dangerous paths. The most significant link with the rest of India was provided by the famous pilgrimage temples of Badrinath, Kedarnath, Gangotri and Yamnotri. But even here, cultural and economic intercourse was more-or-less limited to the pilgrim routes hugging the floors of Garhwal's mighty river valleys. All this changed as a result of India's so-called "Border War" with China in 1962, when the government rapidly constructed a number of roads to the Tibetan frontier, many of which followed the old pilgrimage routes. Private as well as public development schemes followed in the wake of military utilization, and in the last four decades, social and economic changes have been swift and far-reaching.

Despite its proximity to several Tibetan and Buddhist cultures, Garhwal has retained strong linguistic and cultural affinities with the North Indian plains. Its population is overwhelmingly Hindu. Like the plains, Garhwal is viri-patrilocal, that is, a newly-married couple resides in the home of the father of the groom. This is important, for it means that when a young woman is married, she must leave her mait or natal village (*mayaka*), the home of her family and friends, move to a strange place, put herself under the control of her mother-in-law, and physically merge with the body of a stranger, her husband. Students of North Indian society and culture are virtually unanimous that the position of a new bride in a joint family is among the most difficult in North Indian society, and young women often anticipate their marriages with great anxiety. No one who has lived for long in North India can forget those pathetic scenes when a new bride is dragged from her mait weeping and wailing (and sometimes kicking and screaming), to the bus or taxi where her husband and his entourage wait to take her away to her new home, the *sauryas* (*sasural*), her husband's home.

Evidence drawn from Garhwali naming patterns, proverbs, language, "traditional law" interviews with local persons, marriage customs, and folklore, indicates that according to the folk ontology of Garhwalis, persons and the places where they reside have a great deal of influence upon each other (Sax 1990; 1991: Chap. 3). One is not only "what one eats", but also "where one lives", and thus a young woman's nature is fundamentally affected by her natal village. This only adds to the trauma of marriage for her, since it means that she is not only emotionally uprooted, but also physically transformed, by the requirements of married life. Let us investigate this in more detail: precisely what happens to a woman when she shifts residence at marriage?

On posing this question to Garhwali men, a fairly consistent set of answers was received. With few exceptions, they said that a woman's relations with the people and gods of her natal family and village are terminated by marriage, and that a new set of relations is established in their place. Such a perspective can easily be reconciled with the ontological assumption noted above: places and persons mutually (though not exclusively) determine each other; the bride has moved to a new place; *ipso facto* she is transformed. As one of the male informants put it: "Only love remains, but that is something that remains until one's dying day".

Such a perspective is more or less in accord with the formulations' of classical Sanskrit law treatises (*dharmasastra*). Summarizing the *Manavasastra* for instance, Leslie notes that while a man may change his own *varna* through conduct (as in the case of Visvamitra), a married woman's *varna* is determined by that of her husband; she "assumes in the 'oneness' of marriage both the qualities and the status of her husband, merging with him as a river merges with the sea" (1989: 39; see also *Manu* IX.22-4; X.22-4, 42, 67, 70). On the basis of many such passages, Leslie argues that the "ideal oneness" of husband and wife in classical Hindu marriage amounts in practice to a self-effacement of the female. Take for another example the *Stridharmapaddhati* of the eighteenth-century writer Tryambaka, which stresses "the importance of forgetting one's own family and never returning to one's father's house" (Lesle [n.d]: 281), and approvingly cites numerous classical texts to validate his point; for instance Krishna's advice to his younger sister Subhadra on the eve of her marriage (attributed to the Agnipurana), to the effect that she should:

> forget all about us (i.e. her own family), even her mother and father. For this husband alone is a woman's family; the husband alone is a woman's wealth; the husband alone is a woman's religious duty, and her chief austerity (Ibid. 281-82).

The severing of a woman's ties with her natal village and family upon her marriage is intimately related to the idea that the wedding ritual substantially transforms the bride. This is clear in the "orthoprax" *kanyadana* wedding rite as practiced in Uttarakhand. Elementary spatial relationships within it both illustrate and accomplish the joining of bride and groom. Circumambulation of the fire altar is considered by many to be the crucial act of unification; it has "the effect of making the wife his half-body for life" (Inden and Nicholas 1979: 48; see also Campbell 1976 : 90.91; *Manu* VIII. 227; Raheja 1985).[1] In the worship of Ganesa that precedes this act, the bride's priest sits between the wedding couple. After each of the first five circumambulations, when bride and groom resume their places to the west of the fire, the priest continues to sit between them. After the fifth there is a whole series of actions, following which the bride and groom place food in each other's mouths with their hands, signifying that henceforth they are of one body and can consume each other's polluted leavings *jutha*. Now they sit next to each other, but have changed positions: the bride is on the groom's left, the paradigmatic place of the ardhangini, the wife who is the 'half-body' of her husband. During one Garhwali wedding I an elderly married women was seen simply this 'auspicious song' (*mangala git*) during the circumambulation of the fire-altar:

Mangal Git

Gaura made the first circumambulation,

and she is still our unmarried princess..

> Gaura made the second . . . third . . . fourth . . . fifth . . . sixth
>
> circumambulation, and she is still our unmarried princess . . .
>
> After eight circumambulations, Gaura becomes your wife.[2] After nine circumambulations, she becomes your 'half-body'.

Next comes the *gotra-parivartana*, or "changing of the wife's *gotra*", a ritual which also has a transformative effect:

> After gazing on the pole star (*dhruva*), the husband makes his wife recite the following *mantra*: "you are eternally fixed (*dhruva*); may I become eternally fixed in the *kula* of my husband". They then gaze at the star Arundhati, the devoted wife of the star Vasisfha, after which the husband recites this mantra: "As the sky is eternally fixed, the earth is eternally fixed, the entire world is eternally fixed, and these mountains are eternally fixed, so this woman is eternally fixed in her husband's *kula*" (Bhattacharya 1973-1974: 435, in Inden and Nicholas 1979: 48).

I asked the bride's priest at one Garhwali wedding about the claim that Dhuwa (the pole star). "the unwavering one", is invoked when the bride actually changes her *gotra.* He said that this is sometimes done, but that the more common practice in Garhwal is to call Surya (the Sun) as witness, with the special prayer that the couple's "hearts become one, and no enmity remain". He added that the bride and groom are already in fact joined as husband and wife, as a result of the *karma* of their previous lives, and that what the wedding does is to effect the union of the wife with the husband as his half-body.

When a young woman marries in the kaniadana rite she becomes, or begins to become, the "half-body" of her husband. As Fruzetti puts it:

> When a virgin becomes a wife... she is cancelled ("cut off") from her father's collection of ancestors in the line (bangsa bali) [*vamsavali*]. She is now of her husband's *gotra* and is added to his (bangsa bali) [*vamsavali*] (1982: 99 ff.).

Henceforth she will bear children for his lineage, worship the lineage gods of his home and not hers, and observe birth and death pollution for members of her new family (husband, his agnates and their spouses) rather than that of her parents. Conversely, her death or childbirth will result in impurity for her husband's family, not her father's — unless this happens in the father's house. Male informants usually reported that after a woman marries, her focus for such crucial relations as gotra and jati,[3] as well as mortuary obligations and general relationships with the . gods (*devata ke sambandha*) completely shifts, from the natal place to the husband's place. As proof of the pudding, men would often cite the difference in relations of birth and death pollution consequent upon change of *sapinda* relationship,[4] pointing out that after marriage, a daughter needn't observe full death pollution for her parents or for any natal relative. This is also the situation in Bengal, where:

> "An abrupt change is brought about by the marriage of a woman: before her marriage, the impurity caused by her death affects only persons of her father's clan; after her marriage, the impurity caused by her giving birth or dying affects only persons of her husband's clan and no longer those of her father's" (Nicholas 1981: 373; see also Inden and Nicholas 1977: 13-14).

It is primarily the bride, not the groom, who is transformed by the wedding ritual. She is a dangerous 'outsider' entering into intimate relations with a new home and family, and must be transformed so as to render her more congenial to them. Thus the husband's presence is required in only two of the twelve kinds of customary Garhwali wedding rituals enumerated by Lall, several of which are designed toward off inauspiciousness by marrying the girl to objects other than her groom: a pitcher or tree for example (1942: 6-10). Although in many parts of North India a man may be married several times, a woman can undergo the life-cycle rite of marriage (*vivaha sanskara*) only once (Fruzetti 1982: 103), as a Garhwali friend of mine put it:

> A man is like gold or silver. He can be made over many times—into an ornament, a vessel, or whatever, and he remains golden. He can sleep with others and get married (*phera karna*, lit. 'circumambulate' the wedding altar) as many times as he will. But a woman is defiled (*Jutha*) if she sleeps with another, and cannot be married more than once.

For a long while this view of marriage as a complete transformation was accepted by most students of Indian social structure, including many anthropologists. Jacobson provides a rather long list of scholars who stressed "the completeness of the transfer" of a woman after her marriage (1977: 265). Gould is typical of the tendency: he asserts that; "after marriage, a woman is considered to have become a member of her husband's and ceased to be a member of her father's kin group" (1961: 299); only "affective ties" remain, says Gould, and evidently he does not consider them of enough significance to justify extended comment. Gould's reification of "kinship" is typical of anthropological writings of that era: he actually anthropomorphized South Asian "kinship systems" by attributing agency to them, viz.:

> Matrilineal kinship systems purposefully fuse the obligational ties inherent in consanguineal and affinal forms of relationship... Patrilineal kinship systems by their very nature purposefully exclude such overlapping ties (1961: 258).

Local terms, categories or explanations of family relationships are neither mentioned or considered in such analyses.

More recently, students of Indian society have begun to recognize that the male, high-caste perspective exemplified in both classical Hindu law texts and the anthropological writings of a previous generation is but one among many schemes for classifying family relationships, and moreover that indigenous taxonomies of and principles underlying such relationships often provide a more satisfying explanation fcr actual behaviour than do the exogenous theories of social scientists. Prominent among such indigenous principles is that of 'house', 'home', or 'residence,' wnich has been shown to be an important factor in the conceptualization of interpersonal relationships within and among persons and families in diverse regions in South Asia.

Jacobson has shown that in the Bhopal region of central India, a woman's natal relations are not polluted by her death unless she dies in her natal home (1977: 272); there are numerous festivals for which her presence in her natal home is required (Ibid: 275); and that there is "a permanent tie between a married woman and her natal kinsmen" (266); in short that "the ostensible transfer of a woman to her husband's kin group at marriage is in fact only a partial transfer" (Ibid: 281-282).[5] Daniel (1984) has pointed to the important effects that the soil of a given place or village is believed to have upon those who reside there, and more recently, Moore (1985) has shown that the Nayar taravad "is defined by such a house-and-land unit, and not by a sense of matrilineal relatedness", and that for the Nayar, the taravad is "as much about ties to houses as it is about ties to people" (Ibid: 527, 536).

Upon closer examination, it turns out that the principle of shared 'house' or residence was there all along in Hindu ritual/legal texts. With regard to the abrupt change in relations of impurity following a Bengali woman's marriage, Nicholas informs us that "The most common exceptions to this rule occur if she gives birth or dies in her father's house rather than her husband's". Summarizing the text, Nicholas notes that: "Sharing the same house at the time of an impurity is quite similar to the bodily relationship created by marriage" (1981: 373).

Berreman noted several years ago that in Garhwal, divorced women and persons whose adoption into another place had been cancelled were "accepted back without question or ceremony," into their natal places, and made the now-familiar observation that the junior levirate as practiced in Garhwal would amount to incest if the deceased man's wife had been completely absorbed into her husband's kin group (1962a: 526; cf. Jacobson 1977: 275). Summarizing his argument, Berreman wrote that:

> Despite the paramount importance of patrilineal ties in their system of kin relationships as the Pahari conceive it, residence, as I have shown, takes precedence over lineality in certain contexts (1962a: 527).

In contrast to male assertions that females are suddenly and completely transformed by marriage and their subsequent shift of residence, Garhwali women tend to have a more gradualistic perspective, as is shown by excerpts below from interviews with three Garhwali women: Saraswati, an educated young Brahman woman married by the Kanyadan rite twelve years previously; Sucharita, an elderly widow from the relatively low carpenter (*mistari*) caste married who had been forty years previously by brideprice; and Lakshmidevi, a Brahman woman married thirty years previously by brideprice. Of course, the girl's initial separation from her mait is difficult: as Lakshmidevi said:

> Oh yes, the true root is in the mait. From there she has to go. But her brothers and sisters were in that home. She loves and receives love from everyone there first. And it is the root. She takes birth there. It is her source. Only then can she move to another house, right? The beginning (of life) is there. Mother, father, uncle, aunt... all have come from some home. The root is there. And from there,

> she must leave to go to another home. Later she will become attached here [in the husband's home].

Saraswati said that as a young girl anticipating her wedding:

> I did not like it very much. I used to think: "Who knows what he is like?" Yes, I did think it would be nice to have my own family and children, but I also thought: "I must give them up, I must desert them, I must leave...
>
> What could my thoughts be? When I missed them greatly I would weep and wail. I would call those who had lived with me. But my in-laws would not send me. But some people do not feel so badly about it, they say "Let her cry. She is young and healthy. What is she crying about". There is no lack of food or clothing. Many feel compassionate and they send her (to her *mait*).

Similarly Lakshmi said that before marriage she :

> felt very bad (*burii lagi*). I left my brothers and sisters. (I thought) "Where am I going?" But these days, what girl is married at such a young age? I was so small that I thought "How can I go?" and "Where will I go?" But what does it matter if I think it evil? It doesn't matter whether I consider it good or bad.

Sucharita said that before she was married, she saw her future husband:

> wander through our village, and I knew that I had to go in his family. Yearning arises then, but so does fear: who knows how it will be, or what will happen? One is very frightened, child!... One is both afraid and anxious.

During the first few years of marriage, a young bride's mait remains a place of comfort, and if necessary of refuge. Visits by outmarried village daughters (*dhyanis*) to their *maits* are an important feature of married life in Garhwal. When women return to their saurycis after such a visit they wail loudly, embracing their female friends or touching the feet of female elders, begging not to be sent away again. And surely, one of the greatest anxieties of a new bride is that she will not be allowed to return to her *mait*. Most married women eagerly look forward to visiting their *maits*; such visits are very enjoyable. As Saraswati put it:

> If we want to work, we work; and if we don't then we leave it. Everyone in the village honours the girl who has come to her *mait*. Some put money in her hand, some give other things. They give her total respect, (thinking) "This girl is from my village."

In the days of child-marriage, pre-pubescent brides did not normally leave their *maits* or begin living with their husbands until well after menarche. Then as now, young brides were allowed frequent and prolonged visits to their *maits*. Lakshmidevi told us that such "going back and forth" continues for several years, and that in her first year of marriage, she spent nearly four months in her *mail*. Another woman reported that she spent approximately one week per month in her mait for the first year. As Saraswati put it :

> The custom (*riti*) here is that in the first year (the bride) goes back and forth and spends as much time in her *mait* as in her *sasural*. Two or three days in her *mait*, two or three days in her *sasural*. It can go on like this for two or three years after marriage... After I got married I stayed one day here at my sauryas. Then one day at my *mait*. Then after a few days here I went to stay in my *mail* for three months. Then I came back to my sauryas and stayed for ten days, and then again went to my *mait* and stayed another ten days, then returned to my sauryas. So it went for one year.

In Garhwal, there are several ritual occasions for female visiting *mait*, times when it is considered permissible and/or desirable that a married woman visit her *mait*. These include major festival days when one goes 'to eat *barta*' (Hindi *vrat*), i.e., to celebrate Krishna's birthday (Krisna *janmdstami*), 'to eat *bhagwati* (Hindi *dipavali*); or to observe" other major festivals such as *Sivaratra*, *Nandasthami*, and *rakhi* (*raksabandhan*).Navaratra is not usually included in this category, since it is not a particularly important festival in Garhwal. In those regions where Navaratra is observed, it is generally considered a time for collective worship by the agnatic lineage; as inmarried members of that lineage, wives are required to be present in their *suryas* (cf. Bennett 1983: 269). So it is noteworthy that during the Garhwali "equivalent" of Durga Puja — that is, *Nandasthami* the festival of Nanda Devi women are expected to return to their *mait*. Generalizations are difficult, since each region tends to have its own traditions; nevertheless the months of *Jetha* (Hindi *Jyestha*), *Mangsir* (Hindi

Margasirsa), and *Pausa* (Hindi *Pausa*) tend to be favoured times for visiting. These months fall during slack agricultural periods: *Jetha* at the hottest time of the year and the other two months in the dead of winter. Hence parents are not tempted to put their visiting daughters to work in the fields, something that is widely regarded as sinful. From another perspective, the *suryas* needn't give up any of its claims on her labour.

It is thought best if a woman is 'called' to her *mait* by her brother or, if this is impossible, by his son, or the woman's father, or some other male *mait* (resident of the mait). Whoever 'calls' or 'invites' the woman in this way is called the *bulao* or *khedval*. At the end of her visit, a woman's husband, or his brother or father or some other agnate, comes to fetch her back to her *sauryas* from her *mait*. Such arrangements only go to show that even when visiting her natal village, a woman is never entirely independent. She is chaperoned by male relatives, and there are certain places where she must never go unless called, such as a married sister's home. As potential sexual partners, a woman and her sister's husband are kept strictly segregated. We asked Sucharitadevi if sisters ever visit each others' homes after marriage, and she replied:

> No, they don't go. They don't go on their own, never. Now if they are called there, it's another matter. But if you go because you want to, of your own volition, then people there say "What's with her? Why has she come? She has no honor (*ijjat*), no shame, nothing."
>
> Q : But you can visit your brother any time?
>
> A : Yes, one can go there. It is one's right (*hak*). But nowhere else. She (the sister) is of another house (*dusaru ghaur*).

When women visit their natal homes they take prepared food in both directions, but the woman's natal relations take care to ensure that they return more than they received from her husband's family, thus conforming to the hypergamous prestational pattern that is typical of high caste North Indian Hindus, wherein the woman's side refuses to accept any return gift from the man's side. In particular, the sweet called *arasa* is sent back with the returning bride, who is beseiged upon arrival by those seeking one of these much-esteemed treats. *Arasa* is extremely difficult to make; this may be why it is demanded of the young wife, in a manner reminiscent of the Bengali adage noted by Inden and Nicholas, to effect that a woman becomes a true wife only when she can cook iron pellets.

A second context in which women return to their natal villages is for the ritual variously known as *hagarat, dunoj*, or dvara, bali. The Brahmans in my village gave it a Sanskritized name which accords well with the practice: *doharagamana,* 'going repeatedly, going again.' Two or three days after a *kanyadana* wedding, the couple returns to the girl's mait, worships at the village temples and shrines, spends a night or two there, distributes sweets or tea, and departs. Several aspects of this process are deemed essential. First, the principals must act as a couple; the husband must be present, and if he is not, as in a *kumbha vivaha* marriage, then the bride will wait for him before 'repeating.' Second, the bride traditionally rode on a 'Bareilly Dandi', an uncovered palanquin, on the day of the *doharagamana.* This contrasted with the covered red palanquin in which she left her *mait* on the wedding day. Third, the *doharagamana* should take place in the bride's mait, and must take place in a house other than that in which the newly weds will reside.

Following one Jaunsari wedding, after the bride had been welcomed to her new home, I saw a lengthy argument between the family priest, who wanted to return to her *mait* for the *doharagamana,* and the father of the groom, who wanted to get it over with quickly in his own village and not be bothered with yet another march across the river to the girl's mait. The priest won. In extenuating circumstances — for soldiers on leave for instance, who haven't the time to return to the bride's *mait — the doharagamana* may take place in the husband's village, as long as it is in some house other than that in which the couple will reside. In this case the couple will do 'doharagamane' in the husband's village for an hour or two, distributing sweets and/or tea to the crowd of children that inevitably gather: this is acceptable as long as it is not done in the husband's own house.

No one was able satisfactorily to explain this custom to me. My best informant's exegesis was more-or-less the same as everyone else's:

> The road is repeated (*dohara rasta*). When the most auspicious event of all, a wedding, has occurred, then why shouldn't they return? Were they not to return, it would be inauspicious.

A neighbour with functionalist inclinations suggested that the custom allowed the girl's *maiti* relations to get to know the groom, as they wouldn't have had a chance during the wedding. No doubt *doharagamana* has multiple meanings, but among them is certainly a public affirmation of the bride's continuing relationship to her *mait*.

The significant difference between types of palanquin is unambiguous. The virginal bride is taken to her saunyas in a covered red palanquin; the married (and presumably non-virginal) woman returns on an uncovered litter. The palanquin is an icon of virginity, as is shown by the sarcastic way in which a divorced woman who marries into the village is greeted: "Well, you have certainly come in a palanquin (tumi doli mam ayam chha)!"

Despite the great importance Garhwalis attach to a young bride's visits to her mait, they generally decrease in frequency over time. As a woman adjusts to life in her *sauryds*, develops new friendships and alliances there, contributes labour to the household, and bears children and especially sons for her husband's lineage, her position will improve. She is likely to become an auspicious married woman (*sunagini*), and eventually, she may attain a comfortable position of honour and prestige as senior female. This is the ideal life-course of a Garhwali peasant woman and the explicit goal of most young wives, and most women regard it as an appropriate and fulfilling goal. As a woman's affection toward her husband and new family increases, visits to her *mait* decrease. And of course, time also takes its inevitable toll. As one elderly informant whose *mait* was only one kilometre away said, "When my brother has died, my mother and my brother's wife have died, then why should I go to my *mait*? Here my three sons' wives take care of me: why should I go elsewhere?"

A woman recently married into the village where I lived had gone to her *mait* six times in two years, while during the same period another woman married more than fifteen years hadn't visited her mait at all. A third woman married for more than twenty years had also not gone to her *mait* in the last two years, but reported that during the first year of her marriage she had visited two or three times. One elderly woman had visited her mait only once, to participate in the procession of her *mail's* deity, Ghandyal. A neighbour's wife, with two grown sons, had not visited her *mait* for two years, but said that during her first three years of marriage she had visited once every six months or so. The mail of a Brahman friend's wife was a mere five or six kilometres away, and she had visited two or three times in the preceding two years. During her first two years of marriage she visited eight or ten times, she said. During the year I lived in the village, she wasn't planning a visit at all, since there was no one to look after the children in her absence. Lakshmidevi said that:

> Before (having children) I went, but after I had children I went only once a year, once in two years, then four and even five years passed and I did not go. Once I went seven years without returning to my *mait*! (Since my last visit) three years have passed. Of course, sometimes there is a special task (*Ram*). But my home (*ghaur*) is here; my fields and family.

Similarly, Saraswati said that although at first she was more attached to her *mait*, she had come to have more attachment (*lobh*) to her sauryas:

> I have authority here for many things: for taking; for giving, for anything at all; complete authority, authority to cook food. No restrictions at all; I do as I wish. It is just like home — though by this I do not mean that I don't miss my parents. I retain at least that much devotion. If they were in trouble then how could I stay here? It would be nice if I could visit them for two or four davs.[17]

The process of incorporation into the sauryacis tends to be seen by women as a gradual one. It takes a long time, and the women we interviewed told us over and over again that a new bride's many relationships to her natal place cannot be terminated by marriage and a change of residence. Relationships of love (*prem*) and attachment (*lobha*) are particularly enduring, and even after a long and happy marriage, they are never completely effaced. When we asked Lakshmi, who had been married more than twenty-five years, whether she still missed the people of her natal village, she replied:

> Why not? Even now I miss them. Even though I've had children. But it is inconvenient to go there now; there is no time. But that's a different matter; memory continues (*yad barabar*). Absolutely. So sometimes when I miss them terribly I say to myself, "I will go there."
>
> Q : But you have your own children and grandchildren; so why don't you forget about yours *maitis*?
>
> A : O God — I was born there. What more can I say?... It's not that just because my parents have died, I don't have any attachment (*lobh*) there. My uncle and aunt are there.

> My friends and comrades (*sangl-sathi*). I always miss my *maitis*. If I stay alive, I will surely go there. Surely I will get the opportunity to go. I will be able to go when they are well.

For some women, ties to the *mait* remain primary — notably for female ascetics (*mai/jogin/sanyasin*) who, because of divorce or abuse or some other, unhappy marital situation, return to their natal places for extended periods, or for good. One such ascetic, widowed at an early age, described her family's reaction to her husband's death.

> My brother-in-law (who brought me back to my *meti*) said: "Do not take off your nose-ring". (He said) "Our bvari is such a little girl, why should we remove her nose-ring?" But I took it off myself and placed it in a box. Everyone said "Wear it wear it," but I didn't wear it. (They asked) "Why did you take it off?" I said "Which of the widows in our village has a nose-ring? Who is telling me to keep wearing the nose-ring? Why should I put it on?" Also, my hands were covered with bangles. I broke them. Now I was carefree. (I thought), "Now I will live as do the others (widows) in my village. I will become free. My mother and father are (here); I will eat with them. Drink. Then I began to work. began to study, to read and write. Mother didn't say anything, my brothers didn't say anything. Then I began to read the *Ramayana*. My mind was very sharp.

Asked if she would not have remained in her *sauryas* had her husband lived, she replied

> I had no love at all there. And I am not attached to that place. My attachment is in my *mait*. Even now I hardly say that I am from there. Once some people came from there and they said to me "Where are you from?" And I answered "I'm from here (Her *mait*). Why should I say that I'm from that *sauryas*? The name doesn't even come on my tongue. My whole life has passed here.

Of course, this woman's life history was exceptional. Most women live out their lives in their *sauryas*, seeking to balance their feelings of duty and responsibility toward it with their continuing attachment to their *mait*. Despite (or perhaps because of) her low caste status, Sucharita in many ways exemplified the ideal of a Hindu woman who, despite numerous troubles, keeps her own and her families' honour by remaining in her *sauryas*. Asked if she had ever fled to her *mait*, she replied

> No. It never happened. It never got that bad. Women do flee to their *maits* now and then, don't they? They flee for the slightest reasons. They go to their *mait*. I too had some difficulties, but I stayed there. I surely had some sorrows as well as joys, but I stayed there.

Sucharita's remarks about the nature of 'own' (*apana*) and 'others' (*paraya/biranu*) houses reveals much about the ambiguity of the distinction for married women in Garhwal:

> Q : Does a lady ever think that she is in another's home (*paraya ghaur*)?
>
> A : Yes, in the beginning. But after she has children, the *sauryas* begins to feel like her own home (*ghaur*).
>
> Q : So does she think later that now her parents' home is 'other'?
>
> A : No, one's parents' home never seems 'other' (*biranu*) [laughs]. It can never be 'other.' It is one's very own.
>
> Q : You mean that both houses become one's own?
>
> A : No, she shouldn't think of it like that [laughs]. She shouldn't think that way.
>
> Q : When the woman ages and everyone in her *mait* dies, then why does she still remember them?
>
> A : Dear son, a woman remembers her *mait*, when there is trouble in her heart. Something of them remains in her heart. She thinks "Oh God, if my mother and father were alive I could go to them. When someone in her *sasural* is angry at her, or drunk, she thinks "I will go to my *mait*. If I go to my parents, all will be well..." Even though my hair is grey, I still cannot forget my parents, never [laughs]. This is the love (*pyar*) we get from our mother and father. Those in the *sasural* also love us, and we womenfolk should regard these as quite equal. We shoud regard the *mai* and the *sasural* equally. Just the same. But it just doesn't happen.
>
> Q : I've even seen elderly women say to their husbands: "What did I get when I came to your house? I did this, I did that, and yet how much I suffered! But in my parents' house there was comfort.

> A : We shouldn't speak like this. The man will certainly command us. That's the way it is. But we should not camplain: "What have I gotten here, and why did my parents give me to this house? But actually when our parents have given us [to the *sauryas*], we must protect their honour. When they've given us, they've given us. When they have given us, they've done so with a clear conscience — they hardly give us with grief. But if there is suffering (*dukha*) in the *sauryas*... well... everyone suffers in their *sauryas*. But suffering may increase, so it is best to bury it. One should not dwell on (*man mein rakha*) the suffering - the real suffering is the suffering that we keep inside (*peta mein*).

Chhal Puja

Two of the most interesting and dramatic occasions for female visits to their natal places are *chhal puja* exorcisms and ritual processions of local deities. Both of these rituals illustrate the continuing and substantial relationship of a married woman to her natal place. The *chhal puja* is one of the most commonly performed rites of exorcism in Garhwal. It is associated with the deity Masan (from Sanskrit *samasana*, 'cremation ground'), who inhabits graveyards and other unclean, inauspicious, and *tamasik* places. My (incomplete) knowledge of the *chhal puja* was gained mostly through the kindness of a young Brahman exorcist who allowed me to accompany him during two exorcisms, answered my questions, and loaned me his ritual handbooks for photocopying. He learned his 'science' (*vidya*) from his father, who also practiced many forms of exorcism in addition to the chhal puja. Most of my friend's clients (*Jaiman*) are from a nearby village of one-hundred households, from whom he receives two-hundred kilograms of wheat and of lentils every year. Exorcism is a profitable business for him; he earned Rs. 101 as his fee (*daksina*) in the first chhal puja described below.

The exorcist told me that before he was empowered (*siddha*), he was frightened while performing *chhal pujas*, since if a mistake is made, the chhal will return a second time. But his father would stay with him during the ritual, and he has had very few repeat cases. To obtain his power, he says, he had to sit at a burning ground (*smasana*) on a raw (*kachchi*) cow hide, light a lamp in a chicken skull, and recite various *mantras* — a most frightening task. Occasionally he travels as far as thirty miles by bus to perform his exorcisms. He claimed that no castes other than his own (*Dhodyal*, one of the castes of so-called "Gangari Brahmans") are able to do the exorcism; however I know of several local men and women of other castes who are exorcists.

Chhal puja is frequently performed in conjunction with *chhaya puja,* however, either ritual may be performed by itself, depending on the prescriptions of local ritual specialists. As with many other ritual and cultural forms in Garhwal, methods of performing *chhal* and *chhaya puja*— even understandings of what they mean and how they work — vary significantly from place to place. The ritual method (*vidhi*) summarized below is based primarily upon observation of two exorcisms in Chamoli District, and on discussions with the exorcist and other local persons.

Of the various rites performed by or on behalf of married women in Garhwal, *chhal puja* is among the most common. A very high proportion of local married women — something on the order of eighty-five per cent— find that, due to some affliction or another, they are compelled at some point following their marriage to exorcize the *chhal*. The ritual is performed only once in a woman's life. My exorcist friend characterizes the *chhal puja* as a kind of 'share' (*hissa*) that must be paid to the afflicting demon. He says that about ninety per cent of his clients are women who return to their *mait* from their *sauyas* in order to get rid of the demon; such a woman must stay in her *mait* for at least three days, during which time she can't cross any rivers or streams (*nadi nali par nahim hoti hai*). She must return to her *mait* for the *chhal puja* because, quite simply, she acquired the demon there. As one man put it:

> My guess is that it happens like this: girls wander here and there a lot in the *mait.* You've seen my daughter — sometimes she takes the cows down into the ravine to graze, sometimes she goes to the jungle for wood, maybe there's a Ramalila or a Pandavlila and she goes out at night to see it. Somewhere, sometime, some part [of the *chhal*] sticks to her (*koi amsa lag jata hai*), but it never effects her until she goes to her *sauyas.* Then she asks an oracle, finds out that it's a *chhal* from the *mait*, and she goes and gets rid of it. End of story. Not a penny from the *mait.* They don't even have to give the pithaim, although it's OK to buy it there.

It is noteworthy that all expenses came from the woman's *sauryas*. This reverses the typical prestational flow and is in fact the sole instance I know of in which a woman's *maiti* kindred are feasted by her husband's people. Such a reversal is of course thoroughly consistent with the crooked (*tedha*). reversed (*ulta*) character of the rite. The process begins with physical or mental symptoms of demonic affliction. Among the most common symptoms is barenness. When faced with chronic problems of this sort, local peasants consult an oracle (*bakya, puchh karane-wala, puchhari*), who usually belongs to one of the lower castes. The oracle indicates whether a ritual is called for, and where it will be performed. The *chhal puja* usually takes place in a woman's mait. According to another informant, *chhaya puju* never occurs inside a house (*ghar*); furthermore, it is compulsory (*anivarya*) that a woman's husband, her husband's father or her brother participate in the *chhaya puja*. In the first ritual witnessed, the woman's husband accompanied her. In the second, the woman was accompanied by her elder brother. Descriptions of both rituals follow.

The first ritual — a combination of *chhal* and *chhaya puja* — was performed in April 1985. The afflicted woman was a high-caste Brahman about twenty-four years old with no children, married to a Brahman man from a nearby district. The couple had recently returned from the United States, consulted their oracle, and been instructed to return to her mait and perform a *chhal puja*. Before the *puja* began, about fifteen of the woman's natal, male kinsmen were casually playing cards and chatting amongst themselves. The exorcist and his assistants referred to these men using terms (*bhaiyat/svaura*) that are usually taken to indicate the natal kindred from which a woman is ostensibly "separated" or "cut off" by marriage. The *chhal* and *chhaya puja* demonstrate, however, that she remained related to them.

The woman arrived with certain materials required for the *puja* including a sacrificial goat, while the exorcist brought a torn portion of a work-basket (*changatira*) in which had been placed several vulture feathers, fried cakes made of *mandua* (*cynosurus coraconus*) flour, and an image (*dikara*) of Masan-devata that he had earlier fashioned of barley flour and goat hair, with soya beans (*b haft a*) for eyes and vermilion (*kumkum*) for lips. The exorcist cleared a small area, and constructed a 'six-cornered diagram' (*sastakona yantra*) of wheat flour and vermilion. The image was placed in the centre of this diagram, and a lamp of flour-dough was placed before the image. The woman and her husband, via their Brahman exorcist, offered the 'seven-grain mixture' (*satanaj*) — ubiquitous in Garhwali rituals of all kinds — of rice, barley, mandua, *koni* (?), black gram, soya, and *gahat* (?) to Masan. Almost no one present had removed their shoes for the ritual, except for the woman, her husband, and the exorcist. While uttering powerful *mantras*, the exorcist circled rice grains over the woman's head and shook them over the image of Masan.

Similarly he circled the feather, which had been wrapped in thornbush (*jhirani*) and nettle (*bichchhu ghas*) leaves, twice around the woman's head: once clockwise (*sulta*) and once counterclockwise (*ulta*), and shook it over the image. These actions resemble the *nichhvauli* rite in which a sick person's head is encircled with a handful of coins which are then tossed out, removing inauspicious influences. Clearly, certain 'negatives' causing the woman's affliction were being removed from her and transferred to the image of Masan; but although the exorcist later agreed that the effect (*prabhava*) of the demonic self (*pretatma*) of the *chhal* was removed, he denied that there was any particular object in which it was placed — in other words he denied that it was placed in or on Masan, even though that seemed clearly to be the case. While this transfer was occurring, the woman's husband offered Rs. 10 as *sthaniya bheint*, an 'offering to the place' where the ritual was being conducted. The exorcist later told me that he keeps the money and regards it as his 'commission' (*dasturi*).

Next, flat breads that had been cooked on one side only (*rosmt*) were placed in each corner and at the centre of the diagram where Masan sits. All edible substances brought by the woman and her priest: the seven grains, flour, and so forth, were placed on this *yantra*. The fifth bread was for Masan himself to consume. Then the sacrificial goat was brought and the feather was twice circled over both its and the woman's head, and shaken over the image of Masan. The feather was placed behind Masan's image, and water was dribbled on the goat's head. The exorcist whispered a *mantra* into a handful of rice, poured the rice into the left ear of the goat (whose head was held by an assistant), and then poured water over the top of that. Then they watched the goat and waited for a very long time.

They were waiting for the goat to bleat, signifying that Masan had 'accepted the *puja*, Nearly ten minutes passed while the exorcist and his assistant poured more rice and water into the goat's ear, and still he did not bleat. Addressing Masan, one man exclaimed "Why don't you take it? We're giving everything with open hearts (*khula dil*). Take it!" They tried the left ear again, then the right ear. Still the goat didn't make a sound. By the third attempt they weren't even bothering with the *mantra*, but frantically doing anything to get the goat to bleat. Bystanders were urging them to hurry up. Someone suggested that maybe they'd brought a retarded goat. Finally the animal shook its whole body (earlier it had shaken only its head when water was dribbled on it), and people said that Masan had accepted the puja.

The goat was left below, and everyone walked a short distance up the hillside, to a point from where the woman's *mait* was visible, several hundred yards below. According to the exorcist, the *chhaya puja* must always be performed on a ridge, from where the woman can see her *mait*. He also said that this ritual is performed for the fairies (*pari/phari*), and can be regarded as a form of goddess worship that does not involve animal sacrifice (*suddha devi puja*), in contrast to the worship of Masan, a forest god (*ban devata*) who demands blood. The *paris* are thought to be the spirits of young girls who met an untimely death (*alpa mrityu*), by accident or suicide for example. In the *chhaya puja* they demand their share (hissa) of food and drink. They wander about (*bhatakate jate hain*), until their time is complete (*samaya pura ho jata hai*).

In the *chhaya puja*, a small area of ground — about one foot square — was first cleared. A tiny basket called the 'palanquin' or swing' (*doli*) of the *chhaya*, was attached to a branch that had very large thorns. A new diagram was made with wheat flour by the exorcist. Like the first diagram, this was called a *talla mandala* or *talla* mandapa; however, it had a different design. The exorcist's assistant brought an incense brazier on which some hot coals were smouldering. This was set on the ground to the east of the diagram.

Numerous substances and objects were placed around the diagram: red and yellow powder (*pithaim*), a sweet made of sugar, a few handfuls of puffed rice, a banana, and numerous 'ladies' things — cloth, bindis[26] from the bazaar, a necklace, bangles, red and black decorative strings, a comb, a mirror. A fire was kindled to the east of the diagram with the coals that had been brought in the brazier. The exorcist lit the single wick (a red string) of the dough lamp and offered some *haluva*-sweet that had been brought atop a pile of cooked breads. He had brought water in a metal vessel, and he sprinkled this with a branch from the thorn tree. Meanwhile, his assistant began to heat some mustard oil in a metal pot on the fire.

Next, water was sprinkled on the woman, and on a baby chick that she had brought. Both the woman and the exorcist placed some rice grains on its head. The exorcist circled the chick over her head three times and tossed it toward the fire. All presents, food, and so forth that had been offered to the *paris* were placed in the basket, which was circled three times over the woman, and given to an old man to toss into a ravine.

Throughout the ritual, the patient was barefoot, and had been wearing an old *sari* over the top of her regular one. Now she dropped the old *sari* on the ground and approached the fire. The exorcist placed an old blouse on her head, and she bent and looked at her own reflection (*chhaya*) in the oil. A pair of rubber sandals had been placed on the other side of the fire, facing east toward her mait. The exorcist commanded her to "Go, and don't look back!." She stepped into the sandals and went straight home along with her husband, earning her hand-scythe. Suddenly the exorcist arose, poured water into the metal vessel of oil that had been heating on the fire, and simultaneously over-turned it into the coals, producing a dramatic, roaring burst of flame as the woman walked toward the village, without looking back or speaking. According to the exorcist, the fairies are transferred to the oil via the woman's reflection (*chhaya*), and then burned in the fire. The fire at the end of the *puja* was certainly dramatic, but this 'drama' could not have been directed at the patient, since she did not see it.

Next, all participants except the woman and her husband went back down to sacrifice the goat tethered near the image of Masan. The first incision on the goat's neck was quite deep, in order to facilitate bleeding. The blood was allowed to flow all over the barley-flour image of Masan, reducing it to a soggy mess. The carcass was dragged away and a small lamp was lit on the animal's head, which had been left near the Masan image. The exorcist recited a *mantra* into a handful of mustard seeds he had brought, then sprinkled them around the bloodstained area, thus 'closing' it (*bandha karana*) so that the *chhal* could do no further mischief. Then he called for water and waited some time for, it poured the water into his left hand and circled it five times around the Masan image, and left.

Until this point all the male friends and relatives of the afflicted woman — any male from her *mait*, it seemed, who wanted to eat some meat — had been sitting in a nearby field, indifferently playing cards and gossiping, paying little or no attention to the ritual. The cooked *haluva* and breads were passed around, and the goat was rapidly cooked and eaten along with bread and tea. The woman did not consume any of the meat, indeed she did not even come close to the field where the men were sitting. The exorcist later told that such was the custom (*dastura*) of women, but that her husband could eat the meat later if he wished; however, he also declined.

At a second, much attenuated *chhaya puja* for a Rajput woman whose *sauryas* was Kacchi village. Her oracle had told her that the ritual should be conducted west of Kacchi and east of Paral, her natal village. The exorcist and I met the woman and two of her husband's kinsmen in Paral, then proceeded to an isolated spot in the jungle where the men all set to work finding water, cutting wood, and kindling a fire. Then they cooked some food: breads made of wheat flour, jaggery and water, fried in mustard oil; and *haluva* made from rice flour. Meanwhile the exorcist located a shady spot near a thorn tree, where he cleared a small, square area by digging up grass, stones and weeds with his hand-scythe.

This time, the fairies' basket had bamboo rather than thorn-branch handles. No chick was brought, and no red powder was placed in the diagram. Two young females cutting grass strayed close to the area where the *puja* was being performed, and were warned off. This time the *chhal* was shaken over a thorn bush rather than over an image of Masan. The exorcist had to consult his book in the middle of the ritual, when an attenuated version of the *chhal puja* was performed. At the end of the ritual, both the exorcist and his female patient made an offering of pounded rice to the fairies.

A second, more extended ritual illustrated the continuing relationship of a *dhyani* to her natal village in very different ways. This was the procession of Ghandyal, a popular local god. Garhwali deities are periodically taken from their temples and carried from village to village with great pomp and ceremony. In general, the significance of these processions varies according to the gender of the deity: goddesses' processions are conceived of as *vidais*, 'escortings' of an outmarried daughter back to her husband's place after a visit to her *mait* (see above), while gods' processions tend to be thought of as king-like tours through a quasi-royal domain. Elsewhere, We have attempted to show that social relations of male domination and female subordination are reproduced in the processions of the goddess Nandadevi and the rituals associated with them (Sax 1990; 1991). Here we concentrate on the procession of the god Ghandyal, in which I participated in 1984. Ghandyal is the *bhumyal* of numerous local villages, and also the 'gatekeeper' (*dwar-pal*) of the Badrinath temple, the largest and most famous temple in the District, and one that has many ties to the kings of Garhwal (see Galey 1986).

Badarinath priests equate him with the godling Ghantakaran, but residents of Chini, the isolated village in Pauri District which sponsored the procession, identified him with Babarik, who is also known as Aravan in Tamil Nadu (see Subba Rao 1976: 272-73; Cunningham 1970: 99; and Anderson 1971: 28, all cited in Hiltebeitel 1988: 317). Ghandyal's procession occurs but once in a generation: before 1984 it had last occurred in 1952, and before that in 1927. Normally, the god is specially worshipped twice a year following the Spring and Winter harvests: during the light half of the month of *Margasirsa,* and later during the light half of *Asadha*. His special 1984 procession began on the thirteenth solar day of the *Margasirsa* and ended on the ninth solar day of *Pausa*, for a total of twenty — seven days.

It was conceived of as a meandering pilgrimage (*tirtha yatra*) of the god, in which he was taken to a local confluence of rivers (samgam) for a bath, then brought back to be re-established in his home village. The cult of Ghandyal is strongly associated with the dominant local caste of Rajputs: Chini is a Rajput village, the majority of participants in the procession were Rajputs, and indeed the two chief priests of Ghandyal were members of the Rajput castes of *pajni* and *bheda*. On the first day of the procession, I was surprised to hear one of the pilgrims state that Ghandyal refused to eat food prepared by Brahmans; however other pilgrims, embarassed by their companion's frankness, hastened to point out the presence of a Brahman in the procession. Ghandyal was accompanied on his progress by a fierce goddess named Kalinka.

Participants were neither clear nor unanimous about why she came along on the journey; however, most of those asked reported that it was she, not Ghandyal, who consumed the blood of the goat sacrifices and buffalo slaughters that were performed at the conclusion of the procession. On the night before the procession began, several hundred persons, residents of Chini and their guests, danced and sang from dusk until dawn. Next morning a mini-procession led by drums meandered through the village, gathering pilgrims who proceeded to a river below the village for a purifying bath. The group then proceeded to Ghandyal's storehouse (*bhandara*) in a field above the village. There was a great deal of excitement; the crowd had several times to be calmed by the priests, who insisted that the procession would not begin until the sun rose over a nearby mountain. Finally, the first rays appeared; simultaneously a goat was sacrificed and the god's 'sign' (*nisan*) was lofted into the sunlight.

This sign was constructed of a bamboo pole eighteen hands (about thirty feet) long', near the top of which a small crosspiece had been affixed.

On the very top of the pole was a small silver vessel (*kalasa*), and hanging from the crosspiece was a yak-tail, whisk (*chamvar*). As intended, the whole effect was quite anthropomorphic: Ghandyal seemed to tower above us, his hoary beard swaying beneath a glittering silver crown. Behind him fluttered a red-and-white cape perhaps three feet wide and forty feet long; when Ghandyal moved along the mountain trails, one or two pilgrims would follow with sticks to keep this cloth from touching the ground or becoming entangled in overhanging branches. For the first two days, some forty pilgrims took part in the procession. First of all went the drummers, members of the lowest caste called Das. Several yards behind them came men sprinkling water along the trail to purify it. Then came a series of pilgrims bearing different implements and instruments: a lit incense brazier, bell, basket of *puja* materials, yak-tail whisk, iron rod, another bell, more water-sprinklers, small drums, cymbals, a conch shell, raw, husked rice for worship, incense, and brass horns, followed by the *nisan* itself. A crowd would often have gathered at the outskirts of a village before Ghandyal arrived, and when he came in sight many people would become spontaneously possessed, shouting joyful greetings to the visiting god. Then his *nisan* would be carried to the central square (*pandav chauk*) and 'planted' there, after which Ghandyal would be worshipped by the villagers.

As part of the worship, every household in the village was required to make an offering of grain, and the food thus collected was relayed back to Chini by pligrims from there. Ghandyal's pilgrimage terminated in the same village nearly a month later. Again, the day's activities began with a meandering procession down to the river for a bath. Then all the assembled guests, who this time numbered in the thousands, proceeded to a nearby, terraced field where they sat down in a long line to partake of a communal feast. The great majority of these invited guests were local Rajputs. One Chini villager told me that seven and a half quintals (1650 pounds) each of flour and rice, one quintal of lentils, and ten-thousand leaf-plates were utilized for this monumental affair, the largest such feast I ever saw in Garhwal. After it was over, the assembled multitude climbed to the summit, at about 9500 feet, of the neighbouring mountain, where goats and a buffalo were sacrificed, concluding Ghandyal's procession until the next generation once again takes up his *nisan*.

On quizzing some local Brahmans about the reason behind Ghandyal's procession, they told that after a deity had sat in a temple for four, or twelve, or even thirty years, a blight (*dos*) would eventually fall on the countryside. "Why should it?" I asked. "Why not just keep on worshipping him in his temple? Why should a *dos* fall on anyone?" I continued to press them on the point, until one of them answered: "The territory demands it (*ilaka mangta hai*)". One might say that the *dos* is like a disease of the land for which the procession is a cure.

To undertake such a long, involved ritual is a dangerous business. One man complained that 'to stand up Ghandyal' was a great risk, because the villagers must not deviate from a set of strict ritual prescriptions. Were something to go wrong and the god blight the region, the villagers of Chini would be held accountable. For example, he continued, the *nisan* was once accidentally dropped in the river where it floated downstream to a cremation ground and was used by a low-caste man as wood for a funeral pyre. Drought and famine ensued. Another man told me that disaster results if the *dhyanis* of Chini village are ignored or forgotten during this procession. As he put it,

> Tomorrow when we take up his sign, if we fail to go to any *dhyani*, and she sheds a tear and calls out (our names), then her curse will fall on us. So he (Ghandyal) said the same thing: "If you fail to take me somewhere, or if you show me some evil deed and I shed a single tear, it will split the earth."

"We don't have to approach a father or a son (*bap laudu ke pas jana*)", he had said, "but we must certainly go to each dhyani's village." The *dhyanis* of Chini village were required to attend the first day's activities if at all possible, and the bus in which I rode to Chini for the first day for the procession was filled with them. Most important, the route taken by the deity was determined by the residences of his *dhyanis*. The procession was confined to four adjacent land divisions (*patti*) with whom residents of Chini 'have dealings' (*vyavahara chalna*); in other words, where Chini's daughters lived with their husbands. An effort was made to stay in a village where some *dhyanis* from Chini resided (or, failing that, where a Ghandyal temple was located), for each of the twenty-seven nights of the procession. When the god arrived in a given village, and after an initial series of rituals that 'established' him in the central dancing square (*pandav chauk*), villagers would approach the *nisan* to make their offerings. This was always done in a particular order: first locally-resident men, and then the *dhyanis* of Chini village, followed by anyone else who happened to be there.

In one village, I saw a man climb onto a house and call out over the rooftops that it was time for all the *dhyanis* of Chini to come forward and make their offerings (*dhyanis bhyunt*). I also noticed that these women gave five or ten or even twenty rupees, as compared with the Rs. 1.25 given by most other worshippers. It is common in Garhwal to require out-married *dhydnis* to participate in the processions of their village deities. The goddess Bhagavati of Taramath also goes on procession once every few decades accompanied by the *nisan* (newly fashioned for the occasion) of her bodyguard, the deity Timundya. Her procession passes through the villages of all the *dhyanis* of Taramath up to a considerable distance, and each is required to offer one goat, along with a quantity of rice and jaggery, to the goddess.

Those who live at greater distances are expected to remit their contributions via postal money order. Uma Devi, the village goddess of Namuri village, goes to each and every local village where her *dhyanis* reside during her procession, which happens every ten to fifteen years. At such a time, the newly-married *dhyanis* of Namuri must publicly worship her. It was told that formerly the rule was that each newly-married *dhyani* from Namuri had to give a 'tax' or 'tribute' (*vasul*) of twenty-five rupees to the goddess when she came round.

However this was levied only once, so that when Uma Devi came round a second time, ten or fifteen years later, these dhyanis were not required to make any donation. Elderly informants from Chini and nearby villages told that in previous time, a tax (*kara*) was assessed on all the *dhydnis* of Chini during Ghandyal's processions: either one goat or fifty rupees. This 'tax' sas independent of a contribution of rice, which no dhyani could avoid. This amount seemed to be exaggerated; nevertheless the fact remains that in numerous ways — through taxes and tributes, myths and forms of worship, and especially in terms of its route — the processions of Ghandyal reaffirm once each generation that the *dhyanis* of Chini remain daughters of their *mait*, even though they live elsewhere with their husbands. This relationship is conceived of as one of benevolent affection on the part of Ghandyal.

One morning when the procession left a village and began to struggle up a steep hillside toward the next halting place, my assistant noticed that Ghandyal's *nisan* was facing backward. He presumed that this was an error, and told the *nisan*-bearers to rotate Ghandyal so that he would face forward up the hillside. "No," they responded, "we can't do that Ghandyal is having a last look at his *dhyanis*." The *chhal puja* and the procession of Ghandyal both required the presence of out-married daughters in their natal places. Together with *doharagamana* and other occasions for female visiting, they demonstrate that in Garhwal, a *dhyani* does not cease to become part of her *mait* after marriage. The *chhal puja* was evidently intended to be therapeutic; having acquired a demon rather as one acquires an infection, the woman had to return to her mait to slough it off. This fundamental requirement illustrates the simplest form of enduring relationship between a woman and her *mait*; one of substance: the *mait*, or something from it, is literally part of her. In this case, it is a part that she wishes to be rid of, and she must return to her mait for that operation.

The refusal of patients and their husbands to accept any prasada (the cooked goat, etc.) from the ritual, underscores their intention to leave every trace of the *chhal* in the place it came from. Likewise, it is striking that men participating in the feast cared so little about eating such inauspicious food. Evidently, their ('demonic') desire for meat outweighed any reluctance they might have felt. After he returned home, the exorcist fed to his children a banana that had been offered to Masan during the worship; obviously its 'inauspiciousness' did not *disturb* him too much. Might it not be the case that the *chhal,* having been brought back to its appropriate place (of origin), was no longer a threat? What precisely happened to the *chhal*? I am not sure. Clearly, it was transferred away from the woman into the goat, and the goat was then offered to Masan. Later, the assembled males of the woman's natal village ate the goat which had by definition become the transvalued leftovers or *prasad* of the demon.

Do the men then eat the *chhal*? Certainly none of them described the feast in these terms. Rather, they spoke in terms of satisfaction. As one participant in the feast put it, everyone has to eat their fill — not only Masan (whom this man understood to be the afflicting agent), but also Chhal Bhairav (lord of demons) and his subjects (*praja*), who include both demons (*bahiyal*) and men. If any of these were unsatisfied, they could demand that the *puja* be performed again. The language is one of obligations and rights: as one man put it after the feast: "Now everyone has received his share (*hissa*)." Similar language was used in the procession of Ghandyal (and others), where *dhyanis* were obligated to pay a tribute (*kara*) to the deities of their natal villages.

This is perhaps related to the sense of obligation that women continue to feel toward their parents. Indeed, one of the most frequently and clearly stated themes in our interviews was that the attachment (*lobh*) of a woman to her *mait* is largely a matter of responsibility and obligation, she feels that she should try always to be available should her parents have some need or difficulty. Ghandyal's procession was a quasi-royal one; he roamed through his domain taking worship, money and grain from many villages, especially those where one of his *dhyanis* resided.

These women had hardly severed their connections with Chini village after marriage; on the contrary, they were the media through which Ghandyal and his villagers asserted a kind of royal claim on all Rajput lands in the immediate locale. Such expressions of an outmarried woman's enduring relationship to the land and people of her birth have a special place in Garhwali culture; elsewhere (Sax 1991: Chap. 3). I have suggested that this may be an effect of the local brideprice system, which is nearly extinct. However, periodic visits of women to their natal places is attested from all parts of North India, and ritual expressions of this relationship are not all that rare — rather, they have been simply ignored. This leads to an interesting set of questions. Why is it that male high-caste informants tend to emphasize the completeness of a bride's transfer at marriage, and why did an earlier generation of scholars (and some members of the present one) take this as the cultural paradigm for the nature of Hindu marriage in general?

For anthropologists at least, I would suggest that the answer lay in their reluctance to part with analytic categories they had created and reified — in this case, the categories of "kinship" analysis — combined with their theoretical devaluation of the categories of thought and levels of custom actually practiced in the society. In short, they preferred the formal elegance of a schematized "kinship system" to the apparent formlessness of practice. As Nicholas puts it, obsession with agnation is "an anthropologist's fiction, created out of the linear organisation of the genealogical diagram rather than a Hindu conception of relatiohship" (1981: 377). In Garhwali culture, it is not so much the case that women are transferred from one place to another after marriage, as that women and the places they inhabit are mutually determining and, because of womens' movements between places, constantly changing.

Marriott (1976) has argued that South Asian persons are not "individuals" but rather "dividuals" composed of various inputs. The nature of these inputs and the combinations they assume vary according to numerous parameters, creating a fluid system of astounding complexity. Some of the most important of these parameters are time and place which, as the spatio-temporal loci of shifting inputs, may themselves be regarded as complex inputs which partly determine persons' natures. Thus, the qualities of village hamlets and the effects that they have on persons are thought to be due in large part to the presumed natures of the people who live in them; conversely, when a woman changes residence at marriage, her nature and substance are thereby altered. Men say this is a sudden and total change; women tend to have a more "gradualistic" perspective. Neither perspective violates the shared ontology, 'though each is grounded in self-interest. Hence we can say that men and women have different perspective on the effects of local custom, without resorting to the tempting (but ultimately untenable) position that men and women live in different cultures'.

Notes

1. Lall (1942: 89) argues that it is the *anchal* ceremony, rather than the *phera* or circumambulation, that is the crucial unificatory act in Garhwali weddings, and my fieldnotes support his contention.
2. *Bharaja*, lit. "load-bearer."
3. Gotra denotes a 'fictive', exogamous kin group; jdti means literally 'genus' or species', is usually translated "caste".
4. As a noun, *sapinda* refers to that category of relations for whom one observes birth and death pollution; a *sapinda* relationship is a "shared body relationship" (Nicholas 1981: 377).
5. Fruzetti has attributed the continuing relationship of a married daughter and her natal home to shared blood (*rakta*): despite the numerous

transformations of wedding rites and marriage, blood does not change (1982: 21, 119-120 and *passim*).

6. Mr. Chittaranjan Dutt and I separately interviewed about thirty-five Garhwali women of various castes and classes. All names in the interviews below are pseudonyms. Selected transliterations are offered below for those interested in the Pahari dialect.

7. *Ar ta tab tai i ghaur par cha asali jad: Tab takhi bite jayemda phumd. Ja tau tai ghaur par apada bhai-baina chhina. Sab se pyar paill si lagada. Ar takhi bite ran syu ja jad. Takhi bite ta huna sya paida. Utpann. Tabai aun birana ghaur bhi. Haim? Suruat to takhi cha. Tau mam, pita, bhai-baina, kdka, boda, saub tai ghaur par biten Mian. Jad takhi bita i chhan. Ta takh biti aun lukhar ghaur mam.*

8. *Man ka vichar kya hoya? Jab khud lagi ta roya dhoya. Bulyonro cha tab ju dagada mam rail. Tab sasural vald mait bhejadim ni. Ba jo thaim na lagadu buru ta boladan run dya. Jvan-jaman chhan. Rona kilai chhan? Khanai kami ni, pairane kami ni. Kaiyom taim daya a.i janad bhej dindan.*

9. *Chha kabari ghumanu-ghamanu mi janadu chhau ki ve pariar math mina jaun. Lalasd hve jdmda cha. Par daur bi lagadi i chhai kya patd kan hund? Kya humd? Baut daur lagadi chhai buva! Ta daur bi lagadi i chhai par lalasa bhihve jarha.*

10. Such patterns seem to have been encouraged by the nearly-defunct custom of child marriage; see Mountaineer 1860: 200ff.

11. Garhwali women do not traditionally bind the *rakhi*-thread around their brothers' hands as do women in other parts of North India. This is instead done by one's Brahmin *purohit*, which was the usual custom in the plains too, before the seventeenth century (Ann Pearson, personal comm.).

12. But compare Jacobson (1977: 279), who reports that female visits to their natal villages are slightly more frequent during labour-intensive periods such as planting, harvesting, and so forth.

13. Cf. Tambiah 1973: 96ff.

14. *Arasa* is made of rice that is soaked, pounded, strained, mixed with jaggery, then fried in oil.

15. These customs are more-or-less defunct now, since people generally use buses for transport.

16. Compare Bennett's account of the "return of the bride" (*dulan pharkaune*) in Nepal: "[B]y orthodox account the bride should return to her maita only after the fifth night after the *kanyadan* — the night during which according to orthodox tradition the marriage may be consummated" (1983: 91).

17. *Kai chizom bhi adhikar, kai chlj layun se, dyon se kuchh bhi, pura adhikar, khaunai pakanai adhikar. Koi bhi pratibandha ni, jya kara, jamanya kara. Ghaur bhi yan na ki yai ray ghaur mi na jyarh par sraddhd yan raumd chhai ki. Ta kastha bhi holu ki, yi kya khali kan kai rauli? Dux- char din raun cha tab...*
18. Nose-ring, bangles, and red vermilion in the hairpart are auspicious signs of wifehood. Garhwali women remove them when divorced or widowed.
19. *Bvari*, 'little wife', a diminutive term of endearment.
20. *Ham ta prem kuchh chhau ni chhau na vakh. Ar na tu vakho kuchh lobh ni chhau. Ta lobh myaru vakhi chho maite. Abhi bi mi apu thaim (sauryas) thodi bathdndu. Ek bar ta (sauryas) ain ta mila boll "kakhai chhai?" "(Mait) chhaum." Kyo bolan ki (sauryas) chhaum? (Sauryas) ta jib mam andi i na cha. Menita (mait) zindagi katim.*
21. Compare for instance the account of *chhai puja* obtained by Chittaranjan Dutt: "The object (*uddesya*) of this is to obtain offspring (*santan*). Therefore the shadows (*chaya) of the elderly (vrddha*) or of young maidens (*kanya kumari*) are not worshipped. So those women worship the *chaya* who have no offspring, or whose offspring die quickly. In the *chdyd puja* a living chicken (*mungi/kukhadd*), a ram or a goat are given (*chor dena*) in the name of Chhaya Devi. A *jhadkamdi* or a bakya pow-caste ritual specialist] does the *puja*. And ordinary priest (*samanya purohit*) cannot do the *chhaya pujan*. Some people believe that because the shadow of an dchari [Skt. *apsara*] or a *matari* [malevolent female deity] falls on a woman, she cannot give birth to a child, or her children soon die. And the woman has a child (*bachcha*). This pujd is not now prevalent." For cuTfuraT diversity generally within the central Himalyas, see Berremann 1960.
22. *Pithaim*, ground turmeric, sandalwood or vermilion, used to mark the participants (gods, priests, clients, sacrificial animals, containers, implements, drums, etc.) in a ritual, and to transfer substances among them.
23. Torn quarters (*changatira*) of work-baskets (*kande*) woven of local bamboo (*ringol*) are frequently employed in local rituals as vessels for foods offered to low, dangerous, and inauspicious beings.
24. Note that Masan is called a god (*devata*), not a demon.
25. The fifth wheat cake was actually placed behind the image, but it was explained to me that this was symbolic of the center where he sits.
26. The round adornments worn by Indian women on their foreheads.
27. This last action was good dramaturgy. Later the materials were distributed at the exorcist's house.

28. The exorcist told me that the *chhal* was 'sent away' during the *chhaya.' puja*, but this seems unlikely to me. A second participant said that Masan is the same as the *Chhal*.
29. There are a great number of local, endogamous groups whose members consider themselves 'Rajputs'. The traditional local distinction between ('authentic') immigrant Rajputs and local *Khas* Rajputs was adopted by colonial authorities as well as anthropologists, but the appellation *Khas* connotes backwardness and inferiority, and nowadays 'Khasiya' has become a term of abuse. (See Berremann 1972: 14-20 and references therein).
30. *Gaj*, used to excavate a small hole upon arrival in the central square of a village upon arrival, in which to place Ghandyal's nisan.
31. *Jab tak bhaul nisan le janya na, ta kai dhyainl ma ni jaula, unila ams dholela unit go hamu pari hamkar laigo. Uni go hamupar ghat lago. To uni vela bi baule. Agar turmmitai kakhi ni le jala aur kvi buro kam dikhyaila, to myar iki ams chhutan par bhyamkila prithvi phat jali.*

References

Anderson, Mary M. 1971. *The Festivals of Nepal*. London: Allen and Unwin.

Bennett, Lynn. 1983. *Dangerous Wives and Sacred Sisters: Social and Symbolic Roles of High-Caste Women in Nepal*. New York: Columbia University Press.

Berreman, Gerald. 1960. Cultural variability and drift in the Himalayan hills. *American Anthropologist*, 62(5): 774-794.

—. 1962(a) Sib and Clan among the Pahari of North India. *Ethnology*, I: 524-28.

—. 1962(b) Village exogamy in northernmost India. *Southwestern Journal of Anthropology*, 18: 55-8.

—. 1972. *Hindus of the Himalayas*. Berkeley: University of California Press (revised second edition).

Bhattacharya, Surendramohana (ed.). 1973-74. *Purohita-darpana*. 37th ed. Revised by Yogendrachandra Vyakaranatirtha Vidyartha. Calcutta: Saytanarayana Library.

Campbell, J. Gabriel. 1976. *Saints and Householders: A Study of Hindu Ritual and Myth Among the Kangra Rajputs*. Kathmandu: Bibliotheca Hamalayica, Ratna Pustak Bhandar.

Cunningham, Alexander. 1970 (reprinted). *Report of a Tour in the Punjab in 1878-79*. Archaeological Survey of India, Vol. 14. Varanasi: Indological Book House.

Daniel, E. Valentine. 1979. From Compatibility to Equipoise: The Nature of Substance in Tamil Culture. Doctoral dissertation. Department of Anthropology, The University of Chicago.

—. 84. *Fluid Signs: Being a Person the Tamil Way*. Berkeley: University of California Press.

Fruzetti, Lina M. 1982. *The Gift of a Virgin: Women, Marriage, and Ritual in a Bengali Society*. New Brunswick, New Jersey: Rutgers University Press.

Galey, Jean-Claude. 1986. Totalit et hirarchie dans les sanctuaries royaux du Tehri-Garhwal (Himalaya indien). In: Jean-Claude Galey, (ed.), *L'Espace du Temple II: Les Sanctuaries dans le Royaume*. Paris: cole des Hautes tudes en Sciences Sociales (Collection *Purusartha*, 10).

Gould, Harold A. 1961. A further note on village exogamy in North India. *Southwestern Journal of Anthropology*, 17: 30-34.

Hiltebeitel, Alf 1988. The Cult of Draupadi. 1. *Mythologies*. Chicago: The University of Chicago Press.

Inden, Ronald and Ralph W. Nicholas. 1977. *Kinship in Bengali Culture*. Chicago: The University of Chicago Press.

Joshi, L.D. 1929 [1984]. *Tribal People of the Himalayas: A Study of the Khasas*. Delhi: Mittal Publications. First published in 1929 as The *Khasa Family Law in the Himalayan Districts of the United Provinces of India*. Allahabad: Superintendent, Government Press, U.P.

Jacobson, Doranne. 1977. Flexibility in central Indian kinship and residence. In: Kenneth David (ed.), *The New Wind: Changing Identities in South Asia*. The Hague; Paris: Mouton.

Lall, Panna, I.C.S. 1942. *Hindu Customary Law in Kumaon*. Allahabad: Superintendant, Printing and Stationery. United Provinces, India. (Orig. published 1921 in United Provinces Gazette, VIII. 979.)

Leslie, I. Julia. 1989. *The Perfect Wife: The Orthodox Hindu Woman According to the Stridharmapaddhati of Tryambakayajvan*. Delhi : Oxford University Press.

Moore, Melinda A. 1985. A new look at the Nayar taravad. *Man*, n.s., 20 (3): 523-41

Mountaineer, A. 1860. *A Summer Ramble in the Himalayas*. London: Hurst and Blackett.

Nicholas, Ralph W. 1981. *Sraddha*, impurity, and relations between the living and the dead. *Contributions to Indian Sociology*, (n.s.), 15 (1-2): 367-79.

Raheja, Gloria Goodwin. 1988. *The Poison in the Gift: Ritual, cheef word and the Dominant Caste in a North Indian Village*. Chicago: The University of Chicago Press.

Sanwal, Rami, 1976. *Social Stratification in Rural Kumaon.* Bombay: Oxford University Press.

Sax, William S. 1990. Village daughter, village goddess: residence, gender, and politics in a Himalayan Pilgrimage. *American Ethnologist*, 17 (3): 491-512.

—. 1991. *Mountain Goddess: Gender and Politics in a Himalayan Pilgrimage.* New York: Oxford University Press.

Subba Rao; T.V. 1976. Teluga folk additions to the Mahabharatha. *Folklore* (Calcutta), 17 (8-9): 269-75.

13
Culture and Traditions of Himachal

Food and Drink

The Kinners grow Bathua. They take their meals thrice a day—morning tea is a must for all. They do not generally take milk because it is not available in appreciable quantity. Whatever milk their little cows yield they convert into butter which they store in leather pouches. They relish meat. Vegetarians among them are rare. It is strange to note that the eggs, fowls and fish are taboos to all although the modern generation have started io take them. The home-made brew is presented on all special occasions. Even at the time of *puja* and *Havans*, the wine is served as charnamrit to the devotees. It is a common drink for gents but surprisingly the ladies do not like and children are also kept away. Smoking is widely prevalent among the Kinners. The boys also cultivate their habit as their parents do not generally object. While in migration the people will carry a pouch full of tobacco but have their *Hukka*-with them. In the absence of the same, they scoop out two holes in the ground and connect them with a covered passage known as "*Matyang chilam*". In one hole they place tobacco and burning ambers and suck the smoke at the other end lying flat on. the ground. This shows how fond of smoking they are!

The tribals use brasr and bronze utensils in their houses but aluminium wares are used during migration period. The Kinners are a pastoral people both polygamous and polyandrous. Though their main occupation is rearing sheep and goat raising for wool, many tribals are engaged in agriculture and gardening too. The women folk are (beautiful, modest and comely. They are hard working and lively. One can observe a Kinner woman working throughout the day in her fields. She has to level her field and sow the seed single handed. The man is responsible for only ploughing the field once in a year while the poor woman has to do watering, weeding, keeping watch, fencing, harvesting and husking too, throughout the year. On the top of it, she has to take the grain to the market for barter or sale purposes. The Kinners grow bathua, potato, Koda pulses and wild fruits form their staple diet.

Religion

A vast majority of Kinners are Budhists under the influence of Tibetans, they have adopted this religion especially in the Northern half of the Chini subdivision. Almost every village has a Buddhist temple where a lama worships and stays day and night there. They also believe in various Hindu Gods like Badrinath, Maheshwar and Bhagwati. But their worship is catholic to a degree. Wine and meat are offered to the Devatas. Goats are sacrificed in the name of local deities. Involved in blind faiths, the Kinners observe untouchability like Hindus.

On festive days like Diwali, Holi and Shivratri some big fairs are held. Worship of Rama, Ganesh and Krishna is, generally, not known to the Tribals. A girl who is unable to find suitable groom, becomes a Jomo. She remains unmarried and serves her father in his field as a labourer without wage. But she is free to marry a man if she gets a suitable husband, even after years of ordination.

Temple Dance

The Kinners celebrate their festivals with all gaiety. Baisakhi or Beesh is celebrated on the 1st of Baishak. The Goddess is brought out of the temple and a fair is held in the courtyard of the temple. They gather in colourful dress, drink and dance for hours together. Annual worship as Koshme, Shukud, Sazo, Deeval, Flaich, Dakhraini and Sukar constitute some of the festivals celebrated on various occasions. The Badhis celebrate Shivratri. As the fairs and festivals are associated with the religion, there are occasional sacrifices of animals too. Chandika appears to be a cruel Goddess and rules her subjects with a stiff rod. She demands too many sacrifices from them. The Kjnners believe that as she is the well-wisher of her people, it is in their interest to please her by sacrificing animals. She is really a benevolent tyrant.

Evil Spirits

The Kinners believe in evil spirits of many types such as ghosts, ruksas, Khunkch, etc. Banshir is a ghost believed to live in a forest or kail tree. It can assume many shapes of a huge man, jackal, monkey and is believed to be a very cruel spirit but not more than Chan who is supposed to inflict sickness to whom it meets during odd hours of the night.

A man who commits a heinous sin during his life turns into a ghost known as Ruksas and it is supposed that he will never get salvation. Khunkch is believed as a house spirit who can be passed to the other house by selling one's animal or marrying one's daughter. A puja is done toward off the evil spirits.

The people believe that Shukla Paksh is an auspicious occasion for agricultural operations. The tribals prefer Tuesday and Saturday for ploughing and sowing. Before ploughing, the earth is worshipped, by offering a *chilta* or some *sattu.* A stone is also broken on a crossroad to dispel the evil influences.

Hard Life

Life in Kinner region is really hard. No doubt the frequently used old mule path the Hindustan-Tibet road—has been widened from five to eight feet broad over which the traders and tourists; travel safely, the most of the paths in this region are nothing more than tracks, winding over steep and desolate hills. The tribals though facing all these obstacles in life, are honest, frank and hospitable people. In the olden days the guests were treated like God there but due to the hungry eyes of lustful outsiders, ready to exploit their sex norms, the tribals now look upon them with suspicion and hatred. 'Kocha' is a well known term of abhorrence used by the Kinners for outsiders.

Song and Dance

Living a hard life in the utmost liquidity of nature, music has become an important companion of the Kinners. They sing while working in the fields, weeding out the grass, going to the market and at the festive occasions. The gaiety and confidence of the people residing in these valleys find expression in their songs and dances.

There are three types of folk dances enjoyed by the tribals:

(i) Kayang
(ii) Bakayang
(iii) Bonyangchu — Chashimik

The first one is the most popular folk dance of the Kinners. Both gents and ladies participate in it. A leader of the party shouts aloud to inspire the dancers who repeat in a mirthful mood. He takes a cloth from the priest after paying some money and indicates the orchestra to begin playing. The rhythm goes on changing. The gents and ladies join two circles. Women folk lead the party of the lady dancers. All make a chain like circles while dancing. Folk songs are also sung at the occasion.

The other dances are also followed by the orchestra and folk songs.

We are giving here two love songs very popular among the Kinners:

"Tika Sahibas lotash, ang hushyari ham tan ?
Hushyari ta lonma. Pangi, Pangtu Chhang,
Pangi Pangtua Chhang, ang, paimashi birayin,
Pangtu Chhangars lotash, gu tuk pa
Ma big
Gu Tuk pa ma big, gu shueve bitak
Tika sahibas lotash, ang hukum ma ronchis
Ang hukum ma ronchis, ne hala
Ring tan ?
Dak ring ringi bima Khonachn Tanghi
Khonachu Thangi, Nyokche Negiu gore,
Nyokcheu jai, Naryam Pali banthin
Naryam Pati banthin, Ywakshi dhaling gyos,
Ganga Sahay munshi, the wakshi jirjya gyos
Naryum banlhin lotash, gu kin
Rang butak,
Ganga Sahay lotash Kiang rang tha jayin,
And Parmi kochang, yule shwalu chimet,
Kinu tong tong, keto, warkyo zopas
Lanchak."

Translation

"Where is my clever man?"
Asked Tika Raghunath Singh
The clever man is known
As son of Pangtu Negi
Who dwells in Pangi."
"O Pangtu's son
Go and work as Patwari
In my new settlement"
Said Tika Sahib to him.

"I won't go to Tukpa
But to Shuwa."
"This is a disobey to my order."
"Why do you say so Sir?"
The boy had to go there
He met a beautiful girl
Her name was Naryum Pati
She greeted Ganga Sahai from below
And he gave her his
salutation from above.
The girl says:
"I will go with you,"
the boy says
"Please don't do so"
"But why?"
"As my wife is no kind
She will beat you
Please don't do so
And only love
I too will love."

Another song has been composed on a love story of Babu Bhup Singh of the Forest Department who fell in love with a woman of the Lippa village named Sembat. The song goes:

Yochalo denta, Bhup Singh Babu,
Bhup Singh Babu lotesh,
Majang Jangramo
Majang Jangramo, "ijap Lippa bi-tak"
Dakknesh—neshi bima, markhona Lippa,
Manechu dena, "Lippa Mukhiya ham tan?"
Dero ham ketayin? Derota ketak
Barjiu dware,
Barjiu morabo kumo, Barjiu
Nyotang chimet
Barjiu nyotang chimet, sema at
Dang Naryang
Banthin ta Naryang, baho ta sembat
Bhup Singh Babu Lotash, Chhat Kang
Zalmig bitak;
Chhat Kang Zalmig Berang, yutung
Sembat tang gyos
Yutung Sembat tang tang, Thakur

Zolmig boshi gyos
Toling chang mang santang, sembatu
Gare dakhat,
Omsta take Barjiu chimet, hun ta
Hachis tarziu chimet
Bhup Singh Babu Kochyang, marjyad
Ma lan gyos;

Marjyad ma lan lan, gudo
Chagulo kholya gyos
Sembatas dakk loshid,
dhagulo fima firayin
Dhagulo fima firayin, shum
Dorin molang;
Dhagulo he li shetak, sembatu
pralb ton ma.

Translation

Babu Bhup Singh reaches Jhangi village and says, "I will go first to Lippa village." He goes straight up. Reaching near Mane cairn, he asked, "Where is the *Mukhiya*?" He is taken in *Mukhiya's* (Barji) house. Barji has two daughters named Sembat and Naryang who were very pretty.

One day Bhup Singh was going to temple and came across a girl. She was none but Sembat, the daughter of Barji. Captivated by her beauty, he forgot to visit the temple and fell in love. Months rolled on. The love story spread here and there. He makes ornaments for her and adopts her a real lover—may be wife. But this relationship does not continue for a longer period. There is tension and finally breaking off the chain. He takes away her ornaments but the girl is also proud. She says, "You may have the ornaments back. They are worth my two fields price. If I am fortunate, there is no reason to get many ornaments."

Folk dances, obviously, form a part of their cultural life. In the movements of the dance can be detected the basic movements of their body in fulfilling the many tasks the Kinners have to perform in life. Attired in typical colourful brocades, the dancers whirl and circle with regulated movements, depicting the struggle with the nature. Waving and clapping, well-trained footwork, turning heads and a high pitch—all this presents a magical panorama on this land of gods. When the Kinner girl dances, her hills nod, when she sings in a melodious voice her valleys echo and the surrounding nature suspends its movements for a while.

Social Change

Kinner Pradesh is eminently suited for growing fruits, viz., grapes, walnut, almonds, apples and peaches and chilgoza. The Government has realised the need to grow more fruits in this area by plantation and providing new implements for horticulture. Similarly, cattle wealth is being improved by cross-breeding between yak and cow. Zo is an improved variety of ox and is sturdier than the ordinary local bull. Zumoo is another superior type of cow and its average milk yield is almost double the cow's. They are the result of cross-breeding.

The village crafts are also given attention of the Government. The Panchayats have inspired the people to work for the welfare of their region. It is worth noting that even before the Nyaya Panchayats and Gram Panchayats, the Kinners had their own tribal committee to solve internal disputes. The multipurpose cooperative movement in the region has also awakened the people.

But it does not mean that these people have made sufficient progress. In fact, they have many problems. The people are yet to be educated. They require a lot of guidance and help in regard to their agricultural methodology and eradication of social backwardness and poverty.

14

Fairs, Festivals, Rituals and Temples in Western Himalayas

Fairs and Festivals

There are innumerable fairs and festivals which the hill people celebrate. There are fairs at village level, others are at a greater scale. Those at tehsil and district levels draw a fairly big crowd. At a small fair the village god is the centre of worship and all those collecting there can be assumed as his devotees. The fairs at higher level draw more than one deity and amongst these Dussehra of Kullu and Shivaratri of Mandi rank above all as the most splendoured and colourful fairs of the hills. These fairs are a big draw not only to the village gods and the rural folk but also to the traders and visitors from far and wide. The whole town is turned into a mela venue where all people are participants in merry-making. Generally, the fairs are held at a time when the people are free of their harvest engagements. They have returns from their labour done over days and nights and the fairs and festivals give them an opportunity to go for things of their need and choice. Traders from far and near join these festivities and a market emerges with all sorts of things, such as clothes and garments, wool and *pashmina*, leather and furs, hides and skins, metalware and pottery, ornaments and jewellery, fruits and vegetables and all the products—raw and finished—coming from the homes and fields of the ruralites.

Leaving apart those articles, which in a way are indispensable to any household, there are shops to meet everybody's requirements of hosiery and cosmetics, cigarettes and tobacco and spectacles and dentures. The products of native crafts and industries find an easy market in these fairs and festivals. One of the entertainments, particular of the hill folk, on the occasions of fairs and festivals, is the swinging chair that nobody likes to miss. Refreshment stalls and bangle sellers also make a good business. The venue of the fair gets a camp-like look. The visitors enjoy the day-long festivities and many of them can be seen resting and sleeping in the night under open starry sky. Some busy with their lilting tunes are awake the night over. The camp presents a mystic sight as the lamps start lighting up, piercing through the overall mantle of darkness.

One of the common features of all the fairs is the folk dance accompanied by the traditional orchestra consisting of *dhol, nagara, narsingha*, *karnal* and *shahnai*. The evenings are usually marked by drama or skit shows but it is the folk drama, called *banthara* or *kariala* which is heartily enjoyed by the audience. Most of the fairs and festivals are celebrated according to the Hindu calendar but most of them can be conspicuously marked for their local colour. There cannot be a better show-window for the culture of a land than its fairs and festivals. Every fair or festival has an interesting legend about it wherein the local people repose their unflinching faith. Of the countless celebrations it will be suffice to deal with only a few here.

Dussehra

Dussehra of Kullu is one of the most important fairs and festivals of India. One thing notable about the Kullu Dussehra is that it starts from the day it ends elsewhere in the country. Raghunath is the chief deity and other deities coming from all big villages of the Kullu district pay the lord their homage. The idol of Raghunath is taken out on a wheeled chariot while the other gods joining him are on their wheelless chariots, the latter being carried with the help of poles resting on the shoulders of the people accompanying them. The traditional hill orchestra fill the air with mirth and gaiety. The procession, called *rathyatra,* is watched by thousands of people. The *rathyatra* symbolises Rama's march against Ravana. The *rath* (chariot) is kept in the Dhalpur Maidan of the town for five days till the purnamashi (full moon night). One of the main attractions of the Dussehra festivities is a chain of folk songs and dances taking the shape of community rejoicings. The village folk attired in their traditional best abandon themselves to the melodious tunes of the hill orchestra. They sing and dance and it seems as if it is an unending affair. The whole atmosphere is charged with ecstasy, mirth and delight.

Another attraction for the visitors to the festival is a market of shawls, blankets and *gudmas* in a great variety for which the Kullu valley is internationally known.

At the end of the festival, Ravana, Kumbhakaran and Meghnath are ceremonially killed at the bank of the river Beas and the *rath* of Raghunath, joined by thousands of gay people, comes back to its place of start.

Shivaratri

Shiva is the most favourite god of the hill folk and if there is any festival celebrated through the length and breadth of the Himalayas, it is Shivaratri. In the western Himalayas Shivaratri of Mandi ranks above all. Commencing as a festival in the last of February or early March, it develops into a week-long fair. The cult of Shiva being deep-rooted in the Himalayas, Shivaratri fair attracts people from far and wide. On any day at least ten thousand outsiders visit the town and many of them can be seen camping on the premises of the many old temples with which the town is meticulously studded. It is with the melodious din of the hill orchestra that the gods and goddesses on their wheelless chariots, carried on the shoulders of their devotees, throng to the town of Mandi to pay their homage to the great god Shiva.

The fair provides for an annual meeting of the gods with lord Shiva on the one hand and amongst themselves on the other. With a view to giving the hill gods a befitting welcome the town is tastefully decorated and thousands of hill folk attired in their traditional best participate in the fair. The hill gods on their arrival first visit the shrine of Raj Madhav who was considered as the ruling deity of the erstwhile state. When once in the history of Mandi State the Raja happened to be without a heir, Raj Madhav, a form of Vishnu, was installed as the state deity and the administration was pledged to him. The Raja became his representative and ruled the state on his behalf. This warded off in future the tendency of a Raja turning an autocrat or a despot.

The festivities conclude with a *jagara*, i.e. overnight vigil wherein the gods and their devotees both participate. The main events of the ensuing year are forecast and the people are cautioned against the dangers to their life, property and livestock. Before the gods leave the town, they are offered sheets of silken cloth besides fruits and incense. The *puja* is performed after which they take leave of the great god Shiva. The orchestra is played upon and the deities depart with the promise to meet next year again.

Minjar

The week-long festivities of the colourful Minjar fair of Chamba start on the second Sunday of Shravan (August). When was Minjar first celebrated is not known but the present form of the fair is attributed to Raja Sahil Verma who ruled the state in the 10th century. As legend has it the Ravi had its course through the place now known as Chawgan. On one side of the river stands the shrine of Rani Champavati and on the other is the famous temple of Hari Rai. A sage was staying at the Champavati temple and every morning he would swim over the river and visit the Hari Rai temple. As he enjoyed faith and respect of the Chamba folk, they thought of approaching the Raja to so arrange that the Hari Rai *darshan* is easily available to him as well as to the people. On the advice of the sage the Raja arranged a week-long *yajna* (religious sacrifice and oblation) and the lord Varuna—the god of waters—was prayed for changing the river course. The lord obliged and the river changed its course. Since then the event began to be celebrated on a large scale.

The Minjar fair is also associated with an important event in the history of Chamba State. In his fight against a Kangra ruler, Raja Pratap Singh Verman of Chamba emerged victorious and while coming back from Bhatiat, he was given a rousing reception by his people who greeted him with the tentacles of maize and paddy plants. On the conclusion of the fair, i.e., on third Sunday of the month Shravan (August), a procession, which is joined by thousands of local people and mela enthusiasts along with police bands and hill orchestra, starts from Akhand Chandi Palace and goes to the bank of the Ravi. A small platform is raised overlooking the river. A coconut, a rupee or a smaller coin, a fruit and a few paddy tentacles tied in a piece of *lohan*, a type of rid cloth usually offered to the goddess, are usual offerings to the Ravi. Those, who cannot afford to make such offerings, do with paddy tentacles only. Folk songs are sung. The music is again played when the procession is on its way back to Chawgan.

Renuka

The legend goes that a sage, named Jamdagni, had his *ashram* (hermitage) somewhere near the lake where he was living along with his wife Renuka. The sage was murdered by one named Sahasrarjuna. Renuka was a very devoted wife. Struck by the incident, she jumped into the lake, thus putting an end to her life. The lake was named after Renuka, who assumed the status of a goddess after the great sacrifice. The event is celebrated every year from 10 to 12th day of the bright half of the Kartika (November) month at Renuka in tehsil Pachhad of district Sirmur.

Another legend has it that the sage Jamdagni along with his wife, Renuka, lived on a hillock which is still called after him, *Jamu ki dhar*. Both of them were devotees of the lord Vishnu whose penance they held for many years. Pleased at this, the lord wanted to give them a boon. They expressed their desire for a son. They got many but the eldest was the lord himself. He was Parshuram, sixth incarnation of the god Vishnu. Renuka used to fetch fresh water from the river Yamuna every day. One day on her return she came across a nude Gandharva couple. The amorous sight aroused passion in her and the earthen pot in which she was carrying water for her sage husband showed a crack. When Renuka related the incident to her husband, he got annoyed and held it as an act of sacrilege. The sage wanted to punish the wife. All the sons were called up and asked to behead the mother. They all refused but the eldest son, Parshuram, carried out the orders of his father by killing the mother and all the brothers. Jamdagni was pleased with Parshuram and he thought of granting him a boon.

The only reward Parshuram could ask for was the revival of all the dead. The wish was granted and all came to life again. Parshuram did not stay with his parents. Instead he wanted to go for penance some were in Badrinath. Before leaving, he promised to visit his parents once a year. Renuka fair is held to commemorate Purshuram', visit to his mother. On the 10th day of the bright half of the month Kartika (November) the idol of Parshuram, seated in a well decorated palanquin, is taken out in procession which treks the path of some eight kilometres from village Jamu to the site of the lake Renuka. The two deities held as embodiments of the lord Parshuram, from villages Kattah and Masu also join the procession which is attended by hill orchestra. A few folk dancors dressed in long garb with loose sleeves add to the gaiety of the procession as they dance to the accompaniment of the folk music. On the 11th day, i.e., Ekadashi, the son stays with his mother and on the 12th afternoon he takes leave for Jamu with a promise to visit next year.

Lavi

The word *lavi* is derived from the word *loe* which in local parlance means a sheet of woollen cloth. Another meaning of *lavi* is shearing of the sheep. Lavi fair, as the past accounts run, took place twice in the months of Jyeshtha (June) and Kartika (November) which are suited to shearing of sheep, thus making available the wool in abundance. With the changing circumstances the Lavi fair has come to be celebrated only once a year, i.e., sometime in the month of November. As against most of the fairs of the hills having religious background, Lavi is purely a trade fair but imbued with rich traditions.

Sometime back when Rampur and the adjoining areas had no road links, the fair meant a great deal as it provided good marketing opportunities to the people of a vast region including entire upper Simla district, Kinnaur district and Seraj area of Kullu district. The commodities, coming up for sale being uncommon and rare in quality, attracted people and traders from far-off places in India and Tibet. It is difficult to say when and how this fair made a beginning but it can be understood that it cropped up out of sheer necessity of the area producing in abundance commodities like *pashmina*, pashmina-sheets, wool, woollen sheets, *gudma*, namda, carpets, dry fruits like *chilgoza*, walnuts, almond and zeera. Apart from these commodities of common use, the Kinnauri ponies and dogs also come for sale, the latter known for their loyalty and dependence. The gaddis, the handsome tribe of the Himalayas, have them as watchdogs for their herds of sheep.

For days before the fair takes place, the people with their tiny donkeys, ponies and herds of sheep and goats can be seen trekking all along the higher hills of Kinnaur and the adjacent areas. Until 1962 the traders from Kinnaur and Rampur Bushahr had their business contacts with Tibet from where the wool, *pashmina* and other commodities used to come in bulk but the Chinese invasion that year threw everything out of gear. Now with the construction of the national highway, Hindustan-Tibet Road, and opening up of motorable links in Kinnaur, the traders are able to sell off their products direct to the far-off markets. While this change in the trend has considerably benefited the local people, the importance of the fair is increasingly on decline. The fair offers an interesting spectacle as the traders encamp on either side of the river Satluj over a long street during their week-long stay.

Thousands of gay people, dressed in their traditional best, add colour to the camp. The business activities stop as the people prepare for their dusk-to-dawn dancing and singing which gain momentum as the night falls. The tourists, who after braving the hazards of the long hill journey, forget all their fatigue and tiredness as they have the glimpse of the people, mythically known for their striking features and habits of singing and dancing. And as regards the local products the visitors go for, they are not simple souvenirs but the real trophies of this part of the Himalayas.

There are other fairs of which Nalwari figures prominently. Nalwari is a cattle fair and is held at scores of places in the lower Shivalik hills. Of all the Nalwari fairs one held at Bilaspur is the most important and next is that of Sundernagar, earlier the headquarters of the Suket state, and now in Mandi district. All the Nalwari fairs held at different places come in quick succession, so traders from Haryana do a brisk business while they move along with their cattle from one place to another. Since the lower hills are interspersed by valley areas, agriculture is a profitable pursuit of the local populace. The Nalwari fair offers an occasion to the agricultural class to dispose off the old useless cattle and go for the new useful ones, starting thus the year with the hope to have a better yield. At some places, such as Bakloh (Kangra), Karsog (Mandi) and Sabathu (Simla) the fairs are held to celebrate *Sayar* on the 1st of Ashwin (September) and the highlight of the festivities is the sacrifice of the buffalo-bull. The animal is symbolic of the demon which the goddess Mahishasurmardini killed. The fair offers the people to witness show of strength and chivalry as some sturdy youngman advances to slay the buffalo-bull with just a single stroke of *khukri*.

Folk Songs

Folk songs in the Himalayas as elsewhere in the world have been prevailing ever since the language established itself and man became a social animal. These songs—solo and community—mirror the thoughts and emotions of the hill folk in simple, unbecoming and affluent dialect and are sung by the majority of the populace irrespective of any age and caste considerations. However, the best come, in the emotional effusion of the women-folk. Himachal is partly mountainous and partly hilly, decked with open dales and valleys. Its lower and upper parts exhibit different currents so far as their songs and dances go. The songs that erupt along with dances are particularly product of the higher hills and are generally avoided bv the people in the lower hills who have been prone to the sophisticated air of the plains with which they have come in contact for quite sometime past now. The people in the hills are simple and carefree, honest and austere by nature. For centuries they, especially the people in the mountainous region, lived an isolated existence and remained somewhat cut off from the general stream of life in the country. They are hardworking.

In their struggle for life and maintenance they are faced with some unusual oddities and cruelties which they fight out with all the strength and faith they have it their command. The monotony and drudgery are not allowed to obtain indefinitely, rather these are fought with the joy and thrill of the songs and dances. At the slightest pretext the people in the mountainous region air their sweet, melodious, lilting songs to the accompaniment of their dancing limbs. Any religious or festive occasion is a fit opportunity for the people to rejoice by singing and dancing. The peace and splendour of the eternal snows of the Himalayas, the magnificent scenery, the terraced fields, the temples, the palaces and the simple huts and hamlets all serve as the backdrop for many tales and legends which have nicely been told by the unknown bards.

In the lower hills there are *hesis*—a class by themselves — who specialise in singing, dancing and instrument playing and are invited by people on various ceremonial occasions. As against this singing and dancing is a way of community life in the upper hills. Orchestra, which is employed in fairs and festivals, is that of the village deity and the people who join the community dance are not professionals. All those people, who collect on a village fair or festival, participate in dance irrespective of their age, sex and class connections. The notes, that are employed in the music and dance, are limited in range and the rhythm and movement also do not admit of much change, rather they are repeated for quite long. Needless to say the community dance has all the vitality, freshness and musical appeal keeping people bound for hours together. The folk dances, of which nati is the most favoured one on all occasions of pomp and pageantry, are marked by the captivating gestures and gentle movements of hands, feet and body.

The men and women, knitting their hands together in a crescent chain, sing and dance to the accompaniment of *hiransinga*, *karnal*, *dhol*, *nagara* and *thali*.

Community dancing in the lower hills is not much known but the region, like its exquisite miniatures, is bedecked with songs which are simple but have the choicest heart-rending words robed in lilting tunes. The songs in the Himalayas cover a wide range of activities depicting emotions of valour, courage, union and renunciation. Of all these love is the mainstay. There are songs in praise of various gods and deities of which those relating to Shiva are the most common. There are also songs relating to Krishna—the most popular cowherd god of the Hindu pantheon. These songs are of two types—devotional and secular. In devotional songs Krishna is held high in reverence but in others he is treated as a good companion. His activities of love and valour all provide a good theme for the folk songs to thrive on.

Love of Krishna for Radha and else for the gopis (milkmaids) has always been a popular theme with the poets and artists. Perhaps none has for ages figured so well in art and literature as Krishna. There are several songs with of such persons as themes which took to prominence in public life. With passage of time, new persons emerge as heroes. The songs incorporate new names but the contents quite surprisingly remain much or less the same. We can illustrate the point by an example. The European, who first settled in Kinnaur, had married a Kinnjuri woman. In a song about him, his complexion was likened with butter. Now this simile occurs in many songs.

Till recently Simla was not a part of Himachal, though since the formation of the latter it continued to be its head quarters. Also prior to the formation of Himachal, Simla was a place of great attraction for the hill people. It took the fancy of the young lovers. They oftenly thought of escaping to Simla where they could talk and move freely without any fear of social interference or stigma. Simla, as such, occurred very frequently in love songs current all over the hills. There are ballads and songs carrying tales of princes and fairies just as they exist elsewhere but the bulk centres around the common man, his joys and sorrows. There is hardly any aspect of the hillfolk, from birth to death, which is not covered by their songs. Love of rural life and natural setting is expressed in various ways. There are high snow-capped peaks, open valleys, dense forests and meadows, murmuring rivers and streams and along with are the moonlit nights and the clear dawns.

Nature has been so bountiful that the singers can hardly forget to express their gratitude to it. The folk singers have also used a variety of symbols in their praise of nature whose grace and mystery make them worship it as a divine manifestation. Amidst the natural settings of terraced fields and green and grassy slopes there are serpentine roads, zigzag bridle paths and the small hamlets, most of which are kutcha constructions. Besides, there are dwellings of the village gods and deities. Folk songs mirror all this variety and picturesqueness. The hill people are emotionally involved with their environs and the sentiments they express are rustic, simple and pure and much like an uncut diamond.

A classification of the folk songs, as is generally adopted, can also be applied to the songs current in Himachal and other regions of the Himalayas: (i) Love songs, (ii) Religious songs, (iii) Heroic songs, (iv) Festival songs, (v) Seasonal songs, and (vi) Ceremonial songs.

The above classification is only a matter of convenience for those engaged in the study of this part of the great lyrical heritage of the Himalayas and it does not suggest any watertight compartmentilism. The songs under one category may also be covered in the other categories.

Love Songs

What else can be a better theme than love for the young hearts to dwell on. But the love sports are not what easily find favour with the fastidious society. There are social taboos. So when love is not openly accepted, it turns to symbolism. The social system is decried, moral codes are questioned, new values are urged and also rebellion is professed against the order of the day. The feeling of love is eternal. It has continued from the most primitive social system down to the present day society. Of the love songs, quite a good number come from the romantic land of Chamba, such as Phulmu-Ranjhu, Maina-te-Mian, Sunni-Bhunku, Kunju-Chanchalo. To these songs, known by the name of some romantic couples, can be added the love lyrics of Rupnu-puhal, Harisingha-deora and others.

Love lyrics are of two types: those that mirror the joys of meeting, and those that reflect the sorrows of separation.

In scores of songs flowing into the main stream of the hill culture, the best are those that portray the pangs of separation. In a song dear to Gaddi belle, one hears of lovelorn heart:

Tera lagda manda O Gaddia
Tera lagda manda ji O
Ai Patwari khat likhi nion dinda
Karnian saw saw chhanda, O Gaddia
Tera lagda manda ji O
Ikli dukli mein paniengi jannian
Pani pian lai chhamha O Gaddia
Tera lagda manda ji O
Nangay nangay pairen mein Rohar chadhi janian
Pairengi chubhi janda kanda O Gaddia
Tera lagda manda ji O

Here the belle talks of missing her deer Gaddi. She herself cannot write him a letter and, therefore, approaches the Patwari who does not seem to oblige her.

The belle goes all alone to the water-spring where she takes water with both hands put together. The moment again makes her sad. Bare-footed as she is, she climbs up the hill in the hope that she will catch the sudden sight of her home-coming husband and will be filled with immense joy.

Quite a good number of songs spring up round the theme of separation, the young woman suffers because her husband, after marriage, has to go out of his village in search of livelihood. At home there is hardly any occupation which could help him meet new burdens. Traditionally, agriculture has not been much paying in the hills. There are cottage industries but they are not developed on commercial lines. These conditions of paucity forced the youngmen to go out and leave their young wives behind. Folk songs in Himachal echo this pathetic note.

In a song from Mandi the husband has been depicted serving in some far off place. He has left behind a plant of Marua and the lovesick lady never forgets to water it. The plant has grown well with long branches which, the innocent girl thinks, the stupid people cannot break off. She takes it as a happy sign of her husband's well-being. But the growing plant also makes her sad as it connotes that she cannot enjoy the company of her healthy and wealthy husband The song runs:

Sinjdi mein maruae jo pani
Merea hakma ho
Is be marue di lambi lambi larjan
Murkhan nen todi hi ni jani
Sinjdi mein maruae jo pani
Marua ta mera hara-bhara rehanda
Eh ta kisay di hai nasani
Sinjdi mein maruae jo pani
Eh ta kisay di nasani
Kihan kari rehna dassi ja mera o hakma
Muskal lagian namani
Sinjdi mein maruae jo pani

There is another side of separation, that the girl feels because she is married in a distant place. In hills there are no good means of transport and communications. There are rivers and rivulets and no bridges over them. In such conditions the girl sings songs which picture her feelings of separation and homesickness. There are hills all round. The girl looks up in the direction where home of her parents is situated, but the sight is blocked by the hills rising one above the other. She appeals to the high hill to bow down and asks the densely grown pine trees to get aside so that she has a clear view of her father's house. This type of feeling is commonly echoed in songs in all parts of the hills. In a song, *chhinj* current in Bilaspur these thoughts figure as:

Uchchiye muiye dharay thodi jai nawadi hoyan
Minjo payiae day ghar jana

In a *chhinj* current in Mandi the girl asks a crow to fly over to her parents home with a letter. She promises him ample reward in return.

The love-tale of Kunju and Chanchlo has gained so much popularity through the length and breadth of Himachal Pradesh as to have few equals. Here is the duet that narrates a part of their meetings:

Kapaday dhon kanney roan Kunjua
Mukhon bol jabani O
Merey Kunjua mukhon bol jabani O
Hathan bich reshmi rumal Chanchalo
Bich chhalla nishani O
Kali akhian ambey diyan pharan O
Bich atharu nishani O
Merey Kunjua bich atharu nishani O
Adhi adhi rati mati aunda Kunjua
Panj bharian bandukan O
Merey Kunjua, panj bharian banduknn O
Adhi adhi rati asan auna Chanchalo
Ki karna bandukan O
Meriae jinde, ki karni bandukan O
Tun tey chinlo pardes Kunjua
Deija anguthi nishani O
Merey Kunjua, deija anguthi nishani O

Chanchalo weeps while she sets to washing her clothes. She asks Kunju to speak to her. He offers her a ring and a kerchief—the signs of his love. Her black eyes, which look like pieces of unripened mango, are full of tears. She warns Kunju against coming to her in midnight as their enemies with loaded guns are watchful of their meetings. Kunju replies that she dare not fear the guns and that he must see her. Kunju is ready to set out on his journey and before he leaves, Chanchalo asks for the ring, which she feels, will keep the old sweet memories alive.

Gangi is another popular love lyric of Bilaspur district which has travelled to the Suket and Balh valley areas of Mandi district. Gangi is a belle who has become synonym of love and beauty. There is no tragic tinge about the tale. The folk singer takes up Gangi as the character and adds his own compositions to the already current lyrics. Some old lines are replaced by new ones and the process is a continuous chain of making and unmaking. Here are a few lines of the Gangi:

Terey kothey tey bajey tabley
Rati bhi na handey chhorua
Tere bairiyan ney lainey badley
Chand charhi gayo chandrua ra
Hor lobh kiyan ni laga
Chaw laga tere dandarue ra
Nai kanaka ray chaney phulkey
Aj chhori pohane tere
Kal jona vey baganey mulkay

The lover says that the music is going on at the place of her beloved. Gangi warns him not to loiter in the night lost his enemies take revenge. The moon is up in the sky. This cells for a stroll in the moonlit night. The lover admires above all the shining teeth of the beloved. The lover talks of the hospitality of his beloved. He must taste the *phulka* (the traditional bread in India) of the new wheat which he likes Gangi to prepare. It is the hospitality of a single day; the next morning he would be in a land, not his own.

Gambhari is another popular maid around whom a number of songs have been woven in Bilaspur. The following are the lines from a popular lyric about Gambhari:

Khana pina nand laini ni Gambhariae
Khatta ni khana mithha ni khana
Khaney baghan rey kailey
Bandla par nalia khari kawafla
Garmian paundian pakha jhulawey Pistu
Ni Gambhari khaney baga dey kailey
Khasam marey kor ghar karey
Dewar marey hiyan rahna ni Gambhariae
Kaparey phatey main darji te siyawan
Dil jo phatey kiyan sina ni Gambhariae

Here the song portrays Gambhari as a maid who believes in 'eat, drink and be merry'. She does not like things of sweet and sour tastes, instead she is fond of the fresh bananas from the garden. She is on her way to Bandla which can only be reached by crossing steep hills. As the summer sets in, the hot wave begins to blow. She has one, Pishtu, who lulls her to sleep. Gambhari is further painted as one who does not mind missing a husband but she cannot live without the husband's brother. She voices openly her preference for the second sex. Again she talks of her love. Clothes, if tattered, can be repaired but that, she holds, is not the case with love which does not admit of any patch.

Religious Songs

The people of the Himalayas are overwhelmingly religious in their outlook and approach to life. Besides various ceremonies and rituals, their faith also finds expression in the religious songs that sprout on many auspicious occasions. Numerous folk versions of the *Ramayana* and *Mahabharata* are current in the Himalayan region and it is interesting to note how the folk has changed the two great epics and adopted them to suit its own genius.

Janmashtami, Shivaratri and Ramnavami are obviously the three occasions on which prayers are offered and hymns are sung in devotion to Krishna, Shiva and Rama, the three popular incarnations of the Hindu pantheon. Navratras, the nine nights in the months of Chaitra (March) and Ashwin/Kartika (October) constitute another important occasion and prayers are offered to the great goddess. There are scores of other occasions when the local deities are approached with songs sung in their praise. Such deities dot every small or big village of the Himalayas.

When the pilgrims set out on their journey to Naina Devi in Bilaspur or Jwalamukhi in Kangra, they can be seen singing chorus in small groups. A line goes:

Jagdi rahay, jagdi rahay,
jagdambay jot teri jagdi rahay

In this song it is prayed that the sacred flame be ever burning.

A devotional song addressed to the goddess Jwalamukhi runs:

Tun jag ambay raniye, tun jag shera waliye
tun jag lata waliye
Nangi nangi pairi mata Akbar ay a
suney da chhatra chadhaya

The song refers to the goddess Amba who is seated on her vehicle, the lion. It is believed that the emperor Akbar visited the Jwalamukhi temple and greatly impressed by this nature's phenomenon, he offered his prayers to the goddess along with a golden umbrella.

The folk has ever been sensitive to the nature around it. The Dhauladhar range of the Himalayas, with its snow-clad peaks. overlooking the Kangra Valley, has ever inspired a feeling of awe and admiration in the folk-mind which has looked upon it as a living manifestation of the mother goddess. A devotional song in this context runs:

Hay Kangri Dhaulidhar mata
Tain Baikunth basaya
Pan supari bhaint chadhaya maiya
Tain Baikunth banaya
Hay Ka gri Dhaulidhar mata
Tain Baikunth basaya
Suha suha hole maiya anga barajey
Kesari tilak chadhaya
Tain Baikunth banaya
Hay Kangri Dhaulidhar mata

In the song the devout looks upon his own Kangra Valley as nothing short of heaven which he attributes to the bliss of the goddess Dhauladhar. Further he says that the goddess is adorned with the red overgarment and has a vermilion mark on her forehead.

Turning to the Gaddis, a very colourful tribe of the Dhauladhar range, one is captivated not only by the good looks of the gaddi maidens, but also by the menfolk presenting no less a well built physique. Their quaint dress and heavy ornaments and jewellery add to their already good appearance. Equally interesting are the manners, customs and beliefs which mostly centre round their unflinching faith in the Lord Shiva. Nawala is a festival of the Gaddis held in honour of the lord Shiva and *ainchalis* are the prayers they offer on the occasion. *Ainchali* is a long prayer in which the legend about the birth of the universe is related in a simple folk style, which apparently may look rugged but reveals much of their undisturbed pastoral traditions.

Heroic Songs

Earlier to its formation as Himachal Pradesh, the territory was divided into small states, each headed by a Raja or a Rana. While the rulers entered marital relations with each other, they could also be seen, before the advent of the British era, frequently fighting among themselves. These feuds and fights meant unaccounted misery to the innocent people and unnecessary bloodshed but they also witnessed man of unusual bravery. These chivalrous and brave men have gone down in the history of the local people who have repaid their indebtedness by singing them songs known as *har*. In the districts of Sirmur and Mahasu (now Simla), there are quite a good number of such songs as have come to be christened after their heroes. *Hars* of Madna, Kamna and Hukku are songs of this category. Ransi Veer is another saga popular in the hills. It relates to a brave man, Ransingh by name. He revolted against the tyranny of the local regime and was imprisoned first in Delhi and then in Agra. A line of this song reads:

Beto kato, bahu kati, chheori, chhoti,
shirey diney mundley lai

It recalls of the deeds of Ransi, who with a view to propitiating the Lord Shiva, sacrificed his sons, daughters and sons' wives. Ultimately he chopped off his own head, and the lord appeared to bless him.

Recollecting the heroic acts of the ancestors, the folk poet says that they had enjoyed such great reputation as would make great warriors of many states tremble with fear.

Tor nana budhu ra bora kamama
Jodha dora rasti shuneia nama

In winter when people are free of their harvest occupations, they collect at night round a log-fire. It is at this time that the ballads are recited and listened to with keen interest and the unbroken chain may last over several nights.

Gugga is another ballad. As the folk poet is very sensitive to the history and environs, he is first in touch with, he finds no check on his imagination and is generally prone to exaggeration.

Apart from songs that carry the accounts of battle, there are such other songs, as are of no historical significance but they are sung because they have an emotional touch about them and appeal to the individual heart and mind. One such song is the famous *Mohana* of Bilaspur. Mohan's elder brother was in the employment of Raja Vijai Chaned and was implicated in a case of murder. Mohan loved and respected his brother. When enquiries were made into the case, Mohan offered himself as the culprit. Everybody and the Raja himself knew that Mohan was not the real culprit. He was persuaded to come out with the truth and to plead unguilty of the murder. But

Mohan, resolved as he was, preferred the gallows. Mohan, the innocent, was hanged publicly and thousands of people with tears in their eyes witnessed the show. The notes of the tragic tale are:

Tu ni disda O Mohana, tu ni disda
Bhaie riya kitia tey tu ni disda
Terey fikarey bey Mohana terey fikarey
Mera dil laga sukaney, terey fikarey
Aya marna O Mohana, aya marna
Bhaie ri galaya par, aya marna
Phansi charhna O Mohana, phansi charhna
Dino ray bara bajey, phansi charhna
Parwana likhita O Mohana, parwana likhita
Rajey teri phansi ra parwana likhita
Khai pehani ley O Mohana, khai pehani ley
Apni marji ra, khai pehani ley
Dan kari ley O Mohana, dan kari ley
Apni marji ra, dan kari ley
Tu ni bachda O Mohana, tu ni bachda
Rajey ri kalma tey tu ni bachda
Lagya sukney O Mohana, lagya sukney
Tola tola khoon tera lagya sukney
Phansi chadhi gaya bey loko, phansi chadhi gaya
Bhaie ri galaya par phansi chadhi gaya

Mohana is now a very popular song and has echoed all through the hills and dales of Himachal Pradesh and the adjoining areas.

Festival Songs

Himachal, having fairs and festivals, there are songs which are essentially connected with certain festive occasions. Agriculture is the mainstay and with this profession are linked a number of festivals and fairs. All Nalwari fairs give the farmers opportunities to buy or sell their cattle. A festival, centering round the cow and the calf, is Gopalashtami. On this occasion the ladies can be heard singing the following lyric:

Mala doni maldiye, We maley ketha deshey aye
Nalwari Sageta desha aye. the maley ketha deshey aye
Kurunsnetra desha aye, gaia kya kya laie aye
Gai kay rakhi da ra pulla laie aye
Kungu bhari thali/ pini laie aye
Dhup dhapi obarey laie aye

Of all the Nalwari fairs, those of Bilaspur and of Suket are the most famous. The above song bears references to Suket and

Kurukshetra, the former known for its animal fair and the latter for its cattle wealth. What have you brought from the land of Kurukshetra? It is a bundle of grass, a *thali* full of vermilion, cakes and incense for worshipping and feeding the cow. The fairs, which are primarily held in devotion to some deity, have not very often a religious note about them. The atmosphere is gay, the people have a time to let themselves go by the light romantic songs filling the atmosphere.

In a fair held at Mehla (Chamba) in the month of May, people rejoice heartily by singing and dancing. A folk song relating to the fair says;

Mahle dian jataran va lorian da pani
Akola mat pinda dhola be sharabia
Pani kian kari bharna
Chattar gunde dian dakian
Jab say nikli main pani bharne
Gunda laga meri bakhian
Pani kian kari bharna
Chatar gunde dian dakian
Mahle dian jataran to lorian da pani
Gunde de bachani apani akbian, be goriae
Gunda akhian bi chale, teri bakhian be chale
Pod ke sath chali gorian
Mahle dodni di chhayan tithu mile bo
Sange khasam chalora kion milna bo

In the above song a woman asks her husband not to go alone to the Mehla fair and drink the water at Lorian. The woman accompanies her husband to the fair where he asks her to fetch him some cold water. She does not want to move alone as some loafers are loitering about. So both set out; but while on the way, the mischief-mongers are seen side by side. One asks her to meet him under the shade of a soapnut tree. She replies that it is not just possible because her husband is along with her.

Of all fairs and festivals in the Himalayan hills, Kullu Dussehra has assumed nation wide importance. Folk songs and dances are the highlights of the occasion. Various *natis* are sung and danced upon. What a hill belle thinks of Dussehra will be noted from the following lyric of a *nati*:

Mu jana dasami bola dasami lana reshmi thipa mun jana dasami

Tu aije dasami bola, dasami lai chitra pattu tu aije dasami

Mu lagi khane ri bola, khane re ani garira gola, mu lagi khane ri

Tu lai raujia bola raujia ananu bhariai jhola
Jaibe aili dasami bola dasami aiji pahuni meri jaibeli dasami

The belle says that she will go to Dussehra with silken dhatu (a piece of cloth) around the head. To this her lover asks her to wear the *chitra* (square patterned) blanket also which will make her more beautiful. When the belle expresses her desire of taking the coconut, the lover promises her a bag full. He asks her that when she turns up for the Dussehra fair, she should be his guest. The beloved does not like the suggestion, instead she offers to join him as a bride. This is heartily accepted by the boy and both come nearer, and join hands to dance in a *nati*.

Seasonal Songs

Of the seasonal songs there are *chaumasa, baramasa* and *chhinj*. *Chhinj* in lower hills generally means the wrestling bouts and are held when the villagers are free of their harvest occupations. But *chhinj*, connoting a type of song, has nothing to do with the wrestling bouts or show of that type. *Chhinj* are the songs which the ladies of Mandi sing in the month of Chaitra (March/April) alone. If any lady sings *chhinj* sometime other than Chaitra, it is held as a bad omen to her brother. *Chhinj* are the sweetest melodies of the hills.

Angan sadhe chambe da boota, tet baithhya kala kag
Kidhie madhau teri kalia chunja,
kidhie madhau kale pankha
Suine madhau teri kali chunja,
roope madhau kale pankha
Udi jaya, udi juya kaleya kaga,
ik be sandeha lai jaya
Kaisa jo bi dena mera sukh bo sandeha,
bapu jo deni banki chithia
Amma jo hi dena mera sukh be sandeha,
bopu jo deni banki chithia
Kid hie de lad tera sukh be sandeha,
kidhie de lar banki chithia
Paghri de lad tera sukh be sandeha,
patakc de lar banki chithia

The above song takes the form of a dialogue between a maid and a crow. The young maid is married in a far off place and she is sick with the memories of her parental home. She asks the crow to take her letter and deliver it to her parents. In lieu of that message delivery, she promises the crow to get his beak coated with gold, and feathers with silver. The letter is to be delivered to the father and the unwritten message to the mother as is understood that the father is literate and the mother illiterate.

There is a *baramasa* which is sung in the Bilaspur district of Himachal Pradesh during the month of Sawan (July/August). The song features a young wife who is reluctant to send her husband out. When the husband wants to set out, the wife prevents him every month on one pretext or the other. The year beginning with the Chaitra (March) terminates at the Phalgun (February). Now the husband asks his wife the time he should leave. She replies that it is the Chaitra when he will get employment. The song runs:

Phulli ta phulli piya ji nagar bel
Kitti bi phullia phull gulab da
Chaite na jayo piya ji Baisakh nayalyo
Chait mahine kujjan phulia
Baisakhe na jayo piya ji Jeth nayalyo
Baisakh mahine dakha pakia
Jethe na jayo piya ji Har nayalyo
Jeth mahine pakhua jholiye
Hare na jayo piya ji Saun nayalyo
Hare mahine ambua pakade
Saune na jayo piya ji Bhadon nayalyo
Saun mahixne pinga jhutiae
Bhadon na jayo piya ji Sauj nayalyo
Bhadon mahine rati naheriyan
Sauje na jayo piya ji Katak nayalyo
Sauj mahine pittar manaiae
Katake na jayo piya ji Maghar nayalyo
Katak mahine joti jagaiae
Maghar na jayo piya ji Poh nayalyo
Maghar mahine lahepha bharaie
Pohe na jayo piya ji Magh nayalyo
Pohe mahine lahepha adhiye
Maghe na jayo piya ji Phagan nayalyo
Magh mahine githa pujiae
Phagane na jayo piya ji Chait nayalyo
Phagan mahine phagua kheliae
Hoae tan hoae no jo barah mahino
Janae di kun rakhiae
Jayo to jayo piya ji Chait mahino
Jandae di laggi teri naukari

Marriage Songs

Marriage is the gayest and most colourful of all ceremonial occasions connected with social life. Marriage offers a variety of songs. As the preparations are afoot, the songs begin to erupt and fill the air with gaiety and mirth. Several ceremonies connected with the marriage include various songs. These ceremonies are the *patri-puja, lagnotari, tel, lagna, bedi, janitar, phera-ghera, andel* (*dham*) and the dowry-giving. The marriage songs, that the ladies sing in the bridegroom's house are called *sehre* and those in the bride's side are called *suhag.*

The marriage is drawing near and the maid waits for the boy in all her eagerness. Here is a song that gives a glimpse into her heart:

Teri teri khatir khana banaya
Khane ki bela bhi na aya baiman
Lugya dil nahi todna
Hathe laini O mari jana
Teri teri khatir sej bichhaya
Sone ki bela bhi na aya baiman
Teri teri khatir pani mangaya
Pine ki bela bhi na aya baiman

This song, which comes from Simla hills, is called a *gidha*. It is sung by the ladies on the girl's side when only four or five days are left for the bridegroom to arrive.

The song depicts a girl who is waiting for her companion. She is greatly upset. She has prepared a number of dishes. She has laid out the bed. She has brought the fresh cold water of the spring. But all her preparations have gone waste as her mate has not turned up. She cannot now withstand the pangs of separation. She will stab herself with a dagger if her companion fails to join her.

Love of ornaments and jewellery is the first weakness of an Indian lady. In a song the maid appeals to the goldsmith to make all fine embellishments in her ornaments:

Gharde sanara hatha do kanganu
Gharti gharaya barik
Main kian pahanani O, marde jali jali sarik
Gharde sanara kana do kante
Gharti gharaya barik
Main kian pahanani O, jali jali marde sarik
Gharde sanara naka di tilia
Gharti gharayan bark

Main kian pahanani O, jali jali marde sarik

She enumerates one by one all the ornaments, such as bangles for the hands, earrings for the ears, tili for the nose. She feels elated at the idea of her valuable ornaments and jewellery. She also voices the jealousy her relatives feel at her lot.

In a song the bride talks to her brother about the dowry which, she says, is all complete but for one thing, and that is the necklace.

Aj ki ghari, bhaua kal ki ghari,
parsi hi sahure jana, mere bhaua
Daj dan ta bhaua sab kuchh ditta,
ik na ditta gale har, mere bhaua
Kaparc-late ta bhaua sab kuchh ditta
ik na ditta gale har, mere bhaua
Sona chandi ta bhaua sab kuchh ditta
ik na ditta gale har, mere bhaua
Gai bhainsi ta bhaua sab kuchh ditta
ik na ditta gale har, mere bhaua
Bbande kunde ta sab kuchh ditta
ik na ditta gale har, mere bhaua

In the above lyric the dowry has been detailed out as having clothes and garments, gold and silver, cows and buffaloes, metal wares and pots. The only thing, the bride repeatedly insists upon having from her brother, is the necklace. The marriage ceremony is over and the bride is being taken away from her parental home. Her old relatives with tears rolled up in their eyes have collected to see her off. The girl is greatly moved in her emotions which find expression in the following song:

Aj ki dhayari doli rakh meri ma
main purdeshan hoia
Meri doli nu lagde kabe ni ma
mainu bidya karan chale babe ni ma
Meri doli nu lagde kalire ni ma
mainu bidya karan chale vire ni ma
Meri doli nu lagde kane ni ma
mainu bidya karan chale mame ni ma
Meri doli nu lagde kache ni ma
mainu bidya karan chale chache ni ma

In the above song the girl appeals to her mother to detain her *doli* (palanquin) at least for a day. She further describes the adornment of her palanquin and remembers one by one all her relatives—father, brother, uncles, etc., who have come to see her off.

Birth Songs

The songs that are sung on the birth of a son are called *badhai geet* which, in Pahari dialect, have come to be known as *bhayai geet*. With the birth of a son there are merriments all round. It is the sister who comes first to congratulate his brother and his wife who have been blessed with the son. The congratulatory lyric of the occasion sounds as follows:

Uche uche ridhuae ghar vada bhabhiae
Nanad badhai jo ayi, ki sun tu nanaa badhai jo ayi
Au tu nanade, baith tu palange, dukh-sukh laina sunai
Dudh dhawaniye pair dhuau, daintya basanaya deiu
Au to nanade baith tu palang, dukh sukh laina sunai
Kede karne nanade tu ayi
Bhabhiae meriae beta je jaya, nanad badhai jo ayi
Aai ki sun tu cholue laini badhai
Sona chandi lai jo tu nanad, cholue laini badhai
Gai bhainsi lai jo tu nanad, ki cholue deya na jayi

The song is a lengthy one wherein the mother of the new babe offers her husband's sister one by one all the things she could enumerate such as the gold and silver, the pots and vessels, the cows and buffaloes, the dresses and costumes and a host of other things. But all these offers are declined by the *nanad* (husband's sister). The only thing she insists on having is the *cholu* (the long overgarment) but the wife is reluctant to part with it as it is a gift from her father which she has so endearly kept with her. The sister is badly annoyed and while returning to her own home she meets her brother. She gives vent to all her grievances. The brother promises her the *cholu* she is after. Thus assured, she accompanies her brother to the parental house. When she gets the *cholu*, she not only thanks her brother and sister-in-law (*nanad*) but also prays for the well-being of the entire family of her grandfather.

Dance Songs

The songs, accompanying group dances, are called *nati* in Himachal Pradesh. *Nati*, in fact, belongs to the upper hills where it is part of all festivities. There is hardly any fair, social gathering or religious congregation where nati is not one of the highlights. As for themes, *nati* generally talks of love-sports and merriments. Here is an example:

Ladli meri banthaniye
Shigi shigi hande meri ladliye
O ladliye, meri banthaniye
Sulre tu hande meri ladliye
Chaure maide phire ladliye
Batru laye meri ladliye ho
Suthnu laye meri ladliye
Kurtu laye meri ladliyej
Ho ladiye, ho meri banthaniye
Kanthia mangave meri ladliye
Dhatu mangave meri ladliye
Shigi shigi hande meri ladliye

The boy asks his beloved to walk slowly and have a stroll along with him through wide streets of the town. The belle has furnished her the list of demands which includes shoes, trousers, shirt and headwear. Adorned as such the two will have the pleasure of each other's company.

Nati gives vent to a light conversation between the lover and the beloved. Here are a few lines of the *nati*, the like of which are very common in Himachal Pradesh:

Phul phulia samel dandie
Ithi bi ni rahna chhoṛua
Chali jana Suket Mandie
Phul phulia par gunve
Solan salima dekhna
Rat katni dar sunuve

In this *nati*, the belle talks of leaving the native place and moving to a township like Suket, Mandi and Solan where there are good marketing places and recreation like cinema.

Folk and Ritual Dances

Folk dance in Himachal is generally known as *nati* and it is also suggestive of the song and music that go with it. *Nati* collectively connotes the vocal lyric, the instrumental music, the dancing steps and the bodily movements all attuned to rhythm. This part of the cultural fibre combines in it the verve, exuberance and rhythm by which the simple hill folk joyfully abandon themselves. Of all the arts it is the *nati* which gives the participants the utmost sense of fellowship and all-embracing joy. There is hardly a fair where nati, characterised by undulating folk tunes, graceful dance-steps and slow movements of the body, does not become one of its highlights.

In its original folk dance is more akin to rituals than to a form of entertainment but in its popular manifestations it is all entertainment and no ritual. With local patronage on the decline this art is losing its religious and functional value and changes have crept in to suit the tastes and trends of sophisticated urban society.

Dresses and costumes of the folk dancers present a great variety. Generally, any person may join a nati regardless of his or her dress. But in a well organised show the dress is an important consideration. Of a great variety the Pahari cap has been favoured by the men and the dhatu, i.e., square piece of cloth used as headgear, by the women all through the hills. The highlanders in Mandi district prefer wearing round black woollen caps with white loose woollen garments, known as chola or jhaggi, and churidar pyjamas. The tribal gaddis, belonging to the Bharmaur area of Chamba district, use particularly marked quaint dresses. They also have a good number of natis to offer, the main theme being love. Like the gaddis and other tribals people in the Spiti Valley do not change their clothes for dances, but what they wear nor-mally is very fascinating. The men folk can be seen wearing the chhiba (coat), chharing kin go (cap), kira (gachi) and lump (shoes). Women wear the chu/u (long gown), lingche (shawl), lump (shoes) and heavy ornaments and jewellery made either of silver or some cheap metals but rarely of gold.

The dance is started with a few persons who mako a crescent form by joining hands crossed on the back of each other. The orchestra, sitting in the centre, generally consists of two dhols (barrel shaped drums), two nogaras (bowl shaped drums), two karnals (long trumpets) and one shahnoi. At the beginning of the porformnnce the dancors move slowly but later gain momentum with the rising crescendo of the music. Nati tuno is played on the sfiahnais and the dhols and nagaras are bonton to its accompaniment. The karnal is blown intor-mittently. Added to these is the ring of the bhana, a thin metal disc struck by a clapper. People, both men and women, who throng to the mela join the dancers. Some may leave the chain and others may join it but the dance must continue at least for two to three hours.

There is no hard and fast rule on the number of dancers. Generally, the minimum number to form a nati in a mala is 18 and it often swells to 50, 60 or even more. Sometimes men and women in the nati sing in groups. A line is sung in chorus by the men folk and this is then followed by the women. Another method is a dialogue between the two groups. Intermittently some lines are picked up jointly.

There are different types of nati which the various areas of Himachal Pradesh have adopted. The natis named after places such as the Kullu nati, Bushahri nati, Mandi nati, are too broad u base to connote any distinct typos. It is only when a troupe goes out to join some celebrations, it assumes the name of the place it comes from. The two broad typos of nati prevalent in Kullu have been named after the two harvests. The birshu or phirshu nati suggests a welcome to the kharif harvest on the first of Baisakh (April). The other is shayari nati held to welcome the rabi harvest.

The note and tone of a nati are determined by the particular season and underlines the mood and sensitivity that go by it. The shayari and the *birshu* strike a gayful note while a nati presented in the month of Magh (January/February) communicates a sad note and is sweetly suggestive of the separation of two hearts. In fact, the Bada Tyohar, i.e., the grand festival, which falls on the first of Baisnkh (April) and the Magh Sankranti (first day of the month) are two occasions when the people are in a mood of joy and merriment. Singing and dancing are the usual featuros of festivites everywhere. The rassa dance featuring a love legend or a historical event is performed by the people of the interior Sirmur on those occasions.

There are such types of nati as bozuband, ludi, phetiahir and janujangh. They all aro suggestive of some typical physical gestures and formation. In bazuband, a popular nati of any festival, the dancers join each other in a crescent form with arms interlocked like a chain. In a ludi, another favourite dance of the hills, the dancers form a semi-circle but do not join their hands. Here they maintain a short but equal distance from each other. In the community dance, known as phetighir, the dancers form a semi-circle or a circle standing close to each other. The male participants have coloured handkerchiefs in their right hands which they wave as they take steps and move gently or swiftly to the accompaniment of the orchestra. In the janu-jangh, meaning knees and legs, the dancers do not form a circle or semi-circle but stand in a straight line with arms interlocked like a chain. The movements are, of course, mainly limited to the knees and legs.

There are certain natis which are very popular all over Himachal. Of these the lari (bride), shawni, and lilima are attempts to describe the village belle whose physical build, features, gait, manners, colourful apparel and jewellery all help mesmerise the country's youth. There is a nali which the men folk dance with swords in their hands. It is danced to the accompaniment of some saga reminiscent of a battle or war fought in some remote past. One such dance is called kharait. To this category also belongs the burah dance of Sirmur district and is usually performed at Diwali. This community dance tells the story of Sidhu's fort and its acquisition by the Raja. Two other common dances in nati are ludi and banthra, where the movements are swifter. Similarly, the ujagjama and chandhgebrikcr are the other dances of fast tempo. Dhilli and pheti are natis marked for their slow movements. Another nati with slow movement is dohri, meaning double, and connotes the type of formation the dancers should make.

In Pauranik literature the Kinners and Gandharvas have been known as the singing and dancing tribes. Till today the Kinnors have presorved their traditional love of singing and dancing. Their dances are marked by measured steps projecting a graceful style. The music played on instruments like ban (single-sided drum with brass base), bugalf (Ca pair of metallic circular pieces), karnal (a long trumpet), dhol (boating drum) etc, accompany closely each stop, and the pace gathers momentum with the fast playing of the instruments.

Folk and Ritual Dances in Tribal Area

One of the conspicuous features of the tribal life in Trans-Himalayan region with unflinching Buddhist faith, is its colourful dances which may conveniently be seen divided into two groups. One is a folk dance with many types varying according to the types of assemblage, steps, rhythm and beat. The second is a ritual masked dance in monasteries called chham dance.

Folk dance is as natural to the tribals of this borderland as speech to human beings. As generally goes with the tribals their melodies are marked by limited range of tunes in simple keys. Singing, dancing and drinking all go together. The incessant repetition, rather than variety, is what is favoured by all the singers and dancers. The audience is seldom apart from what forms a group of singers and dancers. However, the musicians constitute a different class who take their seat distinctly to give accompaniment to the singing and dancing crowd. The myths, legends, folktales, ballads and riddles which mirror musings, beliefs and traditions of the tribal people come to light. It is either a harvest time or any other festive occasion that the myths and legends are recited. In the winter season when they sit around a warming fire, the old men and women tell folktales and riddles. Earlier in Lahaul the people used to burn with great economy and protect wood of willow, poplar, birch and juniper, the only few species that are scantily seen growing there. The Spiti Valley is more or less devoid of this gift of the nature too. The Spitians have some bushos slacked on the roof-tops of their houses. Of late, the Lahaula have taken to stoves fitted with pipes which serve as outlet for smoke. Some Spitians have also now taken to this technique of cooking and warming.

The tribals in Lahaul and Spiti have a variety of musical instruments to play upon. Every monastery, has a set of musical instruments which is used in temple services and also occasionally on private ceremonies. These instruments include different kinds of gongs and bells, trumpets and horns, flutes, oboes, flageolets, conch shells, cymbals, beating drums and a few others. Many of these are made of silver and copper or both combined with engravings or repouse work carrying symbolic and stylised designs. Of these designs lotus and vajra (sceptre) aro the two very common.

A musical instrument used invariably in liturgical ceremonies and deserving special notice is *kangdum*, also known as *kangling*. It is made of thigh bone of human being extracted of the corpse. Thigh bone is embellished with silver and bronze work before it is finally consecrated as a sacred object. Thigh bone of a woman, who dies in pregnancy, is more valued as the instrument made of it is believed to produce a sound that is peculiarly efficacious for conjuring the benevolent spirits. Thigh bone of *khanduma*, a woman of good and auspicious omens, is seldom missed and it is some learned lama who decides upon the issue on the basis of his astrological calculations.

Gonkhan is a room in a monastery which is generally dark and has mysterious fittings providing an atmosphere for the lamas to evoke or propitiate the terrifying gods resting on a pedestal just opposite the entrance. All sorts of masks, weapons, dresses and ritual objects are generally stored in the *gonkhan* and as the atmosphere is charged with an air of fear, women are not allowed here. A big drum with one leg is seen hanging with the help of two ropes in between the two pillars and the lama beats it rhythmically with a curved stick while murmuring his recitations in a deep guttural voice. Daily worship invoking fierce deities is done by the resident lamas. Besides the grotesquely appearing masks, one among various equipment that create a sense of terror, is the bowl, made of human skull used for offering blood, wine or water to the deities and also for their drinking by the lamas. A sacred masked dance locally known as *chham* is done only by the lamas in the monasteries before a large concourse of spectators on some festive occasion. Since masks are much or less those of the devils, it is also called devil dance. The lamas put on embroidered and brocaded robes of gorgeous colours and the heads are covered with masks made of wood or papier-mache with a thin coat of plaster.

Those masks are prepared by the lamas themselves and like the Tibetan paintings and sculptures know no deviation from what the rules and norms precisely lay down. These precious robes and masks are the property of the monastery and these are kept carefully stored in a room under the charge of a *kardar* (keeper). According to one belief the object of putting on masks of grotesque appearance is to give an idea to the spectators of the types of dread monsters who are met by the soul after it quits the earthly plane. These masks are made after many imaginative figures of monsters, dragons, beasts, devils, imps, spirits and skeletons. The departed soul is frightened and perplexed by these terrifying figures and then the lama or some saint appears to protect it and guide it to a safe end.

The theory obviously is an attempt to establish the supremacy of priesthood over temporal power and command allegiance from simple god fearing common folk. Another belief is that the lamas put on these masks to combat malignant spirits. The figures with demonic appearances are the terrifying defenders of religion or righteousness and also stand for thc horrifying aspects of the Bodhisattvas. Apart from what the popular belief goes, there is some meaning in these plays which the initiates well understand. Killing the evil king is only an allegory, the real meaning is "killing of one's own self".

The dancers appear in eight different masks or there may be more but then they will be grouped in eights. These *krodha* or horrifying manifestations of the eight great Bodhisattvas help the monks to acquire the highest insight. A clover leaf blade oftenly topped by the head of a *khyung* (*garuda*) bird is a very typical ritual attribute called *phurbu*. It is one of the most important weapons of tantric doitios used by the lamas for exorcising evil spirits or pinning down ovil demons. This magic dagger is either made of wood, proferably khadiro, or stool or even cast in bronze. *Phunbus* come invariably in use during ritual masked dance. During the tantric ceremonial the devil is summoned up and a spell is cast on him. It is with the phurbu that he is held fast.

A well-known masked dance lasting several hours features the murder of the evil king Lang-dar-ma. The history of Tibet records that Ral-pa-cen, who ruled from 815 to 835 A.D., was a great religious king to uphold the Buddhist faith. He founded many monasteries and looked to the Indian Buddhism as the only faith of the right type and propagated it through the media of art and literature.

In 817 A.D. Buddhism was severely attacked by the evil king Lang-dar-ma who was Ral-pa-cen's elder brother. The Buddhist followers were persecuted. Later the king Ral-pa-cen was murdered by his opponents and the power was seized by the 'evil king'. The process of persecution continued until 836 A.D. when one of the Buddhist followers murdered Lang-darma. The mystery play is also staged by the Red Hats to mark the birthday of Padmasambhava, the apostle of Tantric Buddhism, on the tenth day of the fifth month of Tibetan calendar. The lamas who dance in this mystery play make some recitation inside the temple in a strictly ritual manner before they actually come on the inner courtyard of the monastery for the performance.

Sissu and other fairs: Sissu is a common fair celebrated all over the Buddhist Himalayas. Its main attraction is always a masked dance but because it is a part of monastic rituals, it is always staged inside the monastery on the attached courtyard. The fair is celebrated on different dates at different places. At Sussur Gompa (monastery) it is held in June, at Gemur Gompa in July and at Mani Gompa of Gondhla in August. Apart from the Sissu fair there are also a number of other fairs in Lahaul featuring masked dance. Phagli, also called Kunh, is a fair of Pattan Valley which is held on amavasa, the first day of the dark half of the month of February (Magh/Phalgun).

It is interesting to note that tho Lahaulas of Pattan Valley celebrate Diwali not on the day when it is celebrated elsewhere in India. As against *amavasa*, the all dark night, it takes place on full moon night and the main feature of the celebrations is illuminations by lighting small sticks of firewood. A similar festival of illuminations is Halda which is celebrated in Gondhla and Gahar Valleys in Lahaul but unlike the fixed dates for Diwali and Phagli it is held on different days in the month of February.

A festival organised on a grand scale in Gumrang Kothi, i.e., in Keylong and round about is Gochi falling sometime in January or February as is decided by the lamas on the basis of their astrological calculations. The main object of the festival is to celebrate jointly the births of all the male children born during the preceding year.

At Thang-gyud monastery a religious festival called *jid-jed* takes place in the month of October and a month later a similar festival called *guitor* is held in the monasteries at Kee, Tabo, Dankhar and

Pin, all in Spiti Sub-division. The masked dance is invariably arranged on these occasions and the purpose is to protect people from diseases and epidemics and ensure health, happiness and all-round prosperity.

On the eve of New Year a dance is acted by the lamas in courtyard of a monastery belonging to the sect of Yellow Hats. The villagers are allowed to witness the show and they take it not as an entertainment but with all religious fervour. This sect was founded by Tsong-Kha-pa (1357-1419 A.D.) who is held by the Gelugpas (Yellow Hats) as an emanation of Manjushri; and Vajra Bhairava, called Dorje Jik-cho in Tibetan, is its chief protector. There is a mystery play called Black Hat Dance. Here the lama does not wear mask, instead he puts on a highly ornate head-dress. This dance is of pre-Buddhist origin. It is some sort of a pantomime accompanied sometime by outcries and interjections.

Another dance of pre-Buddhist origin, i.e., of the times of Bompas, which has continued to this day, is Red Tiger Dance. It is ceremonised at the end of Old Year. The Bon religious practices included cannibalism and human sacrifice which were carried on with a view to propitiating the deities and exorcising the evil spirits. In his attempt to replace Bon cult by Buddhism the great lama Padmasambhava cleverly adopted some of the Bon rituals but only on their face. These devil dances were allowed to continue but the ghastly practices of human sacrifice and cannibalism were virtually put to an end.

These dances are not simple gay and abandon on some lilting tunes but every step and movement of the lamas are carried out strictly according to the rules. The older lamas are the masters to watch if anything goes wrong with the dancers and the musicians. The itinerant monks play religious music on a large drum and cymbals and others with long trumpets and small horns. The music that accompanies the dance is evocative of a particular mood which is dictated by the object of the dance. Whether it is a New Year Dance of the Gelugpas (Yellow Hats) or a dance ceremonising the murder of evil king Lang-dar-ma, the object is sacredly upheld.

Folk and Ritualistic Art

Alpana—a ritual decoration or floor painting executed by womenfolk in Bengal has its parallel in Sathiya of Gujarat, Rangoli or Rangavali of Maharashtra, Aripna of Bihar, Sanjhi of Uttar Pradesh, Mandana of Rajasthan and Madhya Pradesh and Kolam of the South. Himachal Pradesh, a north-western region of the Himalayas, has also age-long tradition of ritual decorations executed on floors, walls and courtyards on all such auspicious occasions as the marriage, birthday, food-taking (*annaprasan*) and sacred thread (*yajnopavita*) ceremonies and also various fairs and festivals. These decorations are easy expressions of women's penchant to live artistically and tastefully. With a devoted mind praying for the family's well-being, a woman observes a *vrata*, executes a pictograph suiting an occasion, worships it and finally it is after distributing of the *prasad* that she takes her meals. Various ritual designs and patterns to appear on the walls, verandas and courtyards of a Pahari household are deeply rooted in the indigenous base of the Pahari culture which has so far been successful in retaining its ancient character.

The designs and patterns are but outward expressions drawn out of the rites and rituals and faith and religion. Ritual decorations are limited to womenfolk, i.e., it is none of men's business. The women who execute these designs and decorations are also not professional but amateurs—the old generation handing down their skills to the new one. This inheritance is held up in its sincerity though the individual has her own imagination to add. Basically the sources tapped in the execution of these decorations are all indigenous, either costing nothing or very negligible. With the advance of civilisation the people in urban areas have switched over to such materials as are easy substitute for the old ones as the latter are now making a fast but gradual disappearance.

In low lying areas of Himachal Pradesh every house has a courtyard attached to it and in its centre there is a plant of *tulsi* (ocymum sacrum) grown on the top of a pedestal. The *tulsi* plant," which has a flavour and great medicinal value, is also an object of worship. One of the ladies in a family would never forget to water the plant early morning. In Sanskrit the *tulsi* has also been named 'Haripriya' and 'Bhutagni'. Bhutagni, as the name suggests, is the destroyer of demons and its ever presence in the courtyard ensures protection against all kinds of evil spirits. As Haripriya, *tulsi* is the beloved of Vishnu. It is to Vishnu that the *tulsi* is ceremonially wedded. The childless lady is more particular about the sacred plant and she marries it either to Vishnu or to one of his incarnations who is her favourite god. In this case the tulsi is accepted as the form of Lakshmi. Amongst the incarnations when *tulsi* is wedded to Rama she is Sita and when wedded to Krishna she is Rukmani. Another form of Vishnu to which tulsi may be wedded is Shaligrama, which in its concrete form is the sacred ammonite usually found on the river bed of the

Ghantki.

The *tulsi* pedestal may vary in its form and size from house to house. In well-to-do families, it takes the form of a lotus well carved out in stones. In others it may just be a simple square construction of stones and mud with brown coloured earth (loshti) and white earth (*makol*) paints on it. These earthen paints so appear as to give rich geometrical patterns or patterns made out of stylised symbols like petals of lotus and rose. To the pedestal is attached a well-chiselled stone image of Ganapati, seated in lalitasan, and marked by elephantine face, a potbelly and four arms. In his right hands he holds a trident and rosary and in the left parasu and modaka-patra.

There is a legend which accounts for the Ganapati's elephant head. Goddess Parvati, his mother, proud of her son once asked planet Shani (Saturn) to look at the beauty of her son. Shani, taking it as an insult, cast his evil effect and reduced the child's head to ashes. Feeling grieved at this Parvati prayed to Brahma, the creator, to undo the evil. Brahma blessed her and said that her son would get the head she first encountered on her way back. It was elephant and Ganapati came to acquire the head of an elephant.

Another legend explains how the Ganapati came to have only one tusk. One day Parshuram came to visit Shiva in Kailash. Ganesh was there on his guard. He did not let Parshuram get in. They had a duel in which Parshuram wanted to use his axe which was a boon granted to him by the- Lord Shiva. As it was a boon from his father, Ganesh did not resist its use but he only allowed it on one of his tusks. The tusk was lost.

Because Ganesh had put up a fight against Parshuram, he was named as Bighneshwar. But by his character, scholarship and deeds he became the god of obstacles. The god is invoked for removing obstacles and also for putting up obstacles but in both cases the purpose must be good and auspicious.

Besides the tulsi pedestal, Ganesh is enshrined also in a niche above the door-frame of the main entrance of a house or a temple in the lower Himalayan areas.

Ganapati with the head of an elephant and the body of a plump man, is now held as the god of learning and success. The god is not only invoked on all auspicious occasions but is also worshipped daily with the prayer to get a good start in the day to follow. In Maharashtra Rangavali is part of Ganesh worship which assumes a great public show but in the Himalayan hills it is all in its subdued form.

The courtyard in a Pahari house is cleaned and painted on all such occasions as the Bada Tyohar, i.e., the New Year Day of the Hindu Vikrami Calendar, andSayar, i.e., the first day of Ashwin month (September) celebrated as first harvest day of the season. Diwali and Shivaratri are other two important: festive occasions when the courtyard gets its unusual uplift. Besides those fixed days on the calendar of the year, the other days are birthday of a new babe, annaprason, mundan and marriage ceremonies.

On the courtyard, studded with a tulsi plant on a pedestal in the centre, is sprinkled cowdung paste which serves as a good background for makol drawings and designs. In local parlance of Mandi (Himacha! Pradesh) it is called lipna. It has an easy derivative in alepan—a Sanskrit and Hindi word used in the sense of painting, more so in the sense of 'plastering' or 'coating with'. The word may also give a striking resemblance with well-known alpana.

In district Mandi of Himachal Pradesh usually the cleaning and decoration of the courtyard and the main doorway is the business of a woman who belongs to a trade caste of cobblers. It is in some big ordinary am that the makol paste is prepared by adding water to the white earthen cakes. This white earthen paste is as good as the white powdered lime used in other parts of the country for white wash or similar purposes. When it is ready, it is with the help of on earthen pot with a small holo at its bottom that the woman paints te floor, giving it variegated designs and patterns.

In many other parts of Himanchal, for example, Bilaspur and Kangra districts, the ladies themselves adorn the doorways and courtyards of their houses. The foot-steps and lotus-petals are particularly marked on the path leading to the chamber where Lakshmi, the goddess of wealth, is an object of worship and offerings. The path is also lighted with earthen lamps on its both sides. This type of ritual decoration is called *likhnu* in local dialect and stands for alepan in Sanskrit and Hindi.

In low-lying areas of Himachal Pradesh, women make attractive designs and motifs on the outer walls of their houses. These are mud-plastered walls which are given coatings of cow-dung paste and white earth paints. The white washed walls serve as background for the simple but forceful designs and motifs. .

The rainy season, particularly the month of Sawan (July-August) has much to offer by way of festivals observed by the womenfolk. Shiva Chautri is observed on the first of Sawan. Symbolical of earthly wisdom the elephant-headed son of Shiva, viz., Ganesh, figures on a piece of paper which is accompanied by a Sanskrit verse. Below this is the chauui meaning 'thirty-four'. Numbers from 1 to 10 are written in sixteen squares in such a way that when added anyway i.e. horizontally, vertically or diagonally, the sum-total is thirty-four.

This chautri is pasted on the main door and also on every door in the house and is considered auspicious—meant to bring in good luck and to drive away evil spirits.

Festivals

Haritalika Teej known as Hariali Tri in Mandi and Chiriyan Ka Vrat in Bilaspur, is observed on third of the lunar half of Bhadon (August/September) for the weil-being or the family. Haritalika is well narrated in Bhavishyottar purana where it takes the form of a dialogue between Shiva and Parvati. The legend goes that Parvati loved Shiva and had resolved to marry him. Her father did not favour this alliance. With a view to win over Shiva, Parvati engaged herself in austerity. Shiva was pleased with her and abducted her from her father's house when she was being given to someone else. Thus, they were married and led a very successful and auspicious life. Parvati, by virtue of her devotion, became an example as the ideal housewife. In fact Gour or Gauri which the ladies worship daily, symbolises everlasting *suhag*, i.e., marital bliss. The young girls, as well as the married women, observe Vrata on this day—the former pray for matches of their liking and the latter for well-being of their family. A general belief is that the girls, who do not observe the Vrata, are destined to remain single and the married ladies are damned for widowhood for as many as seven lives.

On the occasion of Haritalika Teej the women get an opportunity to express their artistic fervour in the form of clay models. These models are prepared over a week or two before the festival day. The centre of worship is Parvati. The main theme of the Haritalika models is the Shiva-Parvati wedding. Parvati worshipping the Swayambhu Linga, representative of the creative union, is the main model. Other models to appear along with are Nandi (bull)—the Shiva family's vehicle, *pohi*—the old married woman who accords a ceremonial welcome to the bride and bridegroom with lighted lamps on a thali, and the music band, especially the shehnai-player.

Clay models of Shiva, Parvati, Ganesh and Kartikeya are made separately with usual skill and dexterity. Ganesh, the elephant-headed deity, commands special attention. Such models as the peacock, sparrow, cow, bull and chariot are favourite with the young lads. The children also favour toy-replicas of kitchen pots and pans. The clay models are made of beaten and well-kneaded clay made out of pure earth with cotton or cloth-rags added to it. The softness and fluidity of the material used are the two factors that go to make the models charming and appealing. When the clay has been modelled into various forms and figures, they are put in shade to get dry. When the images are dried up they are first given a prime coat of rice-water and then a coat of white earthen paint. They are later painted in various brilliant colours to get distinct appearance to various parts of the body, garments and ornaments. After these clay models have been worshipped by the ladies, they are distributed among the children who are very fond of them. While Haritalika Teej is celebrated on a family level in Mandi, it gets a public appearance in Bilaspur where the women of the town collect at a convenient place and arrangements for reciting the Haritalika tale are made.

Rali: Another festival which is marked by clay images is Rali in spring season in Kangra Valley. The legend, that goes with the festival, says that Rali was a young girl who was married to a child named Shankar on the first day of Chaitra (March). It was obviously a matchless marriage. When the marriage party was on its way back, Rali jumped into a running stream thus putting an end to her young life. The child Shankar and Rali's brother Bastu, aggrieved at the loss, could not stand the tragedy and they also jumped into the river. The event, a lesson for the society, became an annual feature and was commemorated by the young girls praying for good matches and happy life.

On the first day of Chaitra (March) the young girls make clay models of Rali, Shankar—Rali's husband and also called Rala, and Bastu —Rali's brother and also called Ralu. The worship of these models continues for a month. For worship purposes, Ralu is the goddess Parvati, and Shankar is the God Shiva.

The young girls of the village carry *dub* grass and flowers in their bamboo baskets to a particular spot where they throw them in a heap. The girls encircle this heap and sing sweet songs. The girls rejoice this way for ten days. Over the heap are placed downwards two branches of tree, each with three fronds. On the two summits are placed two images which stand for Shiva and Parvati. The girls divide themselves into two groups—one joins the Shiva image and the other the Parvati image. Then the marriage between the two is solemnised and this is followed by a feast. On the next Sankrant, i.e., the first day of the month of Baisakh (April) the girls again collect and immerse the images in the flowing water. This immersion ceremony is followed by a ritual weeping.

Sometimes the professional potters prepare big models, almost in life size of all the above characters. While those models are in preparation, to those are added cowries which are but symbols of fertility.

The festival has a striking resemblance in Gangaur of Rajasthan. During the festival which starts on the 1st day of Chaitra (March) both the married girls and unmarried women worship the goddess Gangaur, i.e., consort of Shiva. The gaily dressed girls and women go to a garden each morning with pots of water on their heads. The pots are topped with flowers, leaves and blades of grass all artistically displayed. The grains and *kumkum* are offered to the goddess Gangaur and songs are sung in her praise. The festival lasts for eighteen days.

Beerpanji: is a festival on which a married woman keeps fast for the welfare of her brother. As rituals would have it, the women do not take milk on this day, instead they will have perched grams and a few dry fruits. As no festival is without something artistic about it, on this particular occasion the women will have their pastry-board (*chakla*) and would paint on it with *kumkum* a ritualistic design wherein the two male and female figures represent the brother and sister. Here one can understand the meaning behind the use of *kumkum* which is not only easily available in every household but is also considered auspicious. Kumkum is a sign of marital bliss (*suhag*) for which the brother prays for his sister. This ritualistic design or pattern may either be executed by a single finger of the right hand or some sort of brush made from twigs may be used.

Bahula Chaturthi: On this day which occurs on the fourth day of dark half of lunar month Bhadon (August) all the married women in a family observe fast praying for the welfare of their children. The cow, which is held in deep esteem and serves as a living symbol of motherhood in a pastoral society, is worshipped along with her calf and they are fed with cakes of barley or wheat flour. The women take various fruits at least of a dozen kinds. They prepare garlands of flowers and *doob* and put them around the neck of the cow and calf. Impression of the hands soaked in the paste of wheat flour are marked on their bodies and as many as twelve rounds are taken of them. As against the floor or wall, the cowding plastered winnowing basket (*soop*) serves as the background for the ritual painting wherein pictures of heaven with various deities and figures of cow and calf are drawn in white earth paint. This serves as a tray for the figurines made out of the barley or wheat flour. These figures are offered to the cow and calf when their worship has been performed.

The birthday of Gauri marks an important celebration in the month of Bhadon (August-September). Preparations for proper celebration of the day start some eight days before when barley is sown in a toy *dooly* which has in it an image of Gauri. The image is daily worshipped by all girls and women of the household except the widows. The girls pray for good matches and the women for well-being of their family life. On the birthday of the goddess Gauri, after prayers and worship have been made, the image along with dooly is immersed in the flowing water of a river or stream but the barley shoots are retained and distributed later amongst members of the family who would wear them in their head-dress.

Apparently looking as a festival meant for the happiness of the family, the celebrations, in fact, point out to a rite connected with the fertility cult and are a good artistic and ceremonial expression of the latter.

Purchhath or *Shashthi* is a festival which the ladies observe for the well-being of their children. One of the women executes in white earth a pictograph which is illustration of a story that is related as part of the worship. The cat in the pictograph is the vehicle of the goddess Shasthi. As the legend has it a Raja had seven queens but had no issue. A Sadhu visited the royal palace and delivered a fruit for the queens to take. It was only the eldest who took it in right earnest and a spirit of devotion while the others discarded it. The eldest, who was not beloved to the Raja and was leading a secluded life, gave birth to a son while others did not have that chance. When Raja heard of the news, he visited the Rani who served him the auspicious cakes. The Raja was very happy since he had a hair to succeed him. The festival is a symbol of family's welfare and the *purus,* i.e., cakes of flour and milk fried in ghee make a typical preparation of the occasion.

Navin: Another festive occasion is *Navin* in Chaitra (March) when all the married women in a house observe fast and would join hands in their worship of the mother goddess, Anna-Parmeshwari or Annapurna who is believed to be responsible for bringing in bumper crops and material prosperity. In a corner of the house a small portion of the verandah is plastered either with Joshti, the brown earth, or cowdung to serve as background and on it is painted a square pattern of one metre on each side. The square pattern has a good number of human figures which represent a family consisting of a merchant, his wife, nine sons and their wives. One of the women sitting around this pictograph takes a lead and recites a story of the Navin goddess whose neglect led the prosperous family of the merchant to complete ruins. The goddess is worshipped with a view to propitiating it and finally all the women pray for the prosperity and happiness of their family members.

Hoi Ashtami: *Hoi-Ashtami*, or *Hoi-Ashtami* as it is locally called, is a festival which is celebrated by women in the month of Ashwin (September-October) in devotion to the mother goddess named Hoi. The square pictograph relating to *Hoi-Ashtami* is an interesting one and is generally painted on the wall of a house. If the wall is to be avoided as background, the pictograph may be done on a big square paper which is pasted against the wall. The pictograph here is a miniature representation of the folk conception of universe where not only human figures but also the sun, moon, birds and animals of earth and sea are drawn. Some figures are drawn in such a circular way to appear as Raslila—a common and a very popular theme of painting through all ages. Such groups of words as Jai Hoi Mata, Sita-Rama, Radhe-Shyama and Om in Devnagri script do find place on the pictograph since these are universal expressions adopted by a devoted mind.

Hoi-Ashtami whether it is on a wall or paper, is a pictograph executed in bright colours which are invariably the favourite of all hill folk. The communication of a folk mind is simple and direct but not without imagination and symbolism. The whole pictograph shows a good sense of colour but it may be noted that the folk mind prefers use of contrasts rather than shades.

Kauhra is another type of pictograph which is executed either on a square size cloth or paper which is pasted against the wall and serves as a background for the worship of Ganesha by the wedding couple. The pictograph carries a scene of marriage and some scenes of tho life after marriage. Kauhra is a must on every marriage and if a new one cannot be executed or made available, an old one should serve the purpose. In Kangra there is a living tradition of painting Kauhras in highly tasteful manner and their prices, which range from Rs. 5. to 100, may be fixed according to their respective artistic worth.

In Chamba there is a rich tradition of decorating the entrance of a room with *Bangdwari* on wedding occasions. Bangdwari is a long scroll of paper which is pasted on to the three sides of the entrance—right, left and up. Bangdwari carries elaborate figures and scenes, designs and motifs executed in traditional style and in various pleasing and strikingly glowing colours favourite of the folk.

Shantiniketan did a great job by adopting Alpana and teaching it as a subject of art. This helped not only revitalising it but also making it a popular decorative art. This ritualistic decorative art, as it is prevalent in the lower Himalayas, has more chances of survival as it is primarily a land of cultivators and can hope to keep off the vulgar effects of uncultured urbanisation which is fast taking over many habitations in India.

Pahari Art of Painting

Pahari Chitrakala, i.e., Pahari Art of Painting, is such a widely accepted term now that it hardly needs any introduction. In the course of study by various art critics and historians, Pahari Art of Painting was denominated by various titles, e.g., Rajput Painting. Punjab Hills Painting Kangra Painting etc. The study of Pahari Painting has fairly advanced and all those titles have come for disfavour for one reason or the other.

Rajput Painting included both Rajasthani and Pahari Paintings. Further Rajput Painting only connotes that this art flourished under the patronage of Rajput rulers. This may strike similar to that of Mughal Painting. There is one difference, however. The Rajput Painting encompassed the common masses while the Mughal Art remained largely confined to royal palaces and courts.

Punjab Hill Painting is evidently an obsolete name as it points back to a dead phase of the Punjab history and also excludes from its purview Basohli and Jammu of the Jammu and Kashmir State on one hand and Garhwal of Uttar Pradesh on the other. Further with the emergence of Himachal Pradesh in April 1948 and reorganisation in October 1966, there are no hilly areas left with Punjab.

To call Pahari Paintings, 'Himachal Art' is again not very befitting because Himachal Pradesh, as a political entity, is over four decades old, while the Pahari art phase, with the exception of some individual artists, who have been seen practising the art even today, ceased to exist by the close of the nineteenth century.

'Kangra Painting', as the title goes, assumed much popularity but looking upon the entire canvas, it is a misnomer. Kangra paintings, howsoever good they may be, constituted only a part or a style of the whole art, the other parts or styles being Basohli, Guler, Chamba, Mandi, Bilaspur, Kullu, Garhwal and others.

There is still anotner title—Himalayan Art—which, though a very fascinating one, could not be favoured by the scholars as it connotes a very vast scope. In the field of painting alone, the Pahari art is not all that constitutes the Himalayan art. The Himalayan art is also applicable to all the styles, both folk and sophisticated types—that have flourished in the Himalayan region since centuries past. Obviously it includes the great traditions of scroll (*thanka*) and wall paintings connected with the Buddhist rituals and shrines.

General Introduction

The works of Pahari Painting adorn many a museum the world over and are increasingly attracting art-lovers, historians and scholars alike. Apart from other factors the Pahari Art of Painting, which gives Himachal pride of place in the world of art, is one thing which unequivocally stands for common links in the area ranging from Jammu right up to Garhwal, including of course the present set-up of Himachal Pradesh.

With ever pervading turmoil of social and political changes, the art on the Indian soil remains a search for truth— the truth of divine essence. The art here derives its motivation from the incessant battle between good and evil. Pahari Art, having the general impress of divinity, has covered a vast panorama of Indian life, its history and traditions, its beliefs and customs. Though limited to some hilly parts for its execution, it had for its spiritual content the best that lay in the art, literature and mythology which thrived for centuries past in the Indian sub-continent. The Vaishnava creed, which marked the Sanskrit and Hindi poetry of the period from the eleventh to the sixteenth century was later adopted by the painters of the princely states of the western Himalayas and translated the same into miniature and wall paintings. Surprisingly the art movement flourished at a time when the princely states in the region were not only engaged in mutual feuds and fights but had also been dominated by the paramountcy of the Mughal empire. The Mughal empire had a keen knack for art and architecture which resulted in the building of big palaces and mosques. The paintings got no less importance but the notable thing is that what Mughal artists could not accomplish was achieved by the artists in petty hill states. This makes one surprise as to how a dominated culture stole a march over a dominant empire.

Pahari Art of Painting combines in itself what is traditionally best in the literature, art and music. Dr. Coomaraswamy has aptly remarked, "The work of the Rajput painters deserves to be given an honourable place amongst the great arts of the world." Himself a renowned art-historian, it is much to him that the classical works of Indian painting, including those of Pahari school, were introducted to the western world and found place in many European and American museums and art galleries. Commenting on the Rajput painting, he wrote, "If it is ever possible to write in full the history of painting in India, it is this art of the country itself, which after Ajanta, must form its main theme. Compared with the significance of this religious art, so romantic and impassioned, even in some respects more brilliant, the achievement of the Persian, the Central Asian and Indian painters at the Mughal courts, must be treated as a mere episode."

Painting out the characteristic importance of Kangra School of Paintings he wrote, "Their ethos is unique: what Chinese art achieved for landscape is here accomplished for human love. Here, if never, and nowhere in the world, the Western Gates are opened wide. The arms of lovers are about each others necks, eye meets eye, the whispering *sakhis* speak of nothing else but the sound of Krishna's courtship, the very animals are spell-bound by the sound of Krishna's flute and the animals stand still to hear the ragas and raginis. This art is only concerned with the realities of life; above all, with passionate love-service, conceived as the means and symbol of all Union." Thanks to the wisdom of Dr. Coomaraswamy who through his writings and speeches made us look with interest and feel proud of the legacy which we would have otherwise looked at with apathy and indifference.

Feminine Grace

If one looks to the keynote of the Pahari paintings, he would realise that it is the feminine grace which is so characteristic of the Indian womanhood. Earlier we have its excellent examples in Ajanta paintings and the traditional sculpture.

Dr. Vasudeva Saran Agarwala writes, "The focal point of the Kangra School consists in the flaming beauty of woman. The life of an Indian woman as lived in the idyllic land of love and expressed through the twelve months, the six seasons and the twenty-four hours of the day provides the rich texture of Pahari Paintings. Passionate love enriched by dovotional fooling inherent in the heart of a woman towards the man she loves imparts colour to the charming brocado of the pointer's art. Woman in those paintings alone is real. The man lives and shines under her light as a moth captivated by the warmth of the flame. We do not gather any lasting impression of male beauty in Kangra paintings. But the woman's body, the delicacy of her form, the radiance of her face and indescribable loveliness of her life are subjects in which the Kangra painters excel."

About the portrayal of feminine beauty in Pahari Art, A.K. Coomaraswamy wrote, "The great work of the (Kangra) School was to create a feminine type peculiar to itself and of infinite charm; not robust, like the Rajasthani type, but slender and moving with an irresistible grace, intentionally accentuated by the long lines of the drapery."

Bhakti Movement

One of the reasons, responsible for making Pahari painting truly a great art, is its inspiration in the cult of Bhakti. The eleventh century witnessed the rise of a popular faith—Vaishnavism—the doctrine of personal, passionate devotion towards Krishna, the most popular among Hindu gods.

Jayadeva, the court-poet of Lakshaman Sen of Bengal (1179-1205 A.D.) had come up with his long love poem of *Gita Govinda* which is an allegory of the soul striving to escape the allurement of senses in their search for external peace and is realised through mystical union with God. Krishna is the nod in the form of a cowherd, Radha and other milkmaids are the souls, and 'Dootika' is the messenger maintaining the contact between the two. Apart from the allegorical meaning of soul's yearning for union with the divine, the artists have portrayed amours of Krishna and milkmaids as human encounters.

Radha-Krishna cult owes its beginning to some indefinite past but the Jayadeva's poetry in the twelfth century made a notable contribution by transplanting it on the common social plane. It was further enriched in the fifteenth century by Vidyapati and Chandidas in their varses, characterised by sensuous emotions, spiritual delight and mystic ecstasy. Then comes Chaitanya (1486-1533) who treated God as the supreme lover and the soul of the man as his devoted brids. The Radha-Krishna cult had its sway till the sixteenth century and many mystic poets like Surdas, Keshavdas, Mirabai and others wrote their poems in devotion to and love of Krishna assuming him as their hero in the manner which their varying talent and tastes realised. Marked by brevity of expression and vividness of thought their poems had rich poetic flavour, subtlety of feeling and sensuous delight. These compositions have passed on to us with unabated popularity and appeal even in the present age posing as a disbeliever.

With the rise of Aurangzeb in the Mughal empire the artists had begun to lose the royal patronage and many of them went to the western Himalayan states where the Hindu princes ruled. This region being comparatively peaceful and other things being congenial, the artists chose to settle there. The Rajas gave them a warm welcome in their courts and took keen interest in their works.

Krishna Cult

The most favourite subject of the Pahari paintings was the Radha-Krishna cult which the people of the time thought as the highest state of bliss. Pahari Art did not only make a pictorial record of the mythological legends of the cowherd god Krishna, it gave him meaning and charm much more than the whole of literature about him conveys. It delightfully unfolds him on a plane which can simultaneously be identified as earthly and spiritual, as human and divine. Krishna is an incarnation of Vishnu as the Hindu scriptures record. Krishna is the most popular of all Hindu gods. The Pahari artists, simple and unsophisticated as they were, could not have a better hero to their imagination than Krishna in the Whole history of mankind. It is for the scholars, the devouts and the common folk to see handwork of the old masters whose skill, deftness and dexterity go to combine in the mosu unusual way. In hundreds of Pahari paintings one encounter: the idyllic love scones of Radha and Krishna in such a divine religious and mystical setting as would not easily find a paral-lol. Radha and other milkmaids are charmingly portrayed. It is only the women whoso beauty and grace appeal, there is nothing, so about men. And also it is not the chisullod out features or the exposition of somo limbs or parts of body but the total femininity which lands the femnio figuror: an unusual charm. Of all tho sakhis or gopios (milkmaids) Rndha stands out as one attaining fulfilment. In Pahari paintings while Krishna is deciphered by tho mukut (crown) he wears. Radha is singled out by the role she is entitled to. There is hardly any difficulty in recognising Krishna and Radha in a multitude of figures placed in the painting.

Other Subjects

Next to Krishna, it is the great God Shiva which has figured well in Pahari paintings. Faith in Shiva is older than that in Krishna. The cult of Shiva is deep-rooted and widespread in the Himalayas and it was but natural that the hill artists successfully attempted to paint Shiva in his various forms and manifestations, such as Shankar, Virupaksha, Natraj, Gangadhar and others. While Shiva legend was painted by the hill artists of all places, the Panchavaktra Mahadeva, the five-faced Shiva, was one which was especially favoured by the Mandi artists. In sculpture we find in Mandi stone images of fivo-faced Shiva enshrined in the temples dedicated to Him.

The Hindu epics of *Ramayana* and *Mahabharaia*, Bhagwata Purana, Durga-Saptashati, the love-story of Nala Damyanti, Hamira-Hatha, the incarnations, the nayikas, Ragamala, Baramasa were other main themes which the artists frequently drew upon. The Pahari artists were well conversant with Keshav, Matiram, Bihari, Senapati and other Hindi poets and painted countless pictures based on their poetic works.

Ragamala: Ragamala which means 'Garland of musical modes' has been a popular theme with both the Rajasthani and Pahari painters. In the classical music of India there are six principal ragas or modes of music, and each raga in its turn is wedded to five raginis. These ragas and raginis have their children called *putras*. By raga what one generally understands is passion, melody or song. Every raga has a particular atmosphere to thrive on, A raga cannot and should not be sung out of season. For instance Vasanta and Hindola ragas are associatod with spring. A raga has also an appropriate hour. The raga painting is the usual representation of the emotion.

In National Gallery of Art, New Delhi, there are several Pahari paintings which are illustrative of the Ragas and Raginis, such as Raga Kanhra, Raga Malava (son of Sri Rama), Raga Pancham (son of Bhairava), Raga Lahul (son of Hindola), Raga Kal Naga (son of Deepak), Raga Bhaskar (son of Hindola), Raga Vasanta (son of Hindola), Ragini Suhi (of Mantha), Ragini Kankari (of Megha), Ragini Bhairavi (of Bhairava), Ragini Ahiri (of Hindola), Ragini Gunakali, Raga Hindola, Ragini Devagandhari, Ragini Seehuti, Raga Vinod, Raga Kumbha, Raga Lalit, riagini Swain, Ragin Gandhari, etc.

How these ragas and raginis have been translated in painting may be understood by the following account. Vasanta is illustrative not only of the flowering season but also the yellow garment which the young prince or Krishna wears. In Pahari or Rajasthani painting Vasanta is presented by a scene where Krishna is playing holi with Radha and her maids. Sri Raga is illustrated by Krishna and Radha in a forest, picking beautiful fragrant flowers. Raga Bhairava stands for the God Shiva attended by some maidens. Bhairavi describes the unmarried heroine longing for love. In this situation Parvati is seen worshipping the *Shivalinga* and praying for union with the Lord. The painting, which exhibits dark clouds and rain showers, stands for Raga Megha-Malhar. Raga Kedara shows a band of musicians playing on their instruments. The illustration to the Asawari Ragini portrayed a female snake-charmer and that to the Ragini Todi a woman playing on a Vina and attracting a wild deer. The Ragini Soratha shows a woman stringing a garland and attended by a woman with a fan in her hand, the trees in the background are laden with flowers.

Various Styles

Pahari Art flourished in a very vast area which included princely states like Basohli, Jammu, Punch, Guler, Kangra, Chamba, Mandi, Suket, Bilaspur, Arki, Kullu, Garhwal and a host of other tiny states. Of all these, Basohli could be credited for being the oldest seat of Pahari Painting. Characterised by brilliant and spacious colour, Basohli paintings are marked by bold, frank and animated expression, savage vitality and peculiar disposition of faces of both sexes. Besides, overall simplicity and rhythm go hand in hand with all the paintings of this style. Kangra made its name as the greatest one. Though the best of the paintings originated in the Kangra State, Guler enjoyed the status of being older than Kangra. Chamba and Garhwal also made their own traditions and paintings originating from these two places could be deciphered after their respective characteristics. It was after the taste and talent of the rulers on one hand, and the artists on the other, which together gave a specific character to the paintings of a place in a specific period.

The paintings that were executed in a particular state, were named after it. Earlier when Pahari Painting was a living art, it was not named after any state. It was only a matter of convenience for the scholars that it was put under various titles which it got after the names of the states it thrived in. There is no basic difference amongst various schools or styles so far as the subjects dealt with and the material used by the artists are concerned. The stylistic differences, that developed over the years, were natural as the handling of the brush by different artists of the same or different generations could not follow a beaten track. Whether it was the general public or the rulers, they also had their own liking which had been responsible in shaping the art they were called to patronise.

The Basohli style is different from the Kangra style which will be evident from the figures and landscapes of their respective paintings. The Basohli is quite near the folk style and its figures are bold and colours dark and brilliant. As against this the Kangra style favoured elongated figures that have been painted with hotter skill and delicacy. The artists in the latter case have shown a judicious use of colours and the background of landscape and the buildings also exhibited better handling. The Chamba paintings hold the background in altogether a different style, though it became simpler hero. A crescent-shaped sweep, projecting a very eye-pleasing combination of colours in the background sky is noticeable here. The now trends (it different places and at different times were introduced either by the artists themselves or by the rulers and the general public to whose likings and dictates they responded easily.

Migration: The artists were not always stationary. Some of them moved frequently from one state to another. In fact the artist needed patronage. Every state did not maintain its own atelier but services of reputed artists were often sought everywhere. Sajnu of Kangra was one such artist. Besides his own state, he also worked at Mandi and Kullu, which helped him introduce his style at three different places. Sajnu presented a set of twenty-one paintings illustrating Hamir-Hath to Raja Ishwari Sen of Mandi in the year 1754 A.D. (on the 16th Magh, 1810). It was a time when Sansar Chand was besieged on all sides. Many of thc artists moved to neighbourly states and Sajnu was one of them. There were also gifts of paintings exchanged amongst the states themselves. When a princess of a state was wedded to a prince of another state, she took along with her, not only the paintings which formed part of the dowry, but also some artists. Also when two states developed cordial ties on account of friendship or matrimonial relations, the movement of the artists was frequent.

One of the main factors responsible for migration of an artist was the fame a ruler enjoyed as a lover and connoisseur of art. A state with such a head was a great draw for the artists from various places. Kangra was a great state, in fact the greatest amongst all states of the Western Himalayas. Incidentally it got in Sansar Chand not only a great ruler but also such a lover of art as had few equals in the history of art. Could family be the basis of a style—a question arises and demands careful consideration. For many Pahari artists painting was a family pursuit. For generations the technique of painting was handed down from father to son. That the son inherits the skill of his father is quite probable and the extent to which it is inherited depends on his own nature and intelligence. He may not be the right hair to all his father's traits and there is also a probability that ho may easily surpass his father and ancestors. If the son remains obsessed of his family's achievements, he may not achieve much. But if ho takes family's inheritance on one hand and has on eye for good things outside' on the other, he is naturally better destined.

What determines a style is a ticklish question. The answer does not rest in a single theory. Every theory advanced explains part of the truth. The style is as much a result of the individual cultivation as it is something of a community's mind.

Wall Paintings

Miniature paintings on paper were not the only manifestation of Pahari Art. In fact miniature was the style and technique which was also tried with equal success on cloth and walls.

The wall paintings were executed in almost all the states where miniatures on paper were favoured. There are still good remnants of this art in Arki, Kullu, Mandi, Nadaun, Nurpur, Tira Sujanpur, Chamba, Dada-Sibba, Damtal, Dharamsal, Jammu, Kankhal etc. Many of the paintings have obliterated but those which are left bear testimony to the fact that the entire region of the Himalayas known for its miniatures had also a very rich tradition of wall paintings. The wall paintings were as good as the miniatures on paper—the lines flow with rhythm and energy and the colours appear bright and glowing. The subjects were skilfully handled and they were not different from those of the paper miniatures.

Rumals

While paintings on paper and wall were exclusively the work of male artists, the art that appeared on cloth were mainly the work of womenfolk. Painting was as much an art as it was a fashion. How could then the womenfolk lag behind. They emulated skill and translated it in ombroidery which was a pleasure pursuit of the leisure hours. The cloth substituted the paper, the needle the brush and the threads the colours and pigments. It seems quite natural that in the early stage of its development, the male artists must have helped the womenfolk in the basic drawing which was later embroidered with the felicity and skill so natural with the ladies.

The paintings that were embroidered on cloth have takon a

general name of Rumal i.e. kerchief. But this type of kerchief was not meant for pocket purposes. Generally these rumals were meant for covering tho gifts placed on metal and bamboo trays and baskets on any auspicious occasion such as wedding, birthday, fairs or festivals.

The rumals varied in shape and size. With square and oblong shapes they ranged from a small to a bed-sheet length. The material used in the rumals consisted of an ordinary white *khaddar* cloth as the base and untwisted, unspun raw silk threads in various hues embroidered thereon. The technique employed was that of double satin stitch which resulted in giving the rumal similar expression on both sides.

The subjects, the ladies favoured the most, included the Ras-lila, Nayika-bheda, Radha-Krishna, Shiva-Parvati Ganesh with his Ridhi and Sidhi, and wedding scenes. Besides the kerchiefs, the other products of this craft included wall hangings, hand-fans, dice-board, the bodices (cholis), the cushion and pillow covers, caps, fans and a host of other things. The bodices catching the fancy of the ladies embroidered with the greatest love and care and also they were sometimes studded with small pieces of minor and imitation jewellery and diamonds. The wall hanging carrying a wedding scene, called Kauhra, served as a background decoration for the Ganpati image which formed the chief deity of worship in all wedding ceremonies.

Sansar Chand—The Great Patron

When we analyse the growth and success of this great movement of art the name of Raja Sansar Chand (1765-1823 A.D.) of Kangra stands distinct. Few persons in the history could match his love for art and patronage to the artists. He maintained an atelier where hundreds of talented artists were given regular employment and as a historian puts it they "gained from his gifts and favours." An ambitious king and a kind hearted man as he was, prosperity and peace marked his reign and for sometime, so long as he did not get the twin challenge of the Mughal empire and Maharaja Ranjit Singh, he was a paramount ruler through the length and breadh of the western Himalayan region. A personal devotee of Lord Krishna, he tried to build up his character after his hero. He was romantic by nature but by no means a victim to the abandons of luxurious living. He was a lover of beauty both in art and life. Besides having three queens he also married a commoner named Nokhu. Belonging to a tribe of Gaddi, she was a queen of beauty. The Raja got her from her husband and compensated him with money. The songs carrying the love-tale of Sansar Chand and Nokhu are still very common in Kangra, Chamba and Mandi in the Dhauladhar region of the Shivalik hills of the Himalayas. Their melody makes these folk songs transcend the age barrier with no easy signs of decay or fear of loss in obscurity.

In 1620 the Mughal emperor Jahangir had invaded and captured the Kangra fort. It was since then that the fort, a symbol of power in the western Himalayas, had continued to be under the control of the Mughals. This had given a great setback to the power of the Katochas. Saif Ali Khan, who was incharge of the fort, died in 1781 and Jai Singh Kanhaiya of Batala taking advantage of the situation took it in his fold. By this time Sansar Chand had greatly strengthened his power. In 1736 when he was a young man of 21 years, he got back the fort which had earlier been in the hands of his ancestors for centuries Together. This was a great event in the Katoch reign. The Katoch ruler, thus strengthened, began to invade the neighbouring states which he subjugated one by one. These states included Chamba, Sirmur, Kahloor (Bilaspur), Bangahal and Mandi. Many other tiny states who had not the power to face the Katoch ruler, surrendered to him and accepted his paramountcy.

In his closing years when he had been deprived of his conquests and his glory had faded, he fell in love with a dancing girl Jamalo and spent most of his time in her company in the palace at Nadaun by the side of the river Beas. At this time also his love for art had not declined and he was as zealous for it as in the peak days of his empire. There was, of course, a change in the subjects of his liking. His love for the Lord Krishna, however, continued unabated. The story-tellers, singers and musicians would entertain and enlighten him with the legends of the lord and artists would visit him with their paintings which now centered round the same theme.

The continued success of Sansar Chand made him over-ambitious and he thought of conquering Lahore, then seat of the Sikh empire headed by Maharaja Ranjit Singh. The challenge was easily accepted. In fact, Sansar Chand had no real estimate of tho Sikh might. In 1803-04 his army made a march towards the plains of Hoshiarpur and Bajwara and this was successfully checked by the forces of Ranjit Singh.

In 1805, Sansar Chand invaded Kahloor and annexed some of its areas situated on the right bank of the river Satluj. Apparently a success to Sansar Chand, this proved as the beginning of his decline. The Bilaspur Raja invited Amar Singh Thapa, the Commander of the Gurkha forces and made an alliance with him. The Gurkha Commander with forty thousand soldiers at his command crossed the Satlyj near Bilaspur. The Gurkha forces were joined by 10,000 soldiers of all the states of Bilaspur, Chamba, Basohli and such other small states as were in the neighbour of Kangra and were subjugated by the Katoch ruler. The alliance of these states and the Gurkha Commander was based on the condition that while the Kangra fort would be retained by the Gurkha forces, the states were to be left unmolested. In 1805 at Mahal Morian the fight took place. Raja Sansar Chand fought very brawely but was defeated. The Gurkha Commander also freed Ranjit Ishwari Sen of Mandi who had been in Sansar Chand's imprisonment for no less than twelve years.

It was not a simple defeat for the Katoch ruler, the entire state was put to ruin. In his Kangra Settlement Report, Barnes wrote, "the memory of those disastrous days stands out as a landmark in the annals of the hills. Time is computed with reference to that period, and every misfortune, justly or unjustly, is described to that prolific source of misery and distress...The people, harassed and bewildered, fled to the neighbouring kingdoms, some to Chamba, some to the plains of the Jalandhar Doab. Other hill chieftains incited by Sansar Chand's former oppressions made inroads of anarchy with impunity and aggravated the general disorder. For three years this state of anarchy continued. In the fertile valleys of Kangra, not a blade of cultivation was to be seen, grass grew in the towns and tigresses whelped in the streets of Nadaun."

After his defeat at the hands of the Gurkh; Sansar Chand again thought of turning the wheels of history. He sought the help of Maharaja Ranjit Singh. At Jwalamukhi, where the two met, an agreement was signed whereby the Kangra fort and the adjoining area was to be under the control of Ranjit Singh. In August 1809 the Sikh forces clashed with the Gurkha forces and forced the latter to go beyond the Satluj. This led the Sikhs to have their paramountcy all over the hill states of the Western Himalayas.

In 1809 there were two Europeans in the employ of Raja Sansar Chand. They have also figured in some paintings of that time. When Moorcroft visited Sansar Chand at Alampur in 1820, he wrote of them, "...these men are of use to the Raja and might be of more, but their means are limited...Ranjit Singh has not exacted yet any tribute from him but he claims military service, and put him foremost in his late attack upon the Kahloor Raja, whose forts were taken by the troops and artillery of Sansar Chand under James and O'Briens." (Moorcroft, William and Trebeck, George, *Travels in Hindustan*, New Delhi, Sagar Publications, Reprint 1971, pp. 126, 130).

In his travelogue Moorcroft has given details of Sansar chand in the latter's closing years:

"In the evening I waited upon the Raja at his desire, and found him with his son and grandson in an open building in a garden. Raja Sansar Chand is a tall, well formed man, about sixty. His complexion is dark, but his features are fine an expressive. His son, Rai Anirudh Singh, has a very hand-some face and ruddy complexion but is remarkably corpulent. He has two sons, one of twelve, the other five years of ago, both less fair than himself. Sansar Chand was formerly the most powerful Raja from the Satluj to the Indus. All the potentiates from the former river to Kashmir were his tributaries or dependants, and he was extremely wealthy, possessing a revonuo of thirty-five lacs of rupees. He is now poor and in danger of being wholly subjected to Ranjit Singh. His misfortunes are mainly owing to himself, and his decline presents a remarkable contrast to the rise of his neighbour, and now paramount lord, Ranjit Singh."

Detailing his day-routine Moorcroft writes, "Raja Sansar Chand spends early part of the day in the ceremonies of his religion, and from ten till noon in communication with his officers and courtiers. For several days prior to my departure, he passed this period at a small bangla, which he had given up for my accommodation, on the outside of the garden. At noon the Raja retires for two or three hours, after which he ordinarily plays chess for sometime, and the evening is devoted to singing and naching, in which the performers recite most commonly Brij Bhakha songs relating to Krishna. Sansar Chand is fond of drawing and has many artists in his employ. He has a large collection of pictures, but the greater part represents the feats of Krishna and Balram, the adventures of Arjuna, and subjects from the *Mahabharata:* it also includes portraits of many of the neighbouring Rajas, and of their predecessors. Amongst these latter were two profiles of Alexander the Great, of which Rai Anirudh gave me one. It represents him with prominent features, and auburn hair flowing over his shoulders; he wears a helmet on his head begirt with a string of pearls, but the rest of his costume is Asiastic. The Raja could not tell me whence the portrait came: he had become possessed of it by inheritance." (Moorcroft, William and Trebeck,

George, *Travels in Hindustan,* New Delhi, Sagar Publications, Reprint 1971, p. 144).

Since 1786 when Raja Sansar Chand got his hold over the Kangra fort till 1805, i.e., for two decades, the movement of Pahari art had its peak season. In 1791, a Krishna temple was erected. Three years later, i.e., in 1794 another temple was erected at Tira which was called Sansar Chandeshwar. This temple, assuming its name after the Raja, had a metal image of Gauri-Shankar. In 1824 his Rani, who was a princess of the Suket state, erected the temple Narbadeshwar. Its walls were decorated with brilliant frescoes.

Gulam Mohi-ud-din has written in his *Tarikh-i-Punjab*, "For many years he passed his days in great felicity. He was generous in conduct, kind to his subjects, just as Naushirwan, and a second Akbar in the recognition of men's good qualities. Crowds of people of skill and talent, professional soldiers and others resorted Kangra, mid gained happiness from his gifts and favours. Those addicted to pleasure, who live for the gratification of others, flocked from all quarters and prohltod exceedingly by his liberality. Performers and story-tellers collected in such numbers, and received such gifts and favours at his hands that he was regarded as a Hatim of that age, and in generosity the Rustam of that time." (Hutchison, J. and Vogel J. Ph., *History of the Punjab Hill States*, Vol. I, p. 181).

The Tragic End

The two successive invasions of *Kangra* by the Gurkha and Sikh armies in the first decade of nineteenth century hit hard the art movement in the hills. Raja Sansar Chand (1765-1823), who not only emerged as the greatest of rulers in the western Himalayan states but could also be credited for his unique love for art, had lost his power. But for him, the hill art of painting would not have achieved its heights. The conditions had changed with the rise of big powers and his successor Raja Anirudh Chand had not at all the time favourable to him. The atelier had virtually been wound up and the artists had lost the state patronage. The worst was done by the Kangra earthquake on April 4, 1905 which put practically an end to the overall prosperity of the valley.

Along with thousands of people the artists also lost their lives. Those, who survived this catastrophe, sought employment in the drawing offices of Government departments leaving for good the hereditary pursuits of the great manual skill. With it came the end of this long oriental movement of art which now could truly claim as the last indigenous school of Indian painting.

It is true that the spirit of Vaishnavism, the skill and technique of the artists, the patronage of the Hindu rulers, the landscapes of the Himalayan hills, particularly the Kangra Valley, and the feminine grace of the hill belle all have been collectively responsible for the great movement of Pahari art and its high level of artistic achievement.

Pahari Art Today

As an art movomont it seems that tho Pahari Art is irrevocably lost. What is left of this movement is a treasure of 50.000 works, scattered all over the world. When the art was alleged to have been extinct there appeared a good number of books on it. It was through those books by art critics and art historians that the people at large came to know about this great heritage of the Himalayas. The art museums, galleries and the antique dealers made a hot chase after the works of Pahari Art that were left not only in the royal hands but also the general public in erstwhile states of Himachal and the adjoining areas of Jammu on the north-west and Garhwal on the north-east. The general impression that the Pahari Art is a thing of the dead past is incorrect. The movement with a span of three hundred years had made a gradual disappearance but there area few living artists who still paint in the traditional style. Chandu Lal and Poorna Chand of Kangra Valley and Prem Lal of Chamba are some of the artists whose works have now come to light. Chandu Lal belongs to a family of traditional artists. Lakshaman Dass (father), Ram Dayal (grandfather), Gokul (great-grandfather) and Chhajju (Gokul's brother) were four well-known names who worked for their respective patrons and the general public. Chandu Lal has been at work since his childhood and a painting takes him four to six days to complete. Since he knows his craft well and works continually, the number of his paintings goes well by thousands.

As regards the subjects of his paintings, Chandu Lal has dwelt on a variety of themes, the most favourite being the Radha-Krishna legend. In fact he has tried his hands, and did so very successfully, on a variety of traditional subjects of Pahari school, the noted among them being amours of Radha-Krishna, Nayak-Nayika-bheda and Raga-Raginis. Besides, he has also executed portraits of two great connoisseurs of Pahari Art viz. Raja Sansar Chand of Kangra and Raja Govardhan Chand of Guler which appear faithful reproduction of the old paintings.

Temple Architecture

The Himalayas extensive as they are, have a variety of temple architecture. Low-lying hills or the valloe areas have Shikhara, domed and plat-roofed temples. The mid and higher hills have pent-roofed and tiered roofed (pageda) temples. The high mountainous areas have again flat-roofed temples but in a different where those styles developed. Is not difficult to understand. They fashioned after the geophysical conditions of the various periods.

The Shikhara style developed because living and the valley areas have plenty of stones, particularly in the river-basins, and the area was not very far off and hence they were susceptible to their influences. The domed-shape constituted a style of the eighteenth and nineteenth century when the Mughals were the central power and the sikh found Punjab and its hills as their stronghold. The flat-roofed temples were built largely in the Kangra Valley where the Hindu Katochs ruled for sometime quite favourably.

The mid and higher hills gave rise to two types, which together have come to be known by a general title of hill-architecture. The walls are built of alternating layers of wood and stone but the roof distinguishes the type. There are temples, with pent-roofs and others with pyramidal tiered roofs. These temples, in which there is extensive use of wood, were constructed in the area studded with forests.

The high mountaineous areas such as Ladakh, Lahaul-Spiti and Kinnaur developed flat-roofed gompas because this part of the Himalayas is free of the influence of the western monsoons.

The Shikhara Temples

The Gupta age (400-700 A.D.) was marked by tremendous progress in almost all branches of arts and letters. The building of the structural shrines also made a beginning, although small temples much earlier. These temples were made of bricks and dressed stones. The earlier examples only consisted of a square cella, a small portico and a low platform. Great improvements followed in due course and such elements as covered ambulatory and low tower appeared in the new structures. As the overall tempo of the building activities was great during the eighth century, there followed improvement in the temple architecture leading to a definite concept of what o Hindu temple should be.

A Hindu temple consists of the vimana, or shrine (including tho *garbha griha*), the *antarala* and its Antarala, and the mandapa (assembly hall). The main shrino has inside it the *garbha griha* or sanctuary housing the principal deity to which the temple is dedicated. The vimana is surmounted by a high tapering tower which constitutes the shikhara. The form of shikhara is either rounded or curvilinear and has at its top either a finial (*kalasha*) or an amalaka, that is a circular ribbed stone disc. The inner cella or *garbh-griha* housing the main statue is dark, the only natural light it has is what it shares from the mandapa through its door. A lamp can be seen lighted giving the idea of a divine spirit illuminating the universe steeped in mystery. The door is joined with the mandapa through the antarala, that is a small tibule? The mandapa is a pillared hall where the devotees wait to pay their homage to the deity seated in the garbha-griha. The mandapa shih is joined outside it by a porch called the ardha-mandapa is open in some cases on inside, lift, right and front, and serves as the entrance portico.

In some cases the shrine-room has 'around it a pradak-'shina-path which is a circumambulatory passage meant for the devotes to have a round.

That the Shikhara is totally a style of the plains is a notion which cannot be accepted without reservation. The material, i.e., stone, used in this type of structure is all locally available. True that the plains had powerful tradition of constructing massive structures and comparatively the hills have very less of them, but the fact should not be overlooked that the hills also have some of the best specimens. When the Shikhara style was introduced, the hills also had their share of construction, the first specimen being the eighth century rock-cut temple complex of Masrur (Kangra) in the Gupta style. Jagatrukh temple near Manali (Kullu) also belongs to the early eighth century and is one of the earliest specimens of Pratihar style.

Another important temple, seen a century or two later, was that of Basheshwar Mahadeva built in the Iato Gupta style at Hat (Bajaura) in the Kullu Valley. To the tenth century belongs Mani-Mahesh temple of Bharrnaur (Chamba) built in mid-Pratihar style by Raja Sahil Verman (920-40 A.D.). To Narsingh is dedicated temple in Chamba which belongs to the tenth century. Later, in the beginning of the thirteenth century we see the temple of Baijnath, a great monument of high architectural and sculptural value. A good number of temples in Mandi followed later, the first of which was built by Rani Sultan Devi of Raja Ajbar Sen in the first quarter of sixteenth century.

The temple of Baijnath carries an inscription on stone-slab, still preserved, stating that the architects, employed in its building, were from Kangra. This helps us to opine that the Shikhara style was not solely a product of the plains but it belonged to an era which covered both hills and plains.

In the Himalayan hills a Shikhara temple is a tower like conical formation built entirely of stone and partially decorated with carvings. Such a temple has the usual *garbha-griha*, surmounted by a spire and porch. While some Shikhara temples in the hills have mandapa along with the image-chamber, others less significant are without it. The *amalaka*, appearing in the form of a ribbed stone, is seen at its top. The *amalaka* is some-Times covered by a wooden canopy. This superstructure, a peculiarity of the hills, covered with slates, is meant to protect the main structure against rain and snowfall which is a frequent phenomenon of the mountainous regions and sometimes in its worst. Chamba and Kullu have a fairly good number of such temples. Mani-Mahesh at Bharmaur (Chamba) and Lakshmi-Narain at Chamba proper are Shikhara type of shrines with parasols on the amalaka.

Kullu: Of pyramidal carved temples or Shikhara style there are quite a good number in Kullu district. Of these there is one each at Manglore, Bajaura, Mukraha, Manikaran, Sultanpur, Chakki, and Vashishtha, two each at Sursai and Jagatsukh, and four at Naggar.

Of all thse the nine century Basheshwar Mahadeva *temple* at Bajaura has been rated as "one of the finest monuments of the western Himalayas and a unique example of the later Gupta tradition." Despite the fact that the temple is small, there are some very striking features—the composition, the strength and the carvings all make it a fine monument.

Commenting on the Shikhara style of temple in Kullu, Harcourt wrote, "Of these the Bajaura one is at once the most notable for its ornate carvings, and the figures portrayed on the outer walls and entrance are, I think, certainly to equal anything of the sort I have seen elsewhere in India." (*Himalayan Districts of Kooloo, Lahaul and Spiti*, p. 61)

The sanctum, which measures 8'-6" by 7'-2" and outwardly 13'on each side, has in it a Shivalinga. On the top there is the amalaka. The porch on the east, which has the doorway, contains the river figures of Ganga and Yamuna; and on the south, west and north there are of Ganesha, Vishnu and Durga. Leaving aside the figures on the doorway, the rest are of one size—5'-3" in height. All these figures are nicely carved carrying rich details. The background also carries foliage and small figures. The goddess Durga is shown slaying the buffalo-demon and the two Asura kings. Every porch has at its top the triplet of miniature shrines which is surmounted by a three-faced idol, representing either the three gods, Brahma, Vishnu and Mahesh or the triple form of the great god, Mahadeva alone. The pot and foliages motifs appearing frequently are no less impressive.

Kangra: Baijnath, the name by which the great monument of the Beas Valley stands, is that form of Shiva where he is the lord physician. The temple was built in 1204 A.D. and the town that grew around it has also come to be known by the same name. The earlier name of the place was Kiragrama and this is borne out by the Sanskrit inscription in Sharda script on stone slabs found in the temple. It is learnt from the inscription that the temple was built by two wealthy merchants of Kiragrama, viz. Manyuka and Ahuka who were sons of Siddha. That the architects employed in the great construction were from Kangra itself, is a fact that the hills could rightly feel proud of even today.

The English translation of the inscription reads:

"There is in Trigarta the pleasant village of Kiragram, the home of numerous virtues where the river called Binduka, leaping from the lap of the mountain, with glittering wide waves resembling playing-balls, merrily plays, like a bright maiden in the first bloom of youth. That village is protected by the strong-armed Rajanaka Lakshmana." (*Kangra District*, 1924-25, p. 501).

Kiragrama had been a small state and for generations it owed its allegiance to the state of Trigarta but the relations of the two states were very cordial, the reason being that the daughter of the Trigarta's ruler had been married to the father of Lakshamana whom the above inscription refers.

The temple has much in resemblance with the famous Orissa temples so far as the design and form are concerned. This is also due to the fact that both these shrines originated much or less in the same period. The structural resemblance is particularly noticeable in the flat-roofed mandapa with *rekhashikhara* rising above.

The temple measures 51 X 31'. As is common with many Hindu temples the images of the goddesses Ganga and Yamuna stand at the entrance which is also studded with other deities. On the mandapa are carved a good number of Ganga-figures.

The temple has the main image of a linga enshrined in the *garbha-griha* measuring 8 square inside and surmounted by a spire in the Shikhara style. Outwdraly the sanctum measures 18 each side.

The mandapa, that is an assembly hall, is 20' square inside and has a roof in the pyramid style supported on four large-sized round pillars. In between the image-chamber and the assembly hall is a small ante-room with two pillars. Before the assembly hall there is the porch supported on four columns. Fergusson has made the following observation which is worthy of reproduction: "The shafts of these pillars are plain cylinders of very classical proportions, and the bases also show that they are only slightly removed from classical design. The square plinth, the two trusses, the cavette or hollow moulding between are all classical, but partially hidden by Hindu ornamentation of great elegance but unlike anything found afterwards." (*History of Indian and Eastern Architecture,* 2nd ed., London, 1910, p. 298).

Both Cunningham and Fergusson were of the view that the Baijnath temple had been renovated by Raja Sansar Chand (1776-1824 A.D.) of Kangra, a great connoisseur of art and architecture. But to Sir Aurel Stein, who visited the temple in December 1892, the temple had not undergone such very alterations as the earlier scholars stated. He further held that as mentioned in the inscriptions the doorway of the adytum, i.e., puri was still decorated with the images of the river goddesses but the roof appeared a modern construction.

It may be of some interest to note that while great destructions took place all-round during the earthquake of the 4th April 1905 in Kangra Valley, this temple was not much affected. A nearby temple of Siddhanath, situated at the west-end of the town however, could not survive the catastrophe and was greatly damaged.

Chamba: There are a good number of Shikhara temples in Chamba, most famous of which are dedicated to Vishnu and others to Shiva. There are also a couple of shrines dedicated to the goddess. A Shikhara temple in Chamba has an image-chamber surmounted by a spire but it has no ante-room or mandapa attached to it. This makes them some what characteristically different from the famous Baijnath temple in district Kangra and Bhutnath, Triloknath and Panchvaktra at Mandi. The image-chamber is approached through a porch supported by a couple of pillars. There is a group of six temples in Chamba, out of which three are dedicated to Vishnu and three to Shiva. Of all Chamba shrines, one that of Lakshmi Narain is the most famous. As regards its exact time of construction, nothing can be hold with certainty but as is believed, it marks the advent of Vaishnavism in the hills.

Another temple of the same group is that of Chandragupta which is dedicated to Lord Shiva. Both these temples are believed to have been constructed by Raja Sahil Varman who is credited with having founded the present town of Chamba in about 930 A.D. Another temple falls in between the above two temples and is of a recent date. This temple, dedicated to Radha-Krishna, was constructed by Sadha, wife of Raja Jit Singh, in 1825. Of the rest one is of Gauri-Shankar, another of Trimukh linga, and the last of Lakshmi-Damodar. Besides the above group, there are other two temples dedicated to Hari Rai and Bansi Gopal, both held as manifestations of Lord Vishnu. Hari Rai temple, embellished with good carvings, was erected by Salakara Varman who ruled the state during eleventh century. The Bansi Gopal temple is of recent origin.

As against the above male deities, there are a couple of Shikara temples dedicated to the Devi. They are the Champavati and the Vajreshware temples. The latter, lying outside the town of Chamba, is noted not so much for its architecture but for its sculpture. The stone image is that of the goddess Durga slaying the buffalo-demon.

Outside the town of Chamba, the Shikhara temples of any note in the district are very few. Bharmaur, the ancient capital of the state, has two such temples, viz. Mani-Mahesh and Narsimha. The Mani-Mahesh temple, as the belief goes, was erected by Meru Varman, who reigned about 700 A.D. and the Narsimha temple was erected by Yogakar who ruled about tenth and eleventh centuries.

The temple at Udaipur, just near Chamba, belongs to a Shikhara style but is of a very recent time. The temple which was erected after the death of Raja Udai Singh (1720 A.D.) was named after him and contains three marble idoesd one Narayana, and other two of Raja Udai Singh and his brother Lachhman Singh.

Still another temple of importance belonging to the Shikhara style is that of Triloknath, which has a spire and a porch, the latter profusely carved. It may be noted that this temple is held sacred by both the Hindus and the Buddhists. The temple is looked after by a lama priest and the Buddhists, who flock to the shrine from Lahaul, Ladakh and Zaskar, hold the deity as Avalokiteshwara. The image is obviously an imported one as it is in marble. With transfer of certain pnrganas, the temple is now in the district of Lahaul and Spiti.

Mandi: In the district of Mandi, it is only the town Mandi, which has stone temples in the Shikhara style. A couple of shrines do exist outside, i.e., at Rewalsar but they are not of much significance.

The town abounds in the stone temples and it may be noted that such a good number at such a small place has hardly any parallel elsewhere.

The stone temples in Mandi may be noted for having marked constituents of Shikhara styles, i.e., a cella surmounted by a spire and a porch which, in most case; is decorated with carvings. Some temples are simple single structures consisting of an image inside while others have ante-room or mandapa attached to the image chambers. What is characteristically particular of the Mandi shrines is the trefoil arch which adorns the facade or porch. This arch is supported by the capital of the pillars or pilasters. The brackets on both sides appear as human figurines seated on the head of an elephant and holding the trunk in their hands. In some cases the corners are embellished with the figures of gandharvas, the well-known mythological musicians. This sculptural elegance besides adding to the beauty of the architecture commands a very pleasing effect on the onlooker. The trefoil arch can also be seen in the temples of Triloknath, Bhutnath, Tarna (excluding the main shrine on the top of the Tarna hill) and a host of others.

Of the Shikhara temples in Mandi, which are of architectural importance, Triloknath and Panchvaktra are the outstanding ones. We have earlier noted a Triloknath temple in Chamba-Lahaul but the one at Mandi does not seem much identified with Avalokiteshwara. The temple of Triloknath was erected in 1520 A.D. by Rani Sultan Devi of Raja Ajbar Sen who had been credited with having founded the present town of Mandi. The square sanctuary with 8′-4″ on each side houses a life-sized stone image of three-faced Shiva with Parvati in his lap and mounted on a bull. The porch of the temple is 7′-8″ in length and 3′-6″ in width. The two pilasters may be marked for dwarpala (door-keeper) on each side and the capitals of the pillars carry carvings in floral and animal designs. The two pillars have at their top the trefoil arch.

The Panchvaktra temple, which quite resembles with Triloknath, is situated at a very picturesque site formed by the confluence of the river Boas and its tributary Suketi.

As the name suggests Lord Shiva is the chief deity who has live faces and ten arms. Of the five faces, three are seen from front, the fourth is on the back and the fifth rises upward. The mandapa of the temple rests on four pillars, the bases of which give the appearance of rosette or lotus and the capitals that of flower-pot.

The Temple of Bhutnath, the most frequented shrine, is situated in the midst of the town. With the construction of this temple, Raja Ajbar Sen founded the new township of Mandi, the earlier being on the right bank of the river Beas. This temple has the usual features Shikhara type, such as a small porch and a cella surmounted by a spire. There is also a *sabha-mandapa* which is held as a later addition but is quite in harmony with the main shrine. The facade of the porch carries the usual feature of trefoil arch and the fluted pillars, on which the porch rests; the capitals are embellished with elephant figures.

Another Shikhara temple is dedicated to the god Ardha-narishwar—the idol which has on its right half the image of Shiva and on the left that of Parvati. The bull and the lion, being their respective vehicles, are part of the whole composition. The figure of Shiva has knotted hair on the head, a necklace of human skulls, a musical instrument and a *damru* in the two hands. The figure of Parvati appears with a diadem, an earring and a nosering. The overall appearance of the idol is very clear and easily identifiable. The temple has a porch and an assembly hall and the carvings on the spire mark it out as one of ample artistic merit. The temple suffers from neglect and is not in a good state of preservation.

Greetings and Welcome

Greetings between persons of equal age and status is done by joining both palm of the hands and saying 'Namaskar'. Greetings between an elder and a younger person is done by saying 'Namaskar' with the younger bowing slightly. However, greetings between closely related elder and younger persons is done by touching the feet of the elder who in turn says 'Ashirvad' (my blessings) or 'Chiranjio' (long live). Touching the feet with both hand is more common amongst women who will invariably touch the feet. The younger one generally hugged and kissed by the elder one.

Journey

Whenever a person leaves his house on a journey to any place or on some mission or to join his service or to the house of some relative, an auspicious day and time is selected by consulting the Purohit before starting journey. 'Tilak' is applied by the head of the family on the forehead of the person leaving the house who is given blessings and good wishes for a happy journey and safe return.

Funeral Rites

Funeral rites are also performed strictly in accordance with

'Shastras'. In case of death of an unmarried young man or woman the body is normally buried and not cremated. There is general mourning for a week or so by the entire village or the caste group affected. All celebrations like marriages are cancelled within the caste group or village concerned. However, in case of an adult who is married, the body is cremated. There may be special mourning for 13 days, after which a Puja is performed, called 'Teraween', and feast is given in case of an old man. There may also be a Puja and feast after 12 months known as 'Barsi'. No marriage ceremony takes place in the family concerned for a year and festivals too are not celebrated in the village during that period to mourn the death of a person.

Rituals

Various kinds of rituals practiced, religious or 'Tantrik', have also been prevalent in the hills of Uttarakhand. 'Tantra' is a system of practices involving yoga, meditation, hypnosis, auto-suggestion, Asanas, exercise and self control for the fulfilment of worldly desires as well as the attainment of spiritual knowledge. The knowledge of 'Tantra' has been generally with the few known families in Uttarakhand belonging to 'Brahmin' and Scheduled caste families. The knowledge was passed from one generation to another and it was also one of the traditional occupation of certain families in the hills. 'Tantra' has been practiced both for liberation from evil power as well as for the well being of the person or the family. While the practice of 'Tantra' has come down in the hills, this ancient knowledge is being fully utilised by many internationally known godmen and gurus to provide relief to the needy.

Folk Songs

Folk songs have existed since time immemorial and they have grown with the joys and sorrows of the community concerned. Hill people are strongly attached to their folk songs and folk dances. When these recitals are presented on the stage they do not fully capture the spirit of those outdoor shows as they are basically a community performance in which a person is both an actor and a spectator. Agriculture is the mainstay of the hill people. It is, therefore, natural that agricultural operations figure prominently in folk songs and folk dances.

In fact, folk songs are nothing but poems composed by the community concerned and sung individually or in groups with local musical instruments to back up. Due to the geographical conditions, especially in the hill region, these folk songs do not die but have become part of their rich cultural heritage. The people in rural areas live closer to nature and truth, and therefore, they find it difficult to hide the truth from themselves. The folk songs will invariably reflect the true emotional and other feelings of human beings. The folk songs reflect love for the land where they live with the socio-economic problems of the society. The folk songs of Uttarakhand have also the same background and they also narrate the socio-economic life of the people during various stages of history. Despite socio-economic changes and the advent of the radio and television, folk songs are still sung on various occasions like *Katha* (Tale), *Puja* (Worship), marriages, fairs and festivals. A brief description of folk songs from Garhwal and Kumaon hills are given below.

Folk Songs of Garhwal Region

The folk songs of Garhwal region have come into being due to some peculiar socio-economic problems. Some of these folk songs are born out of the ill-treatment meted out by the mother-in-law to her daughter-in-law. Sometimes it is about scarcity of grains due to drought or famine. As the population kept on increasing, sufficient grain was not available and so by compulsion the people had to come down to the plains for jobs. The sorrows of separation suffered by the women has been expressed in many folk songs of Garhwal. At the same time, there are folk songs composed to narrate various important events of history like the independence movement, bravery displayed by Garhwali soldiers during wars and sometimes in appreciation of the national leaders like Mahatma Gandhi, Jawahar LailNehru and Subhash Chandra Bose. Some of the folk songs portray new fashions continuously overtaking the old ones. The idea behind these folk songs is either to ridicule certain bad customs prevalent in society or to present a satirical view of this. The folk songs are also used as a medium to express sympathy for the suffering, expression of love and compassion or to bring about certain economic or social reforms. Some of the known Garhwali folk songs have been described briefly in the following paragraphs.

Chhopati: These are the folk songs popular in Rawain-Jaunpur area of Tehri Garhwal. 'Chhopati' are the love songs sung between the men and women in the form of questions and answers. The last line of the song sung by one group is repeated by the other group and then carry on with the singing of folk song. Chhopati folk songs are sung with the 'Chhopati' folk dance and thus it is known as 'Chhopati'.

Chounphula and Jhumeila: 'Chounphula' and 'Jhumeila' form part of seasonal dances which are performed from 'Basant Panchami' to 'Sankranti or Baisakhi'. 'Jhumeila' is performed both by men and women but is usually restricted to women. 'Chounphula' is a spinning dance performed by all sections of the community, at night, in groups by men and women. There is no interlocking of hands, but there is synchronisation of movement. Men and women move in opposite directions. During the dance they clap with each others hand. All participants also sing and maintain the rhythm by clapping. 'Chounphula' folk songs derive their names from the Chounphula folk dances. No musical instruments are played during 'Chounphula' folk dances and songs.

Basanti: 'Basanti' folk songs are composed for the coming spring season when flowers bloom and new life spring in the valleys of the hills of 'Uttarakhand'. The folk song is sung individually or in groups in natural surroundings.

Mangal: 'Mahgal songs are sung during marriage ceremonies. These songs are basically 'Puja songs' sung alongwith the Purohits who keep enchanting 'Shlokas' according to the 'Shastras' during the marriage ceremony.

Puja folk songs: These songs are connected with the Puja of family deities. The songs are sung on various religious festivals or on such days when the family has arranged Puja. Puja folk songs are composed in appreciation of deities like Ghanta Karn, Bairon, Heet, Kaluwa, Jakh or any other deities like Sidharth, Chauranginath, Maniknath, Satynath, Gorakhnath, etc., who are also known in other parts of the country. There are other Puja songs connected with 'Tantra' and 'Mantras' to get rid of evil spirits in the body of human beings.

Jaggar: 'Jaggar' falls in the category of ghost and spiritual worship in the form of a folk song or at times combined with dances. Sometimes, Jaggar may also be in the form of 'Puja' folk songs and are sung to worship the various gods and goddesses. In other words, Jaggar is of two types. One to cure illness and the other to invoke the spirit in a human being to bring about the general well being of the community. A typical example is 'Ganganath Jaggar' which is performed by a professional Tantrik from among the scheduled castes men or women. A tale of Dotiyal Prince and his beloved Bhana Joshi, Brahmin girl, is narrated. The love tale ends in the tragic murder of lover. A vocalist sings the tale in a poignant strain and the dancer begins to enact it without elaborate word movement. The climax is built up slowly and then at the critical moment, the spirits of the prince and his beloved are invoked and finally sent back to their heavenly abode to rest. Some of the known 'Jaggar' songs are Darj, Kanchani, Sidua Nirtya, Bhoot Gomila and Anchari, which pertain to worship of evil spirits. There are others like Narsing Nag Devta, Sidhuwa and Devi puja which are performed to please the deity for the well being of the family and the community. Certain types of local musical instruments which accompany Jaggar are Thali, Dholak and Damru. In some Jaggar dance the Damru or Hurka is also used.

Baju-band: This is a folk song of love and sacrifice between the shepherds. It is a love dialogue between a man and woman or between a boy and girl which is sung in the form of a folk song. According to the folk song, the hilly surroundings are covered by forest trees like Banj, Burans, Chir and Deodar, where grazing of the cattle including sheep and goat can be seen. The girl moves behind the boy and gives him her compliments for rescuing her and her goats from time to time from wild animals like the Panther or the Tiger.

Khuded: These folk songs convey the suffering of a woman due to the separation from her husband. The woman curses the circumstances in which she is separated, generally when the husband is away searching for a job and somehow wants to meet him. 'Laman' is another folk song which is sung on special occasions expressing the sacrifice that he is willing to do for his beloved. 'Pawada' also belongs to this category of folk songs where separation is felt when the husband has gone to the battle field. Sometimes these songs are composed to recollect the memorable days the girl spent with her parents before her marriage.

Chhura: 'Chhura' folk songs are sung in the form of advice given by the old to the young one having learnt it out of their experience, particularly in grazing sheep and goats. These songs are sung amongst the shepherds.

Folk Lores of Kumaon Region

Like the folk songs of Garhwal region, the folk lore of Kumaon region have also developed with the history and socio-economic life of the people in Kumaon region. They also form part of the rich cultural heritage of Uttarakhand. While in Garhwal, the folk songs have no category as such defined, the folk lore of the Kumaon region have been classified according to the subject matter they contain. While in the Garhwal region the folk songs have revolved mostly around the hardships suffered by the women due to separation from their husbands or due to the difficult life led by the women with their-in-law, the folk lore of Kumaon region are mostly based on the worship of various gods and goddesses. The folk lore of Kumaon also reflect the love of the people for nature and the beautiful suroundings they live in. One of the well-known Kumaoni folk lore is 'Malushahi', which is based on a love story between a Khasiya boy Malu and a Bhutia girl, Rajula, resulting in a marriage against the wishes of the father of the girl. Similary, there is another folk lore known as 'Ramola'. Other popular folk songs are Bai and Hurkiya Bol which goes like, "Beru Pako Baro Maso O Narena, Kafal Pako Chaita, O Meri Chaila". A brief description of the folk lore of the Kumaon region are given in the following paragraphs.

Aathu: The folk lore of this category are generally composed to give the origin of various gods and goddesses. 'Athwali Rup' and 'Gaura Maheshwara' are two folk lores, the themes of which deal with the origin and life of Shiva and Parwati who are believed to have spent their entire life in the Kedarnath-Kailash-Mansarovar region of Uttarakhand.

Jaggar: Like in the Garhwal region, the aim of Jaggar folk lore is to drive away the evil spirits which may have entered the mind and body of human beings. In the Kumaon region also, Jaggar are performed with local musical instruments consisting of Thali, Damru, Hurki or Dholak, etc. Jaggar is also performed as a part of the grand puja of the local deities. During the later part of history, the life history of Katyuri Kings was also included in Jaggar folk lore probably because of the importance they had gained. The Jaggar folk lore include Ganga Nath, Laksh Begh, Rajsuya Yagya, Gangu Ramola, Sidua, Bidua, Katyuri Bansawali, Mainar and Haru Saim.

Pawada: Like the Pawada of the Garhwal region, the Pawada folk lore of Kumaon has also been composed primarily to convey the statesmanship and battle craft displayed by the kings and the soldiers from time to time. The stories are given in the Pawada folk lores. They are also called Jharo, Katku, Gudoi and Hurkia bol. Some of the known folk lore include Ratanchand, Thimalchand, Rana Rawat, Nar.Singh Dhani, Asandhi, Raja Raila, Biram Dev, Dula Padhani, Bikram Chand, Birsal, Sammauhit and Jamala Bohari.

Jhora: Like the Jaggar, Jhora folklore is also performed with the help of local musical instruments like Dhol and 'Nagara'. They are normally sung at night, on the eve of pilgrimage by the members of the families affected. This is to pray for a successful pilgrimage. Malenanth, Ajaimal, Nraiwali Jaita, Motiyasome and Naulin Baujain are the folklores known in the Jhora category.

Garuri: These are different type of folklore which form part of the Puja of the deities through sacrifice and torture. While the folklore are sung, the person has to undergo torture so as to get rid of illness or the influence of evil spirit the person may be suffering from. It is the oldest method of treatment when medicines and surgery had not even been thought of. Nar Singh, Aide and Vish are the folk lores known in this category.

Riturain: Like the folk song 'Basanti' of the Garhwal region, Riturain (the seasonal folklore) is born out of the appreciation of the nature during various seasons. These seasonal lores like 'Chaiti' is sung during the month of Chaitra when the 'Dhol' and 'Nagara' are played and the folklore are sung and donation in the form of money and grain are collected by the people. 'Goridhana' folklore is also one of this catetary.

Folk Dances

Folk dances likefolk songs are an integral part of any society particularly those living in rural and hilly areas. During olden days, man developed various means of entertainment for himself. Folk dances are generally performed in groups and therefore, became a means of sharing joys and sorrows with other people of the society. In fact, it has worked as a great source of motivation and inspiration to move forward against all odds while man continued his struggle for his livelihood. Some of the folk songs are sung along with the folk dances and accordingly the folk songs and the folk dances derive similar names. Each group or sub-group has distinctive dances. Some of the popular folk dances of both Garhwal and Kumaon have been described here.

Folk Dances of Kumaon Region

Chanchari: 'Chanchari' is more popular in Almora district of

Kumaon region. Originally, the dance was associated with certain rituals or worship of gods and goddesses. Today, it is a secular dance. The 'Chanchari' folk dance is performed both by men and women in a circle. Two half circles are formed by men and women respectively. There are two drummers in the centre who play instruments like the Hurka and Jhanj, and direct the dance along with the verses they sing. The men and the women move in a semi-circle taking a step forward with the rhythm of the song and movement of the body. At times when the number of participants is more, folk dancers make more than one circle, or alternatively, one group of dancers is carried on the shoulders by the other group and the dance continues. Chanchari is also performed during festivals and fairs. The dance also brings out the current happenings in the society and today one can watch the display of all developmental activities, through the performance of 'Chanchari'.

Chhapeli: This is the dance which explains love and romance. Normally, only two persons take part who will sing the love song and dance with the background music provided by local instruments like the Hurka and flute. With the increasing tempo of the dance, the audience also joins in chanting "Hoi-Hoi" during the folk dance. It is a playful dance performed by couples or in pairs.

Chholia: 'Chholia' is performed only by men and is more virile and vigorous in character. The origin can be traced back to the Bhotia warrior. But today, it is restricted to the professional folk dancer. 'Chholia' folk dance is performed with swords and shields only by men and it explains the old marriage custom when the bridegroom's party fought to take away the girl. Though the custom is no more prevalent today, yet the dance is enjoyed with the drummers and trumpeteers, following the dance party. The folk dancers carry red flags which signifies war. When the bride's father moves in with a white flag to avert the battle and the marriage was then solemnised.

Jaggar and Thora: 'Jaggar' and 'Thora' folk lores of Kumaon are connected with the spirits and the worship of local gods. The person affected, performs a dance to worship. While 'Jaggar' is a folk dance performed by an individual possessed by a spirit. 'Thora' is performed in a group and preferably on the day of the festival or before the performance of Puja of the local deities.

Seasonal Dances: 'Savan Shravan' is one of the seasonal dance of Kumaon region which is connected with the cultivation of paddy and maize. Similarly, 'Horka Bol' is recited during paddy cultivation in 'Bhadon' and also during maize cultivation. The name is derived from the instrument used, Horka (drum) and Bol (words). While the singer narrates historic deeds and stories of battles, the men and women dance with the precise coordination of arms, hands and feet to the rhythm of the Horka.

Folk Dances of Garhwal Region

Langvir Nritya: This is an acrobatic dance and is performed by the men folk only. In this dance, a long bamboo pole is fixed at a place. The dancer acrobat climbs to the top of this pole and then balances himself on his stomach the top. Under the pole, a band of musicians play 'Dhol' and 'Damana' while the dancer acrobat rotates on the top of the pole doing other feats with the help of his hands and feet. Although few can perform it today, it has a great tradition behind it. This dance is more popular in Tehri Garhwal region.

Barada Nati: This folk dance is a popular dance of Jaunsar-Bhawar area of Chakrata Tehsil in Dehradun district. The folk dance is performed on the eve of some religious festivals or on the occasion of some social functions. Both boys and girls take part they aim at liberating the soul of the dead person which they believe to have been living in the body of either a goat or another. The dance is similar to the pastorals of Himachal Pradesh or the hunting dance of Nagaland in the dance dressed with colourful traditional costumes. The dance is conducted in a semi-circle to the tune of the music and the folklore being sung in the form of question and answers. Sometimes, the girls have a pitcher balanced on their heads whilst performing 'Barada Nati' dance.

Pandva Nritya: Dussehra and Ramlila are the main attractions throughout the region of Uttarakhand. Accordingly, Pandava Nritya which is related to the story of *Mahabharta* has been very popular particulary in the garhwal region. Pandva Nritya is nothing but a simple narration of the story Mahabharta in the form of dance and music. The narration is mostly enacted on the occassion of Dusshera and Diwali. Pandva Nrity a is more popular in Chamoli and Pauri district.

Bhotia Tribal Folk Dances: Bhotia tribals of Uttarakhand have their typical dances like 'Dhurang' and 'Dhuring' which are connected with death ceremonies.

Fairs and Festivals

The people of Uttarakhand are deeply religious and have great regards to the numerous Hindu gods and goddesses. People dressed in colourful dresses, walk great distances to perform Puja (worship) in innumerable temples located all over Uttarakhand. Most of the fairs or festivals are in one way or another associated with the worship of various gods and goddesses. Today, with the change of time, most of the fairs and festivals also provide entertainment for the rural population of Uttarakhand. Fairs are considered to be the best occasions for every one to look forward anxiously for they provide an opportunity to meet with ones close and—distant relatives. Gifts are exchanged between Kith and kin who meet during these fairs. In addition, sports competition between schools or villages are also organised during these festivals. These fairs and festivals also provide the best opportunity for shopping. Lately small scale exhibitions have also become part of the traditional fairs and festivals.

Normally, all the festivals of the Hindus, that is, Dussehra, Diwali, (Bhagwali), Holi, Janmashtmi, Raksha Bandhan and Ram Naumi to name a few, are celebrated throughout Uttarakhand with a few variations, depending upon local customs. Fasting on the eve of religious festivals like Janmashtmi and Shivratri is common. People pay visit to nearby temples to perform Puja and relish the specially prepared food on these occasions. However, there are many festivals like Asthami or Athe, Baisakhi or Salde Baisakhi, Kartikpurnima, *Phulon ki Sankranti* (Phuldohi), *Singh Sankranti* (Ghee Sankranti), *Makar Sankranti* or *Uttarayan, Kark Sankranti* or *Haryala-Haryas*, Shivratri, Basant Panchami, or Jau tyohar. Nanda Devi and Haryala fair which are organised and celebrated at temples in accordance with local customs and traditions. It is indeed difficult to comprehend the spirit with which these fairs and festivals are celebrated without actual participation. However, an effort has been made here to give a brief description of a few selected traditional fairs which are of great importance to the people of Uttarakhand.

Makar Sankranti

'Makar Sankranti' is the first day of Magha which normally falls on 14th of January every year. It is the auspicious day when the sun crosses over the tropic of cancer and starts moving in the northern hemisphere of the earth. Somehow the festival of 'Makar Sankranti' has gained a place of special importance amongst people of Uttarakhand. In Tehri Garhwal, the day is dedicated to the Pandavas. The people participate in Pandava dances called 'Nauratra'. According to Nauratra, four or five persons act as Yudhister, Bhim, Arjun, Nakul,

Sahdev and a woman acts as Draupadi. This may carry on for nine days and nine nights. On the ninth day a buffalo or goat is sacrificed. In other parts of Uttarakhand, the main attraction of the festival is the game of ball (Gend) which is played between two groups of people. Variations in the game exist in different parts of Uttarakhand. In Tehri Garhwal, the team consists of parents and sons on either side and is played like hockey with no specific rules. In Pauri Garhwal it is played between the people of two adjacent parties without any limitation of ground or the number of participants, and is known as 'Gend ka Mela'. Traditionally the fair turns into a biggest gathering of the year where plenty of shops are established and a variety of goods are made available. Thousands of people take this opportunity to enjoy the fair with their kith and kin who congregate here from distant places. (For more details see following paragraph under the head 'Gend ka Mela').

Basant Panchami

Basant Panchami is celebrated according to local customs. It is also one of the anxiously awaited festivals of the people of Uttarakhand. The green saplings of barley, specially sown for the occasion near temples, are collected and distributed by the 'Aujee' (drummer). The *puja* song is sung, accompanied by the beating of drums in front of each house. Barley was considered to be the proof of holiness and the age old tradition is religiously followed by the people even today. The people stick these saplings on either side of the doors in their houses, with cowdung. 'Magha Panchami' is considered to be a time for better life with the onset of 'Basant' (Spring) and therefore, it is an auspicious occasion for offering green oats to respective family dieties. Special festival food preparations are made and exchanged among the families.

Jhanda Fair

The famous Jhanda Fair is celebrated in Dehradun during the month of March on the fifth day after Holi. The main attraction of the fair is the ceremony for hoisting the holy flag to commemorate the arrival and birthday of Shri Guru Ram Rai. Shri Guru Ram Rai born in 1646, was the eldest son of Shri Guru Har Rai, seventh Guru of the Sikh community. The people take a holy bath in the tank constructed near the Jhanda (flag pole). At one time the whole of Dehradun valley was under the control of Shri Guru Ram Rai who is called Mahanta. As a matter of tradition, the seat of Mahanta is held by the successor Guru who is selected from among his disciples by the living Guru. The disciple or the successor to the living Mahanta generally remained unmarried during his life time. This adds to the holiness and sanctity of the 'Mahanta'. A large number of people visit the Guru to receive his blessings round the year. The gatherings during the annual fair presently exceed three lakhs. The pilgrims mainly come from Punjab western Uttar Pradesh and the hill region of Uttarakhand. The 'Jhanda Fair' lasts for 15-20 days. The wealth of Mahanta has been invested in various educational and other social organisations for the general uplift of the society.

Haryala Fair

Haryala is another festival which is more popular in the Kumaon region of Uttarakhand. This is the festival of rains which is celebrated some time in the month of July on the occasion of Karka Sankranti, the first solar day of Hindu month of Sravana. About ten days before the start of the festival, seeds of five or seven different kinds of grain are mixed and sown in a basket filled with earth. A day before the celebration, when the shoots have come out, the image of gods and goddesses are kept in between the shoots. A *puja* is then performed by a priest and the lady of the house for ensuring good crops during the ensuing months.

The festival also coincides with the marriage anniversary of Shiva and Parvati. The remaining part of the ceremony is observed on the day of Sankranti which is performed by the master of the house. The yellow stem of the shoots is cut and offered to the Gods. Some shoots are tied to the hair of girls. The other shoots are stuck round the door frame with cowdung. At the end of the ceremony the 'Dikaras' (the clay images of Shiva and Parvati and their sons Ganesh and Kartikya) are immersed in the river. The festival is also celebrated in other parts of Uttarakhand with some variations.

Nanda Devi Fair

Nanda Devi is one of the popular fairs of Kumaon region which is celebrated with great enthusiasm, particularly in Almora, Nainital, Bhowali and Kati-ki-Mai during the month of September. Nanda is one of the several names of the goddess Parvati or Durga, who is considered to be a Goddess of war and is worshipped to gain power and strength to defeat any opponent. The three Himalayan peaks in

Uttarakhand region have been named after goddess as Nanda Devi, Nanda Kot and Nanda Ghunti. A number of temples are dedicated to goddess Nanda Devi. The worship of Nanda Devi is accompanied by a 'Havan'. Buffaloes and goats are sacrificed for a period of two days. On the third or fourth day of ceremony, the image or idol of the goddess is taken in a procession to the resting ground where it is placed.

The Nanda Devi festival has its origin in the folk legends. It is said that once two sisters of Chand Raja of Kumaon, named Nanda and Sunanda, were going to the temple to worship the mother goddess. On the way a demon appeared in the form of a buffalo and began to chase and harass them. The two sisters then hid themselves in a nearby banana plantation but to no avail. Then, as the demon was about to attack the two sisters, the mother goddess appeared on the scene and killed them and thus saved their lives. The two sisters were later accepted as divine beings and thereafter worshipped. Accordingly, two images of 'Nanda' and 'Sunanda' are made during the festival and banana leaves are planted on either side of the images. Buffaloes and goats are killed to signify the destruction of the evil spirit. The story in some respect seems to have been adopted by the locals from the legend where goddess Durga was supposed to have killed the buffalo-faced demon, 'Mahisasur', the lord of evil spirits. The festival is celebrated throughout Uttarakhand in one form or another.

Ramlila Fair

Ramlila, the play based on *Ramayana* and written by both Tulsidas or Balmiki, is comparatively more popular in the hills of Uttarakhand. Ramlila is the most anxiously awaited festival. This is the best and the cheapest source of entertainment for the rural folk in addition to the religious importance attached to it. Every village or a group of villages form committees to make necessary preparations for the play of 'Ramlila', including the selection of its cast, rehearsals and the arrangement of necessary-equipment and finances. Donations are collected and funds raised to make the event a success. It is a unique event where one could find plenty of enthusiasm in the old and young alike. In fact, there is healthy competition between the villages in presenting the play of 'Ramlila' and attracting more crowds than the other. Comedies based on the prevailing socio-economic life of the people presented during the play, are real fun for the large number of spectators who come to witness Ramlila. The 'Ramlila' normally last for five to ten days and ends on the day of Dussehra, when the effigies of Ravana are burnt and the final victory of Ram, Lakshaman and Sita is celebrated by taking out procession. It will not be out of context to mention here that the play of 'Ramlila' presented by people of Uttarakhand are equally popular in the big cities like Delhi, Mumbay and Lucknow. It is presented with the same amount of vigour, enthusiasm and dedication as displayed by them in their native place.

The Autumn Fair

The Autumn fair or the Summer fair organised at the hill resorts of Mussoorie and Nainital are the latest addition to the cultural life of the people of Uttarakhand. These modern fairs are primarily meant for the benefit of tourists and are organised during the peak period of the tourist season at these hill stations. The fairs are organised under the auspices of local municipal boards. The programme includes Dances, Drama, Music, Sports and other talent contests in various fields. The seasonal fairs and festivals have been attracting thousands of tourists every year.

The aim of these festivals is not only to entertain but also enlighten the tourists and the visitors on the art, culture and folklore of Uttarakhand region. Indirectly these festivals are aimed to improve the socio-economic life of the people. Gradually, these fairs are becoming more popular and soon many more hill stations will join the race. Autumn fairs have already been organised in Joshimath Narendra Nager and Ranikhet.

Gend Ka Mela (Fair of the Ball)

There are many other fairs of local importance. One of them is known as 'Gend ka Mela'. The fair is popular in Dada Mandi, Katghar and Thal Nadi in Kotdwara Tehsil of Pauri district. It coincides with Makar Sankranti which generally fall on the 14th January every year. It is on this day that the Hindus all over the country take a holy dip in the river to start afresh, the year of the god. 'Makar Sankranti' has its own religious importance. 'Gend Ka Mela' is celebrated as an annual fair in this part of Uttarakhand and the people anxiously wait for the day to come. People in their colourful dresses congregate here from villages five to six miles away to take part in this fair. Temporary shops are erected for the fair and for two to three days it turns into a place of great joy and fun where people mingle with and meet their relatives and gifts are exchanged.

The main attraction of the fair is the 'Ball' game. It is not exactly known as to how the game, came into being. However, it is a unique game which can not be witnessed in any other part of the country. The rules of the game are also unique. There are two teams representing the two geographical areas generally based on the boundary following the natural course of a river or fields. There is no limit to the number of persons who can take part. Also there is no limit to the size of the ground. The game generally starts around ten or eleven o'clock in the morning with the beating of drums. The balls is of the size of a Basketball and weighs about ten to 15 kg and is filled by some solid material. It is well stitched and covered by leather. The ball is in the possession of one team at a centrally selected place and the opposing team is given a signal to move into capture the ball and take it away to their area. While the struggle to snatch and take possession of the ball continues in the centre, a large number of other participants join in the fray. The ball may or may not be in the possession of a particular team, but the opposing team tries to push the whole crowd to their side. It requires a lot of stamina, strength and dogged determination to get into the centre and pull the ball out of the crowd. Since the ball itself weighs 10 to 15 kg it requires at least 4 to 5 persons to carry it and to keep it under their control. There is no time limit. The struggle may carry on with the fluttering of flags and the beating of drums till late at night, when the people start returning to their homes. Quite a large number of people do get injured during this struggle. The team which has more stamina and determination will ultimately take the ball to their area and as soon as the opposing team has surrendered, the game is over. The winning team celebrates the victory with the beating of drums and dancing. The visitors can only enjoy the game by actually watching it.

Magh Mela of Uttarkashi

'Magh Mela of Uttarkashi' is celebrated in Uttarkashi on the day of 'Makar Sankranti', which falls on the 14th of January every year. In the olden days, people used to gather to have a dip in the holy river Bhagirathi (Ganga) and thereafter the idols of various gods and goddesses were carried in a procession accompanied by the beating of drums and special puja performed. At that time, the fair used to be combined with the establishment of a bazaar during the period of the *Mela*. In this bazar various items from cottage industries used to be sold and purchased under the barter system. Large quantities of home made woollen garments also used to be sold and purchased during this *Mela*. In recent years, the *Mela* has changed its colour and outlook. Today, agricultural and industrial exhibitions are also arranged during the *Mela* period. This, combined with cultural programmes, turns it into a very enjoyable fair where thousands of people gather and share the joy and fun with their kith and kin. However, the traditional religious celebration continues to be the star attraction of the Mela even today.

Customs, Rites and Rituals

The customs, rites and other rituals practiced by the people of Uttarakhand are essentially based on Hindu religon. These customs are deep rooted and are strictly observed by people of all castes, i.e., Brahmin, Kshatriya, Vaishya and Shudras. All customs and traditions are influenced by their belief in spirits and superstitions, the innumerable Hindu gods and goddesses. A brief description of various ceremonies and rites performed by the people on various occasions is given in the following paragraphs.

Birth

As usual, the birth of a son is considered more auspicious than that of a daughter. On the birth of a child the woman is segregated for all purpose for a few days until a 'Puja' is performed for the purification of the woman. 'Nam Karan' (christening) ceremony is also performed on another auspicious day. Later on, in case of a son, at the age of 3, 5 or 7 another ceremony called 'Chura Karam' is performed with great enthusiasm, when the head of the child is shaved off and is introduced to schooling by making him write a few letters on a 'Takhti' (wooden board). A special 'Puja' and feast is arranged on this occasion. All these ceremonies are done strictly in accordance to scriptures read on the occasion by the 'Purohit' (Brahmin who is responsible to perform *Puja* and other rituals according to Hindu scriptures).

Marriage

Even to this day, the higher caste people (Brahmins, Kshatriyas and Vaishyas) do not approve marriages of their daughters with grooms from lower caste. Brahmins and Rajputs will willingly take a girl from a lower caste, but marry their daughters only to a boy of a higher caste. There are prohibitions against marriages between the same clan or caste. With the present trend in the country and the changing outlook of Hindu society, widow marriage are also being solemnised, where acceptable, with their relations and other members of their families. 'Polygamy' is not common now but Polyandry is still practiced in some areas of Chakrata Tehsil of Dehradun district. Marriages among the tribes (Boksa, Tharu and Bhotiyas) are solemnised with certain variations in accordance with tribal customs.

Usually, the marriages are pre-arranged. Having selected the girl, further negotiations are done on the basis of matching the horoscopes of the prospective bride and bridegroom. The horoscopes are studied by a 'Purohit' or an Astrologer from both sides. Status of the family and the caste are the main prequisites for negotiating any marriage offer. A small ceremony is held when the proposal is accepted by changing Teeka (Vermillion) at the residence of the prospective bride. This is followed by an engagement ceremony on an auspicious day when a 'Necklace' is also presented to the girl. Marriage is fixed on another auspicious day. In addition, a feast is also given as in other parts of the country.

Traditionally the marriage procession is led with a white flag called 'Nishan' which represents the bridegroom. This is followed by the local band consisting of a *Shehnai*, piper and a pair of drummers and a *Nagara*. This in turn is followed by a white 'Palki' in which the bridegroom is carried. The last man of the marriage procession carries another flag which is red and represents the bride. On arrival at the brides residence a reception is given in accordance with local customs and rites and a feast is given to the marriage party. Thereafter, 'Nath' (Nose ring) ceremony is performed at a pre selected auspicious time when the 'Nath' is presented to the bride. Next day the betrothal ceremony takes place at a specially erected 'Bedi' which includes 'Havan' and the bride and the bridegroom complete seven rounds (Phera) of the sacred fire as per rituals conducted strictly according to the *Shastras* (Hindu scriptures) read by the *Purohit*. At the end, dowry or gifts if any, according to the status of the family, are given to the bridegroom. After a normal feast, the marriage party leaves the house of the bride. While returning, the marriage party is led with the red flag, followed by the red 'Doli' of the bride and the

Palki of the bridegroom. The white flag remains at the end. Various other rituals and 'Puja' are gone through till the bride finally steps into the house of the bridegroom. There is no 'Gauna' (Second marriage) system in Uttarakhand like in the plains but once again immediately after the marriage the bridegroom is required to come to the house of the bride and take her to his house on another auspicious day. Thereafter, the marriage is considered to have been finally solemnised.

Index

A

Adi Shankaracharya, 53, 56, 59, 64, 65, 67, 68, 72, 73, 84, 86, 151, 152, 160
Adi Tribe, (Arunachal Pradesh), 15, 21, 43, 44, 45, 46
Advait Vedanta, 100
Agriculture Calamities, 120
Ain-i-Akbari, (Abul Fazal), 94
Airy God, 157
Ajanta, 263, 264
Ajanta Paintings, 263
Aka-Nishi, 15, 21, 30
Akas, 21, 37
Akash Ganga, 74
Akbar, 237
Akhand Chandi Palace, 226
Alakananda, 55-61, 63, 64, 76, 77, 87
Alberuni, 94
Alexander the Great, 274
Alvars, 111
Amarnath, 98
Amarnath Cave, 15, 16
Ancient Hindu Temples, 50
Ane-Duisi, Sun Mother, 31
Angamis, 28
Angrichogba and Black Magic, 21
Animal Sacrifices, 17
Animism, 15, 19, 20, 27, 148
Animism Belt, 29, 30
Annapurna, 260
Ao Nagas Deities, 36
Apa-Tanis, 37
Arakam Yoma, 23
Ardhanareshwar, 74
Arjuna, 59, 61, 110
Arki—Kankhal, 270
Arunachal Pradesh, 20, 23, 26
Ashtadhyahi, 106
Asoka, 19, 23, 26
Assam
- and Burma, 28
- Hill Tribals, 26
- Plains, 15, 20

Asva Layana Griha Sutra, 18
Aurangzeb, 265
Austric
- Culture, 116
- Or Dravidian Culture, 18

Avalokiteshwara, 282
Avanti Varman, 15
Avantipura, 15

B

Baandhara, 59
Babrubahan, 22
Badri
- Temples, 66
- Vishal, 59

Badrikashram, 56, 59
Badrinath Dham, 55, 56, 58, 59, 60, 63
Badrinath, 71, 72, 86, 94, 100, 103, 113, 114, 151, 152, 227
Baila (UP), 145
Baila Rajputs, 134, 138
Bairat, 123
Balabhadra and Subhadra, 103

Baluchs, 32, 38, 41
Banderpoonch Mountain, 77
Bango, Halo, Pakya Spirits, 35
Basohli—Garhwal, 268
Bathua, 215
Beas Valley, 280
Bengal and Assam Doars, 20
Betrothal Ceremony, 164, 189
Bhagavat Gita, 56, 61, 103, 104, 106, 108
Bhagavat Purana, 105, 267
Bhagirathi, 76, 88
Bhai Tewar, 176
Bhai Tika Ceremony, 176
Bhairavas and their Types, 20
Bhairon, 127
Bhairon-Tangi Birs, 124
Bhavishya Badri, 85
Bhigrauli (HP), 145
Bhima (Bhimsen), 59, 69, 72, 122, 123
Bhotia Cultural Area, 26, 30
Bhotias, 18, 19
Bhotias Traders, 67
Bhutnad (Himachal Pradesh), 145
Bilaspur, 258
Bilaspur, Basohli, Chamba, 273
Birth Songs, 245
Bissu Spring Festival, 140, 141, 142, 143
Bissu-Mond Festival, 136
Black Hat Dance, 253
Bon and Buddhist Faiths, 24
Border War, 181
Botha Mahasu, 124, 126
Brahma, 148
- Kapal Ghat, 65
- Kund, 57

Brahmanical Sculptures in Nepal, 20
British
- Policy, 27
- Religious Policy, 28

Buddha, 61, 110
Buddhism, 15, 19, 20, 23, 25, 29, 30, 56, 57, 59, 77, 81, 84, 96, 99, 110, 151, 152, 160, 216, 252
- Icons, 21
- Spirits, 33
- Tibetan Forms of-, 23
- Viharas, 60

Buddhists, 26, 42, 252
- and Jains Icons, 151

Belt, 23, 46
- Communities, 25
- Monks, 40
- Rituals, 19, 30, 42
- Shrines, 19
- Viharas, 63

Buddhists, Ladakh—Arunachal, 42
Burma, 21

C

Caste System, 20
Chaitanya, 53, 265
Chaitanya School, 23
Chakmas of Chittagong Hills Tracts, 23
Chakra Tirtha, 66
Chalda Mahasu, 125
Chamba, 261, 272, 273, 278, 281, 282
Champawat Temple, 154
Chandanwari, Pishughati, Sheshnag, and Panchtarani, 16
Chandragupta Vikramaditya, 106
Chandragupta, II, 99
Chandu Lal, Artists, 276
Chaturbhuja Singavahini, 57
Chaukhamba Mountain, 77
Chaumu God, 157
Chhal Bhairav, 208
Chhaya Puja, 196-198, 200, 201
Chhel Puja Exorcism, 196-198

Chhetris and Artisans Castes, 167
Child Marriages, 164, 189
China, 181
Chinese
- Art, 264
- Invasion, 228
- New Year's Day, 173

Chini Village, 203, 205, 206, 208, 216
Chitai Temple, 154
Chola
- Bronzes, 50
- Kings, 50, 51

Chorabari Tal, 82
Chortan, 26
Christian
- Belt, 27
- Missions, 27, 28
- Tribals, 30

Christianity, 15, 28-30, 114
Classical Dances, 49
- Bharatnatyam, 49
- Odissi, 49

Corbett, Jim, 88
Cremation and Exposure, 37
Cult of Dead, 37
Cult of Shiva, 266
Cu-Natca Ceremony, 39

D

Daflas, 31, 37
Dakshprajapati, 148, 149, 153
Dalai Lama (6th), 25
Dalton, Gen., 28
Dance Songs, 245
Dangariya, Oracle or Shaman, 159
Dards, 38
Dev Prayag (Confluence of Alakananda & Bhagirithi), 57, 58, 88
Devadasis, 50
Dhauladhar Range, 237, 272
Dhauli Gang, 57, 58
Dialect,
- Tankhul Dialect, 29
- Thado and Kuki Dialect, 29
- Sirmaur, 227
- Chamba, 247
- Kinnaur, 228
- Kullu, 228, 279
- Lohit, 46
- Mandi, 229, 247, 256, 258
- Sirmaur, 238
- West Siang, 46

Divorce, 167
Doms, Austric Race, 115, 116
Donyi-Polo, Animistic Religion, 44, 46
Dowry, 269
Draupadi, 59
Dravidian
- Gods, 18
- Temple Architecture, 113

Dudhganga, 71
Durga-Saptashati, 267
Dussehra of Kullu, 223, 224
Dwarka, 71, 94-96, 103, 113

E

Exorcist, 178
- Dress, 180
- Principal Kinds, 179

F

Faces of Shiva, 74, 82
- Kalpeshwar, 74
- Kedarnath, 74
- Madmaheswawr, 74
- Parvati, 74
- Rudranath, 74

Fairs and Festivals, 223-299

Festival, Fagali (Buddhist), 18
Festivals, 51, 53, 171
- Badrinath-Kedarnath, 65
- Brahmotsavam, 51
- Magh Festivals, 131-136, 139, 140
- Mond Festival, 144-146

Five Badris, 81
Five Kedars, 81
Five Prayags, 81
Folk and Ritual Art, 253
Folk Dance, 224, 246, 247, 249, 290
- Of Garhwal Region, 291
- Of Kumaon Region, 290

Folk Songs, 229, 285-287
- Chhopati, 286
- Of Garhwal Region, 286

Folklores of Kumaon Region, 288
Funeral Rites, 98, 167, 284

G

Gaddis, 15, 17, 30, 32, 33, 41, 46, 237
Gaddis Cultural Areas, 17
Gandhara, 23
Gandharvas, Celestial Musicians, 52
Ganga, 88, 95, 97
Ganga and Yamuna, 77, 81, 114
- Figures, 279

Gangaur of Rajasthan, 259
Gangetic Plains, 15
Gangnath Temple, 156
Gangotri, 57, 71, 72, 74, 76, 95, 114
Garhwal, 15, 81, 88, 89, 148, 150, 187, 189, 196, 197
- and Uttar Pradesh, 262
- Hills, 56
- Himalaya, 56-58, 60, 68, 71
- Region, 289

Garhwali
- Rituals, 185
- Weddin, 184, 185

Garos, 31, 37
Garuda Gumpha, 60
Gaumukha, 76, 77
Gauri Kund, 76
Gelugpa Monastery, 24
- Arikadum, (Arunachal Pradesh), 24
- Basgo (Ladakh), 24
- Dungham (Bhutan), 24

Golden Tselling (Bhutan), 24
- Karsha (Zanskar), 24
- Lahaglin, 24
- Mune (Zanskar), 24
- Padung, 24
- Phugtal (Zanskar), 24
- Rangdung, (Zanskar), 24
- Sanglangphe, 24
- Saspol (Ladakh), 24
- Shankar (Ladakh), 24
- Spituk (Ladakh), 24
- Surcharg (Lumla), 24
- Taidung, 24
- Tailing (Bhutan), 24
- Tashi-Tselling (Bhutan), 24
- Tharpa-Choling (Sikkim), 24
- Tikse, (Ladakh), 24
- Tirpa (Kalimpong), 24
- Twang (Arunachal Pradesh), 24

Gelugpa Sect, 24
- Features, 24

Ghepan, God of Naga Cult, 19
Gita, 129 see also Bhagavat Gita
Gita Govind, 265
Gita, 129
Glaciers, 56, 57, 59, 77, 81, 96, 99
Gangotri, 77
Gaumukh, 57

God Apa—Tanis, 34
God Vishnu, 123
Goddess Kalinka, 203
Goddess Lakshmi, 60, 64
Golu Devta 158
Golu Temple Almora, 154
Gori Ganga, 155
Govardhan Math Puri, 100
Great Buddhist Council, (Kashmir), 23
Griha Sutra, 18
Gugga Ballads, 238
Guhamitra, 20
Gujjar, 15
Gupt Kashi, 59, 72
Gurkha Names, 163
Guru Govind Singh, 56
Guru Nanak, 56
Gurung Village, 161
Gurungs, 167, 170, 179

H

Hanuman Chatti, 77
Haridwar, 95, 96
Haritalika Teej, 257, 258
Harsha, 99
Hemkund Sahib, 56
Hidimba, 33
Hien Tsang, 99
Hill Miris, 31, 37, 39
Hill Miris Spirits, 34
Himachal Pradesh, 181
Himalayan Buddhists, 38
Himalayan Tribes, 38
Hindu
- Art of Nepal, 20
- Belt, 15, 16, 20, 21, 46
- Katochs, 277
- Marriage, 183
- Philosophy, 100
- Pilgrims, 16
- Reformers, 19
- Ritual/Legal Text, 187
- Traditions, 91
- Trinity, 30

Hindu, Buddhist and Jains Shrines, 114
Hinduism, 15-17, 19-22, 28-30, 44, 92, 100, 103, 110, 114, 121, 128, 147, 160
- and Buddhism, 27

Hindustan Tibet Road, 217, 228
Hoi Ashtami, 261

I

Idlong—Imphal, 27
Immigrants, 122
Imphal, 28, 29
Imra, 32
India and Tibet, 40
Indian
- Classical Artists, 263
- Classical Music, 57
- Paintings, 275
- Social Structure, 185

Indo-Gangetic Plains, 95
Indo-Greeks, 148
Indra-Killa Mountain, 38
Infant Mortality, 118
Inheritance, 170
Inscription in Sharda Script, 280
Inscriptions, 50
- Cangu Narayana Temple, 19
- Deo-Patana, 19
- Lajapal, 19
- Tabahal, 20

Islam, 15, 16, 27, 29, 114
Islamic Belt, 26
Itmov, 30

J

Jaggar Folklore, 289
Jahangir, 272
Jaidev, 111
Jamdagni (Rishi), 17, 226
Jammu – Bilaspur, 16
Jaunsar-Bawar, 115-118, 121, 125, 128, 129, 144, 145
- Festivals of-, 130
- Wedding, 191

Jed-Jed, Religious Festival, 252
Jerusalem, 99
Jhalrai, Katyuri King, 15
Jhecha, 15, 17, 18, 20, 33, 38, 41, 46
Jhelum, 15
Jhulaghat Pancheshwar Area, 157
Joshimath, 56, 60, 67, 72, 74, 85, 86
- Theological College, 68
- Trading Post, 67, 68, 69

Jwalamukhi, Kangra, 236
Jyotirlingams, 108
Jyotirlingas, 71, 73, 94, 152, 153
- Temples details, 153

K

Kabul—Dacca, 27
Kafir Goddesses, 32
- Suranji—Shuman, 32

Kafir Gods, 32
- Imra—Shomde, 32

Kail Bisht, Flute Player Folk God, 157
Kakpeshwar, 83
Kama Kund, 87
Kama Prayag, 87
Kamakoti Peetham Kanchipuram, 100
Kanchenjunga, 20
Kangra, 24, 261, 271-274, 279, 280
- Earthquake, 275

Kullu and Hamirpur, 16
- School of Paintings, 263, 264
- Settlement Report, 273
- Style, 268, 269

Kanishka, 23
Kanyakumari, 92
Kar-Gyupa Sect, 24
Karna, 58
Karna Prayag (Confluence Pindar Ganga-Alakananda), 58, 59
Kashmir, 15, 16, 23, 24
Kashmir Pandits, 16
Kashmir's Hindu Tirtha, 15
Katoch Rulers, 272, 273
Katyuri Kings, 289
Kauravas, 66
Kedar Temples, 74
Kedarganga, 76
Kedarnath, 58, 59, 71, 72, 74, 81, 95, 114, 151, 152
Kedarnath Mountain, 71
Kedarnath, Badrinath, Gangotri and Yamunatri, 56
Keshava Prayag, 59
Kesvara Linga, 20
Khasa (s), 115, 116, 118, 120, 129, 130
- Cultural Life, 130
- Festivals, 130
- Groups, 115

Khasi, 31
Khasi Hills, 16, 27, 29
Khasi Hills—Chin Hills, 27
Khasi Women, 27
Khasis and Meiteis, 26
Khasis, 27, 29, 37, 44
Khoas, 37
King
- Bhagirath, 75

- Daksha, 86
- Garib Niwaj, 22, 23

Khongtekcha, 21
- Puranjaya, 67
- Pururava, 84
- Swargadev Assam, 22

Kinnaur, 231
Kinnauras, 19
Kinner Region, 217
Kinners, 215, 216, 217
- Folk Dances, 217
- Folk Dances, Love Songs, 218
- Folk Dances, Pradesh, 221
- Folk Dances, Types, 217
- Religion, 216

Koltas, 122, 127, 131, 133, 134, 136, 137, 141
Krishna, 109-111, 113 see under Lord Krishna also
Krishna Cult, 266
Krishnadevaraya (Vijayanagar), 112
Kukis, 26, 28
Kukis Shaman, 44
Kulu, 15, 17, 18, 23
Kumaon, 147, 148, 150, 154-160, 181, 288, 289
Kunti, 122, 123
Kurukshetra, 72, 98
Kurukshetra War, 72
Kushan Kings, 148
Kuwari Pass, 87

L

Ladakh and Zanzkar, 282
Ladakh to Mishimi Hills, 23
Ladakh—Arunachal Pradesh, 23
Lahaul, 19, 249, 252
Lahaul and Spiti, 250, 282
Lake,
- Manasarovar, 55, 58, 98, 99
- Nainital, 149
- Satopanth, 59
- Vaitarini, 74

Lakshaman Sen (Bengal), 265
Lama Marpa of Lahrang, 24
Lama's Incarnations, 25
Lamas and Their Types, 25
Lang-Dar-Ma, 251, 252
Lavi, Trade Fair, 227, 228
Lepchas, 15, 30, 33, 179
Lhota Nagas Spirits, 36
Likhnu, Ritual Decoration, 256
Lish, Alexander B, 29
Lohita, 15
Lord Badrinarayana, 60, 65, 68
Lord
- Indra, 75
- Krishna, 171, 173, 183, 230, 231, 265, 266, 271, 272
- Krishna, 56, 59, 61, 68, 73, 87, 103, 104. 105
- Mahadeva, 88
- Ram, 75, 103, 105
- Shiva, 55, 61, 66, 71, 84, 86, 93, 171, 225, 237, 256, 257, 281
- Vishnu, 55, 57, 59, 60, 65, 84, 92, 93, 95, 97, 227, 254, 276, 281, 282

Love Songs, 232-234

M

Madhavacharya, 59
Madhuganga, 71
Magars, 167, 179
Magar Village, 161
Magical Incantations, 17
Magico-Religious
- Rites, 121
- Practices, 120

Mahabharat, 44, 56, 58, 59, 61, 65, 69, 72, 94, 103, 105, 108, 274

Mahapadama Nag, 16
Mahapadma Sar, (Wular Lake), 16
Maharaja Ranjit Singh, 271-273
Mahasu (Deota), 117, 121-123, 129, 140, 142, 144
Mahayana
- and Hinayana, 26
- Buddhism, 110
- Hinayana Belt, 23

Majariyat System, 19
Mana, 87
Mana Village, 66
Manchus in China, 40
Mandakini, 55, 57, 58, 71, 73, 76
Mandi, 272, 282, 283
Mandi and Kullu, 269
Mandi Stone Images, 267
Mangal Git, 183
Mani
- Gompa, 252

Mahesh, God, 17
Manipur, 15, 16, 21, 22, 27, 28
Manipur Culture, 27
Manipur Kalika, 22
Manjushri, 253
Mansuna, 74
Mao Nagas, 37
Marcho Bhotias, 85
Marriage Songs, 245
Masked Dances, 251
Mata Worship 18
Mathura—Punjab, 23
Matrilineal System, 187
Megalithic Cult, 116
Meitei (s), 21, 27, 29
Meitei Languge, 28
Mendaura, 137, 138, 139
Menial Class, 162
Migration of Artists, 269
Mijis, 37
Mikris, 44
Minjar Fair of Chamba, 226
Mirabai, 111
Miris, 21
Mishmi (s), 35, 45
- and Naga Cultural Areas, 15
- Shaman, 43

Missionary Activities, 29
Monasteries, 252
- Dankhar, 252
- Kee, 252
- Pin, 252
- Tabo, 252

Mond Rites, 146
Moni—Nirmati Gods, 32
Monpa Family of Twang, 25
Monpas, 46
Mount
- Kailash, 55, 58, 59, 68, 92, 99, 109, 151

Meru, 52, 55
- Nanda Devi, 59
- Neelkantha, 59, 60
- Trisul, 59

Mourning Rites, 167
Mughal Artists, 263
Mughal Empire, 265, 271
Mun, 179
Mun, Lepchas Shaman, 42
Mundas (Central India), 19
Mundas of Bihar, 116
Musical Instruments, 141, 250
Muslim Invasions, 23
Mythology,
- Hindu, 55, 104
- Noctes, 45
- Singphos, 45

N

Nag Puja, 19
Naga Cult, 15, 16, 18, 19
Naga, Karkotak, 20

Nagarjuna, Buddhist Teacher, 23
Nagas, 28, 43
- Angami, 44
- Ao, 31, 36, 44
- Kabui, 31
- Kukis, 31
- Lhota, 36, 40, 44
- Quireng, 31
- Sema, 31, 40, 44

Nag-Worship, 16
Naina Devi (Bilaspur), 148, 149, 236
Naked Dance, 121
Nalwari Cattle Fair, 229
Nana, Greek Goddess, 148
Nanda Devi, 74, 148, 149, 158
- Festival, 189, 296
- Mount, 150
- Yatra, 150

Nanda Prayag, (Confluence Nandakini and Alakananda), 58
Nandakini, 57, 76, 87
Naothingkhong, Meitei King, 21
Nar Narayana, 84, 110, 114
Nar and Narayana Sages, 71
Nar Parbat, 63, 68
Narad Kund, 84
Narasimadeva (Orissa), 111
Narayana Parbat, 63, 68
Narsimha Temple Joshimath, 64, 68
Narsingh Badri, 85
Narwaris of Nepal, 20
Nati, 248
National Gallery of Art, 267
Neelkanth, 74
Nepal, 19, 174
Nepalis Hindus, 20
Newards, 30
Nilamatapurana, 15
Nilganga, 77
Nin-ma-pa Monasteries, 24
Nin-ma-pa Sect, 24
Nirvana, 91
Nishis, 46
Nishis and Hill Miris, 42
Nityananda, 56
Noctes, 21, 31, 36, 39, 43
Noctes—Singphos, 37

O

Oaths and Ordeals, 129
Omens, 129
Omkareshwar, River Island, 92

P

Padma Naga, 16
Padmasambhava, 252, 253
Pahari
- Art, 266, 270
- Art of Paintings, 262, 263
- Cultural Area, 16, 17, 20, 30, 33, 42
- School, 263, 264, 276
- Shaman, 17

Paintings,
- Basohli, 262
- Bilaspur, 262
- Chamba, 262, 269
- Guler, 262
- Kangra, 262, 264
- Kullu and Garwal, 262
- Mandi, 262
- Miniature, 270

Pahari, 263, 264-268, 276
Punjab Hill, 262
Rajput, 264
Pallas, Peter Simon, German Naturalist, 40
Pallavas and Cholas, 112
Panch Kedar, 72, 73
Panchkroshiyatra of Kashi, 98
Pandava (Brothers), 69, 56, 57, 59, 66, 72, 74, 76, 81, 98, 122

Pangi-Lahaul and Kinnaur, 26
Parshuram, 227, 255
Parshuram Kund, 46
Parvati Temple, 74
Pashupati, 20, 30
Pashupati Astra, 66
Pattigrew, William, Scottish Missionary, 28
Peak,
- Chandrashila, 82
- Chaukhamba, 82
- Kedarnath, 84
- Nanda Devi, 68
- Hathi Parbat, 74
- Nanda Devi, 74
- Trisul, 74

Pindadan Ceremony, 98
Pindar Ganga, 57, 76, 87
Places of Pilgrimage in India, 100-101
Plates, Phayena Copper-, 21
Polytheism, 40
Poorna Chand, Artists, 276
Pre-Harappa Period, 32
Prem Lal Chamba, 276
Punjab Plains, 15
Puranas, 96, 108, 109
Puri, 71

Q

Queen Ahilyabai (Indore), 63

R

Radha and Krishna, 266, 267, 276
Radha-Krishna Cult, 265, 266
Ragas and Raginis details, 267-268, 276
Ragamala, 267
Raghunatha, Deity, 18, 224
Raghunathmath, 88
Raja
- Chandra Kirti Singh, 27
- Gambhir Singh, 27
- Ishwari Sen of Mandi, 269
- Jai Singh of Manipur, 22
- Pratap Singh Verman, 226

Raja Chola (Thanjavur), 112
- Sahil Varman, 281
- Sahil Verman, 226
- Sansar Chand, 269, 271-274
- Sansar Chand, 275, 276
- Udai Singh, 282
- Vijaya Chand, 238

Rajatarangani, 23
Rajput Paintings, 262
Ram and Sri Krishna, 129
Ramanandi Cult of Vaishnavism, 22
Ramanujacharya, 56, 59, 111
Ramayana and Mahabharata, 21, 236, 267
Ramcharitmanas, 111
Rameshwaram, 63, 71, 76, 92, 94, 103
Rani Guleria, 77
Rath Yatra, 50, 113, 224
Rawal Nambudris Community, 60
Rawani-Jaunpur Area, 286
Red Hats, 252
Religious
- Architecture, 49
- Ceremonies (In Nepal), 161
- Songs, 236

Renuka, 226, 227
Renuka Fair, 227
Rigveda, 104
Rigveda Vishnu, 104
Rishi, 110
- Badrayana, 60
- Dattatreya, 110
- Ganga, 55, 60
- Gautam, 59
- Kapila, 59, 110

- Kashyap, 59
- Narada, 110
- Narada, 59
- Veda Vyasa, 110

Rishikesh, 57, 58, 72

Ritual Dances in Tribal Area, 249

Rituals, 17, 41, 42, 44, 53, 196, 200, 201, 205, 246, 285

- and Festivals, 97
- Hindu, 19
- in Great Himalaya, 181
- of Animism, 44

River

- Akash Kamini, 82
- Alakananda, 71, 95
- Brahmputra, 55
- Gandaki, 107
- Ganga, 55, 56, 57, 65, 74, 75, 76, 92, 129
- Godavari, 92
- Imphal, 23
- Indus, 55
- Mandakini, 82, 95

Ravi, 226

- Saraswati, 59
- Yamuna, 55, 227
- Yen-Isuei and Lena, (Siberia), 40

Rohilla Invasion, 154

Roman Catholics, 29

Roopkund, 87

Rope Dancing, 120

Rudra Prayag, 57, 87, 88

Rudraganga, 74

Rudranath, 83

S

Sabarimala, 97, 98

Sacred Pools, 71

- Retah, 71
- Rishi, 71
- Rudra, 71
- Udak, 71

Sacrifices and Rituals, 41

Sagar, 75

Sahasranama (Vishnu), 111

Saivite, 15

Saivite Practices, 17

Sakya-pa Sect, 24

Saptapuris, 93-95

Saraswati, 71

Sassur Gompa, 252

Satapatha Brahman, 110

Sati, (Parvati), 86, 88, 94

Satluj, 273

Sect,

Shaivas, 96

Sri Sampradaya, 111

- Vaishna, 106
- Vaishnavas, 96

Serampore Mission, Christian Missionary, 29

Shaivas, 83

Shaivites, 108

Shakti, 147, 148, 152

Shaman, 17, 33, 158, 159

Shamanism, 20, 40, 41

Shantineketan, 262

Sharda Math Dwarka, 100

Sherpas, 179

Shikhara Style, 278, 280, 282, 283

Shillong, Centre of Higher Education, 29

Shilpa Shastra, 49

Shiva, 103, 108, 109, 114, 147, 148, 149, 151, 152 see under Lord Shiva also

Shiva Temple Kumaon, 152

Shivapurana, 81

Shivratri of Mandi, 223, 225

Shrine of

- Raj Madha, 225
- Jambalu Devata, 17
- Kulang, 17
- Majharh, 17

Silcher, 28
Silk Weavers of Kashi and Kanchipuram, 50
Singphos, 39
Singphos Spirits-Nats, 35
Sissu Fairs, 252
Skandpurana, 59, 82, 83, 92, 108
Snake Worship, 18 –
Society, 43, 44

- North Indian, 180
- Primitive, 41

Sources of Names, 162
Spirit World, 128
Springs, 64

- Kurmadhara, 64
- Narada Kund, 64, 65
- Prahlald Dhara, 64
- Rishiganga, 64, 65
- Tapta Kund, 64

Sulungs Belief, 39
Sun/Moon Eclipses, 116
Supernatural Powers, 17
Swargaduari, 71
Swargarohini, 72
Swargarohani Mountain, 66

T

Tagins, 31
Tamangs, 170, 179
Tamangs—Rais, 179
Tangsas Spirits-Śang, 36
Tantric

- Buddhism, 252
- Cults, 21

Tapovan, 87
Taxila, 23
Tehri Garwal, 125
Temple

- Architecture, 51, 63277
- Badrinath, 64, 181
- Baijnath, 278-281
- Bansi Gopal, 282
- Bhutnath, 283
- Champavati, 226, 282
- Dance, 216
- Dwarkadesha, 113
- Gangotri, 76, 181
- Hanumana, 16
- Hari Rai, 226
- Hari Rai, 282
- Jagannath of Krishna (Puri), 92, 113
- Jagatrukh, 278
- Jwalamukhi, 237
- Kedarnath, 73, 181
- Kedarnath-Badrinath, 152
- Krishna, 16, 275
- Madhyamaheshwara, 74
- Mani-Mahesh, 278
- Martand, 16
- Meenakshi, Madurai, 98
- Nanda Devi, 83, 151
- Nandaghanti, 83
- Narayana, 16
- Narsimha, 282
- Of Badrinarayana, 63, 65, 68
- Of Bagulamukhi Mata, 16
- Of Brahma, 16
- Of Chamunda Mata, 16
- Of Chantpurani, 16
- Of Charanpaduka, 65
- Of Hatkioti, 16
- Of Hidimba Devi, 16
- Of Jwalamukhi Mata, 16
- Of Kaliwari, (Shimla), 16
- Of Kangrawali Mata, 16

- Of Laikasa, 22
- Of Lakshana Devi, 16
- Of Ma Chamunda, 57
- Of Malinithan (Arnachal Pradesh), 16
- Of Markula Devi, 16
- Of Mritunjaya Devi, 16
- Of Pahari in Assam, 16
- Of Panthoibi, 22
- Of Sakti Devi, 16
- Of Sandhya Devi, 16
- Of Tamreshwari Devi, (Arunachal Pradesh), 16
- Of Tara Devi (near Shimla), 16
- Of Tarna Mata, 16
- Of Vaishno Mata, 16
- Of Vishnu, 16
- Omkareshwara (Ukhimath), 72
- Pandukeshwar, 68
- Pashan Devi (Nainital), 149
- Pashupatinath (Nepal), 73
- Raghunath, 57
- Ram, 16
- Ramanathaswamy, 63, 76
- Shankaracharya, 16
- Shiva and Gauri, 73
- Siva, 16

Towns, 49
- Madurai, 49
- Varansi, 49

Trilokinath, 282, 283
Trisul, 83
- Varadaja, 97
- Vasudev, 68
- Yamunotri, 77, 181

Tewar, (Dewali), 176
Thapa, Amar Singh, 272
Thumkando (HP), 145
Tibet, 19, 24, 59, 67, 68, 181, 228, 251
Tibetan
- and Buddhist Cultures, 181
- Paintings and Sculptures, 251

Tirupati, 97
Titip District, 21, 23.
Trade, 27
Traders and Tourists, 217
Tribal, 20, 27, 215
- Beliefs and Practices, 116
- Koch and Bodas, 20

Tribes, Khamptis and Singphos, 23
Tripura, 15
Tulsi (Haripriya, Bhutagni), 254, 255
Tungnath, 74
Tunguz Tribe, 40
Type of Naga in Nepal, 20

U

Uddhava, Friend of Krishna, 61, 64
Ukhrul, 28, 29
Upanishads, 49
Urvarishi, 67
U-Thlen, Khasi God, 37
Uttarakashi, 72, 77, 83
Uttarakhand, 181, 285-287, 293, 297
Uttaranchal, 95, 181

V

Vaishna Saints, 106
Vaishna Sect, 106
Vaishnava Devi, 97
Vaishnavas, 106, 107, 108
Vaishnavism, 21, 22, 23
Vajra Bhairav, 253
Valley
- Alakananda, 81
- Bhagirathi, 81
- Brahmputra, 20, 21
- Gondhla and Gahar, 252
- Indus, 30

- Kangra, 237, 276, 277
- Kashmir, 15
- Kullu, 278
- Mandakini, 71
- Manipur and Tripura, 15
- Of Flowers, 56, 59
- Of Kullu, 15, 122
- Pattan, 252
- Spiti, 247, 250

Vasanta and Hindola Ragas, 267
Vashishtha Kund, 57
Vastu Shastra, 49, 52
Vastupurusha Mandala, 52
Vasudhara Waterfalls, 65, 85
Ved Vyasa, 66
Vedant School of Hindu Philosophy, 84
Vedas, 18, 49, 66, 92, 104
Vidyapati and Chandidas, 265
Vijradhara as Adi Buddha, 24
Vishni's Iconography, 107
Vishnu, 87, 103, 114, 147, 148, 152 see under Lord Vishnu also
- Avataras, 105
- Ganga, 65, 84, 85
- Prayag, 58, 59, 87
- Purana, 105
- Temples, 107
- Badrinath, 107
- Guruvayur, 107
- Kanchipuram, 107
- Srirangam, 107
- Tirupati, 107

Vishnu's
- Avataras details, 110
- Char Dhaam, 114
- Mythology, 105

W

Wall Paintings, 270
Wanchos, 36, 40, 43, 44
War Gods, 34
Weaning Ceremony, 163
Witchcraft, 41, 177
Wizard, 178
Wular Lake (Kashmir), 16

Y

Yamnotri, 71, 76, 77, 78, 96, 114
Yardesh, 38
Yellow Hats (Gelugpas), 253